The Mighty Wurlitzer

The Mighty Wurlitzer

HOW THE CIA PLAYED AMERICA

Hugh Wilford

HARVARD UNIVERSITY PRESS
Cambridge, Massachusetts
London, England

Printed in the United States of America

First Harvard University Press paperback edition, 2009.

Library of Congress Cataloging-in-Publication Data

Wilford, Hugh, 1965–
The mighty wurlitzer : how the CIA played America / Hugh Wilford.
p. cm.
Includes bibliographical references and index.
ISBN 978-0-674-02681-0 (cloth : alk. paper)
ISBN 978-0-674-03256-9 (pbk.)
1. United States. Central Intelligence Agency. 2. Intelligence service—United States. 3. Cold War. 4. Political culture—United States—History—20th century. 5. Public-private sector cooperation—United States—History—20th century. 6. United States—Politics and government—1945–1989. I. Title.
JK468.I6W45 2008
327.1273009'045—dc22 2007021587

For Patty

Contents

Illustrations

Illustrations follow page 148.

Abbreviations

ACCF	American Committee for Cultural Freedom
ACEN	Assembly of Captive European Nations
ACUE	American Committee on United Europe
ADA	Americans for Democratic Action
AFFJ	American Fund for Free Jurists
AFL	American Federation of Labor
AFME	American Friends of the Middle East
AFSCME	American Federation of State, County, and Municipal Employees
AFV	American Friends of Vietnam
AID	Agency for International Development
AIF	Americans for Intellectual Freedom
AIFLD	American Institute of Free Labor Development
AMCOMLIB	American Committee for Liberation
AMSAC	American Society of African Culture
ANG	American Newspaper Guild
ANLCA	American Negro Leadership Conference on Africa
ARCI	Aid Refugee Chinese Intellectuals, Inc.
BSO	Boston Symphony Orchestra
CAA	Council on African Affairs
CCF	Congress for Cultural Freedom
CCNY	City College of New York
CIA	Central Intelligence Agency

CIG	Central Intelligence Group
CIO	Congress of Industrial Organizations
COI	Coordinator of Information
CORAC	Council on Race and Caste in World Affairs, Inc.
CORE	Congress of Racial Equality
COSEC	Coordinating Secretariat of the International Student Conference
CPUSA	American Communist Party
DCI	Director of Central Intelligence
DD/P	Deputy Director/Plans
EAG	Europe-America Groups
ECA	Economic Cooperation Administration
ERP	European Recovery Program
FBI	Federal Bureau of Investigation
FO	Force Ouvrière
FTUC	Free Trade Union Committee
FYSA	Foundation for Youth and Student Affairs
HIACOM	Harvard University International Affairs Committee
IAFWNO	Inter-American Federation of Working Newspapermen's Organizations
ICFTU	International Confederation of Free Trade Unions
ICJ	International Commission of Jurists
ILG	International Ladies' Garment Workers' Union
IOD	International Organizations Division
IRC	International Rescue Committee
ISC	International Student Conference
ISI	Independent Service for Information on the Vienna Youth Festival (later Independent Research Service)
IUS	International Union of Students
KGB	Committee for State Security
KIM	Young Communist International
MEDICO	Medical International Cooperation
MI6	Secret Intelligence Service (United Kingdom)
MIT	Massachusetts Institute of Technology
MO	Morale Operations
MoMA	Museum of Modern Art

MSU	Michigan State University
NAACP	National Association for the Advancement of Colored People
NCFE	National Committee for a Free Europe (also Free Europe Committee)
NCL	Non-communist left
NKVD	People's Commissariat for Internal Affairs (forerunner of KGB)
NL	*New Leader*
NSA	United States National Student Association
NSC	National Security Council
NTS	Narodno-Trudovoy Soyuz
NYU	New York University
OCB	Operations Coordinating Board
ONI	Office of Naval Intelligence
OPC	Office of Policy Coordination
OSO	Office of Special Operations
OSS	Office of Strategic Services
PPS	Policy Planning Staff
PSB	Psychological Strategy Board
PSI	Public Service International
RFE	Radio Free Europe
RL	Radio Liberation (after 1964, Radio Liberty)
SAC	Société Africaine de Culture
SAK	Central Organization of Finnish Trade Unions
SDS	Students for a Democratic Society
SLU	St. Louis University
SMAP	Student Mutual Assistance Program
SMM	Saigon Military Mission
SO	Special Operations
SOBSI	All-Indonesian Central Labor Organization
SWP	Socialist Workers Party
UAW	United Automobile Workers
UNC	University of North Carolina
USIA	United States Information Agency
WAY	World Assembly of Youth

WFDY	World Federation of Democratic Youth
WFTU	World Federation of Trade Unions
WIDF	Women's International Democratic Federation
YAF	Young Americans for Freedom
YPSL	Young People's Socialist League

The Mighty Wurlitzer

Introduction

W. Eugene Groves was, all who knew him agreed, a young man of tremendous promise. Class valedictorian at his Indiana high school, he continued to shine as a member of the track team at the University of Chicago, where he studied physics and served as president of the student association. After graduating in 1965, he won a Rhodes Scholarship to Oxford and then, a year later, returned home to run for the presidency of the United States National Student Association (NSA), a post that had served several previous holders as a stepping-stone to high public office. By the age of twenty-three, the student politician had already come a long way from his hometown of Columbia City (population 5,500), where his father worked as a carpenter and his mother presided over the local Cancer Society.[1]

It was just as he was preparing to launch his NSA presidential campaign that Groves learned a secret about the organization that would change his life forever. Despite its appearance as a free and voluntary center for American student groups, the association was, its current president, Philip Sherburne, informed him, secretly funded by the Central Intelligence Agency. This arrangement, Groves learned, dated back to the first years of the Cold War, when the Soviet Union had launched a concerted effort to win the ideological allegiance of young people in western Europe by appealing to such idealistic causes as world peace and progress. Rather than making this appeal directly, communist propagandists did so covertly, through so-called "front" organizations—groups of private citizens outwardly serving some independent purpose who were in fact financed and controlled by Moscow.

Confronted by this challenge, senior U.S. government officials decided to respond in kind. The CIA, vested with broad, unspecified powers of covert operation by its legislative charter, the National Security Act of 1947, began making secret subsidies to the National Student Association (founded, incidentally, in the same year), first through wealthy individuals posing as private donors, then, more systematically, via fake charitable foundations created specially to act as funding "pass-throughs." Students in the NSA's international affairs division, who had been "groomed" by undercover intelligence officers attending NSA summer seminars and who were sworn to official secrecy, then helped channel the money abroad, where friendly foreign student organizations spent it on various activities intended to combat the influence of communist fronts. By the time that Eugene Groves was let in on the secret in 1966, the NSA's international program had expanded beyond western Europe to include new areas of Cold War strategic significance, among them South America, Africa, and Southeast Asia.

The revelation left Groves in an agonizing quandary. Described by friends as "warm and open," he was instinctively repelled by the elements of secrecy and deception involved in the relationship between the CIA and the NSA, not least of which was the requirement that those students who had sworn the secrecy oath—or, to use the Agency's own operational terminology, been made "witting"—conceal the truth about the NSA's funding from those who were "unwitting."[2] An earnest believer in the principles of citizen action and voluntarism, Groves was also dismayed by the U.S. government's apparent disregard for the NSA's independence as a nongovernment organization. Finally, while no long-haired student radical—he habitually wore a dark suit with a vest and, if quizzed about his politics, would describe himself as a "liberal" or "reformer"—Groves was profoundly disturbed by what he perceived as terrible errors in recent American foreign policy, particularly the war in Vietnam. The student leader's first instinct, therefore, was to try and "get the rascals out" by revealing all.[3]

As he pondered his situation, however, Groves began to imagine the dreadful consequences that might befall his beloved NSA if he were to go public. Its reputation as an international representative of the nation's youth, already under attack from youth groups both to its left (such as the Students for a Democratic Society) and its right (the Young Americans for Freedom), would be damaged beyond repair; shadowy figures in Washington might extract revenge by revoking its officers' draft deferments or canceling its tax-exempt status; individuals such as Roger Pulvers, an NSA exchange student studying in Warsaw, might find themselves in personal danger. And what of the possible risks to Groves himself? "Will they shoot me on a street corner when they find out that I know without having signed a security oath?" he wondered.[4]

In the end, Groves's hand was forced by the news, casually dropped into conversation by former NSA president and prominent liberal activist Allard Lowenstein, that a muckraking California magazine, *Ramparts*, was about to run a story exposing the CIA link, based on files pilfered from the association's headquarters by a disgruntled former officer. A hastily convened series of meetings between NSA leadership and CIA officials followed. Groves, who by now had been elected president, was outspoken in his condemnation of the clandestine contract between the two organizations. "My antagonism flustered some of the agents, who frantically accused me of undermining all the free world institutions that had been so painstakingly created over the last fifteen years," he recalled later.[5] Eventually, after consultation with the White House, the CIA gave permission for the NSA to draft a preemptive press statement admitting to and repudiating the relationship. Despite grave personal misgivings, Groves agreed that, prior to its release, he would conceal the story from inquiring reporters and other officers of the organization who were still unwitting. He also secured Roger Pulvers's recall from Poland, explaining to the bewildered and tearful student in a London hotel room that a CIA analysis had concluded it was dangerous for him to remain behind the Iron Curtain.

The story eventually broke in February 1967 when the *New York Times* simultaneously published an advertisement for the *Ramparts* exposé and a statement by the NSA. If the latter was intended to staunch the flow of revelations, it failed miserably. To the horror of Groves and countless other Americans, the *Times* went on in the weeks that followed to print a series of reports revealing covert CIA sponsorship of an astounding variety of other U.S. citizen groups engaged in Cold War propaganda battles with communist fronts. High-ranking officials in the American labor movement, it emerged, had worked clandestinely with the Agency to spread the principles of "free trade unionism" around the world. Anticommunist intellectuals, writers, and artists were the recipients of secret government largesse under the auspices of the Congress for Cultural Freedom (CCF) and its many national affiliates. University professors, journalists, aid workers, missionaries, civil rights activists, even a group of wealthy women known as the Committee of Correspondence, all had belonged to the CIA's covert network of front operations.[6]

The effect of the *Times* revelations was shattering. The Congress for Cultural Freedom was plunged into controversy, as illustrious American and European intellectuals argued bitterly about who among them had been witting of the CIA connection; wracked by resignations and reviled by younger writers, the disgraced organization sank into obscurity. The powerful president of the American Federation of Labor–Congress of Industrial Organizations (AFL-CIO), George Meany (who, newly available documents show, personally attended meetings with CIA chiefs in the early 1950s), resolutely denied there ever having been any secret dealings between his organization and the federal government; his statements were greeted with skepticism at home and protest abroad, where many American labor programs were abandoned for fear of violent retaliation against U.S. personnel. Dozens of other front operations collapsed under the impact of the revelations, leaving reputations and friendships in tatters. One unwitting officer of the Committee of Correspondence, who had worked for years trying to raise donations from private sources, never forgave colleagues who had known that such fund-raising was unnecessary because the CIA was bankrolling the organization and yet had allowed her to carry on because her activities helped preserve the Agency's cover.

As for the National Student Association, it weathered the storm better than most front organizations, refocusing its efforts on domestic issues and in the process actually increasing its membership. The last tie between the NSA and the CIA was severed in August 1967, when the student group took over the title and mortgage payments on the Washington brownstone that had served as its headquarters since 1965.[7] Having managed this transaction and seen out the rest of his presidency, Eugene Groves, once apparently bound for a glittering political career, retreated into private life. "The world [has] los[t] its innocence," he told the NSA's 1967 congress. "I want to get out."[8]

The ignominious demise of the CIA's covert network in 1967 presented a stark contrast with the circumstances of its creation nearly two decades earlier. Then, in the late 1940s, there had been very little doubt that such measures were necessary to defeat what was perceived as a menace to the survival of the "free world." True, the United States had the upper hand in many dimensions of the rapidly developing Cold War. Economically, it was clearly the strongest power on earth, as was shown by the unprecedented scale of the Marshall Plan aid program; and it still enjoyed sole possession of the atom bomb. However, in an equally important theater of this new kind of international conflict—the ideological struggle between capitalism and communism for the "hearts and minds" of nonaligned peoples around the world—its advantages were far less obvious. The Soviet Union could call upon communists' considerable experience of constructing front organizations, a tactic perfected by the Communist International, or "Comintern," during the 1930s and revived when the Communist Information Bureau—"Cominform"—was established in 1947, shortly after the proclamation of the Marshall Plan, in order to coordinate pro-Soviet Cold War propaganda. Even the British were ahead of the Americans in this game, boasting such "publicity" agencies as the Cultural Relations Department and the Information Research Department. Something had to be done quickly, lest the United States squander its economic and military superiority in the Cold War by losing the moral argument.

Fortunately, Americans did have a few advantages in the battle for hearts and minds. To begin with, there were some people around who knew about communist front tactics because they had once been communists themselves: such men as novelist and former Comintern officer Arthur Koestler, now a fanatical anticommunist, and Jay Lovestone, onetime leader of the American Communist Party turned chief foreign policy advisor to George Meany. It was the inveterate schemer Lovestone who devised the CIA's earliest covert operations in the field of international labor politics, secretly channeling millions of dollars to anticommunist trade unionists in Europe and further afield; Koestler helped carry the fight into the world of intellectuals and artists, organizing the 1950 rally in West Berlin out of which grew the Congress for Cultural Freedom. As the CIA was to discover, employing such ideological zealots in its covert operations could lead to serious practical complications. Still, in the first days of the Cold War, the expert advice of these men proved invaluable.

Moreover, in attracting supporters to its front organizations, the CIA could harness the American people's much-vaunted love of association. "A nation of joiners" was how historian Arthur M. Schlesinger, Sr., famously described his compatriots in 1944, echoing Alexis de Tocqueville's observation of more than a hundred years earlier that "Americans of all ages, all conditions, all minds constantly unite."[9] The potential Cold War applications of this trait were first spotted by diplomat and scholar George F. Kennan, who, recently declassified government records reveal, deserves recognition not only for having invented the idea of "containment" but also for being the principal architect of the CIA's covert network. "Throughout our history, private American citizens have banded together to champion the cause of freedom for people suffering under oppression," noted Kennan in a crucial planning paper of 1948. "Our proposal is that this tradition be revived specifically to further American national interests in the present crisis."[10] There was, of course, a strong element of expediency, even opportunism, about this tactic, just as there was in the Comintern's and, later, the Cominform's propagandistic appeals to "fellow travelers'" desire for world peace. That said, none of the U.S. front organizations of the Cold War period were merely official fabrications; all drew strength, to greater and lesser degrees, from the spontaneous energies of American associationalism.

Last, but not least in importance, the U.S. government could count on its citizenry to show it an extraordinary measure of goodwill and support in its crusade against communism. This was in part the legacy of World War II and the recent experience of total mobilization against a global threat to freedom. It also reflected the peculiarly intense anticommunism of the era, which served as an extremely strong cohesive force in postwar American society, binding together disparate groups in a powerful ideological consensus. To be sure, there always were those who felt uneasy about the secrecy involved in front operations (by aping the tactics of their totalitarian enemy, were not Americans in danger of becoming the thing they despised?) or feared the possibility that such activities might distract the CIA from what was supposed to be its cardinal purpose, the acquisition and analysis of foreign intelligence. By and large, though, there was little public inclination to question the wisdom or the ethics of the means by which government officials conducted the Cold War. Indeed, for at least the first decade of its existence, until the early 1960s (a period often referred to within the Agency as the "Golden Age" and identified with the leadership of Allen W. Dulles, Director of Central Intelligence between 1953 and 1961), the CIA enjoyed a reputation for competence and probity that now, many years and intelligence scandals later, is hard to credit. As one Agency officer recently remarked, "There was almost nobody in this country that I couldn't go to . . . and say 'I'm from the CIA . . .' and at the very least get a respectful reception and a discussion."[11]

It was against this background of perceived international crisis and domestic political consensus that the CIA constructed an array of front organizations that Frank Wisner, the Agency's first chief of political warfare, liked to compare to a "Mighty Wurlitzer" organ, capable of playing any propaganda tune he desired.[12] In the roughly twenty-year period before the revelations of 1967, there were three broad phases of front operation mounted by the CIA—or, if you like, tunes played on the Mighty Wurlitzer. First, there were organizations intended to provide a cover for émigrés and refugees from the communist-bloc countries, who were viewed as a potential secret army capable of infiltrating and undermining the Soviet empire from within (although the theme of "liberation," or "rollback," would fade after the abortive Hungarian uprising of 1956). Then, in rapid succession, came a series of operations designed to shore up civil society in western Europe against communist destabilization, most of which mobilized groups on the so-called non-communist left (or "NCL," in the Washington parlance of the day): trade unionists, intellectuals, and students. Finally, as the Cold War began to spread into new theaters in the so-called Third World during the late 1950s and early 1960s, the CIA secretly sponsored a host of new programs, often ostensibly concerned with development or modernization, but also intended to ensure that the "developing nations" did not succumb to communism. These programs tended to involve what would later be labeled "minority" groups, such as women and African Americans.

Of course, these distinctions were not hard and fast: the different phases overlapped, with some front organizations operating in two and a few in all three. Also, despite often having very different ideological and regional orientations, the groups that made up the CIA's covert network had certain basic features in common. For example, all were composed of private American citizens who had preexisting links to similar groups overseas, often based on some shared identity: generational in the case of the student groups, racial in the case of the African American organizations, and so on. These links provided the CIA with the cover it needed to influence strategically important sectors of foreign populations, but they also tended to set up a tension within the groups between members' nationality as Americans on the one hand and their transnational identities on the other.

Partly in order to manage this tension, the Agency sought some degree of control over its front operations. It exercised this control through individuals located within the organizations concerned, normally salaried officers such as executive directors or secretaries, who were witting about the true source of their funding and pledged to secrecy—although just how much control the Agency exercised, and how many witting as opposed to unwitting members the groups contained, remain questions of lively controversy even today.

Finally, while their politics might have varied in other important respects, the groups were united by a shared ideological conviction so important it was almost an article of faith: all were anticommunist. In the early years of the Cold War, when the anticommunist consensus was at its height, this belief was enough to ensure that the CIA's front operations remained secret. Later, however, as the consensus began to disintegrate under the strain of the Vietnam War, secrecy became impossible to maintain, and the scene was set for "the biggest security leak of the Cold War," as Eugene Groves called the *Ramparts* revelations in his 1967 report to the NSA congress.[13]

Writing the history of the Mighty Wurlitzer is not an easy task, given the shroud of official secrecy that still surrounds it today, fifty years on. The CIA has declassified only a tiny proportion of the presumably vast cache of records generated by this sprawling operation, preferring instead a policy of releasing groups of documents relating to specific, already well-known moments in its history, such as, for example, the Guatemalan coup of 1954. The job is not impossible, however. For one thing, while the CIA's operational records remain tantalizingly out of reach, the front organizations themselves have generally left behind substantial and publicly accessible collections of their working files, many of which contain strong traces of their relationship with their clandestine patron. For another, there already exists a small corpus of scholarly monographs and articles about particular front operations, written by intrepid souls using often highly ingenious research methods to overcome official secrecy.[14]

Valuable though this literature undoubtedly is, there are at least two respects in which it strikes the present author, at least, as inadequate. First, there simply is not enough of it. Granted, quite a lot has been written about CIA patronage of the arts, especially American abstract painting, including the most important book published in the field to date, Frances Stonor Saunders's enterprisingly researched and entertainingly written *The Cultural Cold War.*[15] Surprisingly little, however, has been written about other sectors of the CIA's covert network, and next to nothing on activities that were targeted at areas of the world outside of western Europe.

The other main problem with the existing literature about this subject, which has less to do with coverage than with interpretation, became apparent to me as I researched my previous book, a study of how U.S. Cold War front operations affected Britain and, in particular, the British left. The tendency has been to portray the CIA as very much the dominant partner in the patronage relationship, with the front groups obliged to toe the official line, thanks to the Agency's control of the purse strings. The most influential expression of this interpretation is Saunders's *Cultural Cold War*, whose British title, *Who Paid the Piper?*, extended the musical metaphor first employed by Frank Wisner to suggest that the CIA was calling the tune of the artists who received its covert subsidies. Yet this notion seemed at odds with the evidence I was uncovering about front operations involving literary intellectuals and trade unionists on the non-communist left. To start with, some of the ex-communists involved, Jay Lovestone and Arthur Koestler, for example, thought they knew best how to fight the Cold War and often disagreed with official policy. Moreover, the CIA could not always dictate how the money it secretly disbursed was spent, with left-wing literati sometimes purloining it for purposes that had little or nothing to do with the superpower conflict. The CIA might have tried to call the tune, I concluded, but the piper did not always play it, nor the audience dance to it.[16]

This book, therefore, has two main aims. One is to provide the first comprehensive account of the CIA's covert network from its creation in the late 1940s to its exposure twenty years later, encompassing all the main American citizen groups involved in front operations, not just in Europe but in the Third World as well. The other is to portray the relationship between the CIA and its client organizations in as complete and rounded a manner as possible, combining intelligence history with the specific social history or histories of the groups concerned. My hope is that, by telling both sides of the story, the groups' as well as the CIA's, I will shed new light not only on the U.S. government's conduct of the Cold War, but also on American society and culture in the mid-twentieth century.

Finally, a few words about the principles of selection underpinning the structure of this book. Although my survey of CIA front operations is intended to be comprehensive, it is not exhaustive. It is highly likely that we still do not know the identity of all the groups that received covert subsidies. One, Patrick Peyton's Family Rosary Crusade (described in Chapter 8) has only just come to light. In any case, it would be impossible to discuss in detail between the covers of a single volume every committee and project that is known to have been CIA-financed. Instead, what I have chosen to do is identify the main groups within American society that participated in the covert network and devote a chapter to each, concentrating on the activities of the most important organizations and individuals involved. This means that certain front operations, those that involved only a handful of U.S. citizens (in other words, ones that did not mobilize a distinct social group) and served little purpose beyond providing a funding conduit to foreign recipients, will receive merely passing mention.[17]

What follows, then, is the story of how the CIA attempted to mobilize a cross-section of American society in the Cold War struggle for hearts and minds—to "play" America as if it were a giant musical instrument—and how U.S. citizens at first followed the Agency's score, then began improvising their own tunes, eventually turning harmony into cacophony.

ONE

Innocents' Clubs

THE ORIGINS OF THE CIA FRONT

One day in late October 1940, during the first year of the Nazi occupation, two hunters were making their way home through woods just north of the small French town of Montagne, near Grenoble, when the excited barking of their dogs drew them to an old oak tree. Propped up against the trunk, almost concealed by drifting autumn leaves, was the badly decomposed body of a man, its head almost entirely denuded of flesh. Around the neck was a knotted cord, which had apparently snapped after having been suspended from an overhanging branch. A search of the corpse carried out later that day by the town's mayor and coroner turned up documents that revealed the body as being that of a German citizen named Willi Münzenberg. Unclear as to just who this man was, and not wanting to attract the attention of the Gestapo, the French officials rapidly reached a verdict of suicide, despite the absence of a note and the body's failing to display injuries usually associated with self-inflicted hanging.[1]

If the inhabitants of Montagne had not heard the name Münzenberg before, there were many in Europe—and, for that matter, several in the United States—who had. Born in 1889, the son of a violent, alcoholic innkeeper in southeastern Prussia, the handsome young radical had cut his teeth organizing communist youth in local factories, earning a reputation with the German authorities as a sort of professional malcontent. "He gave the impression," recalled the novelist Arthur Koestler, "that bumping against him would be like colliding with a steam roller."[2] Struck by his ideological fervor and tactical ingenuity, Leon Trotsky brought

Münzenberg into the small circle of Marxist intellectuals that surrounded exiled Bolshevik leader Vladimir Ilyich Lenin in Zurich. Münzenberg was not, however, in the company of Russian revolutionaries who in 1917 famously boarded the train that carried them in a sealed compartment to the Finland station in Petrograd. Instead, he moved to Berlin and, as the highest-ranking Bolshevik outside the Soviet Union, set about leading the western world into revolution.

Münzenberg's first major assignment was to raise money for victims of the ghastly famine that swept the Volga region of Russia in the early 1920s. Despite massive incompetence in the actual handling of funds and an obsession with discrediting outside humanitarian interventions such as Herbert Hoover's American Relief Association, Münzenberg's famine appeal was a propaganda coup, generating considerable sympathy for the Bolshevik regime, not least in the United States, where the Friends of Soviet Russia committee "literally raised more money in its first two months than it knew what to do with."[3] Out of these early efforts grew the so-called Münzenberg trust, a vast media empire of newspapers, publishing houses, movie houses, and theaters which, "on paper at least," stretched from Berlin "to Paris to London to New York to Hollywood to Shanghai to Delhi."[4] The financial profitability of these ventures has probably been overestimated—Münzenberg's most recent biographer thinks that the "Red Millionaire" was in fact a poor businessman who lost rather than made money for Moscow[5]—but their effectiveness as instruments of propaganda has not. Particularly successful were Münzenberg's various "front" groups, committees superficially devoted to some undeniably benign cause, such as anti-imperialism, peace, or antifascism, whose real purpose was to defend and spread the Bolshevik revolution. Using such devices as letterhead adorned with famous names, spectacular cultural festivals, and carefully stage-managed mock trials, these organizations proved irresistible to politically well-meaning progressives, whose participation made them, in effect, "fellow travelers" of the international communist movement. Münzenberg referred to the front committees as his "Innocents' Clubs."[6] "These people have the belief that they are actually doing this themselves," he once told an associate. "This belief must be preserved at any price."[7]

The apotheosis of the front tactic came in August 1935, when the Seventh World Congress of the Communist International proclaimed the

People's Front against fascism. The Popular Front, as it was known, lived up to its name. In the United States, for example, writers and artists flocked to the antifascist cause. Just returned from the front line in the Spanish Civil War, Ernest Hemingway told the Second Congress of the League of American Writers that fascism was "a lie told by bullets."[8] Movie stars such as Melvyn Douglas, Paul Muni, and James Cagney sponsored the Hollywood Anti-Nazi League. "This machine kills fascists," proclaimed the guitar of hobo balladeer Woody Guthrie. And these were only the most conspicuous converts. Across the whole spectrum of American society, citizen groups gravitated to the Front. African Americans, already impressed by communists' apparent sympathy for their civil rights (the International Labor Defense, which saved nine young black men accused of raping two white women from a legal lynching in Scottsboro, Alabama, was a branch of Münzenberg's International Workers Relief) joined the National Negro Congress. Factory workers in heavy industries, long regarded as untouchable by the established trade unions, formed the rank-and-file of communist-led organizing drives that coalesced in a new national labor confederation, the Congress of Industrial Organizations. Student protestors, attracted by the campus campaigns of the American Student Union, formed a national mass youth movement some thirty years before the university strikes of the 1960s.[9]

Of course, for every U.S. citizen who joined a front organization, there were many more who kept their distance. For anticommunist Americans, then and since, the Popular Front was cheap political theater, a marionette show in which foreign puppet-masters pulled the strings of the naïve and foolish. Recently this view has apparently been vindicated, in dramatic fashion, by a series of documentary revelations that followed the collapse of the Soviet Union and end of the Cold War. First, historians who gained access to the archives of the Communist International and the U.S. Communist Party (CPUSA) in Moscow discovered papers showing that not only had American communists received large sums of cash from the Kremlin (rumors of "Moscow gold" had circulated for years without hard evidence to back them up) but also that the CPUSA leadership, including no less a figure than the Party's General Secretary throughout the Popular Front era, Earl Browder, had actively connived in spying by Soviet agents in the United States during the 1930s and early 1940s.[10] Then, in 1995, the National Security Agency revealed the existence of

VENONA, a top-secret Cold War signals intelligence operation that had succeeded in decoding a number of messages between Soviet diplomats in America and Moscow that had been intercepted during World War II. Here was proof that many of the claims about Soviet espionage made in the reckless, overcharged, anticommunist atmosphere of the late 1940s and early 1950s were in fact true. Julius Rosenberg, executed for treason in 1953 and long afterward thought to be a victim of judicial murder, was indeed an "atom spy." Many of the U.S. government officials accused of espionage by the emotionally unstable "blonde spy queen" and FBI informer Elizabeth Bentley really had, it turned out, passed government secrets to the Soviets. There were even intercepts strongly suggesting that Alger Hiss, the suave, patrician New Dealer at the center of the period's most controversial spy case, was a Soviet agent after all (although Hiss's defenders are disputing this interpretation of VENONA even now).[11]

Given the new evidence, it is hardly surprising that many commentators have concluded that the American communist movement was a mere automaton, the unswervingly loyal servant of the Kremlin. Such a verdict on the CPUSA leadership is, it seems, inescapable. Yet it does not entirely account for the motives and aspirations of ordinary communists, the vast majority of whom were never involved in anything remotely resembling espionage. (Even the most generous estimate of the number of spies within the Party, 300, seems small when placed in the context of a total membership during World War II of some 50,000.)[12] For the average member of a Popular Front organization—a Jewish fur-worker dismayed by the rise of anti-Semitism in Hitler's Germany, a student inspired by the Republican cause in the Spanish Civil War, an African American protesting Mussolini's invasion of Ethiopia—the communists might have deserved praise for their efforts resisting fascism, but supporting the Soviet Union was far down his or her list of priorities, under other, more pressing concerns, such as fighting unsafe working conditions, challenging the injustices of racial segregation, or alleviating the hardship caused by unemployment. True, in the background were the Soviet paymasters and their agents in the United States, the apparatchiks of the CPUSA; but the fronts would never have got off the ground if they had not also reflected the particular values and needs of the groups they represented.

Ironically, for Willi Münzenberg himself, the man who, to quote Koestler again, "produced Committees as a conjurer produces rabbits out of his hat," the advent of the Popular Front marked the beginning of the end.[13] Forced to abandon Germany for France after Hitler's rise to power, he strove to maintain Stalin's favor as, one by one, his old Bolshevik friends disappeared. It was not long before the Gestapo spies who shadowed him in Paris were joined by agents of the NKVD (the predecessor organization to the KGB). Expelled from the German Communist Party in 1938, he began feeling out contacts in the western intelligence services, raising the intriguing possibility that, had he survived the war, he might have been on hand to advise the CIA as it began setting up its own front operations in the late 1940s. Such an outcome was not to be, however. After France fell to the Wehrmacht, he fled south toward the Swiss border, disappearing in late June 1940 somewhere between Lyons and Grenoble. Precisely how he met his end remains a mystery, although there is general agreement among historians that the coroner's verdict of suicide was unsound. As Trotsky's assassination in Mexico in the same year showed, Stalin's reach could be long and deadly.

A few weeks after Willi Münzenberg's disappearance, a shortish man with a ruddy face and blue eyes boarded a Pan American Clipper flying boat bound for London via Lisbon. William J. Donovan was an American hero. Born in 1883 to Irish immigrant parents in Buffalo, New York, he had starred as quarterback for Columbia University, emerged from World War I as one of the most heavily decorated veterans of the American Expeditionary Force, and amassed a small fortune as a corporate lawyer on Wall Street. For all the wealth and adulation, though, "Wild Bill" carried about him a palpable air of frustrated ambition. Apparently bound for high political office in the 1920s, he was passed over for the post of attorney general in Herbert Hoover's administration, then defeated in New York's 1932 gubernatorial race. Banished to the political sidelines, he channeled some of his prodigious energies into lengthy foreign excursions in North Africa, Spain, and the Balkans, where he indulged a taste for spying he had acquired during the Russian civil war of 1919. His mission to London of July 1940 was tailor-made. In addition to investigating German Fifth Column activities and the state of Anglo-American naval intelligence collaboration, Donovan was personally charged by his Columbia classmate, President Franklin Delano Roosevelt, with reporting on Britain's ability to withstand the Nazi advance. (Roosevelt wanted to help the British cause but was stymied by American anti-interventionism and the consistently defeatist dispatches he was receiving from his Ambassador to the Court of St. James, Joseph P. Kennedy.) Here then was both an excellent opportunity to learn from the British masters of the secret arts and an unexpected entrée into the White House.[14]

This time, Donovan did not squander his chance. Fêted by the British—the king, Prime Minister Winston Churchill, and Colonel Stewart Menzies ("C," or the chief of MI6) all granted him personal audiences—he returned to the United States with the message that FDR wanted to hear: Britain could repel the Nazi horde, but only if America sent more destroyers. Now performing the function of the crippled president's "eyes and legs," Wild Bill began lobbying in earnest for something he had desired fervently for years: an American national intelligence agency.[15] There already existed several organizations tasked with gathering and analyzing information bearing on the nation's security: the Army's venerable Military Intelligence Division, or G-2; the Office of Naval Intelligence; the newly created Office of Inter-American Affairs (overseen by a precocious scion of one of the country's wealthiest families, Nelson A. Rockefeller); and, of course, J. Edgar Hoover's Federal Bureau of Investigation. But these agencies' intelligence efforts were badly fragmented, and none of them was equipped to carry out the sort of secret political warfare that other nations were waging with ever greater skill and sophistication.

In pushing for a central body that would combine the functions of espionage and covert operation, Donovan ran up against several obstacles—including the opposition of bureaucratic rivals like the formidable Hoover, conservative qualms about adding further to government powers already vastly augmented by the New Deal, and a deeply ingrained American dislike of spying ("Gentlemen do not read each other's mail," Secretary of State Henry Stimson had famously pronounced when some deciphered Japanese messages landed on his desk in 1929).[16] Still, helped by some well-placed words of support from his British friends, in particular William C. Stephenson (the secret agent code-named "Intrepid"), Wild Bill persevered and in July 1941 was rewarded by his appointment as Coordinator of Information (COI), a new position vested with considerable powers of oversight over the existing intelligence agencies.[17] The Irish altar boy had at last arrived in the American establishment.

Accompanying Donovan in his wartime ascent was another middle-aged corporate lawyer who, though different in background and temperament from Wild Bill, nonetheless shared his sense of unfulfilled potential—and his fascination with the clandestine. From the age of seven, when he wrote a history of the Boer War that was published by his proud family, Allen Dulles appeared bound for great things. The grandson of one secretary of state and nephew of another, he had served with distinction in several U.S. missions during World War I, discovering in the elegant Swiss city of Bern a penchant for espionage that was, as writer Burton Hersh has noted, "damned near glandular."[18] He was also a member of the American delegation to the Versailles peace conference, advising Woodrow Wilson as the president attempted to make the world safe for democracy. After these heady early experiences, however, nothing else quite measured up. Like Donovan, Dulles made a great deal of money out of the law and investment banking, and tried unsuccessfully for political office—in his case, a Manhattan congressional seat—while continuing to travel and dabble in intelligence. The weight of his family's expectations was burdensome, especially because next to the "somber granite edifice" that was his older brother John Foster Dulles, he could not help looking lightweight.[19]

The eve of World War II found Dulles as genial and raffish as ever (qualities that apparently made him irresistible to women—his sexual conquests, in addition to his long-suffering wife Clover, included the queen of Greece, a daughter of Toscanini, and Clare Booth Luce) but drifting professionally. This explains why, when Wild Bill Donovan invited him to run the New York office of the COI in 1941, he leaped at the chance. In November 1942, after a year spent gathering data on the Nazis and perfecting his spying tradecraft under the tutelage of William Stephenson, who shared his office building in New York, Dulles returned to Bern as Donovan's European second-in-command.[20] He spent most of the rest of the war in Switzerland, "a prisoner in Heaven."[21]

By this point, of course, the United States was a belligerent power, and the COI had been reconstituted as a military agency, the Office of Strategic Services. Wild Bill Donovan's OSS has been the subject of much mythmaking regarding its contribution to both the eventual Allied victory and the later creation of the CIA. In fact, the organization was excluded from most of the major theaters of the war, badly hampered by friction with rival services and Donovan's notoriously poor administrative skills (which one subordinate likened to a person "pouring molasses from a barrel onto the table"), and involved in some frankly harebrained schemes, including a plan to drive Hitler insane with lust by showering his headquarters with pornography.[22] For all that, there were individual acts of astonishing bravery, such as those performed by the Jedburghs, who in 1944 parachuted into occupied France to help the resistance cut Nazi supply lines ahead of the Normandy landings, not to mention the unsung efforts of the nine hundred or so Washington-based scholars in the OSS's Research and Analysis branch, who strove to retrieve and analyze every available scrap of information on the Axis powers.[23] There were also some notable espionage coups, such as Dulles's success in establishing links with anti-Hitler elements in Germany, including the Abwehr officers who plotted to assassinate the Führer in 1944.[24] For all his managerial shortcomings, Donovan deserves credit for having called into existence, almost overnight, a remarkably diverse and dynamic organization, which at the very least proved a considerable nuisance to the enemy—and partly laid the foundations of America's postwar intelligence establishment.

Notwithstanding a tendency among boosters of the CIA to talk up the Agency's dynastic descent from the OSS because of the latter's aura of heroism and derring-do, there were a number of incontrovertible continuities between the wartime agency and its peacetime successor, not least in the area of covert operations. To begin with, despite neither having any domestic responsibilities—indeed, both were expressly forbidden from operating at home—the two organizations showed the same tendency to reach inward into American society in order to discharge their secret missions abroad. Academics, émigrés, and labor officials all moved into and out of Donovan's covert network, sharing their expert knowledge and contacts in foreign countries and blurring the boundaries between the official and the civil realms as they went—much as the spies themselves seemed not to distinguish between government service and personal duty (Donovan never collected any salary during his time as Coordinator of Information, falling back instead on his considerable private means).[25] Then there was the OSS's clear orientation toward covert action, as opposed to the less glamorous (but, many would argue, more worthwhile) business of information collection—its penchant not only for paramilitary sabotage and subversion but also for the subtler arts of "psychological warfare," propaganda designed to undermine enemy morale and strengthen that of allies. "Persuasion, penetration, and intimidation . . . are the modern counterparts of sapping and mining in the siege warfare of former days," believed Donovan.[26] No wonder, then, that in addition to a Special Operations (SO) branch, his spy agency had a whole division devoted to MO (Morale Operations), in particular the production of materials designed to suggest widespread demoralization among ordinary Germans and Japanese.[27] This prioritizing of covert operations, including "psy-war," over espionage was one of the OSS's more significant (and, arguably, regrettable) legacies to the CIA. Finally, it is possible to detect several social and political similarities between the two services: a common practice of recruiting their staff from elite universities such as Yale (not for nothing was the OSS nicknamed "Oh So Social"); a distinct predisposition toward internationalism, produced in many cases by the officers' experience of living and fighting alongside foreign partisans during the war; and a surprising amount of liberalism, even leftism, again often the result of close wartime dealings with communist-dominated resistance movements. Indeed, several conservative critics complained, not without justification, that Donovan was harboring communists within the OSS.[28]

Of course, it would not do to exaggerate the leftward leanings of the Office of Strategic Services. Equally powerful—and, in terms of the later development of the CIA, historically more important—was an impulse toward *anti*communism. Take Frank G. Wisner, for example, chief of OSS operations in the central Balkans during the latter stages of the war and the man responsible for implementing the CIA's earliest covert operations. The Mississippi-born, powerfully built Wisner, who as well as earning top grades at the University of Virginia narrowly missed out on a place in the U.S. sprint team at the 1936 Berlin Olympics, was ostensibly in eastern Europe to spirit downed Allied airmen out of Nazi-occupied territory—an operation he carried out with dazzling success, rescuing nearly two thousand flyers. But his real mission was to report on communist attempts to take over the region as the German occupation ended. Rapidly establishing himself in Bucharest as a major broker of Rumanian politics (and enjoying the lavish hospitality available at the intrigue-ridden court of King Michael), Wisner built up HAMMERHEAD, a highly productive network of anticommunist espionage agents whose findings won him a reputation in Washington as a prophet of postwar Soviet intentions.

"This place is wild with information," reported one 1944 cable home, "and Wisner is in his glory."[29] Shortly before leaving Rumania in February 1945, Wisner's growing hatred of the communist system acquired an obsessive, even apocalyptic intensity when he impotently witnessed the herding of ethnic Germans onto trains bound for forced labor camps in the Soviet Union. "My husband was brutally, brutally shocked," recalled his wife, Polly. "It was what probably affected his life more than any other single thing."[30] A few months later, when he was in Germany extracting intelligence about the Soviet Union from defeated Nazis, one of his lieutenants, the young Harvard historian Arthur M. Schlesinger, Jr.—himself no slouch in the anticommunism stakes—was taken aback by Wisner's ideological fervor. "He was already mobilizing for the Cold War," Schlesinger recalled later.[31]

But the Cold War had not started yet. Granted, cracks were appearing in the Grand Alliance even before the declaration of victory in Europe. Meanwhile, Franklin Roosevelt's death in April 1945 ushered into the White House a plain-spoken, midwestern machine politician who soon "tired of babying the Soviets" (as he told an aide after just a few months in office).[32] However, Harry S. Truman was no fan of the OSS and seems to have taken a strong personal dislike to the "Black Republican leprechaun," William Donovan.[33] More convinced than ever of the United States's need for a permanent secret service, and personally reveling in his role of American spymaster, Wild Bill had begun arguing as early as September 1943 for the extension of the OSS's lifetime beyond the end of the war. Again, however, he encountered resistance at every turn, some from the usual quarters, such as Hoover's FBI; and some in less expected places: it now appears that FDR himself authorized the leaking to the press of a memorandum from Donovan outlining his vision of a peacetime intelligence agency, which resulted in a storm of negative reports in the anti-Roosevelt press in February 1945. "New Deal Plans to Spy on World and Home Folks," read a headline in the *Chicago Tribune*, "and Super Gestapo Agency Is Under Consideration."[34] Wild Bill ploughed on manfully, but the game was up. Eventually granted access to the Oval Office, he presented Truman with an envelope containing his spy agency blueprint, which the new president tore in two and handed back to him. The OSS was formally dissolved in September 1945, with Research and Analysis hived off to the State Department and all the other branches going to the military. Demobilized by the end of 1945, Donovan, Dulles, and Wisner all returned reluctantly to their law practices in New York. It was, Dulles told John Kenneth Galbraith, "an appalling thing to come back, after heading a spy network, to handling corporate indentures."[35] History, it seemed, had passed him by again.

George F. Kennan was suffering from one of his chronic maladies—a debilitating combination of cold, fever, sinusitis, and toothache. Still, he had waited a long time for a chance like this, and he was not about to let it slip through his fingers. Princeton-educated, intensively trained at the U.S. foreign service's elite school for Soviet specialists in the Baltic city of Riga, and steeped in Russian culture and history, Kennan had watched for years from his middle-ranking post at the American Embassy in Moscow as well-intentioned but naïve New Deal officials let Stalin and his despotic regime get away, literally, with murder. Now, however, in February 1946, the Truman administration was uncertain as to how to handle its erstwhile ally. Some of the new president's advisors counseled that Truman continue his predecessor's wartime policy of cooperation, while others advised taking a hard-line stance. The State Department cabled the U.S. mission to Moscow requesting clarification of Soviet intentions. Kennan's superiors were at last asking for his opinion, and, as he later put it in his memoirs, "by God, they would have it." Dictating to a secretary from his sickbed, the chargé d'affaires composed a 5,540-word telegram, "all neatly divided, like an eighteenth-century Protestant sermon, into five separate parts," which gave eloquent voice to his long pent-up personal frustrations, love of the Russian people, and hatred of Bolshevism.[36]

There was, Kennan's "Long Telegram" explained, no possibility of continued cooperation with the Soviet leadership. A number of factors, including an instinctive sense of national insecurity and the expansionist imperatives of Marxism-Leninism, had made communist Russia into "a political force committed fanatically to the belief that with [the] U.S. there can be no permanent *modus vivendi*, that it is desirable and necessary that the internal harmony of our society be disrupted, our traditional way of life be destroyed, the international authority of our state be broken, if Soviet power is to be secure." This threat was all the more terrifying because, in addition to its vast internal resources, the Soviet Union had at its disposal "an elaborate and far-flung apparatus for exertion of its influence in other countries, an apparatus of amazing flexibility and versatility, managed by people whose experience and skill in underground methods are presumably without parallel in history." Not only that, western societies contained a "wide variety of national associations or bodies which can be dominated or influenced by such penetration," including "labor unions, youth leagues, women's organizations, racial societies, religious societies, social organizations, cultural groups, liberal magazines [and] publishing houses." In these circumstances, the only "manly" course of action open to the United States (Kennan was fond of using such gendered language to make his point) was to contain Soviet expansion with "the logic of force" in the hope that structural weaknesses within the communist system, chief of which was the Stalin regime's lack of legitimacy in the eyes of ordinary Russians, would lead to its eventual disintegration.[37]

It was an emotional, rhetorically overwrought performance, which sat uneasily with Kennan's later, much-vaunted reputation as a Cold War "realist"; but, for an audience grasping for ways to make sense of the bewilderingly complex postwar world, it hit home. Recalled from Moscow in April 1946, Kennan toured the United States, giving as many as thirty lectures on the Soviet challenge before taking up residence at the National War College in Washington, where he developed his notion of strategic "containment" into an article published the following year in the influential journal *Foreign Affairs* under the pseudonym "Mr. X."

Meanwhile, events seemed to be conspiring to confirm Kennan's analysis of Soviet behavior. In March 1946, while speaking in Fulton, Missouri, Winston Churchill used the phrase "Iron Curtain" to describe Moscow's growing control over communist-dominated governments in eastern Europe. A year later, with the Soviet Union sending probes into areas of the Mediterranean and Middle East previously controlled by the British, President Truman appeared before Congress to request huge appropriations to aid the threatened governments of Greece and Turkey. A few months after the "Truman Doctrine" committed the United States to a global policy of saving "free peoples" from communist aggression, Secretary of State George C. Marshall used a June 1947 commencement address at Harvard to outline a massive program of financial assistance to the war-devastated economies of Europe. Predictably, the Soviets refused to take part in the Marshall Plan and, in October, at a conference of eastern European communist party officials in Warsaw, revived the Comintern (which Stalin, in a wartime gesture of goodwill, had abolished in 1943) in the shape of the Communist Information Bureau, or Cominform. Soon the Cominform was launching Münzenberg-style front operations all over the west, peddling a seductive image of the Soviet Union as a champion of world peace and the war-mongering United States as its principal enemy. The briefly fluid international situation of the immediate postwar period had frozen into a bipolar world order in which two ideologically opposed enemies used every means available to them, short of direct military confrontation, to frustrate the ambitions of the other.

It was against this background of deepening international tension that the Central Intelligence Agency was conjured into being. The first step toward the establishment of a peacetime foreign secret service had been taken in January 1946 when, in a mock ceremony in the Oval Office perhaps intended to mask his profound anxiety about the dangers of creating an American gestapo, Harry Truman appointed his trusted friend Rear Admiral Sidney W. Souers the first head of the interim Central Intelligence Group (CIG), conferring on him a black cloak and wooden dagger and pronouncing him "director of centralized snooping."[38] The CIG was to function as a White House "news desk," furnishing the president with digests of information gathered by the intelligence divisions in the State Department and armed services.[39] With the arrival in February of the Long Telegram, however, and the alarming deterioration in American-Soviet relations that followed, support grew for a more powerful centralized body with its own research and analysis capability. Following a series of congressional debates—the U.S. secret service was the first in history to originate in parliamentary legislation—a national security bill was enacted on July 26, 1947, creating both a Central Intelligence Agency and a National Security Council (NSC) to advise the president. Mention of the Soviet Union was conspicuously absent from the National Security Act and the debates leading up to it. Nonetheless, an important clause of the Act, which authorized the CIA to perform unspecified "other functions and duties related to intelligence affecting the national security," would later be invoked as legal justification for anti-Soviet covert operations.[40]

That was still in the future, however. In the first years of its existence, the CIA, reflecting the temperament of its director, the amiable but ineffectual Admiral Roscoe H. Hillenkoetter, steered clear of political warfare, preferring to stick with the more gentlemanly business of intelligence gathering. Not surprisingly, this squeamishness exasperated the "Park Avenue cowboys," the rambunctious corporate lawyers who had run the OSS and, since that organization's demise, had been lobbying for a revival of special operations to counter the new totalitarian threat. Joining the Park Avenue cowboys in their calls for stronger anti-Soviet measures were the "Dumbarton Avenue skeptics," a cadre of anticommunist Sovietologists who, during the war years, had gathered in the Georgetown home of future ambassador to France Charles "Chip" Bohlen to express their dissent from the foreign policy of the Roosevelt administration.[41] At the head of this coalition of "determined interventionists" was George Kennan, an ardent advocate of covert operations and psychological warfare, who in May 1947 was effectively handed control of U.S. Cold War strategy when he was chosen by George Marshall to head the powerful new State Department body, the Policy Planning Staff (PPS).[42] Thanks to his authorship of the Long Telegram and the "X" article, Kennan has long been recognized as the chief architect of the American foreign policy of "containment." It is only recently, with the release of newly declassified government documents, that historians have come to appreciate the extent to which his definition of containment anticipated the more aggressive strategy of "liberation" more commonly associated with the administration of President Dwight D. Eisenhower and his secretary of state, John Foster Dulles.[43]

The first significant victory for the determined interventionists came in December 1947, when the National Security Council gave the CIA its covert operation charter in the shape of top-secret directive NSC 4-A, instructing Director of Central Intelligence (DCI) Hillenkoetter to undertake "covert psychological operations" against the Soviet Union.[44] The Agency used its new powers in the spring of 1948 to prevent communist victory in elections taking place in Italy, distributing anticommunist literature, providing pro-western newspapers with scarce newsprint, and conducting a disinformation (or "black") propaganda campaign under the leadership of future counterintelligence chief James Jesus Angleton.[45] The communists were defeated at the polls, whether as a result of the U.S. intervention or the conservatism of Italian voters is not entirely clear. But the interventionists were not satisfied. Moscow was tightening its stranglehold over eastern Europe—witness the brutal coup that had taken place in Czechoslovakia in February—and, under Hillenkoetter, the CIA's approach to political warfare still lacked conviction. On May 4, 1948, in an atmosphere of near war-panic caused by the Soviets' launch of the Berlin blockade, Kennan's Policy Planning Staff presented a plan for "the inauguration of organized political warfare" that involved the creation of a new "covert political warfare operations directorate within the Government."[46]

If the Long Telegram provided the theoretical rationale for the overt dimensions of U.S. Cold War foreign policy, the PPS's May 1948 memo supplied the intellectual basis for its covert aspects. Kennan's first aim was to persuade government officials who still had qualms about a democracy's conducting covert operations in peacetime that political warfare was not only proper, it was also necessary given the circumstances in which the United States currently found itself. Other nations had long accepted the legitimacy of this kind of warfare: the British, for example, had made extensive use of it, and its conduct by the Soviet Union was "the most refined and effective of any in history." American politicians needed to overcome the "popular attachment to the concept of a basic difference between peace and war" and "recognize the realities of international relations" (note the appeal to realism and easy assumption of the right to bypass popular opinion, both typically Kennanesque moves). Doing so might come easier if they realized that they were already engaged in an overt form of political warfare without knowing it: such measures as the Truman Doctrine and the Marshall Plan were, after all, originally conceived as responses to Soviet provocations. Covert operations of whatever kind—"clandestine support of 'friendly' foreign elements, 'black' psychological warfare, and even encouragement of underground resistance in hostile states"—were in this sense merely an extension of existing U.S. government policies. In any case, the country's "international responsibilities" were now such that, "having been engaged by the full might of the Kremlin's political warfare," Americans had no choice but to respond in kind.

Having demonstrated, at least to his own satisfaction, the ethical propriety of covert action, Kennan then proceeded to describe "specific projects" that the United States might undertake. A possible first step was to set up public "liberation committees," which would serve as foci for "political refugees from the Soviet world" to foment resistance to the communist regime. "This is primarily an overt operation," the memorandum explained, "which, however, should receive covert guidance and possibly assistance from the Government." The example of Comintern-funded front organizations was not explicitly cited here—the justification offered was the patriotic one that private U.S. citizens would eagerly participate in such committees because of a long American tradition of voluntary association in support of "people suffering under oppression"—but the spirit of Willi Münzenberg could be detected in the passing observation that the communists had "exploited this tradition to the extreme, to their own ends and to our national detriment, as witness the Abraham Lincoln brigade during the Spanish Civil War." Another suggestion was the "support of indigenous anti-Communist elements in threatened countries of the free world, . . . a covert operation again utilizing private intermediaries." A reference to communist-inspired industrial strikes in France intended to disrupt the delivery there of Marshall aid suggests that Kennan already had particular U.S. labor groups in mind for this purpose. Third, the memorandum raised the possibility of "preventive direct action in free countries"—that is, paramilitary operations—but only as a last resort, when other political and psychological methods had failed. Finally, Kennan recommended the establishment of an entirely new government body, under the cover of the National Security Council but answerable to the Secretary of State, which was to have "complete authority over covert political warfare operations."[47]

In just one document, George Kennan had set the agenda for all of the United States's front operations in the first years of the Cold War. Here, in embryonic form, were the CIA's émigré organizations, its covert labor program, and its many other clandestine efforts to aid the European "non-communist left" using equivalent American groups as go-betweens. Ironically, though, the immediate effect of Kennan's proposals was to reduce the Agency's control over covert operations. While his recommendation that the State Department take complete control of political warfare from the CIA was rejected (thanks to a combination of half-hearted resistance by Director Hillenkoetter and a reluctance on the part of foreign-service traditionalists to give a home to the "dirty tricks" brigade), such was the sense of crisis pervading Washington in the summer of 1948 that Kennan's idea of creating a new government body devoted exclusively to covert operations won widespread support. The result was a compromise whereby the CIA was to house the new organization—supply it with "quarters" and "rations," to employ the military parlance still in common use at the time—and the Secretary of State (meaning, in effect, Kennan's PPS) provide it with policy guidance. NSC directive 10/2, approved on June 18, 1948, superceded NSC 4-A by creating an Office of Special Projects endowed with powers to conduct "any covert activities" related to "propaganda, economic warfare; preventive direct action, including sabotage, anti-sabotage, demolition and evacuation measures; subversion against hostile states, including assistance to underground resistance movements, guerrillas and refugee liberation groups, and support of indigenous anticommunist elements in threatened countries of the free world."[48]

To carry out this mission, the intellectual Kennan turned to the men of action, the Park Avenue cowboys. William Donovan's best days, it was generally agreed, were now behind him, so Kennan's first pick to head the new political warfare outfit (whose name was soon changed to the deliberately more opaque Office of Policy Coordination, or OPC) was Wild Bill's European deputy, Allen Dulles. Mistakenly believing that he would become Director of Central Intelligence in a Republican administration following the 1948 presidential election, Dulles declined the invitation. Kennan then turned to the former chief of OSS eastern European operations, the hard-driven Frank Wisner, who had rejoined government service in 1947 as a State Department official overseeing intelligence operations in occupied Germany.[49] As the Assistant Director for Policy Coordination, Wisner lost no time in recruiting to the OPC men like himself, OSS old boys and professionals with European experience, in the process creating, in the words of one recruit, future CIA Director William Colby, "the atmosphere of an order of Knights Templars, to save Western freedom from Communist darkness."[50]

The new recruits were assigned either to headquarters in Washington (housed in a collection of dingy huts strewn along the Mall) or undercover positions in diplomatic posts and military bases abroad. The Washington-based personnel were split into five "Functional Groups"—psychological warfare, political warfare, economic warfare, preventive direct action, and "miscellaneous"—and, in deliberate imitation of the Marshall Plan, six geographical divisions, the heads of which controlled the field staff.[51] In practice, however, OPC officers abroad, who were usually second-in-command at their embassy, enjoyed a large measure of autonomy, often initiating their own operations, or "projects," as they were called.[52] The independence of individual officers was mirrored by that of the organization as a whole, which, although housed by the CIA and guided by Kennan's PPS, was practically nonaccountable thanks to the broad mandate of NSC 10/2 and Wisner's secret access to the unvouchered "counterpart funds" set aside for Marshall Plan administrative expenses, which amounted to roughly $200 million a year.[53] The determined interventionists had triumphed: covert operations had at last acquired truly effective organizational form.

Such were the origins of the CIA's Mighty Wurlitzer. Willi Münzenberg had pioneered the front organization in Berlin, then during the 1930s watched it take root in the United States, that society of inveterate joiners. With the approach of World War II, a group of "fading Wilsonians"[54] who habitually thought of their private and the public interest as one and the same thing, overcame an innate American aversion to government secrecy and established the nation's first central intelligence agency. (The great expansion of federal power that had taken place under the New Deal made this change much easier to accomplish than it might otherwise have been.) Immediately after the war, as Soviet-American friendship gave way to enmity and the OSS was revived in the shape of the CIA, George Kennan grafted the communist front tactic onto the new Cold War U.S. intelligence apparatus. All that was needed now was for the dashing young Ivy Leaguers in Frank Wisner's Office of Policy Coordination to translate this plan for political warfare into action.

TWO

Secret Army

ÉMIGRÉS

As George Kennan and other "determined interventionists" discussed possible means of not only containing the spread of communism but also rolling back the Soviet empire in a campaign of liberation, they kept coming back to the same idea: the possible usefulness to their cause of the numerous exiles from the communist world now living in the west. In the immediate aftermath of World War II, American occupation forces in Germany had gathered a great deal of valuable information from former Nazis with special knowledge of communist Russia, such as Reinhard Gehlen, who had been Hitler's chief of military intelligence on the eastern front. By the summer of 1946, the War Department was systematically spiriting away to the United States Germans who had desirable "technical" expertise (and, often, terrible records as war criminals) in a secret operation code-named "Paperclip."[1] Kennan and his fellow interventionists now advocated taking a similar approach to the many thousands of eastern-bloc citizens who were either crowded into prisoner of war (POW) and displaced person (DP) camps in Germany or scattered around various western capitals: captured Russian soldiers who had fought with the Nazis against their own communist government, refugees from Baltic and Balkan territories "liberated" by the Soviets, and disillusioned ex-communist intellectuals. As well as being exploitable for intelligence purposes, this drifting, desperate population could be deployed in anti-Soviet political warfare operations, both paramilitary and psychological. The mere fact of the presence in the west of these political refugees testified to the hatefulness of communist rule and the possibility of escape from it.

How, though, to harness this "potential secret army?" Various suggestions were considered. Kennan proposed the creation of a political warfare school to train exiles in "air support, communications, local security, counter-intelligence, foraging, sabotage, guerrilla tactics, field medicine, and propaganda." Two veterans of the OSS, Stanford-educated guerrilla specialist Franklin Lindsay and State Department-trained Sovietologist Charles Thayer, came up with a plan "to extract for U.S. advantage disaffected foreign nationals from Soviet-dominated areas." Shortly before taking over the Office of Policy Coordination, Frank Wisner, who had toured German DP camps in 1947 while working for the State Department, led a high-level study group investigating the "Utilization of Refugees from USSR in U.S. National Interests." When the group reported in May 1948, it made particular play of the exiles' "fortitude in the face of Communist menace" and know-how "in techniques to obtain control of mass movements," including "Socialist, trade union, intellectual, moderate right-wing groups, and others." Wisner wanted to see the relaxation of U.S. immigration controls and a secret government disbursement of $5 million to expedite the recruitment of these "natural antidotes to Communism." The resulting program, Operation Bloodstone, echoed its predecessor Paperclip by admitting a number of war criminals. As Harry Rositzke, a Soviet expert in the CIA, explained, "It was a visceral business of using any bastard as long as he was anti-communist."[2]

The employment of such elements in intelligence-gathering and paramilitary operations was clearly something that had to be done secretly. Psychological warfare, however, was a different matter. Inspiring resistance within the "captive" populations of the eastern bloc and demoralizing the communist leadership were goals that could only be achieved with public pronouncements by anticommunist exiles. The problem was how to lend support to such exiles without at the same time discrediting them by making them look like American agents. The answer lay in Kennan's May 1948 memorandum on political warfare: the formation of "a public American organization" to "sponsor selected political refugee committees" that would receive "covert guidance" and "assistance" from the government.[3] In addition to providing U.S. officials with the ability to deny plausibly that they were subverting a foreign government in peacetime, this stratagem would have the advantages of creating the impression of voluntary humanitarianism among American citizens and, at the same time, helping educate the U.S. public in the moral issues of the Cold War.

In April 1949, Kennan wrote Secretary of State Dean Acheson asking for the go-ahead to launch "one of the principal instrumentalities for accomplishing a number of our most important policy objectives."[4] Acheson in turn contacted diplomatic elder and veteran anti-Bolshevik Joseph Grew, who agreed to chair the new organization. Meanwhile, corporate lawyer Allen Dulles, still without a government position yet exerting a growing behind-the-scenes influence over the emergent U.S. intelligence apparatus, attended to the legal practicalities, filing a certificate of incorporation with the State of New York in May. On June 1, 1949, Grew held a press conference, announcing the formation of the National Committee for a Free Europe (NCFE) (a name later shortened to the Free Europe Committee) and introducing a group of sponsors that, in the words of Frances Stonor Saunders, "read like *Who's Who in America*," including Dwight Eisenhower, Arthur Schlesinger, Jr., and Cecil B. DeMille.[5] Shortly afterward, Dulles accepted the post of executive secretary, leaving the more visible job of NCFE president to DeWitt C. Poole, a State Department expert on anticommunist propaganda who, as a young official in the U.S. Embassy in Moscow, had witnessed the Bolshevik revolution and, during World War II, managed émigré relations for the OSS. In 1951, Poole was succeeded by Time, Inc., senior executive C. D. Jackson, previously Eisenhower's head of psychological warfare operations during the war.

According to outward appearances, the NCFE was an independent organization spontaneously formed by private American citizens, "one of those innumerable voluntary associations which make up democratic society," as Grew put it.[6] In fact, the New York–based corporation was a proprietary of Frank Wisner's Office of Policy Coordination (OPC), which provided it, as per Kennan's 1948 memo, with both secret guidance and funding, the former arriving in the shape of verbal or written directives from Washington, the latter a weekly check fetched from the Wall Street offices of investment bank Henry Sears & Co.[7] Details of these arrangements were divulged to employees on a strictly "need-to-know" basis and only after a careful security vetting. There was, however, no shortage of clues as to the committee's real nature. When questions of policy or the organization's budget came up, "witting" officers would refer mysteriously to "our friends in the South" or the "Sponsor" (the committee itself was the "Fund").[8] Government classification codes appeared on internal committee memoranda, as did handwritten annotations with the initials "F. W."[9] The whole operation had an oddly sleek feel to it for "a struggling young organization of European refugees." Visitors to the NCFE's headquarters expecting to find themselves in a "barren loft" discovered instead a plush suite of offices on the third floor of the Empire State Building.[10] This high standard of accommodation reflected the generosity of the OPC's patronage. "Contributions" received by the committee during the financial year 1951–52 alone amounted to $18,017,864.[11]

The obvious wealth of the NCFE created an urgent need for a cover story. This was provided by the "Crusade for Freedom," a public fund-raising drive devised by Abbott Washburn, an ex-OSS officer and public relations expert who was seconded from food conglomerate General Mills for the purpose.[12] Earlier in the century, the PR genius Edward L. Bernays had adapted such covert techniques as the front organization for commercial purposes, creating, for example, the Tobacco Society for Voice Culture, an apparently independent group dedicated to promoting the message that smoking improved people's singing, on behalf of one of his clients, Chesterfield cigarettes.[13] During World War II, the U.S. public relations industry was pressed into the cause of strengthening civilian morale through the War Advertising Council (later renamed the Advertising Council), which encouraged the public to buy war bonds and conserve war materials.[14] Now, Washburn was being invited to draw on this tradition of secret salesmanship and government service in order to "sell" the Cold War to the American public—and, in doing so, provide a plausible explanation for the large sums of cash sitting in the coffers of the National Committee for a Free Europe.[15]

Launched by General Eisenhower on Labor Day, 1950, the Crusade for Freedom employed a number of ingenious devices to stimulate the support of ordinary Americans. A "Freedom Bell," cast (like the Liberty Bell in Philadelphia's Independence Hall) in an English foundry, was transported around the nation on the "Freedom Train" before being shipped to Europe and, during an emotional ceremony watched by a crowd of 400,000, installed in the tower of the Schöneberg Rathaus in Berlin.[16] Echoing the "Campaign of Truth" launched earlier in the year by President Truman, radio appeals exhorted audiences to donate "truth dollars" to the cause, with celebrities such as actor Rock Hudson assuring listeners that the NCFE was "supported entirely by contributions by American citizens."[17] Civil air patrols "bombed" suburban neighborhoods with preprinted "Freedom-grams" to be signed and sent to NCFE headquarters for distribution in eastern Europe.[18] Although Washburn's campaign raised only $2.25 to $3.3 million a year during the 1950s, a fraction of the NCFE's total expenditure, it did manage to divert attention from the organization's main source of funding and succeeded in imaginatively involving the American public in the plight of the captive nations. Its ubiquitous images and slogans became as familiar to 1950s Americans "as Ivory soap or Ford automobiles."[19]

Given such a wealth of covert patronage and public support, one may ask, just what did the NCFE do? Much of its early activity consisted of efforts to relieve and rally the eastern-bloc refugees who were drifting into the United States. Attempts were made to form effective working groups, or "National Councils," representing all the democratic political elements—socialist, Catholic, and peasant—in each of the Iron Curtain countries, with the OPC trying to control council membership.[20] Individual émigrés undertaking research projects on aspects of the communist system were supported by regular grants from the NCFE. Brutus Coste, for example, an eminent Rumanian diplomat and scholar who was working on a project entitled "Democracy in Russia," received a monthly stipend of $300.[21] This interest in subsidizing academic endeavor with a possible intelligence dividend was evident also in several more ambitious initiatives undertaken in the NCFE's first years. The organization established its own publishing house, Free Europe Press; a "Mid-European Studies Center" for newly arrived refugee scholars in New York; and a "Free Europe University in Exile" to educate eastern European émigré youth, housed in a chateau near Strasbourg, France.[22]

Such activities remained an important part of the NCFE's program, but by 1950, as U.S.-Soviet relations plumbed new depths and the Cold War turned hot in Korea, the emphasis shifted to more aggressive forms of psychological warfare, which involved piercing the Iron Curtain itself. One method employed extensively by the NCFE had been tried and tested against the Nazis in World War II but now looks surprisingly low-tech. Staff would travel to sites on the borders of the Soviet Union's "satellite" nations and release balloons. Carried eastward on the prevailing winds, the balloons would explode once they had reached a height of 30,000 or 40,000 feet, showering propaganda materials—leaflets denouncing communist leaders, fake currency, and anticommunist "newspapers"—on the captive populations below. (One tongue-in-cheek proposal—to advertise the sexual prowess of American men by scattering extra-large, U.S.-manufactured condoms stamped "medium"—was abandoned at the planning stage.)[23] The first such operation was launched from an open field near Regensburg, West Germany, in August 1951. The balloons floated toward the border with Czechoslovakia as planned, but then, to the consternation of the watching crowd, began drifting back. Fortunately for the NCFE officers present, the wind changed direction again, and the balloons eventually reached their target.[24] Similar launches were carried out throughout the early 1950s; protests from eastern European officials were met with the claim that the U.S. government had no control over the actions of a private group of freedom-loving American citizens. Some 300 million pieces of propaganda were dropped over the "denied areas" before the practice was discontinued in the wake of the failed Hungarian uprising of 1956.[25]

By the mid-1950s the balloons were functioning merely as adjuncts to a technologically more sophisticated form of psychological warfare. Like so many "psy-war" tactics employed by the United States in the Cold War, the use of radio to propagandize eastern European populations had been pioneered by the Bolsheviks. On November 7, 1917, a message from Lenin to the Russian people was transmitted from the cruiser *Aurora*, anchored at Petrograd, in Morse code. Later, during World War II, the people of Finland were "softened up" for Soviet annexation by intimidatory radio broadcasts.[26] Now it was the anti-Bolsheviks' turn to take to the airwaves. During the NCFE's press launch in June 1949, Joseph Grew described a plan to "put the voices of . . . exiled leaders on the air, addressed to their own peoples back in Europe, in their own languages."[27] The State Department already had a foreign broadcast arm, the Voice of America, but it was designed to inform foreign audiences about the United States and was constrained from carrying out explicit propaganda by its overtly official ownership. The NCFE's aim was to set up a station to act as a sort of surrogate home service for the Iron Curtain countries, an alternative to the communist-controlled media, with separate national desks enabling

Polish émigrés to speak to Poles, Hungarians to Hungarians, and so on. Radio Free Europe (RFE) first broadcast to Czechoslovakia on July 4, 1950, from a former Luftwaffe base in Lampertheim, near Frankfurt, using a transmitter loaned it by the U.S. Army. The following year, with more powerful machinery at its disposal and a new headquarters situated in the beautiful surroundings of Munich's Englischer Garten (with rehabilitated German spy chief Reinhard Gehlen helping to provide the base security), RFE expanded its operations to Poland, Hungary, Romania, Bulgaria, and Albania.[28] By 1953, the station boasted 252 American and 1,526 foreign employees. It gathered broadcast materials from eight news bureaus; operated twenty-six transmitters, including cutting-edge facilities in Portugal; and provided "saturation broadcasting" to the captive nations.[29]

The tone of RFE's early broadcasts was shrill and hectoring, reflecting both the ardent anti-Bolshevism of the National Committee for a Free Europe and the more aggressive Cold War stance adopted by the U.S. government after 1950. (NSC 68, signed by President Truman in September 1950, effectively militarized Kennan's doctrine of containment by calling for a massive arms buildup to defeat communism.) In November 1950, DeWitt Poole instructed the station's managers to attack communist leaders "and tear them apart, exposing their motivations, laying bare their private lives, pointing up their meannesses, pillorying their evil deeds, holding them up to ridicule and contumely."[30] Gradually this approach moderated, as programmers attempted to build RFE's reputation as a legitimate news source and began introducing more lighthearted items intended to appeal to a wider audience. Nonetheless, the denunciatory impulse remained, as was demonstrated to startling effect in 1954, when the Voice of Free Poland broadcast a series of interviews with Josef Swiatlo, a colonel in the Polish security service who had defected during a shopping trip to West Berlin. As the former head of counterintelligence in Poland, Swiatlo had seen the private files of many of the country's leading communists—indeed, he had compiled several of them himself. He now divulged their contents, including lurid details of financial corruption and personal scandals, to RFE's presumably outraged Polish listeners. It was a propaganda coup for the new station, one made to appear all the more dramatic by subsequent political developments in Poland, which included a purge of senior intelligence officials, a spate of communist self-criticisms, and, in 1956, the ushering in of the more moderate Gomulka regime.[31]

The National Committee for a Free Europe enjoyed several successes, not least in the realm of broadcasting. Years later, after the disintegration of the eastern bloc, such dissident luminaries as Lech Walesa and Vaclav Havel testified to the importance of RFE in nurturing the flame of resistance in the captive nations.[32] Reviewing the NCFE's program in its entirety, however, one cannot help being struck by the organization's operational problems, its many failures, and the unintended consequences of several of its actions. The NCFE's scholarly projects, for example, were fraught with difficulties and disputes. In France, the University in Exile was subject both to harsh attacks by the left-wing press and attempts to penetrate it by French intelligence. Its American planners argued about its admissions criteria and the selection of staff, while its students fell prey to a creeping demoralization, some calling it the "tragic bordello."[33] Meanwhile, back in the United States, attempts to organize the émigré population into distinct National Councils ran up against even greater obstacles. An NCFE progress report compiled in January 1950 noted the apparent inability of both Yugoslav and Polish exiles to form single councils, concluding that "it is in this department of our work that the most harassing problems have arisen."[34] By 1952, the Poles still lacked an organization that could qualify for NCFE recognition, the Rumanians were in a similar state of disarray, and both the Czechoslovakian and Hungarian councils were badly split.[35] A high-level government committee formed to review all U.S. psy-war programs reported in 1953 that "efforts to form national councils . . . have largely been frustrated by the bickerings and jealousies common to émigré politicians."[36]

It is certainly arguable that the NCFE's problems with the National Councils were related to a historic tendency among exiled political leaders to internal factionalism and ideological extremism. Macaulay's description of English refugees in seventeenth-century Holland might have applied equally well to the eastern European émigrés of the Cold War era: "A politician driven into banishment by a hostile faction generally sees the society which he has quitted through a false medium. Every object is distorted and discoloured by his regrets, his longings, and his resentments. Every little discontent appears to him to portend a revolution. Every riot is a rebellion."[37] Certain characteristics unique to this particular exile community, however, made it especially fractious and ungovernable. First were the obvious rivalries between certain nationalities, such as the animosity between Poles and Ukrainians. There were also ethnic conflicts within particular exile communities—for example, the tension that existed between Czechs and Slovaks. Finally, often overlapping with these other divisions were profound political differences between and within groups. Émigrés from socialist or social democratic backgrounds accused exiles with right-wing beliefs of harboring fascist sympathies (sometimes with good reason), while the latter denounced the former for alleged communist leanings. Some political conflicts were even more obscure. According to one internal Office of Policy Coordination memorandum, Polish social democrats were among those calling for their compatriot, the famous anti-Stalinist writer Czeslaw Milosz, to be denied a visa to enter the United States because they objected to his continuing to call Poland's economy "socialist"—they interpreted this as a slander on socialism.[38]

The problems caused by exile factionalism potentially extended far beyond the National Councils. There was always the danger that outsiders would get dragged into intramural disputes, opening the NCFE up to unwelcome external scrutiny. Security was a problem anyway, given the ease with which refugee populations could be infiltrated by communist agents. Émigrés also had the inconvenient habit of boasting to one another about successful bids for U.S. government patronage, and a number of them had guessed correctly at the real source of the NCFE's funds. Most worrying for the OPC was exile leaders' readiness to complain to elected politicians if they did not get what they wanted from the NCFE. Many U.S. congressmen represented districts dominated by eastern European immigrants and therefore took more than a passing interest in the official conduct of the Cold War. During the 1950s, with domestic anticommunism reaching a fever pitch, several widely reported attacks were made on the RFE by right-wing Republicans, who were goaded on by disgruntled émigré constituents. And as if all this was not enough, exile conflicts often spilled over into the day-to-day operation of RFE. The Czech service, for example, faced repeated attacks by ethnic Germans who had been expelled from the Sudetenland and perceived RFE as an obstacle to "German-West Slav understanding."[39]

This is not to say that the OPC simply stood back and let the émigrés do whatever they wanted. Granted, the desk chiefs at RFE were selected by the National Councils, and the NCFE made much of the editorial freedom enjoyed by the émigré programmers, but the station's administrative structure included a number of circuit breaks designed to give the Americans some control over what was broadcast. As with staff at the NCFE's headquarters in New York, any employee in Munich made witting of the OPC's patronage was required to swear a secrecy pledge. An American "policy advisor" held daily briefings with the desk chiefs, at which he laid down editorial guidelines formulated in Washington. He also read through transcripts of programs on each of the different language services (but only after they had been aired). Every month intelligence officers in the United States would review tapes of a day's output, chosen at random, to double-check that the policy advisor's guidance was being followed.[40] Taken together, these measures persuaded the Americans that, despite the sense of autonomy felt by the émigré staff, in fact it was the Americans who were in charge. Some congratulated themselves on the ingenuity of these arrangements. In 1952, William E. Griffith, the American policy advisor in Munich during the early 1950s and later a major academic expert on communism based at the Massachusetts Institute of Technology's Center for International Studies (another institution with connections to the CIA), told a colleague, using words reminiscent of Willi Münzenberg's contemptuous attitude toward his "Innocents' Clubs," "This feeling of freedom is indispensable. That it is in fact an illusion, albeit a convincing one, is even more so."[41] Not everyone was reassured, however. In 1955, Frank Altschul, former head of the NCFE's radio committee, informed Allen Dulles (then Director of Central Intelligence) that the "audit of scripts is not comprehensive enough . . . to insure the early detection of deviations from the line laid down."[42]

As well as giving the Americans a false sense of security, attempts to impose control on the émigrés could produce unexpected and unwonted results. In 1951 Dulles was overheard at a Washington dinner party telling fellow guests that "these refugees had never lived so well in all their lives, . . . that they [were] getting too big for their britches, [and] that they would have to do what our people . . . told them to do or else."[43] The following year the NCFE issued a directive to all émigré organizations based in the nation's capital to relocate to New York—a move presumably intended to bring them more firmly under NCFE supervision and make it less easy for them to hobnob with conservative congressmen. Disgusted by this "unwarranted" and "overbearing" behavior, the exiles complained to officials in the Truman administration that the NCFE's diktat threatened to "reduce them to the status of paid American agents" and, furthermore, invited "a major propaganda attack on American exploitation and abuse of émigrés and displaced persons" (the last comment sounding suspiciously like a veiled threat to leak the plan to the press).[44] Meanwhile, in Munich, refugee broadcasters balked at what many regarded as heavy-handed American management techniques. When the NCFE overruled RFE advice and launched a balloon operation designed to complement the Swiatlo broadcasts by scattering written accounts of his revelations over Poland, relations with the Polish desk broke down altogether. "Poles are now asking Poles," one sympathetic American reported to the NCFE, "who is the worse master, the Russian or the American?" The fallout from this incident was extensive. Polish-American congressmen wrote furious letters to Secretary of State John Foster Dulles; communist propagandists pointed to evidence that a hidden hand was manipulating the RFE; and Swiatlo himself, incensed by negative references to him in the balloon materials, threatened to sue the NCFE for $10,000.[45] The incident culminated with Robert E. Lang, the RFE's American director, resigning his post in protest.

As Lang's resignation showed, the OPC could not even count on the passive obedience of the private American citizens acting as its front men. Such NCFE officers as DeWitt Poole had, after all, been in the anti-Bolshevik game much longer than a sophomore like Frank Wisner. They were also backed up by the clout of the prestigious names that had lent themselves to the NCFE board, and they were sufficiently well connected in government circles to appeal decisions they did not like directly to the White House. "It has to be borne in mind that the Fund is directed by individuals not only of some public stature but possessing specific experience in the fields of diplomacy and psychological warfare," an anonymous memorandum from a NCFE officer (probably Poole himself) warned the OPC in 1950. "If an ostensibly private instrumentality is desired which will do no more than carry out automatically directions from Washington, a different type of personnel will have to be found for the Fund." The memo concluded, "A long step would be accomplished simply by recognizing the Fund to be a partner on an equal footing, subject only to the final authority of the Government on points of public policy."[46]

From the first, the NCFE appears to have felt that its "friends in the South" were paying it insufficient attention and failing to come up with good-quality anticommunist intelligence for use by RFE. "We receive with some regularity a daily selection of what is purported to be significant news items," complained Frank Altschul in 1950. "Only the fewest of these items are of any use at all." At the same time, NCFE and RFE managers resented excessive meddling in their business by OPC officers. Lang was particularly sensitive on this score, fulminating about "intrusion in each and every element of our affairs by characters on the operating side of our friends' organization."[47] Most controversial of all were attempts by the OPC to use the RFE's airwaves to broadcast code messages to resistance fighters behind the Iron Curtain. Although senior CIA officials have denied that the station was ever used for this purpose, there is evidence that the Polish section, at least, was directed to air "several special messages."[48]

The balance of power in this relationship appears to have shifted periodically. On one occasion a showdown between NCFE/RFE staff and their OPC case officers was won by the former, with the spies either resigning or being reassigned to other projects.[49] Shortly afterward, however, Dulles used a "full dress RFE meeting" in his office as an opportunity to slap down Lang. "Are you telling me, Mr. Dulles, that this is 'it'?" the station director demanded, after hearing the DCI expound the official line on broadcast policy. "I don't know if we will ever see anything 'itter'," responded Dulles.[50]

Given his experiences with the NCFE, it is small wonder that, when he turned his attention from satellite nation refugees to émigrés from the Soviet Union, Frank Wisner would have taken a rather different approach. The American Committee for Liberation for the Peoples of the USSR (the last words of the name changed several times during the early 1950s, but the first half remained constant, often abbreviated to "AMCOMLIB") was incorporated in Delaware in January 1951, after Frank Lindsay, deputy chief of OPC, had dealt with the necessary paperwork. (With its relatively lenient corporation laws, Delaware became the spies' favorite state for registering front organizations.)[51] There was little of the fanfare that had accompanied the establishment of the NCFE, and few of the new organization's officers were household names. Rather than enlisting "old boys" like Dulles and Wild Bill Donovan, Lindsay turned to low-profile academics and journalists with expert knowledge of Soviet affairs. AMCOMLIB's first president was Eugene Lyons, a senior editor at *Reader's Digest* and author of *The Red Decade*, an influential exposé of communist front tactics in 1930s America. While the famous publisher of *Time*, Henry Luce, had been involved in discussions leading up to the organization's launch and sat on the board of the NCFE, the post of secretary was filled by Allen Grover, Luce's less well-known vice-president and general factotum.[52] Grover told AMCOMLIB's first board meeting that there would be no public fund-raising activities along the lines of the Crusade for Freedom. Instead, money would come from "personal friends of committee members."[53] Generally speaking, the new organization departed from the example set by the NCFE in that AMCOMLIB adopted a more secretive and, so Wisner and Lindsay must have hoped, manageable structure. Its basic aims, however, were much the same as those of the older group: organizing the émigrés into an effective political warfare force and equipping them with a radio station capable of reaching listeners behind the Iron Curtain—in this case, within the Soviet Union itself.

The trouble was that the Soviet émigrés proved no less conflict-ridden than the exiles from the satellite countries. To begin with, the "minority" nationalities, especially the Ukrainians, were just as opposed to Russian domination as they were to Bolshevism and were determined to use the anticommunist cause as a vehicle to assert their national independence. This naturally made the job of crafting a unified anti-Bolshevik movement all the more difficult. And that was not all. Even within the Russian émigré community there were profound political divisions. On the left were the Mensheviks, a small but influential group of social democrats who had fled Russia following 1917 and, after years of wandering the west, had fetched up in New York, where they congregated around the *New Leader*, an anticommunist labor weekly. Among the brilliant intellectuals and incorrigible intriguers who made up the Menshevik "Foreign Delegation" were the much-revered but slippery business manager of the *New Leader*, Sol Levitas; the redoubtable "Kremlinologist" David Dallin; and Boris Nicolaevsky, an eminent historian of the Russian Revolution and wily political operator. The Mensheviks were united in their opposition to Stalinism but could not agree among themselves about whether to jettison Marxism as well. Their uncertainty on the "Marxist issue" alone was enough to condemn them in the eyes of the émigré right. Advocates of the restoration of the Russian monarchy, or Czarists, were a dwindling minority in the émigré population, but there were many others who embraced one form or another of conservative nationalism. The Narodno-Trudovoy Soyuz (NTS), or National Union of Labor Solidarists, a well-organized and ideologically aggressive faction of "Great Russians" who flirted with neo-fascism, was increasingly popular. The Vlasovites, veterans of the military units of captured Russian soldiers formed by the Nazis during World War II under the command of the charismatic general Andrei Vlasov, were rather vaguer on questions of doctrine, but were fervently nationalistic and anti-Bolshevik.[54] Together, these various groups constituted a political powder keg, with their would-be American patrons unwittingly poised to light the fuse.

Attempts to impose some order on this mélange were already underway by the time that AMCOMLIB appeared on the scene. In January 1951, an OPC officer, former journalist Spencer Williams, rented an inn on the outskirts of the Bavarian town of Füssen to accommodate a meeting of Russian exile leaders. As representatives of the main émigré organizations assembled in an atmosphere of brooding enmity, Williams tactfully retired to the pleasant town of Garmisch, forty miles away.[55] The meeting did not go well. Discussions got so badly bogged down over the "unification" issue—how much independence the Russians should concede to the national minorities in the struggle against Bolshevism—that it barely got around to the question of liberation.[56] The NTS delegates present, suspecting that the Americans were in cahoots with the Mensheviks, particularly Boris Nicolaevsky, staged a walkout, causing Williams to cancel the inn reservation after just a week. For their part, the Mensheviks, who were already dismayed by the U.S. authorities' readiness to employ émigrés with fascist pasts, returned to New York feeling that they had been used as American agents. ("I wonder why Americans, every time they undertake something along the Russian line, never fail to call on people who are hopelessly compromised," Nicolaevsky once remonstrated with an OPC contact.) In a *New Leader* article entitled "The Wrong Russians Again," David Dallin berated AMCOMLIB for trying "to give orders" and "interfering in the smallest details."[57] Considering that the work of the American Committee was supposed to be secret, it is hardly surprising that Dallin's outburst earned him the organization's undying hostility.[58]

Next it was the turn of AMCOMLIB's European director, journalist and publicist Isaac Don Levine, to try persuading the exiles to pull together. His efforts appeared, on the surface at least, more successful. In August 1951, after "considerable back-and-forth negotiations, and some emotion," the main Russian organizations (which, following some further factional splits, now numbered five) met at Stuttgart and, prodded by Levine, managed to agree to a common policy on the nationalities question.[59] (The London *Economist*, noting the presence at the event of the aging Alexander Kerensky, who had served briefly as Russian prime minister before the Bolshevik revolution, joked snidely about AMCOMLIB "lifting Kerensky from the dustbin of history.") A follow-up meeting attended by representatives of six non-Russian émigré groups (the Ukrainians stayed away) took place in a Wiesbaden hotel in November, leading to the formation of a "Coordinating Center of the Anti-Bolshevik Struggle." The following summer, Levine even succeeded in persuading the exiles to set up a commission to sponsor the launch of a new radio station.[60]

The appearance of progress, however, was deceptive. Shortly after the Wiesbaden conference, the conservative NTS, which had access to sources of covert patronage other than the CIA, including British intelligence, led a breakaway movement of Russian nationalists unhappy with the concessions that had been made to the minority nationalities. Relations between the Russians and non-Russians left behind do not seem to have improved as a result; indeed, by the summer of 1953, they had broken down altogether. AMCOMLIB decided that enough was enough and withdrew its support for the Coordinating Center, announcing, "It is regrettable that the political forces of the emigration have not had the foresight and statesmanship to lay aside their internal differences and unite in presenting a common front to the Kremlin."[61] From that point on, the radio project would be developed independently of the émigré leadership. Still, AMCOMLIB did not completely give up its hopes of forging a unified exile movement, which one Russian onlooker reckoned had already cost it about $8 million.[62] In 1954 C. D. Jackson, who had moved on from the presidency of the NCFE to become President Eisenhower's Special Assistant for International Affairs (which meant, in effect, chief planner of U.S. Cold War psychological warfare), grew so exasperated with AMCOMLIB's continuing "exilitis" that he called a series of meetings with senior CIA managers, telling them "to pull [themselves] together and evolve some practical policy." "Forget about trying to unite political exiles," he instructed one intelligence officer. "Get the political exiles out of the way, preferably Peru . . . and just go to work."[63]

Meanwhile, in March 1953, AMCOMLIB's new radio station began broadcasting to the Soviet Union from the former operations building of Oberweisenfeld airport in north Munich.[64] Radio Liberation (after 1964, Radio Liberty, or RL) experienced many of the same problems as its Munich neighbor, Radio Free Europe, although there was little sense of camaraderie between the two: the eastern Europeans who worked at RFE looked down on the "slouching tatterdemalion staff" of RL, which soon acquired the nickname "Radio Hole-in-the-Head."[65] Its clandestine patrons in Washington tried to exert influence by posting undercover staff to RL's Lilienthalstrasse offices. The pretense fooled no one. "I doubt that there was a single stoker or sweeper," wrote one American employee, "who did not have some inkling of the true state of affairs."[66] Protecting the base against Soviet penetration was also a daily challenge. The deaths of two émigré employees in 1954—one a Belorussian writer whose body was fished out of the Isar River, the other the chief of the Azerbaijani desk found garrotted in his apartment—both smacked of the KGB.[67] Nevertheless, internecine strife carried on unabated, with Great Russians pitted against the nationalities, and Mensheviks versus the NTS. The latter were eventually banned from the station by its director of broadcasting, Howland Sargeant, a former assistant secretary of state and head of the Voice of America. Under Sargeant's management, Radio Liberty also moved away from the highly aggressive tone it had adopted in its first broadcasts, becoming a trusted news source for such dissident Russian intellectuals as Andrei Sakharov and Alexander Solzhenitsyn.[68] It was thanks in no small part to this approach that the station avoided the sort of disaster that befell Radio Free Europe in 1956 and drove one top CIA officer to the edge of insanity.

For Frank Wisner, the man charged by George Kennan with the task of breaking up the Soviet empire, the intractability of the émigrés connected with the NCFE and AMCOMLIB was only one in a long and growing list of problems. To begin with, the paramilitary side of the liberation campaign was faring no better than the psychological. In 1949, the Office of Policy Coordination had become involved in the first U.S. attempt of the

Cold War era to overthrow a foreign government, the communist regime of Albanian dictator Enver Hoxha. British spies had come up with the idea of using the island of Malta—still a UK colony at the time—as a base for infiltrating specially trained émigré agents loyal to the exiled King Zog into the small Balkan country. "Whenever we want to subvert any place, we find that the British own an island within easy reach," remarked Wisner, whose OPC put up the funds for the operation, codenamed BGFIEND.[69] This first test of rollback ended in dismal failure. Hoxha's counterintelligence service rounded up the Anglo-American agents with an efficiency that suggested advance knowledge of their arrival. The source of the tip-off was later identified as H. A. R. "Kim" Philby, who in his role as Washington-based liaison between OPC and MI6, had attended planning meetings for BGFIEND. The Anglophile Wisner, who had liked and trusted Philby (the British mole's nickname was borrowed from Wisner's favorite writer, Rudyard Kipling), never forgave this act of treachery. (For his part, Philby later contemptuously described the American as "a youngish man for so responsible a job, balding and running self-importantly to fat.")[70] Still, this misadventure did not deter the OPC from carrying out further agent drops behind the Iron Curtain, in the Baltic states, and even in the Ukraine, all leading to the same tragic denouement.

Wisner was also facing difficulties closer to home. In October 1950, after the CIA had failed to predict the outbreak of war in Korea, the pliable Roscoe Hillenkoetter was replaced as Director of Central Intelligence by the former U.S. ambassador in Moscow and Eisenhower's chief of staff during World War II, General Walter Bedell Smith. "Beetle" was a very different proposition from "Hillie." Irascible, foul-mouthed, plagued by stomach ulcers, he was (as one wit put it) "even-tempered": that is, always angry.[71] Furthermore, the new DCI did not care much for Wisner's OPC, which in its first two years of existence had expanded at a dizzying rate, spinning off "projects" like a giant Catherine wheel. (The Central Intelligence Act of 1949 had made it even easier for Wisner to engage in covert operations by exempting the CIA from congressional budgetary and accounting requirements.) Smith had never been a fan of psychological warfare; in his view, it was too costly, its effectiveness was unproven, and it exposed the United States to the risk of scandal. "If you send me one more project with goddamned balloons," he once snarled at a cowering subordinate, "I'll throw you out of here."[72] Moreover, as a midwesterner of humble origins, Smith felt little sympathy for the Ivy League, dilettante types who flocked around Wisner. More to his liking were the quiet-spoken professionals in the CIA's Office of Special Operations (OSO), the Agency division responsible for intelligence collection, or espionage, as opposed to covert action. Observing the parking lot at CIA headquarters, where the Chevrolets and Fords driven by OSO officers stood alongside the MGs and Jaguars owned by OPC-ers, Beetle determined to bring Wisner and his crowd to heel.[73]

Shortly after Smith's arrival, the OSO and the OPC were submerged in a new entity, the Directorate of Plans. In January 1951, Allen Dulles, at long last back in from the Park Avenue cold, took up the position of Deputy Director/Plans (DD/P), Beetle's second-in-command for covert action and espionage. For Wisner, who had enjoyed almost absolute operational freedom for the previous two years, this amounted to a "severe double demotion."[74] Smith was not done, however. A series of staff cuts, clearly aimed at culling the more cavalier elements of the OPC, resulted in as many as fifty forced resignations. "I don't care whether they were blabbing secrets or not," said the general to an underling. "Just give me the names of the people at Georgetown cocktail parties."[75] Next, a Project Review Committee was set up to scrutinize the covert operation proposals coming into OPC headquarters from its field staff. Beetle also demanded access to cable traffic between Wisner and his officers. Finally, the DCI approved the creation of an additional layer of Washington administration to contain the enthusiasm of the OPC sharpshooters, the Psychological Strategy Board (PSB), an interdepartmental committee designed to coordinate the government's rapidly proliferating political warfare effort.[76] In October 1953, President Eisenhower replaced the PSB with the Operations Coordinating Board (OCB), a body vested with enhanced powers of approval and supervision over CIA covert operations.

At the same time that Wisner was becoming increasingly boxed in by bureaucratic constraints, he and his colleagues in covert operations found themselves under renewed attack from the forces of domestic political reaction. The vulnerability of the CIA to criticism from congressmen with immigrant constituencies has already been noted. In the summer of 1953, it was the turn of Joseph R. McCarthy, junior senator from Wisconsin and anticommunist demagogue supreme, to take on the Agency. With its shroud of official secrecy, aristocratic social demeanor, and whiff of New Deal–style big government, the CIA was an obvious target for McCarthy; the surprise was that the assault was so long in coming. In the event, Allen Dulles (who had succeeded Smith as DCI in February 1953) stood firm, refusing to yield up the senator's intended victim, Dean Acheson's Yale-educated son-in-law William Bundy, who had made the mistake of contributing to Alger Hiss's defense fund.[77] When McCarthy then tried going after other CIA officers, he was foiled by an ingenious deception operation devised by counterintelligence specialist James Angleton.[78] Tired of chasing false leads, McCarthy transferred his attentions to the U.S. Army, becoming embroiled in a series of televised hearings that eventually led to his downfall. Dulles's stance, which compared very well with the more submissive posture of his brother John Foster over at State, helped foster the CIA's reputation as a safe haven for anticommunist liberals in Red Scare America. However, it did little to alleviate the problems immediately facing Wisner, who was himself the subject of an FBI security investigation focusing on his wartime romance with a celebrated Romanian anti-Nazi, Princess Caradja.[79]

Wisner liked to boast of his ability to play any tune he wanted on the CIA's Mighty Wurlitzer of Cold War covert operations. Yet, in truth, the task of trying to manage such a vast array of projects and "assets" had begun to control him. Friends noticed that his usually ornate but measured southern mode of speech was acquiring a prolix, hectic quality. He smoked and drank too much. A habit of flexing the muscles in his forearms during meetings grew into a nervous tic. Part of the problem was his personal relationship with Dulles (whom Wisner had succeeded as Deputy Director/Plans). True, the new CIA Director did not have the martinet-like qualities of Smith, and he was far more favorably disposed toward covert action than his predecessor, but Dulles undermined his (surprisingly thin-skinned) deputy by reaching down the chain of command and interfering in ongoing operations, as well as displaying an ill-disguised favoritism toward lieutenants who, unlike Wisner, shared his Yankee origins. Physical and mental exhaustion also took their toll: after working for six days a week from eight in the morning to the same hour at night, the DD/P would often don evening dress and head off to some Georgetown party where, likely as not, Cold War strategy would feature in the dinner conversation. Nor did Sundays provide any relief from this whirl: indeed, the

Sunday night party, at which guests would dine, drink, and dance until two or three on Monday morning, was a Georgetown institution. Above all, there was the simple fact that Wisner, with his fierce ideological conviction and fragile sense of self, was not well suited to the role of spy. This was a job that demanded the jovial pragmatism and inner coldness of someone like Allen Dulles.[80]

Meanwhile, even true believers in rollback were starting to lose their faith. In 1952, a "murder board" set up by Frank Lindsay, one of the chief planners of the exile strategy, weeded out about a third of OPC projects. Lindsay also wrote a nine-page memorandum to Wisner and Dulles, "arguing point by point why Kennan's notion of a counterforce was not working."[81] "Having spent a fair amount of time with guerrilla organizations, I already knew that they fight for their own purposes," he later explained to an interviewer. "You don't direct them. . . . They take on a life of their own."[82] The irony was that rollback was expiring at just the time that an administration identified in the public mind with a foreign policy of containment was giving way to one that, rhetorically at least, espoused liberation. Of course, this did not mean a cessation of covert action. Indeed, as is discussed in later chapters, Eisenhower and John Foster Dulles believed clandestine foreign interventions to be a relatively inexpensive, and conveniently deniable, means of waging the Cold War. The success of CIA-staged coups in Iran in 1953 and Guatemala in 1954 (which, recently published documents reveal, owed as much to good fortune as effective planning) strengthened this bias. However, as these two operations showed, the geographical focus of covert activity was shifting away from the Soviet empire, which, as Lindsay put it, "seemed impervious," toward regions of the developing world, such as central America and the Middle East, where defenses against penetration were weaker (and the stakes for the U.S. economy higher).[83] Even Wisner was growing more cautious in eastern Europe. Hence, when rioting broke out in East Germany in June 1953, he heeded the advice of CIA colleague John Bross not to try and equip demonstrators with arms.[84] Still, he did not give up on his dream of one day liberating the east; the memory of the hopeless civilians herded onto boxcars in 1945 continued to haunt him.

Wisner's crisis came in 1956, and it was the émigrés who were at least partially to blame. Among the satellite nations targeted by the NCFE, the one perceived as most susceptible to psychological warfare was Hungary.

Consequently, while observing the State Department's injunction against calls for armed rebellion, RFE made particular efforts to inspire Hungarian resistance "through appeals to religion, invidious comparisons with life in the West, and invocations of the tradition of nineteenth-century freedom fighter Louis Kossuth."[85] In October 1956, fighting broke out in the streets of Budapest, followed by the installation of Imre Nagy, a communist moderate, as head of government. At first the Russians appeared content to let events take the same course as they had in Gomulka's Poland, and withdrew their troops to the border. When, however, Nagy announced his intention of taking Hungary out of the Warsaw Pact, Soviet tanks rolled back into Budapest. In the bloody fighting that followed, thousands of Hungarians were killed, along with 669 Russian troops. Later, 300 resistance leaders, including Nagy, were executed.[86] The Eisenhower administration loudly protested the Soviet action, but did not intervene militarily. Liberation was exposed as a sham.

This is not the place to relate the complex controversy about Radio Free Europe's role in the origins of the Hungarian uprising.[87] Suffice it to say that an internal review of the Voice of Free Hungary's broadcasting at the time of the unrest in Budapest found that, while announcers had not explicitly promised western military support to the demonstrators, nonetheless, "for much of the time neither the American management of RFE nor the head of the Hungarian service was in control of what was transmitted" and (to quote a senior CIA officer's summary of the findings) the tone used by the émigrés "was more exuberant and optimistic than the situation warranted."[88] Certainly, Frank Wisner felt responsible for what had happened. On an inspection tour of European CIA stations at the time, the Deputy Director/Plans rushed to Germany and then on to Austria, where he stood at the border watching helplessly as Hungarians attempted to flee. "People [were] killed by the Russians as he stood there, in his sight," recalled a colleague. "It was a profound emotional shock."[89] Returning to the U.S. embassy, Wisner frantically telephoned Washington, pleading with the White House to commit troops, all to no avail. His behavior grew manic. An operations man in Athens, the next stop on his tour, remembers him dictating cables to headquarters that simply did not make sense. By the time of his return home, Wisner was on the verge of a complete breakdown, "rambling and raving all through dinner, totally out of control."[90] Three years later, he was eased out of his duties as DD/P and given the largely ceremonial role of station chief in London. In 1965, at the age of fifty-six, Frank Wisner took his own life.

As well as effectively destroying Wisner, Hungary signaled the final abandonment by Washington of both the main strategic goal identified by Kennan in the late 1940s, the disintegration of the Soviet empire, and the principal tactic used to achieve that purpose, the covert use of eastern-bloc émigrés. A few irreconcilables, such as C. D. Jackson, still banged the rollback drum; and some CIA money continued to find its way through the NCFE to exile organizations, such as Brutus Coste's Assembly of Captive European Nations (ACEN) (which, like the National Councils, caused its share of headaches for its covert patron). Most, however, accepted that the future of American policy in eastern Europe now lay in the encouragement of gradual reform—"evolution, not revolution." In May 1958, the National Security Council decreed that government officials should no longer work as closely with the "national committees" because "there [was] no evidence that émigré politicians [had] any significant following in their homelands." And in a message clearly intended for the American management of RFE and RL as well as the Voice of America, the NSC discouraged "the use of U.S. Government facilities to convey messages of exiled leaders."[91] The fading of rollback was accompanied by the death, in February 1959, of one of its most stalwart advocates, Wild Bill Donovan, whose last substantial act of government service had been helping Hungarian refugees over the Austrian border three years earlier.[92]

Of course, this is not to say that the CIA gave up using émigré leaders altogether. Exiles would form an important element in agency programs for new theaters of operation, most notably Fidel Castro's Cuba (with equally little success). Neither would the front group tactic Kennan had borrowed from the communists be discarded. Indeed, its use in liberation proved to be one of its less significant Cold War applications. The CIA front only really came into its own in the other major field earmarked for covert action in Kennan's 1948 political warfare plan: the "support of indigenous anti-Communist elements in threatened countries of the free world."

THREE

AFL-CIA

LABOR

In March 1951 an FBI wiretap picked up the following conversation between former OSS chief Wild Bill Donovan and Jay Lovestone, onetime leader of the U.S. Communist Party (CPUSA) and now chief foreign policy advisor to the American Federation of Labor (AFL):

> *Lovestone:* I'm just about to start a fight with your friends.
> *Donovan:* Who? . . . Mr. [Walter Bedell] Smith? . . . I'm glad to hear it. . . .
> *Lovestone:* You see, I'm nobody's stooge, or agent, or lackey.
> *Donovan:* What's the basis of it, Jay?
> *Lovestone:* The basis of it is that . . . they're trying to tie me down to certain things I won't accept. . . . They can go plumb to hell. . . .
> *Donovan:* Well, they're very foolish, Jay. You can be one of the greatest assets they have, as I told them.[1]

Besides showing how disaffected with the CIA the retired American spymaster had grown by 1951, this dialogue reveals two important characteristics of the CIA's front program in the first years of the Cold War. One of these was the Agency's readiness to employ in its covert operations members of the so-called non-communist left (NCL)—that is, trade unionists, socialists or social democratic politicians, and even former communists like Lovestone—mainly because of their preexisting links with similar elements in western Europe. The other was the tendency of the NCL groups involved, especially the ex-communists, to chafe against the constraints imposed on them by clandestine official patronage. These two factors are the dominant themes of the United States's first major campaign in the Cold War contest for western hearts and minds.

Jay Lovestone's life story reads like a strange, shadowy, even sinister version of the classic American narrative of the poor immigrant boy made good. The son of a Polish rabbi, Lovestone emigrated to the United States in 1907 at the age of nine and grew up on New York City's Lower East Side, a lanky and startlingly blond-haired adolescent with a reputation as a tough neighborhood boxer and magnetic soapbox orator. Like many other cash-strapped but bright young Jewish men of his generation, he attended New York's City College, where he thrived in a gladiatorial atmosphere of aggressive intellectualism and factional radicalism. After graduating in 1919, he rose rapidly to the position of general secretary in the newly formed CPUSA before being deposed by Stalin during the 1929 Comintern congress in Moscow for his "deviationist" position on the question of American "exceptionalism." "Who do you think you are?" the Soviet leader shouted at the rebellious U.S. delegation. "Trotsky defied me. Where is he? Zinoviev defied me. Where is he? Bukharin defied me. Where is he? And you! Who are you?"[2] Lucky to escape Russia, Lovestone returned to New York and organized a tight-knit communist opposition group known as the Lovestoneites. (The ability to inspire intense personal devotion in his followers appears to have been one of Lovestone's greatest political assets, along with powers of sexual attraction that led to a string of affairs with women in his coterie.) He also began building bridges to the American trade union movement, courting the patronage of anticommunist labor leaders like the dynamic head of the New York garment workers, David Dubinsky, who needed Lovestone's help flushing Stalinists out of their unions.

By the end of the 1930s, Lovestone had despaired of regaining Stalin's favor and completed his transformation from CP apparatchik into a particularly fanatical and ruthless anticommunist. "The son of a bitch is okay, he's been converted," said Dubinsky in 1941, as he introduced Lovestone to George Meany, the cigar-chomping Irish plumber from the Bronx who minded the finances of the nation's foremost trade union center, the American Federation of Labor.[3] Soon the former communist, whom even

Stalin recognized as an "adroit and talented factional wirepuller," was established as Meany's number-one advisor on international labor affairs, and was given considerable latitude to operate overseas under the AFL's imprimatur.[4] This arrangement was institutionalized in 1944 by the creation of the Free Trade Union Committee (FTUC), a semiautonomous labor foreign policy unit funded by Dubinsky's International Ladies' Garment Workers' Union (ILG), run from a cluttered cubicle in the ILG's Broadway headquarters by Lovestone and represented on the ground in Europe by an extremely able and energetic young Lovestoneite named Irving Brown. Later, the separate status of the FTUC would give Meany the ability to deny charges that the AFL had directly handled covert CIA subsidies.

During the war years, the OSS ran a labor desk under the charge of union lawyer and future Supreme Court Justice Arthur J. Goldberg, who employed the bustling Brown in several clandestine operations against the Nazis (hence Lovestone's friendship with Donovan).[5] In 1945, with the disbanding of the wartime secret service, the U.S. government effectively abolished its political warfare capability in the labor field. The Lovestoneites filled this vacuum with a foreign policy of their own, geared to exporting the principles of AFL-style "free trade unionism"—in particular, workers' freedom from any form of political control—and thwarting communist attempts to win the allegiance of European labor. Their most characteristic tactic was surreptitiously fostering splits in Popular Front–style alliances of communists and socialists or social democrats, a maneuver the Lovestoneites had pioneered in factional struggles for control of the United Automobile Workers (UAW) during the late 1930s. In France, for example, Brown egged on former resistance fighter Léon Jouhaux, leader of the new union federation Force Ouvrière (FO), to quit the communist-dominated Confédération Générale du Travail while at the same time promising Italian socialists "suitcases of money" if they broke away from the Confederazione Generale Italiana del Lavoro.[6] He also resorted to more direct methods, such as channeling AFL support to the Corsican union leader of the Marseilles docks, Pierre Ferri-Pisani, whose members beat up communists trying to disrupt the landing of Marshall Plan supplies. The crowning achievement of "Lovestone diplomacy" came at the end of the decade, when the international labor congress, the World Federation of Trade Unions (WFTU), which included Soviet as well as western organizations, split apart and a new anticommunist alliance, the International Confederation of Free Trade Unions (ICFTU), was born. Small wonder that Brown, whom *Reader's Digest* described as "an entire diplomatic corps and a one-man OSS," felt inclined to boast, "our trade union programs and relationships have penetrated every country of Europe. We have become . . . an army."[7]

Considering this prehistory of voluntary and highly effective anticommunist agitation, it is hardly surprising that Frank Wisner should have wanted to team up with Jay Lovestone. Not only was the latter supremely knowledgeable about the Cold War enemy—"He is better informed on the subject of Communist theory as well as its activities than anyone I know," Donovan once told a colleague—his hatred of Stalinism was such that he even felt compelled, during an audience in the Sistine Chapel, to lecture Pope Pius XII on the subject (prompting the pontiff to respond, "But, Mr. Lovestone, I too am anti-Communist").[8] More important still was the fact that, by virtue of their association with the AFL, the Lovestoneites enjoyed unrivaled connections to the trade union movement in western Europe, a crucial battleground in the propaganda Cold War, given European labor's vast postwar power, both economic and political, and its historic susceptibility to communist influence. Here, then, was the perfect cover for U.S. government-sponsored political warfare of the sort envisioned by George Kennan: a group of private American citizens, with conspicuous access to sources of nonofficial financial support, aiding "indigenous anti-Communist elements in threatened countries of the free world." There was also the precedent of the OSS's labor operations and the tradition of tolerance of, even sympathy for, non-communist left tendencies bequeathed to the CIA by World War II.

Lovestone and Wisner were formally introduced by the Free Trade Union Committee's chairman, photo-engravers' leader Matthew Woll, in December 1948.[9] The FTUC received its first payment from the Office of Policy Coordination, $35,000, the following month. This and subsequent subsidies were disguised in the FTUC's accounts as donations from private individuals and referred to in the code language Lovestone soon evolved for his secret dealings with Wisner as "books" or "volumes" from the OPC's "library."[10] Such payments soon overtook AFL contributions as a source of revenue for the FTUC: whereas by the end of 1949, union subsidies added up to a mere $56,000, "individual gifts" totaled some $203,000.[11] Having been laundered by Lovestone in New York, OPC funds were transferred to Brown in Europe via a variety of different bank accounts. The FTUC's European representative also received payments directly from Marshall Plan officials or American embassy personnel drawing on the so-called counterpart funds.

Aided by his wife and secretary, Lillie, the indefatigable Brown then piggybacked the OPC monies to anticommunist labor elements all over the European continent. Some of these, such as Jouhaux's Force Ouvrière and Ferri-Pisani's Mediterranean Vigilance Committee in France, or the socialist unionists in Italy's new anticommunist labor center, the Confederazione Italiana Sindacati Lavoratori, had already benefited from the genuinely private largesse of the AFL. Correspondence between Brown and Lovestone, who demanded regular reports from his lieutenant about events in Europe, contained frequent references to the purchase of "French perfume" or "spaghetti." (There was more than a hint of tongue-in-cheek humor about the code words invented by the Lovestoneites, who had been using secret language ever since the 1920s, when the U.S. communist movement was compelled to adopt an underground or "illegal" existence.) "Lumber merchants" was Lovestoneite code for a new addition to the FTUC's list of clients: socialist members of the Central Organization of Finnish Trade Unions (SAK), who from late 1949 became a major recipient of concealed U.S. government assistance.[12] Reflecting a tendency for OPC front groups to overlap and sometimes become entangled, the FTUC also backed the exile operations of the National Committee for a Free Europe, including an International Center for Free Trade Unionists in Exile housed in the Paris offices of the Force Ouvrière, and an NCFE Labor Contacts Division in New York, designed to act as a focus for émigré eastern European unionists in the United States.[13]

Although the best known and most effective, Brown was not the only FTUC field agent handling OPC subsidies, nor were covert labor operations confined to western Europe. Lovestone had a network of agents, mostly ex-communists like himself, spanning the entire "free world." In Indonesia, an old follower, the outspoken Harry Goldberg, ran a training program designed to rally noncommunist labor groups against the WFTU-affiliated All-Indonesian Central Labor Organization, SOBSI. (Lovestone later moved Goldberg to Italy after the latter publicly accused President Ahmed Sukarno of an "outstanding lack of statesmanship.")[14] A former labor education officer in the U.S. military government in Japan, the brilliant but neurotic Richard Deverall, presided over an FTUC bureau in Tokyo until he too was recalled due to his habit of accusing U.S. embassy staff of being secret communists. Willard R. Etter, another ex-government officer whose excessive anticommunism had gotten him in trouble with his superiors (he was sent home from the U.S. consulate in Shanghai after claiming to have discovered a nest of communist agents there) set up shop on Formosa (Taiwan) and trained Chinese nationalists to carry out espionage and sabotage on the communist mainland. In February 1950, Wisner, his fascination with paramilitary "rollback" operations as yet undimmed, approved a six-month "laundry budget" for Etter of $145,472.[15] The FTUC, it seemed, had an agent in every major theater of the Cold War, functioning, in the apt phrase of Lovestone's biographer, Ted Morgan, as a sort of "anti-Cominform."[16]

Before the CIA's front operations were exposed, American trade unionists who went abroad to fight communism in foreign labor organizations during the early years of the Cold War tended to be portrayed in writings on the subject as disinterested, even heroic, defenders of political freedom.[17] After the revelations of the late 1960s, this view was exchanged for the image of a puppet on a string, with the individuals involved now depicted as so many stooges, or "patsies," of the American national security state.[18] In recent years, with the opening to researchers of Jay Lovestone's voluminous personal files, a third picture has emerged.[19] This presents a far more complicated relationship than was previously painted, one in which both sides jealously guarded their independence and even fought each other for control of covert operations.

The first issue to come between the OPC and FTUC was, perhaps predictably, money. To be sure, Lovestone was glad of the extra income coming from his "luncheon friend," Wisner—it had been clear for some time that the AFL's subsidies were not enough on their own to support the sort of activities that were needed to win the Cold War contest for labor's allegiance.[20] But his long experience in anti-Stalinist political warfare meant that Lovestone was bound to resent any attempts by the OPC to tell him how its money should be spent. He adopted a simple definition of his new patron's role: it was to provide large quantities of cash, then leave the actual job of fighting communism to himself and his agents. Lovestone's attitude toward the professional spies with whom he dealt was condescending, even disdainful. They were raw novices in the struggle against Stalin, dashing perhaps, but lacking in substance. The code name he invented for them summed it up: they were the "Fizz kids."[21]

Unfortunately for Lovestone, the OPC did not share this interpretation of its role. Although generous, its subsidies were not indiscriminate. Rather, they were carefully targeted, reflecting the U.S. government's strategic priorities in the Cold War. Hence, when in 1950 the focus of international tension in Southeast Asia shifted from China to Korea, support for Willard Etter's insurgency operation on Formosa dried up, leaving several of his agents stranded on the Chinese mainland, where they were soon captured and executed. Lovestone was appalled. "I curse the day I ever introduced you to that pack of bribers and corrupters in Washington," he told Etter.[22] Meanwhile, Brown's operations in Europe were constantly stymied by the failure of the OPC to honor the financial pledges Wisner had made to Lovestone. "Volumes" for "the lumber people" were promised and then withheld; delays to the "French budget" meant Brown was unable to purchase any "perfume"; having assured Lovestone "that there would be five cook books for the spaghetti chefs," the Fizz kids "backwatered and doublecrossed" him.[23] To add insult to injury, the OPC also demanded that Lovestone provide a fuller accounting of his spending than the AFL had required, CIA security chief Sheffield Edwards even opening the FTUC's mail to monitor its expenditures.[24] Lovestone was infuriated by what he perceived as "petty snooping" and "insolent bookkeeping."[25] In April 1951 he told his CIA liaison, Samuel D. Berger, that he was on the verge of instructing "Irving, Goldberg, Deverall and all our other friends to pack their grips, close their shops, and come home. You see," he continued, "I am not a nylon merchant—black market or otherwise. I do not intend to lend aid and comfort to any attempt of second-class bookkeepers determining the policies of our organization."[26]

No less deplorable from Lovestone's point of view were signs that the OPC was attempting to usurp his control of FTUC field operatives. Etter, for example, was approached with an offer of a large salary if he performed "extra-curricular" activities or took full-time employment with "another organization."[27] Similar efforts were made "to drive a wedge" between Lovestone and his most valuable asset, Brown, but the latter loyally resisted the OPC's blandishments.[28] When the co-option of Lovestoneite personnel failed, the OPC went outside the apparatus of the FTUC altogether, using other Americans in the field, such as Rome labor attaché Tom Lane, instead.[29] Lovestone, who appears to have had a low opinion of government officers in general, thought this tactic extremely foolish, not least because it increased the possibility of exposure. "In view of the type of rich dishes that Uncle Tom has been serving up, a number of my friends will not touch any spaghetti shipment," he complained to Lillie Brown in March 1951. "They don't want to be involved in such filthy kitchens."[30] Worse still, the OPC would invoke the name of the AFL in operations that had nothing to do with the FTUC. Brown in particular objected to this practice because it threatened to tarnish his personal reputation in Europe. He and Lovestone retaliated by withholding intelligence from the OPC; withdrawing from involvement in other front operations, such as the Congress for Cultural Freedom; and refusing to cooperate with a CIA agent in Brown's office, Leon Dale.

It is not hard to understand the OPC's reasons for sometimes bypassing the FTUC. Lovestone was a notorious intriguer, and there were those in the intelligence service who (as one spy put it) "couldn't quite accustom themselves to the fact that we were giving money to the former head of the Communist Party."[31] Official concerns about security can hardly have been allayed by the assignment to the FTUC staff in June 1950 of Carmel Offie. Among the many eccentric characters to be found in Lovestone's circle, Offie was surely the oddest. The son of poor Italian immigrants, grotesquely ugly, and flamboyantly homosexual, the "Monk" (his ironic Lovestoneite code name) had risen through the ranks of the U.S. foreign service by dint of his extraordinary skills as a political fixer and "modern-day court-jester"—in Paris during the 1930s, he had arranged dates for the young John F. Kennedy and played bridge with Wallis Simpson. In 1947, however, he was caught using the diplomatic pouch for unauthorized currency transfers (he also smuggled rubles, diamonds, and, on one occasion, three hundred Finnish lobsters).[32] Flung out of the diplomatic corps, Offie was picked up by Wisner on the recommendation of Chip Bohlen (Kennan was another admirer) and given special responsibility for émigré affairs. He soon made himself indispensable to the OPC chief, hiring a family cook as well as locating potentially useful "good Germans."[33] When, however, Joe McCarthy began sniffing around the OPC, dropping hints in the Senate about a "convicted homosexual" occupying a "top-salaried important position" in the CIA (Offie had been arrested for "perversion" in 1943 after soliciting an undercover policeman in Washington's Lafayette Park), Wisner felt obliged to move him over to the FTUC, where he functioned as Lovestone's OPC liaison.[34] As well as adding to the CIA's apprehension about the security of FTUC operations (Sheffield Edwards reckoned Offie "about the worst of the OPC employees . . . some of whose backgrounds were horrible"),[35] this move fueled the Lovestoneites' tendency to defy the orders of the "Fizz kids" because the disgruntled Monk increasingly sided with the unionists against the spies.

Underlying the mutual security concerns of the FTUC and OPC were a host of largely unspoken social and ethnic tensions. At this time, the CIA still recruited most of its entry-level staff from the Ivy League universities, while its upper echelons were dominated by military top brass and corporate lawyers. It was therefore perhaps only to be expected that many senior intelligence officers would feel uncomfortable working alongside the ex-radical, immigrant-stock proletarians who staffed the FTUC. "In general, the Fizz kids are continuing their marked anti-labor and anti-Semitic tendencies in addition to their incompetence," Lovestone once told Brown.[36] This instinctive mistrust was reciprocated, with interest. On being introduced to him, Polish émigré Joseph Czapski immediately noticed that Lovestone, in his conversation, constantly "expressed a 'class line' that had nothing to do with political and ideological issues. Specifically, L[ovestone] was expressing the fact that he is a plebeian and a Jew."[37] In his transactions with the CIA, the ex-communist articulated his grievances about the Agency's behavior in language dripping with class consciousness. "These people are purely socialites whose names appear in the Social Register, who look for excitement and who confuse thrills with results," he once told Brown. "I have not minded being a janitor in the firm, but Irving I do not want to be a janitor whose functions are increasingly devoted to carrying out strange tenants' garbage."[38] It cannot have helped that the OPC case officer originally assigned Lovestone, Pinky Thompson (or "Stinky" as the Lovestoneites called him, on account of his fondness for bouts of heavy lunchtime drinking), was "an affluent Philadelphia clubman with a plantation in Georgia where Wisner went shooting each year."[39] It was no surprise that the humbly born Italian American Offie fit in better at ILG headquarters. In short, the alliance between the FTUC and the CIA was an unnatural one of New York and Georgetown, Lower East Side and Upper West Side, City College and Princeton, that only the strange circumstances of the secret Cold War crusade against communism could have brought into being.

In late 1950 the already stormy marriage of the Free Trade Union Committee and Office of Policy Coordination grew even more tempestuous when Lovestone began to suspect that Wisner was flirting with another labor suitor, the AFL's industrial rival, the Congress of Industrial Organizations (CIO). The CIO had by this date shed the communist associations that had characterized its early existence, purging its communist-led affiliates in 1949 and, in the same year, walking out on the World Federation of Trade Unions. As well as signifying the final extinction of the American Popular Front, these actions prepared the way for the CIO's rising star, Detroit auto workers' leader Walter Reuther, to assert his immensely attractive personality abroad. Emulating the example of the AFL, the CIO dispatched a European representative, Reuther's younger brother Victor, to open an office in Paris in 1951. The CIO also succeeded in building up considerable influence within the government agency responsible for administering the Marshall Plan in Europe, the Economic Cooperation Administration (ECA), whose head, Milton Katz, favored the notion of a "dual-track" labor foreign policy involving the two American labor federations on an equal footing.[40]

Lovestone was dismayed by these developments, in part simply because he was possessive of his foreign turf, but also because there was a deep ideological and personal animosity between him and Brown, on the one hand, and the Reuther brothers on the other. The latter had never forgotten or forgiven the part played by the Lovestoneites in the splitting of the UAW during the 1930s. On their side, Lovestone and Brown regarded the Reuthers, former socialists who placed as much emphasis on the promotion of economic growth abroad as on fighting communism, with the same sort of contempt they showed the Fizz kids, referring to them sneeringly as the "YPSLs" (members of the Young People's Socialist League). As Lovestone explained to his intelligence liaison, Sam Berger, "Victor

Reuther might be a very nice guy. If I had an eligible daughter and she was in love with him, I would not interfere with her desire to marry him. But to put Victor Reuther and Irving Brown on a par in carrying on the frontal struggle against totalitarian Communism and its machinations . . . is enough to make, as Stalin said, a horse laugh."[41]

Whether these remarks were passed on to the OPC is not known. What is clear is that the professional spies did not share Lovestone's factional agenda: their main concern was to improve their access to the non-communist left, and the CIO, whose social democratic politics played rather better with European labor than the business unionism of the AFL, was able to provide them with contacts that the FTUC could not. Also, next to the Lovestoneites' brand of obsessive, negative anticommunism, the positive, constructive approach of the Reuthers was bound to seem more appealing, especially to those younger intelligence officers who liked to think of themselves as belonging to the non-communist left or, at the very least, the liberal center. Finally, the CIO, with its roots in the "corporatist" politics of the New Deal era, simply seemed a more natural government partner than the AFL, which, ever since its founding in the late nineteenth century by British cigar maker Samuel Gompers, had avoided entangling official alliances.

Lovestone's growing suspicion that Wisner was interested in initiating a relationship with the CIO was confirmed during a meeting held in the office of the Director of Central Intelligence in Washington on the morning of November 21, 1950. The purpose of this gathering was to allow the new DCI, Walter Bedell Smith, to meet with the international staff of the AFL and review the covert operations they were jointly undertaking. In attendance were George Meany (identified in coded minutes taken by Offie as "Mr. Plumber"), Woll (Photographer), Dubinsky (Garment Worker), Lovestone (Intellectual), Smith (Soldier), and Wisner (Lawyer). After an opening exchange of pleasantries between Woll and Smith, Lovestone took the opportunity to remind those present that the AFL had been active in the foreign labor field long before "Mr. Soldier's employers" and that the federation's total expenditure on international activities since 1945 far exceeded that of the OPC. The DCI then invited comments on possible future operations, "and the discussion moved to bringing another organization into the work." Wisner admitted "that there had taken place certain conversations on this subject." Then, one by one, the AFL officers announced their objections, citing "the organization's" (the CIO was never referred to by name) "inexperience, its insecurity and penetration by unreliable elements." Meany was particularly vocal on this score, "mentioning dates, names, and places" of communist infiltration. The official response was emollient: Smith declared himself "much impressed" by the unionists' arguments, and Wisner laid out the tough conditions that any other organization would have to satisfy before receiving covert funding, including the existence of an established foreign apparatus and the swearing of secrecy oaths. After some further discussion of information exchange, the drafting of a Charter of Operations to formalize the partnership (it is not clear if any such document was ever produced), and specific operations in South America, Germany, and France, the meeting broke up in a reasonably amicable atmosphere, with Smith reassuring the unionists that "he did not for one moment regard funds provided by his organization as a subsidy for the labor movement," and Woll stating "that the chief value of labor in foreign operations was its independence from government influence."[42]

Wisner's comments were, of course, designed to leave the door open to possible dealings with the CIO, and in the months that followed the AFL-CIA summit, Lovestone's worst fears were confirmed. In December, Allen Dulles arrived in the Agency, bringing with him as his assistant a young ex-OSS officer by the name of Thomas W. Braden. This development was significant for several reasons. As Deputy Director/Plans, Dulles was (Braden later recalled) "very much interested in the labor movement" and believed that the CIO should be folded into CIA covert operations.[43] Braden, to whom Dulles gave the responsibility of liaising with the CIO's international officers, was favorably disposed toward Brown ("There should be a book called 'The Guy Who Won The Cold War' about Irving," he later told Brown's biographer),[44] but was less impressed by Lovestone, particularly his habit of providing "just a chit under an assumed name" to acknowledge receipt of a covert subsidy, rather than detailed accounts. "I thought he was an asset," the CIA officer remembered, "but I never thought we had to go by his prescriptions."[45] On his side, Lovestone was bound to resent Braden's new influence over his affairs: with his craggy good looks, heroic military record, and a dilettanteish postwar résumé that included spells at Dartmouth College, the Museum of

Modern Art, and the OPC's front organization in the field of European federalism, the American Committee on United Europe, Dulles's lieutenant must have struck the ex-communist as the archetypal Fizz kid. In contrast with this naturally fraught personal relationship, there seems to have been an instinctive political sympathy between the liberal Braden, who had been "idealistically pro-labor since the days of the New Deal," and the social democrats of the CIO.[46]

The relationship between the CIA and the CIO is less well documented than the FTUC-OPC collaboration, but some evidence does exist. In 1967, the year of the "revelations," a great deal of media attention focused on a statement by Braden that on one occasion in the early 1950s he had flown to Detroit and handed Walter Reuther $50,000 in $50 bills, which the UAW president then sent to his brother Victor in Europe, where it was spent bolstering anticommunist unions in West Germany.[47] Victor responded to Braden's claims by alleging that the CIA officer had attempted to recruit him as an agent during a meeting at the U.S. embassy in Paris in 1952, asking him to perform a role within the CIO similar to that played by the AFL's Irving Brown. According to his own account of the incident, Reuther "categorically rejected" this proposal "on the spot," a decision that received the strong approval of CIO leader Philip Murray when it was reported to him shortly afterward.[48]

Dramatic though these encounters between Braden and the Reuther brothers undoubtedly were, they serve to distract attention from what appears to have been a more important link between the CIA and the CIO provided by the latter's British-born Director of International Affairs, Mike Ross, who transmitted disguised Agency subsidies to Victor Reuther's Paris office. According to Braden's later recollection, Allen Dulles would periodically ask him, "Have you seen Mike Ross lately? You ought to go and see him, Tom, maybe he needs ten thousand dollars."[49] This claim is supported by evidence in Ross's papers at the George Meany Memorial Archives in Maryland, which contain scattered references to the relationship, including a coded letter from "T," as well as by documents in Irving Brown's files, such as a letter of May 1952 in which Lovestone informed his European deputy that "Squinty" (Dulles) had just let slip "that Tom B. is his contact with Mike Ross."[50] Lovestone, who was already "convinced that Victor and his friends are operating . . . with the aid of substantial injections from Dr. Fizzer," was predictably outraged by this admission.[51] "The more I hear of what these fellows do," he told Brown, "the more I feel this is a disgusting outfit and situation."[52]

Combined with the other tensions in the relationship, the Fizz kids' affair with the CIO led to a series of bitter showdowns between the Office of Policy Coordination and the Free Trade Union Committee in early 1951. Infuriated by the antics of "uninformed and irresponsible sophomores," Brown berated senior CIA officials in Washington and then, accompanied by Offie, confronted the staff at the Rome embassy who had been feeding government money directly to Italian socialists.[53] In March, Lovestone approached Dulles with the proposal that, in the future, the Agency subsidize the FTUC by means of blanket grants, a move clearly designed to increase Lovestone's operational independence.[54] Not surprisingly, the Deputy Director/Plans refused to play along, instead coming up with a demand of his own: the removal of Offie from the FTUC payroll as a condition of continued CIA funding. The Monk was charged, so Lovestone reported to Brown, with "giving too much confidence to outsiders" (an allegation that, when it reached Offie's ears, provoked him to exclaim, "we are not whores . . . to be used . . . by politically incompetent dilettantes").[55] By this stage, AFL leaders such as Dubinsky were advocating a complete end to relations with the CIA. Tensions came to a head at a meeting between the FTUC and Smith ("the super-duper Fizz kid")[56] on April 9, 1951, which "degenerated into a shouting match."[57] According to Dubinsky's later account: "We told them they would ruin things [in Italy], but they wouldn't stay out. General Smith kept sounding more and more dictatorial at our conference. Finally, Lovestone said to him: 'You're a general, but you sound like a drill sergeant.' When he protested, I told Smith, 'You're not telling us what do; we are from the labor movement.'"[58]

This angry exchange, more reminiscent of a failed wage negotiation between management and labor than a covert operation, neatly captures the contradictions at the heart of the CIA-FTUC partnership. On one side were professional spies wanting to exert the maximum degree of control possible over the activities they were financing, concerned about security and uninhibited by loyalty to any one private group, yet at the same time constrained by their need for concealment and access to certain noncommunist left elements that only the Lovestoneites could provide. On the other were representatives of the American labor movement entirely confident of their own ability to carry out covert operations, indeed positively jealous of their independence in the field, yet bound to the CIA by the purse strings of covert patronage. It was a marriage of convenience, beset by mutual suspicion and resentment.

At the same time that the AFL leadership was clashing with the CIA directorate, another reshuffle was taking place within the Agency that would further reduce the influence of Wisner—and, therefore, Lovestone—over covert labor operations. Since moving to his new position in Washington a few months earlier, Tom Braden (or, to give him his new code name, "Homer D. Hoskins") had come to the conclusion that management of the OPC's front projects, spread out as it was between the organization's various geographical divisions, lacked focus and coherence.[59] What was needed, he decided, was a single unit responsible for mounting a concerted worldwide campaign against the Soviet propaganda offensive. Predictably enough, when Braden took this proposal to a meeting of the divisional chiefs, chaired by Wisner, it was overwhelmingly rejected. Braden responded by going straight to Dulles's office and offering his resignation, only to learn that the DD/P had already overruled the head of OPC.[60] Shortly afterward, a new entity was created within the Directorate of Plans, the International Organizations Division (IOD), with Braden as Division Chief assisted by a Deputy and Branch Chiefs. The IOD assumed responsibility for managing all front groups from the regional divisions. Although formally under Wisner's authority, Braden "just went over his head" and reported directly to Dulles.[61]

With the CIO-leaning Braden now in charge, signs that the CIA intended reducing Lovestone's power multiplied. The clearest of these was an attempt to circumvent Henry Kirsch, the Lovestoneite who directed the National Committee for a Free Europe's Labor Contacts Division in New York. The FTUC's relations with the NCFE were strained anyway, due to Lovestone's dislike of the organization's officers, whom he regarded as "over-priced Executives" (DeWitt Poole, in particular, was "an incompetent, empty fool") and its courting of right-wing émigrés, including "pro-Nazi Bulgarians, pro-Nazi Romanians, and pro-Nazi Hungarians."[62] At first Lovestone was pleased when another member of his circle, Leon Dennen, was brought in by the NCFE to help run the Free Trade Unionists in Exile center in Paris. (He was also amused by rumors spread by the CIO that the physically unimposing Dennen was meant to serve as Brown's bodyguard: he and Brown agreed that the arrangement would work better the other way round.)[63] Soon, however, he realized that the ex-Lovestoneite's primary allegiance was no longer to labor and that the move was really designed to eliminate Kirsch from the loop. "I suppose Henry will be another case of the Monk," Lovestone forlornly told Brown (Offie had eventually been removed from the FTUC payroll in June 1951). "He will be punished for being loyal to the AF of L."[64]

Lovestone took his complaint to a meeting with Kirsch and the NCFE president, C. D. Jackson, at New York City's Vanderbilt Hotel in October 1951. Again, the discussion seemed to owe more to bad industrial relations than spy-craft. After listing the AFL's contributions to the work of the NCFE, Lovestone described various "anti-labor trends" in the organization and demanded a greater say in the planning of its operations. Jackson, a zealous advocate of free enterprise, retorted that he had hired Dennen as an individual, not a representative of American labor, and would "not have any AF of L stooges" in the NCFE.[65] This confrontation permanently soured personal relations between the two men (in 1954 Jackson described Lovestone as "an intemperate, dishonest, ruthless Communist who had only changed his allegiance and not his tactics")[66] and dealt the coup de grâce to the collaboration between the FTUC and the Free Europe Committee. Shortly afterward, Lovestone broke off all contact with the NCFE and Matthew Woll resigned from its Executive Committee. Jackson considered retaliating by withdrawing funding for the Paris-based labor Center in Exile, but was dissuaded by Allen Dulles, who allegedly said, "We have enough trouble with Lovestone as it is."[67] In correspondence with George Meany, Lovestone tellingly accused the NCFE of lacking the "spirit of collective bargaining."[68]

Meanwhile, the FTUC-CIA partnership was drawing unwelcome attention from conservative outsiders similar to that visited on the NCFE and its sister émigré organization, AMCOMLIB. A right-wing journalist, Westbrook Pegler, wrote a series of vituperative but well-informed columns alleging that Lovestone and Brown were communist agents who had succeeded in suborning U.S. foreign policy. The Lovestoneites suspected that Pegler had been primed by hostile elements within the CIA. In January 1953, Offie told Brown that the journalist's "informants are in Fizzland who are giving him this stuff to discredit primarily labor, then Dubinsky, you and Jay, and to show in a sinister underlying rhythm that all these people who 'run' things are Jews."[69]

The following year, it was the turn of President Eisenhower's assistant secretary for international labor affairs, Spencer Miller, to fling the mud. Miller, an unstable anti-Semite and obsessive anticommunist, believed that Lovestone was part of an international Jewish conspiracy to undermine the United States, describing him to the FBI as "a Rasputin-like character who desires to dominate the labor picture throughout the world."[70] Miller eventually resigned his post after testifying before the House Committee on Un-American Activities that there was a ring of communist agents in the Department of Labor and that Lovestone was their "kingpin."[71]

As if this public probing of the CIA's labor operations was not enough of a security worry, an ongoing FBI espionage investigation had Lovestone being trailed by G-men, his mail opened, and, as already noted, his telephone tapped. Evidently, J. Edgar Hoover was intrigued by the FTUC. He suspected that it was somehow mixed up with the CIA, but he was not quite able to figure out the relationship and was deeply apprehensive about the Lovestoneites' communist pasts. "We should be alert to Lovestone, Offie, and Brown, as I have grave doubts about this trio," he told a colleague. The Monk's sexuality appears to have caused Hoover particular concern. "It seems to be an inherent part of a pervert's makeup to be also a pathological liar," he reflected.[72]

While the Lovestoneites had to battle anti-Semitism, McCarthyism, and homophobia on their right flank, their left was being peppered by charges of corruption, cynicism, and class betrayal. Their enemies in the CIO, especially the Reuther brothers, had long resented their splitting tactics. "Jay was divisive," Victor Reuther told Ted Morgan. "If you had three people in the room and he was one of them, you had three caucuses."[73] Now, as the CIO's influence spread within the foreign policy apparatus, this view also began to be held by some U.S. government officers. Most of the individuals selected for the new labor attaché program shared Lovestone's preference for straightforward anticommunist political warfare, often because they owed their appointments to his influence. Elsewhere, however, especially in the Economic Cooperation Administration and U.S. information services, a CIO-like emphasis on productivity and government partnership prevailed, with the result that the official "labor diplomacy" effort in the Cold War reflected the internal divisions of the American labor movement.[74] A Reutherite perception of Lovestone even spread into the CIA itself, turning some intelligence officers into "whistle-blowers."

One such whistle-blower was Paul Sakwa. A young World War II veteran who during the late 1940s organized retail clerks and undertook research for the CIO while writing a master's thesis at Columbia University, Sakwa was hired by the CIA in 1952 after having been judged a security risk by both the Department of State and the Department of Labor. Assigned to Paris as an officer in the French Branch of the Western Europe Division, he soon reached the conclusion that, whatever good they might have done initially, Irving Brown's operations in France, especially his funding of the Force Ouvrière, were now positively harmful. "Elections were influenced if not purchased outright, union dues remained uncollected, organizing activities ceased," Sakwa reckoned. Back in Washington, he complained about Brown's activities to Tom Braden, who, to Sakwa's surprise, agreed to cut subsidies to the FO. Later, after he had moved to Belgium under cover as Assistant Labor Attaché, Sakwa confronted George Meany in a similar fashion while escorting him and his wife around a fair in Brussels. Meany, however, proved less receptive than Braden, ordering Sakwa out of his car as they were on their way to a dinner function. (Mrs. Meany, who evidently agreed with the CIA officer, was likewise commanded to return to the hotel lobby.) "What began as an effort to promote and defend democracy," wrote Sakwa later, "evolved into operations designed to thwart real, incipient, or imagined Communist threats at the expense of democracy itself."[75]

After peaking in 1950, CIA subsidies to the FTUC declined steadily throughout the decade, falling to a mere $10,109 by 1958.[76] By that date, the FTUC's position within the American labor movement had been seriously undermined, thanks to the merger in 1955 of the AFL and CIO and the creation of a joint International Affairs Committee. In December 1957, following much infighting between the two federations' international affairs staffs, it was eventually agreed that the FTUC should be abolished. This move did not, however, signal an end to CIA interests in the labor field. To be sure, the focus of Lovestone's work shifted away from covert operation toward intelligence gathering, which he carried out in league with his new controller in the Agency, James Angleton, who would squirrel away reports from the ex-communist's worldwide chain of agents in the "JX Files."[77] Irving Brown, however, remained as active as ever, carrying out operations for the Agency on a freelance basis. (He had always enjoyed higher regard from the professional spies than his boss, and by 1960 personal relations between the two had become strained.) Also, as is discussed in later chapters, the CIA found other American unionists, based within the U.S. affiliates of the international trade secretariats, who were prepared to engage in clandestine work for their government.

Newly available evidence shows that the old imagery of puppet masters and marionettes fails utterly to capture the complexities of the partnership between the Lovestoneites of the AFL and the "Fizz kids" of the CIA. Granted, the labor officials involved seem never to have been troubled by what would become the main issue of controversy in 1967, the ethical propriety of secret subsidies. Nonetheless, the numerous documented incidents of conflict between the two parties reveal the AFL representatives as bringing to the relationship a definite agenda of their own—and, for that matter, of having a conception of a "labor" interest that they were keen to protect from meddling by the executives of the CIA. It is even possible to detect a whiff of labor militancy in some of the top-level meetings of 1950 and 1951 that the AFL rarely displayed in postwar industrial relations. Perhaps the most appropriate metaphor for the FTUC-CIA liaison is one specific to this particular field of front operation: management-worker conflict. "The relationship worked satisfactorily until the Corporation began to try to dictate to the worker," claims an undated memorandum in the Lovestone papers. "The worker refused to conduct itself as being 'bought,' resented the crude attempts at infiltration, and particularly resented the Corporation threatening to use the co-worker if the worker didn't play ball the way the Corporation wanted to play it."[78]

FOUR

A Deep Sickness in New York

INTELLECTUALS

In March 1949 the Communist Information Bureau staged its most startling provocation of the whole Cold War. That month, New York City's Waldorf-Astoria Hotel, an Art Deco edifice of midtown Manhattan elegance, hosted a gathering of Soviet and American intellectuals, the Cultural and Scientific Conference for World Peace. Modeled after the World Congress of Intellectuals for Peace held in Wroclaw, Poland, the previous August, where eminent Marxist thinkers such as Hungarian aesthetician Georg Lukács had denounced "the drift toward fascist imperialism in the United States," the New York conference was intended to rally American intellectuals against the anti-Soviet foreign policy of their government.[1] Similar Cominform-sponsored efforts to appeal to intellectuals' dread of another world war—the Stalin Peace Prize, the Stockholm Peace Appeal, the launch in Paris of the monthly review *Défense de la Paix*—were eliciting a strong response in western Europe: the First World Peace Congress, held in Paris in April 1949, drew over 2,000 delegates. The communist organizers of the New York event, whose sponsors included such luminaries of the American Popular Front as Paul Robeson, F. O. Matthiessen, and Lillian Hellman, must have hoped to strike a similar chord within the United States itself.

If so, they were to be bitterly disappointed. Indeed, the New York conference was nothing short of a publicity disaster. The State Department derailed preparations by refusing to grant visas to would-be European participants. Conferees arrived at the Waldorf to find anticommunist vigilantes, alerted by the Hearst press, parading on Park Avenue. Most unnerving of all was a series of disruptions staged by anti-Stalinist American intellectuals within the hotel itself. Organized by New York University philosophy professor Sidney Hook, who had rented a honeymoon suite on the hotel's tenth floor to serve as headquarters, Americans for Intellectual Freedom (AIF), as this group called itself, asked deliberately awkward questions of the Soviet delegates, issued misleading statements in the name of the conference's organizers, and, on the final day, at the aptly named Freedom House, staged their own public meeting, which was so well attended that speeches had to be broadcast via loudspeakers to an overflow crowd in Bryant Park. "We had frustrated one of the most ambitious undertakings of the Kremlin," Hook congratulated himself later.[2]

The battle at the Waldorf marked a turning point in the Cold War struggle for hearts and minds. The failure of the conference signaled the final extinction of the Popular Front as a force in American cultural life (at just the same time communists were being driven out of their last labor stronghold in the CIO), and the AIF's counterdemonstration was the opening U.S. salvo in a conflict that would come to be known as the "cultural Cold War"—the Soviet-American contest for the allegiance of the world's intellectuals. The following year, in June 1950, Frank Wisner's Office of Policy Coordination would fund an anticommunist rally in West Berlin directly inspired by the example of the AIF, out of which was to emerge the CIA's principal front operation in the cultural field, the Paris-based Congress for Cultural Freedom. Over the course of the next decade, the CCF would become one of the west's main defenses against the ideological appeal of communism and a dominant institutional force in western intellectual life.

Before examining the impact of the CIA's covert patronage, as administered through the Congress for Cultural Freedom, on American culture (the subject of the next chapter), it is first necessary to relate the history of the CCF's New York–based affiliate, the American Committee for Cultural Freedom (ACCF), and its attempt to mobilize U.S. intellectuals in the cultural Cold War. As will soon become evident, this means telling a story very like that of the Lovestoneites' Free Trade Union Committee in that it features a group of ex-communists helping to invent the weapons with which the CIA fought the Cominform, then their being sidelined as the spies attempted to professionalize their front operations. The main difference between the ACCF and the FTUC was that the intellectuals were, if anything, even more troublesome clients for the Agency than their counterparts in labor.

When Hook countered the Cominform's peace offensive by appealing instead to the concept of intellectual freedom, he was speaking to a distinct ideological tradition on the American non-communist left that dated back to the early 1930s. There emerged then in New York a group of intellectuals who, although riven by internal conflicts of one sort or another, were united by certain strong ideological bonds.[3] One of these was a shared sense of alienation from the dominant, liberal political culture of the 1930s, the product in most cases of a Lovestone-like upbringing in an environment of Jewish, immigrant, working-class socialism (although the group was also joined by several upper-class, gentile bohemians whose rejection of New Deal politics could be interpreted as a form of radical conservatism). Following from this, the New York intellectuals, as they would later be designated (sometimes with the "i" in "intellectuals" capitalized, reinforcing their sense of themselves as a definite—and important—community or movement), also shared a strong allegiance to highbrow culture, in particular the most complex forms of modernist literary experimentation, which they consistently defended against political attack from both the left and the right.

Most crucially, and again inextricably tied up with their other affinities, the group was bound together by its hatred of Stalinism. Like Lovestone, most of the New York intellectuals had passed through or close to the communist movement in the early 1930s, and they remained in its orbit until the end of the decade, an element of its Trotskyist "left opposition" (the Lovestoneites were the "right opposition"). Afterward, although several of them tried hard to invent new forms of non-communist radicalism, most became preoccupied with fighting Stalinism, to the exclusion of other, positive political commitments—a condition that Irving Howe, one of the more enduring radicals in their number, diagnosed as "Stalinophobia."[4] Later still, during and after the 1960s, their peculiar combination of fervent anti-Stalinism and cultural elitism would cause the New York intellectuals to become identified with the neoconservative movement in politics and the arts.[5]

Within this group, two individuals stand out for the important part they played in the cultural Cold War. Sidney Hook was the archetypal Jewish New York intellectual: brilliant, pugnacious, a fearsome polemicist; poet Delmore Schwartz nicknamed him "Sidney Chop" for his implacable performances of logical argumentation.[6] Born and raised in one of the worst immigrant slums in turn-of-the-century Brooklyn, Hook worked his way through CCNY (like Lovestone, he was a member of Morris Cohen's famous philosophy class) to graduate school at Columbia, where he became a disciple of the illustrious Pragmatist John Dewey. Although strongly influenced by Marxism—indeed generally acknowledged as America's leading Marxist thinker thanks to his magnum opus, *Towards the Understanding of Karl Marx*—Hook was an ardent anti-Stalinist who loudly protested the Moscow show trials of the late 1930s, in which Stalin used the courts to purge his political enemies. Hook went so far as to organize a commission of inquiry, chaired by his mentor Dewey, which traveled to Mexico to question the exiled Leon Trotsky. In 1939, after much of the American left had rejected the Dewey commission's finding that Trotsky was innocent of the charges leveled against him by Stalin, Hook formed another group, the Committee for Cultural Freedom, to act as a focus of opposition to the Popular Front. (As several historians have noted, some New York intellectuals, such as diehard radical Dwight Macdonald, thought the committee's brief too "negative" and joined instead the League for Cultural Freedom and Socialism, which put equal emphasis on anti-Stalinism and democratic socialism.)[7] The late 1940s found Hook increasingly alarmed by the threat of Soviet expansion into western Europe and casting around for other organizational weapons with which to fight the anti-Stalinist cause. An attempt to hijack Macdonald's anarcho-pacifist Europe-America Groups (EAG) for this purpose failed, as did an effort to replace EAG with the more straightforwardly anti-Soviet Friends of Russian Freedom (whose statement of aims was eerily like that of the CIA émigré front AMCOMLIB). Hook's 1949 counterrally at the Waldorf was the culmination of this two-decades-old organizational history.

Less visible than Hook, but arguably more influential behind the scenes, was another NYU philosophy professor, James Burnham. If Hook epitomized the plebeian, immigrant New York intellectual, Burnham—taller in stature, gentler in expression, more elegant in appearance—belonged to the small minority of native-stock, patrician rebels who also were members of the group. Born into a wealthy Chicago family, Burnham received his education at a Catholic boarding school in Connecticut, then Princeton and Balliol College, Oxford.[8] After taking up his appointment at NYU in 1929, he was gradually drawn into the world of New York sectarian radicalism, emerging as a leading theoretical light of the new Trotskyist faction, Max Shachtman's Socialist Workers Party (SWP), before losing his faith in socialism after the Nazi-Soviet Pact of 1939 and being driven from the SWP the following year. The 1940s saw Burnham move from a position of bleak political detachment, as expressed in his widely read 1941 treatise *The Managerial Revolution* (whose "nightmare vision of a world divided among three perpetually warring totalitarian superstates" strongly influenced George Orwell's *1984*), to fierce partisanship in the Cold War.[9] *The Struggle for the World*, published in 1947 but based on a paper Burnham had written for the OSS in 1944, depicted international communism as a conspiratorial movement bent on global domination. The book urged American leaders to use all the means at their disposal, including political and psychological warfare, to resist Soviet expansion. "The summons is for nothing less than the leadership of the world," proclaimed Burnham, in language verging on the apocalyptic. "If it is reasonable to expect failure, that is only a measure of how great the triumph could be."[10]

Shortly after this announcement, Burnham himself enlisted in the struggle for the world, joining the OPC as a full-time advisor on anticommunist political warfare. Burnham's role in the OPC was secret, but it is possible to piece together a fairly detailed picture of this New York intellectual's duties as covert operative from clues scattered throughout his personal papers at the Hoover Institution in California. A Princeton classmate, journalist Joseph J. Bryan III, now head of the OPC's Psychological Warfare Workshop (the unit responsible for coming up with the oversized condom proposal for the Free Europe Committee), first approached Burnham in the hope of engaging his services "as an expert consultant."[11] Evidently, Burnham himself must have raised the matter of his Trotskyist past, because in a subsequent letter Bryan felt the need to reassure him that "the chief of my branch" (in other words, Frank Wisner) did not share his "apprehension about possible embarrassment to the administration."[12] In any event, by July 1949 the philosophy professor had obtained the necessary security clearance to begin his consultancy with the

OPC.[13] In August he moved his household from New York to Washington, claiming that he was taking a sabbatical from NYU to work as a "freelance writer."[14] Burnham began his new job in October. He never visited the OPC's offices on the Mall, where his identity was concealed by the code names "Hamburn" or "Kenneth E. Hambley"; he wrote regular memoranda and planning papers from an upstairs office in his rented Georgetown townhouse, which also provided "cover for contacts, intelligence de-briefings, planning, and actions in connection with various official needs and projects."[15] Even the most routine of intellectual activities now served as a disguise for Burnham's new work. In November 1950 he used an invited lecture at the prestigious Groton School in Massachusetts (alma mater of many prominent figures in the early CIA) as cover for a trip to deal with various pieces of OPC business in New York City.[16]

According to E. Howard Hunt (a CIA officer before achieving notoriety as one of Richard Nixon's White House "plumbers"), in the years that followed, Burnham provided the OPC with advice on "virtually every subject of interest to our organization."[17] A particular area of expertise was émigré affairs. Burnham was OPC's main point of contact with the group of Polish exiles gathered around the Paris-based journal *Kultura*, including the charismatic Joseph Czapski, with whom he developed a proposal for a refugee institute that would eventually become the NCFE's Free Europe University in Strasbourg.[18] He also intervened on behalf of Czeslaw Milosz with the American immigration authorities, liaising with the exile relief organization the International Rescue Committee to expedite the Polish writer's visa application (but only after having interviewed Milosz personally to satisfy himself that rumors he was a Soviet agent were baseless).[19] Indeed, counterintelligence appears to have been one of Burnham's main functions, with the ex-Trotskyist using his inside knowledge of the communist movement to advise the OPC about possible infiltration of its front operations. He was perennially suspicious on this score, once even suggesting that Allen Grover, AMCOMLIB's secretary, was known within Time, Inc., as a "comintern representative."[20] At the same time, Burnham peppered the OPC with a constant barrage of proposals for anticommunist psychological warfare: the circulation of "rumors and stories about Stalin's health"; the creation of stock cartoon characters lampooning communist officials; "desirable semantic changes" in American propaganda, such as the use of the word "colony" instead of "satellite" to refer to the captive nations in eastern Europe, so as to associate the Soviet Union with imperialism.[21] According to one former CIA officer, Miles Copeland, Burnham was even consulted by Kermit Roosevelt when the latter was planning the 1953 coup in Iran.[22] Copeland himself also looked to the eminent ex-communist intellectual for enlightenment about the great ideological issues of the day, an attitude echoed by Burnham's admiring OPC aide, Warren G. Fugitt, who years later fondly recalled afternoons spent in Burnham's Georgetown living room "with the likes of Max Eastman declaiming in front of the fireplace, Raymond Aron waiting for us to ask precisely the right question, and Arthur Koestler furious about something."[23]

This, then, was not a simple case of the OPC "using" Burnham. If anything, the New York intellectual was performing a role similar to that played by the "Park Avenue cowboys" in the years immediately after World War II, trying to fasten his own anticommunist agenda onto the U.S. government. Although heartened by the Truman Doctrine and the Marshall Plan, Burnham remained doubtful that the liberals in charge of official policy toward the Soviet Union truly appreciated the nature of the communist threat or understood how best to combat it. "The only morsel of hope that I've swallowed during these months is from my southern excursion," he told his colleague and confidant Hook in December 1948, in an oblique reference to his first contacts with the OPC. "The people there seem to understand what is, and what should be done better than any other group of which I know." However, Burnham's enthusiasm about America's new secret service officers was qualified. "They do not," he remarked to Hook, "know how to implement their knowledge and willingness. We ought to be able to find some way to help them—and ourselves—there."[24]

What was really needed, Burnham believed, was the experience and expertise of intellectuals who had once been communists themselves. With this in mind, he attempted to put Hook in touch with the OPC. He also tried to arrange a meeting in Washington between former Comintern officer Arthur Koestler and "a dozen or so persons to which you might be a severe and needed teacher."[25] Still, Burnham's Cold War commitment continued to run ahead of that of the Truman administration. A paper he presented to the OPC in or about 1950, "The Strategy of the Politburo, and the Problem of American Counter-Strategy," echoed his book of the same year, *The Coming Defeat of Communism*, by urging an aggressive campaign "on the most massive scale" designed to bring about "the disintegration of the communist élite."[26] Burnham's advocacy of rollback, soon to find its most famous expression in his *Containment or Liberation?* (1953), was associated with a growing political conservatism, which manifested itself in a populist identification with "the masses" and—ironically, considering his radical background—an increasing dissatisfaction with the OPC's NCL strategy. In short, Burnham was not merely advising official opinion—he was actively trying to shape it.

Much the same was true of Sidney Hook. Although the evidence concerning Hook's ties to the CIA is less detailed than it is for Burnham, certain things are clear. One is that he performed consultancy work for DCI Walter Bedell Smith, who set great store by Hook's "profound and accurate knowledge and appreciation of Communist political philosophy."[27] Hook also consulted with the Psychological Strategy Board, the body created in 1951 to oversee and coordinate official anticommunist propaganda efforts; he corresponded with its first director, Gordon Gray, and wrote Gray's successor, Raymond B. Allen, even before Allen had taken up the position, to offer his advice on psychological warfare. "This subject has interested me for years," Hook told Allen, "and I have watched despairingly as we have lost one round after another to the Kremlin."[28]

This work never turned into full-time employment for Hook, though, as it did for Burnham. Indeed, there appears to have been some reluctance on the part of the OPC to contact Hook at all: in January 1949, Burnham expressed surprise that his colleague had not yet "heard from my friends," interpreting this as "a very bad sign."[29] This might have had to do with security concerns. Whereas Burnham had so far escaped investigation by the FBI, Hook had been the subject of an Internal Security Case in 1943, after J. Edgar Hoover had spotted a *Daily Worker* article describing him as "the chief carrier of Trotskyite bacilli" at NYU.[30] Another possibility is that Hook had earned a reputation in government circles for being too opinionated and outspoken. In April 1948, for example, he had blasted the State Department for its "utter ineptness" in failing to adopt an "aggressive approach" in its radio broadcasting: "Whoever formulated this policy doesn't understand the world he is living in, is abysmally ignorant of Central Europe, and ought to be retired to some field where he can do less damage to the fight for democratic survival."[31] Like his fellow professor, Burnham, Hook assumed a distinctly didactic attitude to government officials. In September 1948, after spending a week consulting with General Lucius D. Clay and other administrators of the American occupation zone in Germany, he wrote Burnham, informing him, without any apparent irony, that "they have accepted my diagnosis of the situation in Europe."[32]

In any case, Burnham and Hook appear to have developed a working relationship in which the former liaised secretly with the OPC in Washington while the latter publicly managed day-to-day front affairs in New York. This was the basis of what was perhaps their single most important contribution to the U.S. effort in the cultural Cold War, their role in the planning of the Congress for Cultural Freedom.[33] A month after leading the resistance to the March 1949 Waldorf conference, Hook traveled to Europe to help with the organization of a similar rally against the Paris World Peace Congress (for which Carmel Offie and Irving Brown secretly arranged OPC funding). While there, he met with Melvin J. Lasky, a young New York intellectual working for the American military government in Germany, where he edited the politico-cultural review *Der Monat* (a model for the later journals published by the CCF, such as *Encounter*). Hook and Lasky discussed the possibility of creating a permanent body of anticommunist intellectuals to act as a democratic counterweight to the Cominform. In August, Lasky talked with Ruth Fischer, a former Comintern officer and sister of Gerhart Eisler, head of Cominform operations in East Berlin, about her plans to stage a massive anticommunist demonstration in West Berlin, "giving the Politburo hell right at the gate of their own hell," as she put it.[34] This idea was taken up by Michael Josselson, a CIA officer stationed in Berlin who had witnessed the Americans for Intellectual Freedom rally in New York earlier in the year ("We should have something like this in Berlin," he had told a friend in the AIF), and was passed up the line to Frank Wisner in Washington.[35] Formal approval of the project was not granted until April 1950, but by this point Lasky was enthusiastically pressing ahead with arrangements, inviting a dazzling array of intellectual celebrities to Berlin for a conference to be held in June. Meanwhile, Burnham took over the planning at the American end, disbursing funds, drafting the conference program, and securing travel documents for the American delegation. He and his wife, Marcia, traveled to Germany on June 15, eleven days before the Congress was due to begin, both their tickets paid for by the OPC (her presence in Berlin was "necessary to make certain that the other delegates shall regard me as a private individual," he explained to his employers).[36] Hook traveled on June 25, his absence from NYU covered by a substitute teacher whose salary of $150 had been paid by the OPC via Burnham.[37]

The Congress for Cultural Freedom met at Berlin's Titania Palast over four oppressively hot late June days, each of which witnessed, in the words of CCF historian Peter Coleman, "moments of high drama—defections from the East, political conversions, intellectual confrontations."[38] The ex-communists were dominant throughout, both in public, with Arthur Koestler "censoring and lecturing the delegates" (as an anonymous report in the Lovestone papers put it), and behind the scenes, where an unofficial steering committee composed of Koestler, Burnham, Hook, Lasky, and Irving Brown met every evening over a nightcap to plan the next day's business.[39] The ghost of Willi Münzenberg was discernible in the plan for a permanent body, which was adopted in the months afterward and whose structure resembled, in the words of Frances Stonor Saunders, "a mirror image of a Cominform *apparat*." As Burnham explained in one of his OPC memoranda, "The basis and aim of Soviet strategy imply the basis and aim of the only feasible American counter-strategy." (The philosopher's analyses of the Soviet system and proposals to destroy it often had a decidedly Marxian flavor; another ex-communist, Louis Fischer, once described Burnham as "communistically anticommunist.")[40]

As the CCF was established on a permanent footing, however, with headquarters in Paris under the command of Josselson and national affiliates dotted around the "free world," the ex-communist influence waned, replaced by a corresponding professionalization of the operation's management, much as there had been in the OPC's labor program. The first hint of this development came in April 1949, after the OPC-sponsored rally against the Peace Congress in Paris had descended into organizational chaos. Dismayed by reports of a stage-invasion by a group of anarchists, Frank Wisner voiced his apprehension that the plan to create an organization of anticommunist intellectuals (or "little Deminform," as he called it) might turn "into a nuts folly of miscellaneous goats and monkeys whose antics would completely discredit the work and statements of the serious and responsible liberals." As it happened, the Congress for Cultural Freedom passed off without any major hitch; indeed, it was considered one of the OPC's first big successes, with President Truman himself reported to be "very well pleased." Nonetheless, Wisner was deeply unhappy about one aspect of the conference. Several months earlier, when giving the operation the go-ahead in April 1950, he had insisted that Lasky and Burnham keep a low profile in Berlin, because both were closely associated in European eyes with U.S. officialdom and might provoke suspicion about the Congress's backing. Burnham obeyed this edict, presumably because, as an OPC employee, he had received an explicit command; but the exuberant Lasky, at this stage unaware of the CIA connection, was all too visible at the gathering. Wisner was "very disturbed" by this "nonobservance" of his directive and insisted on Lasky's exclusion from the new organization as a condition of continued funding by the OPC. Initially Josselson, who like Burnham had remained discreetly behind the scenes in Berlin, defended Lasky, claiming that "no other person here . . . could have achieved such success." When it became clear, however, that Wisner really would withhold OPC funds if his demand was not met, Josselson backed down and advised Lasky to take a "well-earned vacation."[41]

Another early casualty in the OPC's takeover of the CCF was Arthur Koestler. Having dominated the June 1950 rally, the Hungarian-born writer was now determined to have his say in shaping the Congress as a permanent entity. Not surprisingly, given his training in the Münzenberg apparatus, he thought that the new organization should concentrate on full-frontal political warfare, staging Popular Front–style mass rallies in western Europe and propagandizing behind the Iron Curtain.[42] For this reason he backed Louis Fischer, another former Comintern officer (and a fellow contributor to the classic statement of disillusioned ex-communism, *The God That Failed*) for the post of secretary-general. Fischer's candidacy also received the support of Irving Brown, at this stage the main conduit of OPC funds to the Congress.

Gradually, however, it became apparent that the CCF's emergent bureaucracy did not share Koestler and Brown's vision. In particular, Michael Josselson believed that, rather than engaging in spectacular political confrontations, the organization should adopt a "soft-sell" strategy, winning intellectuals to the western cause in the Cold War by fostering a sense of cultural community between America and Europe. Fischer was dumped in November 1950 (Brown, for one, detected prejudice against ex-communists in the decision)[43] and Josselson's friend, Russian-born composer Nicolas Nabokov (cousin of the novelist, Vladimir), chosen instead. Not only did Nabokov share Josselson's preference for cultural as opposed to political warfare, he was also the favored candidate in Washington, where during the war years he had been adopted by the set of anti-communist Russophiles surrounding George Kennan. Plans for a mass rally in Paris in the summer of 1951 were abandoned in favor of a festival celebrating western cultural achievements of the twentieth century. Koestler resigned from the CCF in July, telling a friend that he had been "made to withdraw in a gentle and effective way."[44]

A similar fate awaited James Burnham. Although he had agreed to stay out of the limelight in Berlin, the New York intellectual exerted a powerful influence on the CCF during the first months of its existence, consulting with the OPC over Nabokov's appointment, helping establish affiliates in Asia, and managing the CCF's affairs in America. Like Koestler, Burnham wanted the new organization to use Comintern-style political tactics in the struggle for hearts and minds.[45] Reflecting his emerging political conservatism, he also thought that the CCF should function as a true "anti-Communist front," embracing the "non-Socialist Right as well as [the] traditional Left."[46] He was therefore dismayed by signs that key personnel within the Paris secretariat, such as Director of Publications François Bondy (ironically, one of Burnham's own nominees), intended to appeal solely to the center-left. Another of Burnham's contacts in the CCF offices, Louis Gibarti (once one of Münzenberg's top propagandists and the man credited with recruiting Kim Philby as a Soviet agent), echoed Brown by reporting a growing hostility in CCF circles toward former communists who had traveled to the political right.[47] By the summer of 1951, the CCF had, after a period of political and tactical uncertainty, emerged as an organization of the non-communist left, concerned chiefly with cultural diplomacy as opposed to political warfare. This development reflected the rise of Josselson's influence over the Congress's affairs, and the decline of Burnham's.

By late 1951 the days of Burnham's collaboration with the CIA were numbered. The relationship had been marred from the beginning by tensions of the sort that had undermined the partnership between the OPC and the Free Trade Union Committee. As early as December 1949, Burnham felt moved to complain about his new employer's failure to reimburse expenses he had incurred traveling to New York on covert official business, claiming that this was symptomatic "of a way of doing business that can't stand up against the competition in the field where we are now trying to operate." Irritation turned to rage a few months later when he learned that Polish émigré Joseph Czapski was being given a cold shoulder by the National Committee for a Free Europe. "This is a goddamned outrage," he told the OPC and complained on another occasion, "It is still infinitely easier for communist fronts to get money than for anti-communists to do so."[48] What appears to have upset Burnham most, though, was a series of security lapses that threatened to expose his employment by the OPC and thereby wreck his reputation as a free-thinking intellectual (a concern reminiscent of Lovestone and Brown's complaints about overspending on labor operations in Italy). The worst of these lapses occurred in October 1951, when intelligence officer C. Hawley Oakes gave away more than he should have done in a conversation with Burnham's principal contact in India, an intellectual and politician named Minoo Masani. "This act, besides being an incredible violation of security, political intelligence, and ordinary horse sense, has jeopardized the results and future possibilities of three years of work," ranted Burnham. He went on to demand Oakes's summary firing, an internal investigation, and the establishment of an operational rule to prevent such gaffes ever occurring again. His memo to Frank Lindsay was entitled "An Act of Idiocy."[49] Burnham shared the Lovestoneites' view that the government's political warfare agencies were peopled by "stock brokers, academic social scientists, lawyers, investment bankers, [and] members of café or conventional society out for a fling at secret missions and Washington salons" who lacked a genuine "hatred of communism." To the extent that the United States had been resisting the communist menace, charged the author of *Containment or Liberation?*, it had been "trying to do so without anti-communists."[50]

The death blow to Burnham's career in intelligence was the McCarthy issue. Like other ex-communists in New York intellectual circles, Burnham was ambivalent about the red-baiting antics of "Tailgunner Joe." Granted, the junior senator was an unscrupulous demagogue, but in communist penetration of executive agencies he had hit on a real threat to national security. The New York intellectuals also found the spectacle of American communists invoking the protection of civil rights guaranteed them by a constitution they were seeking to overthrow very difficult to stomach. For these reasons, Burnham ended up siding, if not with McCarthy himself, then against those anti-McCarthyites who saw excessive anticommunism as a greater threat to civil liberties in America than communism itself. For the liberal anticommunists who staffed the covert-action branches of the CIA responsible for front group operations—several of whom were themselves the victims of McCarthyism—this position was unacceptable. "A number thought him 'too' hard-line, and a few went so far as to label him a 'fascist,'" one former intelligence officer told Burnham's biographer, Daniel Kelly. Some even feared that Burnham might try to help McCarthy when the witch-hunter turned on the Agency in 1953. By April of that year, the New York intellectual's consultancy contract was terminated. "It is not clear whether Burnham left the CIA voluntarily or was pushed out, though the latter seems more likely," writes Kelly. "What is certain is that he resigned under a cloud."[51]

Of the eminent ex-communists who had helped create the CCF, it was Sidney Hook who remained most closely involved with the organization. In addition to acting as the American representative on its Executive Committee, Hook was the founding chairman of the Congress's U.S. affiliate, the American Committee for Cultural Freedom. The roots of the ACCF, which first met at New York University's Faculty Club on Washington Square in December 1950 and received its certificate of incorporation on January 5, 1951, can be traced to the prior organizational history of the New York intellectuals, in particular the Committee for Cultural Freedom, which Hook had created in response to the Nazi-Soviet Pact in 1939.[52] However, the ACCF also had another, less obvious dimension. As far as the CIA was concerned, its main purpose was to support the international program of the Congress for Cultural Freedom by creating, as Tom Braden put it later, "the impression of some American participation in the European operation."[53] In addition, during a crucial phase of the CCF's early existence, after the Free Trade Union Committee had withdrawn from the cultural field and before the Agency began setting up fake foundations as financial conduits to its fronts, the ACCF functioned as one of its parent organization's main sources of funding.

It is possible to infer something of the scale and nature of this "backstopping" operation from the Burnham papers. Covert government money arrived at the ACCF's offices on East Forty-Fourth Street either directly via Burnham (in March 1951 and again in May, for example, the OPC consultant paid his NYU colleague Hook $1,000)[54] or, more often, via other front organizations, principally the NCFE.[55] The funds were then dispatched abroad by the ACCF's executive secretary, Pearl Kluger, an ex-Trotskyist who in the late 1930s had run the Dewey commission of inquiry and was sufficiently trusted by Hook and Burnham to be made "witting" of the CIA connection. Using this method, the OPC disbursed $2,000 to the organizers of a conference in New Delhi intended to secure a foothold for the CCF on the Indian subcontinent; $3,500 to Japan in an effort to kickstart a national affiliate there; and $15,000 to underwrite a series of anticommunist youth rallies in Berlin.[56] Although Burnham, mindful of the injunction against the CIA's operating within the United States, made it clear to Kluger that the funds were "primarily for use abroad," some money also found its way to eastern European émigrés in New York, whose fuzzy national status allowed a slight bending of the rules. The beneficiaries of this covert patronage were the wily Menshevik Boris Nicolaevsky and his partner, Anna Bourgina, who received several installments of $2,000 for the research they were undertaking on a "Black Book" about Soviet repression of cultural freedom.[57]

The Burnham papers also hint at some of the operational problems involved in this complex and devious exercise. Kluger, confronted with the task of managing the international CCF's finances and, at the same time, providing cover for the ACCF by organizing public meetings in New York, felt increasingly overburdened and underresourced. "When I complained to our friend that Santa Claus did not come down the chimney this month," she told Burnham in March 1951, "he said he had not understood that this was a six-months Christmas."[58] With such large sums going out to so many different parts of the globe, it was not always possible to keep a close eye on how CIA funds were actually spent. A banker's draft of $1,000 sent to organizers of the CCF affiliate in India simply disappeared; Burnham suspected an Indian editor of purloining it for his magazine.[59] Nicolaevsky was spotted walking the corridors of the Voice of America's offices, presumably in search of further handouts. "Is some of Bourgina's money as well as some of the other funds which he collects from various agencies and institutions going to finance his present intrigues?" wondered Burnham.[60] The intellectuals' habit of appropriating CCF subsidies for their own private purposes, which was to become a chronic problem in the United States's cultural Cold War effort, helps explains why the ACCF's "donor" requested a monthly accounting of the organization's spendings, in a move reminiscent of earlier attempts to monitor the FTUC's outlays. "Unless the donor is completely informed of the American Committee's activities," Pearl Kluger was told, "he is not in a position to approve further grants of money for the development of the Committee's projects."[61]

Then there were the security risks inevitably involved in running a front operation from public offices in the heart of New York City. Kluger, whose experience of watching out for Stalinist agents dated back to her days with the Dewey commission in Mexico, was constantly vigilant for signs of communist infiltration. In February 1951, she urged Burnham to investigate a "Vogue Travel Service" housed in the same building as the ACCF after a Committee member had recognized a Stalinist veteran of the Abraham Lincoln Brigade entering its offices. "I know I need not point out the advantages a travel agency has for our 'friends,' mail from all parts of the world, people travelling around, etc.," she pointed out.[62] A few months later, Kluger "played dumb" when "asked numerous questions concerning the financing of the Committee" by an "over-eager" visitor claiming to be from the State Department.[63]

Reports such as these, combined with the ongoing need to separate funding for foreign and domestic operations, persuaded the OPC to adopt extra security measures when the ACCF began handling the large sums of money required to mount Nicolas Nabokov's 1952 Paris arts festival. To ensure that festival business was not "mixed up in the other activities of the organization," Burnham instructed that a new checking account be set up "under the joint control of Sidney Hook and Pearl Kluger in covert understanding with an OPC representative."[64] A "Festival Account" was duly opened at the Rockefeller Center branch of the Chase National Bank, and a first payment of $40,000 deposited on October 11, 1951.[65] Meanwhile, an OPC officer by the name of Albert Donnelly arrived in New York to take charge of "all necessary negotiations for the Festival."

ACCF office staff were given firm instructions not to interfere. Phoning "any person in Washington," for example, "including Mr. B.," was strictly out of the question. "Mr. Donnelly has certain telephone facilities at his disposal which make any further indiscretions of this nature unnecessary."[66]

By the beginning of 1952, the CIA had also begun experimenting with what soon became its favorite method of laundering subsidies to its front organizations: the dummy foundation. This device was ingeniously simple. As Tom Braden explained, "We would go to . . . a well-known rich person and we would say, 'We want to set up a foundation,' . . . and pledge him to secrecy. . . . And then you would publish a letterhead and his name would be on it, and there would be a foundation." The "rich person" in the case of cultural operations was Julius "Junkie" Fleischmann, the heir of a Cincinnati gin fortune and patron of several opera companies, ballet troupes, and theatrical productions—"The American Maecenas for the world of culture," as Michael Josselson once described him.[67] Junkie, who was already helping the NCFE with the Crusade for Freedom, began posing as an "angel" of the CCF in 1951: the cover story for Albert Donnelly's presence in the ACCF office was that he had been hired as "Mr. Fleischmann's assistant."[68] In January 1952, Fleischmann was installed as president of the newly incorporated Heritage Foundation, whose purpose was officially recorded as aiding "those selected organizations, groups, and individuals which are engaged in increasing and preserving the cultural heritage of the free world." By the time of Nabokov's festival in April, the flamboyant Fleischmann was well known in CCF circles, and the Heritage Foundation, renamed the Farfield Foundation in August, was firmly established as a plausible source of the organization's clearly abundant funds. As far as the CIA was concerned, the ACCF had now performed its main practical function and could therefore take a backseat to the strategically far more important CCF.

Unfortunately for the Agency, this view was not shared by the American Committee for Cultural Freedom itself. By 1952, the organization had grown into a high-profile body of several hundred members engaged in a busy program of public activities.[69] The question of how widely knowledge of the CIA connection was shared in this group remains controversial, but it does seem clear that most of the organization's officers and executive-committee members suspected some secret government involvement. Diana Trilling, for example, who ran the ACCF's Administrative Committee during the mid-1950s, knew even before she joined the organization that the Farfield Foundation was a fake. The only question in her mind "was whether it was a conduit . . . for the CIA or the State Department." She nonetheless carried on her work for the ACCF "because I did not believe that to take the support of my government was a dishonorable act." She added, "Nobody did at that period—that interpretation is the result of a significant change in our political culture. I never liked the secrecy but was willing to live with it because I thought we were doing useful work."[70]

Like the Lovestoneites of the FTUC, witting members of the ACCF seem not to have been troubled ethically by the organization's secret funding. What concerns they felt were either tactical (another Executive Committee member, labor official Arnold Beichman, objected "not so much for moral reasons as because I felt certain that someday the whole tawdry business would be exposed") or (again as with the FTUC) related to the question of the organization's independence.[71] In October 1951, Hook told Burnham that several members had become so upset about the arrangements for the Paris festival that they were on the verge of resigning. As Burnham reported to the CIA, there was "a general feeling of uneasiness about the relations of the Committee with 'the government,' and a half-conscious feeling by the Committee members that they are being exploited for purposes over which they have no real control." An effort should be made "to counteract this uneasiness, and to forestall any public disruption of the Committee."[72]

Whatever it was that the New York intellectuals in the ACCF knew or did not know about the CIA's hand in their affairs, it did not prevent them from treating the organization as if it were a genuine, privately run committee, indeed, as if it were their own. The most obvious indication of this lack of regard for the ACCF's intended tactical function as cover and backstop for the international CCF was the Executive Committee's support for the two strategic options advocated by Koestler and Burnham in 1950 yet rejected by the CCF's leadership: the adoption of an overtly political position and the inclusion of conservative elements in a united front against communism. The first of these policies, which reflected the

New York intellectuals' intense anti-Stalinism and conviction that they knew best how to wage the cultural Cold War, even led the ACCF to question the tactics of its parent body. Sometimes this criticism was implicit, as when the ACCF took steps to protest Soviet violations of human rights or rebut communist anti-American propaganda to which the CCF had not responded.[73] At other times, it explicitly disputed the relevance to the Cold War of the CCF's cultural activities: Nabokov's festival was a particular target for denunciation by the New York intellectuals, who clearly thought that the neutralist atmosphere of the French capital was rubbing off on the CCF's officers.[74] The CCF was understandably annoyed by these attacks from within its own camp and took an increasingly stern line with its American affiliate during the early 1950s. Hook found himself having to mediate between the two organizations, trying to explain the CCF's cultural strategy to his comrades in New York while at the same time defending the ACCF's hard-line political pronouncements to members of the CCF's Executive Committee in Paris.

The other main tendency of the ACCF, toward a broad, inclusive membership policy (a late victory for Burnham, who had advised Hook to advertise the new organization "outside of the old radical and avant-garde circles" among "more conventional 'American' types"), resulted in a body that resembled, in the apt phrase of historian William L. O'Neill, "a Popular Front of anti-Stalinists, something like the League of American Writers in reverse."[75] At first, the ACCF's right and left wings—the former composed mainly of such ex-communists as Burnham and AMCOMLIB's Eugene Lyons, the latter of socialists, liberals, and a few mavericks like Dwight Macdonald—managed to coexist, perhaps partly because potentially disruptive individuals in the New York intellectual community were either not invited or refused to join.[76] (The launch of the journal *Dissent* in 1954 gave the nonconformists an alternative base around which to rally.) In March 1952, however, growing tensions about the organization's position on McCarthyism erupted in a blazing row during a conference at the Waldorf-Astoria Hotel after Burnham's ally Max Eastman defended McCarthy and accused liberals who saw him as a greater threat to American cultural freedom than communism of "divided loyalty." On this issue the ACCF intellectuals split along fairly clear doctrinal lines, similar to the division in the labor movement between the Lovestoneites of the AFL and the social democrats of the CIO. "By and large," observed Chicagoan novelist James T. Farrell, who later succeeded Hook as ACCF chairman, "the New York ex-radical intellectuals are not likely to be strongly anti-McCarthy." Arthur Schlesinger, Jr., one of the organization's leading anti-McCarthyites and a prominent Cold War spokesperson for anticommunist liberalism (his widely read 1949 work, *The Vital Center,* described the non-communist left as "the standard to rally the groups fighting to carve out an area for freedom"), agreed with Farrell, complaining of "some deep sickness in certain sectors of the New York intellectuals." "The *New Leader* variety of ex-Communist is really too much for me," he told his old friend, Nicolas Nabokov, shortly after he had been hissed by the audience at an ACCF forum for giving a "mild, Anglo-Saxon address" on the subject of anticommunism. "The whole thing left a very bad taste in my mouth and considerably diminished my enthusiasm for the Congress which, in this country, at least, has become an instrument for these bastards."[77]

Schlesinger, a former OSS-er, was in regular contact with senior officers of the CIA, briefing them about developments within the ACCF and putting a rather different spin on events from Burnham. (The two men were bitter enemies, the ex-communist referring sniffily to the "vital left-of-center" and the liberal describing *Containment or Liberation?* as "an absurd book written by an absurd man.")[78] When Frank Wisner, whom Schlesinger saw frequently on the Georgetown dinner party circuit, learned about the Waldorf row over McCarthyism—the last subject he wanted to see being aired in public, with its potential for arousing anti-Americanism abroad and its sensitivity for the CIA at home—he was appalled. "I can understand how . . . a group of American private citizens interested in cultural freedom would feel that it would have to take a position on McCarthyism," Wisner told a CIA colleague. "However, that is not the nature of the American Committee for Cultural Freedom which . . . was inspired if not put together by this Agency for the purpose of providing cover and backstopping for the European effort." Steps had to be taken immediately to repair the damage. Ideally, Wisner would have preferred "that the entire debate on this subject, from the beginning, be expunged from the record." If this was not possible, then at the very least, "an appeal to unity and concord . . . might be successful."[79]

It is not clear if such an appeal was made, although Frances Stonor Saunders speculates that a letter from Nabokov to Schlesinger urging him "to do everything you can to prevent a split in the American Committee" might have been prompted by the CIA.[80] What is certain is that the Agency took a much closer interest in the ACCF's affairs after the Waldorf dustup than it had before. (The only government officer present at the 1952 conference was a staff member of the Psychological Strategy Board, who was apparently unaware that the ACCF was an Agency front.)[81] The Deputy Chief of the International Organizations Division, Cord Meyer, asked Schlesinger to send him minutes of Executive Committee meetings on a regular basis, and Michael Josselson urged the more moderate members of the ACCF, such as sociologist Daniel Bell, to try to keep the hard-liners in check.[82] The latter, however, persisted in their ways. In 1954, an attempt to settle the McCarthy issue once and for all by publishing a scholarly monograph on the subject (James Rorty and Moshe Decter's *McCarthy and the Communists*) led to a walkout by the ACCF's most right-wing members, who deemed the book too critical of the Wisconsin senator. Leading the way was James Burnham, no longer obliged by his contract with the OPC to have any dealings with an organization he had come to regard as "a narrow and partisan clique."[83] Released from his ties to both the CIA and its intellectual front organization, the ex-communist was free to develop his growing interest in conservative thought, joining William F. Buckley, Jr.'s *National Review* in 1955 and later earning a reputation as a forerunner of neoconservatism.

By September 1954, Michael Josselson, who had never been convinced about the necessity of the ACCF in the first place, had decided that enough was enough, and informed Sol Stein, the organization's new executive secretary, that the CCF was terminating its monthly grant of $500.[84] This was bad news indeed for the Committee. Junkie Fleischmann's Farfield Foundation had continued shelling out to the ACCF for a while after Nabokov's 1952 festival, with John F. Dailey, Jr., of the foundation's Wall Street office sending Hook $2,500 a month for deposit at the Rockefeller Center Chase National.[85] This assistance stopped in January 1953, however, and no regular funding source was found to replace it.[86] Stein, a resourceful and creative cultural Cold Warrior, managed to keep the ACCF afloat through 1953 by garnering gifts from private angels, including Dave Dubinsky of the International Ladies' Garment Workers' Union (which gave $2,000) and Henry Luce (whose contributions came in the form of Time, Inc., stock).[87] He even enlisted the services of a

New York public relations firm, Harold L. Oram (a well-known fund-raiser for left-liberal causes who was associated with several other CIA front operations), in an effort to promote the ACCF among private philanthropists.[88]

Despite Stein's hard work, the search for a regular donor to replace the Farfield Foundation proved fruitless. Especially galling was the ACCF's failure to land a grant from the Fund for the Republic, a prominent liberal foundation run by the opinionated former chancellor of the University of Chicago, Robert M. Hutchins.[89] Hook blamed a history of intellectual controversy between him and Hutchins for the Fund's repeated rejections of ACCF grant applications, but this is probably too simplistic an explanation. The liberal philanthropies appear to have deliberately frozen out the ACCF after the McCarthy imbroglio of 1952, perhaps at the discreet bidding of the CIA. In any case, Josselson's monthly grant of $500 was an emergency measure to tide the Committee over until the Hutchins group had reached a decision on a funding bid by Stein. When that proved unsuccessful, the intelligence officer had the pretext he needed for turning off the financial tap.

The New York intellectuals were not put down so easily, however, and resorted to a number of stratagems to ensure the ACCF's continuation. Even as he lobbied CCF headquarters, threatening the possibility of the ACCF's reforming as an extremist, right-wing rump if it went out of business, Stein went over Josselson's head with a direct petition to the chief of the Operations Coordinating Board, Edward Lilly, listing the organization's various contributions to the international cultural Cold War effort (and conspicuously omitting mention of the 1952 Waldorf conference).[90] Meanwhile, individual officers and members of the Executive Committee begged personal donations from Junkie Fleischmann with such persistence that the American Maecenas must have begun to rue the day when he agreed to front for the CIA.[91]

When these methods failed to secure the ACCF's survival, its leaders went straight to the Agency itself. During a gloomy meeting of the Executive Committee, where it was reported that (according to the later recollection of Diana Trilling) "we now lacked money even for the next month's rent," Norman Thomas, the much-revered socialist leader and Trilling's predecessor as chair of the organization's Administrative Committee, declared that he "could see but a single solution: he would 'phone

Allen.'" (It was later disputed whether or not Thomas was acting at the instruction of the ACCF or on his own. Still, as Trilling pointed out, "None of us could fail to know that 'Allen' . . . was Allen Dulles, head of the CIA," an old family friend and Princeton classmate of Thomas.) Trilling remembered Thomas returning to the meeting "to tell us that a check for a thousand dollars would be in the mail the next morning." In fact, correspondence in the ACCF's papers suggests that the money was slower in materializing. On April 27, 1955, Stein wrote Thomas requesting that he make "a follow-up telephone call" to remind Dulles "of his interest in our work and suggest that speed is essential in coming to our assistance." Believing that it "would do harm rather than good to call Allen D. without some more immediate excuse," Thomas bided his time until the following Sunday, "on the fair chance that Dulles may be up in the country this weekend" (they owned neighboring houses on Long Island). Finally, around the same time—the circumstances are less well documented—Hook approached Cord Meyer concerning the Committee's plight.[92]

These combined efforts paid off a week later, on May 9, 1955, when the ACCF was awarded $10,000 by the Farfield Foundation to fund its reception center for visiting European intellectuals, and a further $4,000 by the Asia Foundation (a CIA proprietary analogous in function to the Free Europe Committee) to help establish a similar facility for Asian visitors.[93] ("It was mostly your own good work and your own powers of persuasion that turned the trick," Thomas wrote Stein. "I am happy to think I had a little to do with the proposition in certain quarters.")[94] Both donors were at pains to emphasize that their grants were intended to assist the ACCF's international work, not its domestic agenda. Indeed, in the case of the Farfield Foundation, there is more than a hint of pique in the tone of its letter to the ACCF confirming its grant award, suggesting that the foundation's trustees were put out by the sudden directive from the CIA that they step in to bail out the American Committee:

> With respect to that part of its program relating to the Congress for Cultural Freedom, it has been Farfield's practice to support the international headquarters of the Congress, rather than individual national branches. The Directors have been somewhat reluctant to part from their usual procedure, and have done so only because they believe that

> the American Committee deserves support in its activities which relate to the international program of the Congress for Cultural Freedom.[95]

Arthur Schlesinger, leader of the liberal opposition to the New York intellectual majority in the ACCF, must have expressed similar views to Cord Meyer, judging by a letter penned by the latter on May 16. "Thanks for your note, and I agree with much you have to say about certain members of the present Executive Committee in the outfit in New York," wrote Meyer.

> We certainly don't plan on any continuing large scale assistance, and the single grant recently made was provided as the result of an urgent request directly from Sidney H. and indirectly from Norman T. Our hope is that the breathing space provided by this assistance can be used by those gentlemen, yourself, and the other sensible ones to reconstitute the Executive Committee and draft an intelligent program that might gain real support from the Foundations. If this reconstitution of the leadership proves impossible we then, I think, will have to face the necessity of allowing the Committee to die a natural death, although I think this course would result in unhappy repercussions abroad.

"I much appreciate what you have done in terms of sitting on top of the loose talk," Meyer concluded. "I hope that the two of us can get together soon to discuss this whole problem in some detail."[96]

Meyer's hopes of salvaging the ACCF were destined to be disappointed. Indeed, rather than behaving more responsibly, the rejuvenated Committee became embroiled in a fresh round of controversies about communism and the Cold War. In the fall of 1954, it weighed in on an ongoing legal battle between Freda Kirchwey's *Nation* and Sol Levitas's *New Leader*, enlisting Wild Bill Donovan in defense of the latter's freedom of speech. (Art critic Clement Greenberg had used the *New Leader*'s pages to characterize the left-liberal *Nation*'s foreign editor, J. Alvarez del Vayo, as an apologist for the Soviet Union, prompting Kirchwey to bring a suit for $200,000 in damages against Levitas and his publication.)[97] Next, in early 1955, came a second embarrassingly public split over McCarthyism, when Sol Stein wrote another liberal New York journal, *The New Republic*, criticizing its sympathetic coverage of Owen Lattimore, the State Department Asia expert who had been hounded out of his job for alleged communist activities, and the ACCF's leading anti-McCarthyites (among them Schlesinger) dispatched follow-up letters dissociating themselves from Stein's comments.[98] A year later, in February 1956, Arthur Miller (whom the ACCF had defended in 1954, when the American Legion of Glenwood Landing, Long Island, tried to close down a production of *Death of a Salesman*) provoked another bout of unfavorable publicity by issuing a public statement declaring a neutral position in the cultural Cold War after receiving simultaneous invitations from the ACCF, AMCOMLIB, and the Union of Soviet Writers to join with them in celebrating the seventy-fifth anniversary of the death of Fedor Dostoevsky. "The facts, I believe, make it absolutely impossible for either the American or Soviet civilizations to honestly 'claim' Dostoevsky," pronounced Miller, "and unless I am altogether mistaken all these celebrations are designed with that aim. Were he alive today I believe he would be in trouble in America for certain of his views, and in Russia for others."[99]

If Meyer thought that the "hot-heads" of the ACCF might cool down after these ventings, he was very much mistaken. "Any time they come across anybody who disagrees with them and has what they call a 'soft attitude,' they are immediately galvanized into action," observed James Farrell of his colleagues on the Committee. "Like many husbands and wives, they come to life when they have a good argument." The most spectacular flare-up of all came a month after the Miller fiasco, in March 1956, when one of the CCF's honorary chairmen, British mathematician and philosopher Bertrand Russell, protested the imprisonment of Morton Sobell, a suspected accomplice of husband and wife "atom spies" Ethel and Julius Rosenberg, as a gross miscarriage of justice, akin to the "atrocities" perpetrated by "other police states such as Nazi Germany and Stalin's Russia."[100] Without consulting the CCF, the ACCF fired back a public response challenging Russell's account of the Sobell case as "totally mistaken" and questioning the propriety of "an officer of the Congress for Cultural Freedom" making "false and irresponsible statements about the process of justice" in the United States.[101] This was not the first time that the Briton and the New York intellectuals had come to blows. Several spats with the *New Leader* in the early 1950s were followed by two incidents involving the ACCF and a Popular Front–style anti-McCarthy group, the Emergency Civil Liberties Committee, which led to the CCF's

Honorary Chairman—a touchy man at the best of times—threatening to resign his post.[102] On both occasions, Russell allowed himself to be dissuaded by more moderate members of the ACCF, acting at the behest of Michael Josselson in Paris, who feared losing the prestige of Russell's name in Asia. After the public reprimand of 1956, however, not even the famously charming Nicolas Nabokov could prevail upon Russell to stay with the CCF. "I do not want to have anything to do with people who behave like your friends of the American Committee," the philosopher loftily told the composer. Thanks to the actions of the ACCF, the CCF had lost, as Josselson put it in a furious letter to Hook, one of its "biggest attractions."[103]

By now, the NYU professor was tiring of his role as an intermediary between the international CCF and its rebarbative American affiliate. On the one side, Hook faced constant recrimination from Josselson, who appears to have blamed Hook personally for the out-of-control behavior of his fellow New York intellectuals. On the other, when Hook did try to restrain the ACCF, he was accused of taking a "pro-Paris" position, and worse. During a meeting of the Executive Committee on October 12, 1955, Hook was dismayed when Sol Stein introduced a resolution calling on the CCF to intervene in Indonesia against the communist-backed President Sukarno. Hook vehemently opposed this proposal, believing it to be an "open foray into politics" that had nothing to do with cultural freedom, and succeeded in striking any reference to it from the minutes.[104] After the meeting, Diana Trilling viciously attacked Hook, describing his actions as "one of the most shocking experiences of my intellectual career" and strongly implying that he was acting directly on instructions from the ACCF's mysterious backers in government:

> Who and what is the authority from whose eyes and ears this sin of ours must be kept, Sidney? Of whom are we are so afraid that we cannot talk or commit speculations, even our mistakes, to paper for fear of the punishment that will ensue? Are we free men and women joined in a free democratic enterprise or are we the pitiable puppets of the Kremlin, trembling lest we take a wrong line or vote the wrong way?[105]

Caught between New York, Paris, and Washington, it is perhaps no wonder that, after Russell's resignation, Hook began considering his own position in the CCF.[106]

As it turned out, though, it was Hook's successor as ACCF chairman, James Farrell, who was first to snap. The novelist and critic, one of the best exponents of the "proletarian" literary genre of the 1930s, had never felt comfortable as chair of the ACCF, partly because he feared that his new administrative duties might distract him from his writing, and partly because he felt at odds with the "anti-Communist snobbery" of the "old Bolsheviks" in the organization.[107] The strain began to show during a CCF-sponsored tour of the Middle East in the summer of 1956. In June, Farrell wrote Radio Free Europe from Jerusalem, extending a "hand of friendship" to communist writer Howard Fast, who had just publicly recanted his Stalinism; Hook intervened, cabling RFE to request that it "not use statement for time being." Shortly afterward, "terribly tired and worn out," Farrell "got boiled on beer" in Beirut and "wrote an incoherent letter on the back of a menu" to the notoriously isolationist *Chicago Tribune*, stating that U.S. foreign aid was wasted on its recipients and that Indian intellectuals in particular believed that their best policy was "to flirt with Communists, insult us, and perhaps get more money out of us."[108]

After returning home, perhaps sensing that the Executive Committee was gearing up to ask for his resignation, Farrell (again, it would seem, in his cups) telephoned the *New York Times* shortly before midnight on August 27 to report that he was voluntarily giving up the ACCF chairmanship. The following day he composed a more sober explanation of his decision, citing the organization's failure "to sink our roots deeply into American life," its lack of understanding of conditions abroad, its obsession with fighting an increasingly insignificant communist threat at home, and its tendency to subjugate culture—ostensibly its primary concern—to politics.[109] The whole sorry episode provoked a predictable response from Josselson, who berated the rest of the ACCF leadership for failing to contain the damage caused by Farrell's outbursts. However, one cannot avoid the suspicion that the CCF director was secretly pleased by the ACCF chairman's actions, which, as one observer remarked, appeared "calculated, with deliberation or not, to injure the Committee."[110] Indeed, a cable from Farrell to Josselson suggests that the former might have been "put up" to his resignation: "Have broken up American Committee," wrote Farrell. "Your advantage. . . . Have kept my word."[111]

Whether or not Josselson willed it, Farrell's resignation, coming so soon after the Russell affair, sounded the death knell of the American Committee for Cultural Freedom. In 1957, it suspended its active life, bequeathing its remaining funds—the remnants of the Asia Foundation grant and a few Time, Inc., shares—to the *New Leader* and the New York intellectuals' premiere cultural organ, *Partisan Review*. Even in this moribund state, however, the ACCF remained the focus of ex-communist factional infighting. In 1960, for example, after the organization had been reactivated as a tax shelter for *Partisan Review*, one of its directors, Diana Trilling, became embroiled in a feud with the magazine's editors over what she perceived as their wavering on the communist issue, leading to her noisy resignation from the ACCF board.[112] The same year Sidney Hook participated in his last meeting of the CCF's Executive Committee. "My inactivity by this time was not unwelcomed," he later wrote, "since I was regarded by the Parisian directorate as a representative of the obnoxious American Committee for Cultural Freedom."[113]

The CIA's difficulties with the ACCF illustrate even more vividly than its experience with the Free Trade Union Committee the potential pitfalls of front operations. Like the Lovestoneites, the New York intellectuals seem not to have had many qualms about accepting secret subsidies. Otherwise, though, they were almost impossible to manage. As former communists themselves, they shared Lovestone's belief that they had a much better understanding of the Cold War enemy than the U.S. government, claiming what almost amounted to ownership rights to anti-Stalinism. This conviction was reflected in the persistence with which they advocated certain Cold War tactics—all-out political warfare, alliance with conservative elements, noncooperation with liberal "anti-anticommunists"—even in the face of obvious official disapproval. Nor did it help that, despite their willingness to accept covert patronage, they were extremely sensitive about their intellectual independence. In much the same way that the doctrine of "free trade unionism" motivated the FTUC to resist not just communism but excessive CIA interference in labor affairs as well, so the New York intellectuals' allegiance to the concept of cultural freedom often placed them at loggerheads with U.S. government policy in the cultural Cold War.

Just as with the Lovestoneites, the New York intellectuals' marriage to the CIA was an entirely expedient union, brought about by a short-lived coincidence of strategic aims. Looking at the relationship from the intellectuals' point of view, it is possible to see acceptance of the Agency's patronage as a self-interested measure designed to help them achieve certain independently held goals at a time when financial backing from established liberal philanthropies was being withheld. Later, as strands of the New York intellectual community fed into the neoconservative movement, new sources of institutional support would become available in the shape of conservative corporations and think tanks, and the need for an alliance with secret federal agencies would pass.

FIVE

The Cultural Cold War

WRITERS, ARTISTS, MUSICIANS, FILMMAKERS

Spying and writing have always gone together. In Britain, where the modern intelligence agency was born, intellectuals moved smoothly back and forth between secret government service and the literary life, some, like journalist Malcolm Muggeridge, even spending the morning at the typewriter before consulting with MI6 after lunch.[1] Somerset Maugham, Compton Mackenzie, Graham Greene, Ian Fleming, John Le Carré: all placed their powers of observation and divination at the disposal of the British secret state while mining their experience of intelligence work in their fiction. It was not just a case of satisfying the reading public's apparently insatiable appetite for the espionage novel. There seemed to be some basic connection between the roles of writer and spy: both were iconic, even heroic, figures in modern culture, necessarily detached from ordinary society, yet gifted—cursed, perhaps—with unique insight into the darkest realms of human existence. "I, from very early, lived a secret life, an inward life," Le Carré once told an interviewer. "I seemed to go about in disguise."[2]

In this respect, the spies of the CIA were no different from their British counterparts. Indeed, the "man of letters" was, if anything, even more conspicuous a figure in the upper echelons of the American secret service than in MI6. During World War II, Norman Holmes Pearson, a noted Yale professor of literature and editor, with W. H. Auden, of the five-volume Viking *Poets of the English Language*, ran "X-2," the London-based counterespionage branch of the Office of Strategic Services. After the war, when the OSS was resurrected as the CIA, the task of counterintelligence—protecting one's secrets from theft by rival agencies—was inherited by another "Yalie," James Jesus Angleton, whose obsession with hunting for "moles" later came to verge on paranoia. A founding editor of the influential "little magazine" *Furioso* and friend of Ezra Pound, Angleton (who inspired the "complex and convoluted" character of Hugh Montague in Norman Mailer's CIA novel, *Harlot's Ghost*) was known, among his many other code- and nicknames, as "the Poet."[3] One of Angleton's several protégés in the Agency, Cord Meyer, had edited the Yale *Lit* and published short stories in the *Atlantic Monthly* before becoming a spy.[4] He used his position as Deputy Chief, then Chief, of the International Organizations Division to recruit to the CIA a number of young critics and poets associated with John Crowe Ransom's *Kenyon Review*, house organ of the New Criticism, a rigorously formalistic method of reading literary texts.[5]

Of course, once one was in the CIA, writing had to take second place to spying. Unless, like E. Howard Hunt, one was specifically tasked with improving the Agency's public image by penning flattering fictional portrayals of it, the challenge of fighting the international communist movement and all its devious stratagems was so demanding that it left little time for the literary life.[6] Besides, men like Tom Braden, who during the war had run missions for the OSS in occupied France, were impatient to return to the fray, to abandon the contemplative life for the active. Moreover, even if there was little opportunity to write poetry in the heat of the Cold War, there was another, no less honorable part for these CIA officers to play in the process of artistic creation, one for which, by dint of their patrician backgrounds and educations, they were extremely well suited: that of cultural patron.

As well as being a political, an economic, and (only when other methods failed) a military conflict, the confrontation between the United States and Soviet Union was a clash of cultures. The communists were fond of pointing toward their cultural achievements as proof that they, not the western bourgeoisie, were the true heirs of the European Enlightenment. Witness the excellence of Soviet cinema, theater, dance, art, music, and literature. The United States, in comparison, was a cultural wasteland, its few artists treated as mere ornaments by its capitalist class, and its workers cretinized by the idiotic products of its culture industries.

Faced with these charges, which appeared to find a receptive audience among intellectuals in western Europe, Americans responded by accusing the Russians of disregarding the inherent value of culture, of subjugating art to the dreary dictates of a totalitarian political ideology. Not only that, the picture of the United States as a bastion of philistinism was, so they claimed, badly outdated. In fact, America was the seedbed of the most creative impulses in modern culture, as was shown by, for example, the influence of Pound and T. S. Eliot over modernist poetics. With Europe enfeebled by its recent political convulsions, and many of its artists seeking refuge across the Atlantic, it now fell to the United States to protect and nurture the best cultural traditions of western civilization.

Yet there were problems with this set of claims. American politicians were hardly known for their appreciation of modern art: indeed, one congressman, Representative George A. Dondero of Michigan, won himself considerable publicity by loudly denouncing the "horde of foreign art manglers" as a "pen-and-brush phalanx of the Communist conspiracy," while even the president himself, Harry Truman, once famously declared of a Yasuo Kuniyoshi semi-abstract painting, "If that's art, I'm a Hottentot."[7] This sort of Babbittry inhibited U.S. government officials who wanted to counter communist propaganda by publicly displaying works of homegrown modern art. One traveling State Department exhibit, "Advancing American Art," which featured work by, among others, Adolph Gottlieb, Arshile Gorky, and Georgia O'Keefe, was the target of such vitriolic attack that it had to be canceled in mid-tour and its contents sold off as surplus government property (they fetched a mere $5,544).[8] Combined with the effects of this sort of cultural vigilantism was a fundamental contradiction. The whole point of American art was supposed to be that it was free, the unfettered expression of individual consciousness: this was what distinguished it from the agitprop produced by the Soviet Union's "artists in uniform." How, then, could the U.S. government openly mobilize American culture in the Cold War kulturkampf?

In these circumstances, it fell to the CIA to shoulder a large share of the burden of official artistic patronage during the first years of the Cold War.[9] The Agency's principal front organization in the so-called cultural Cold War was the Congress for Cultural Freedom, the body created in 1950 to counter the Cominform's "peace offensive." Under OPC officer Michael Josselson's skillful stewardship, the CCF evolved into one of the most important artistic patrons in world history, sponsoring an unprecedented range of cultural activities, including literary prizes, art exhibits, and music festivals. The CCF's location in Paris, the citadel of western European Cold War neutralism, reflected the CIA's desire to carry "the battle for Picasso's mind" (as Tom Braden later described it) to the communists.[10] It also indicated that, ironically, anticommunist American literati stood to gain less from their government's patronage than their uncommitted European fellows. Nonetheless, American writers, artists, and musicians were involved in the CCF's international program as part of the CIA's efforts to "showcase" U.S high culture for the benefit of neutralist foreign intellectuals. Agency subsidies as a result had domestic repercussions in America—or, to use intelligence parlance, "blowback."

This fact, combined with the prominence of many of the individuals concerned, has ensured that, among the CIA's numerous front operations in the Cold War, the CCF has attracted the most attention from historians. For many years after the existence of the Agency's covert network was exposed by investigative journalists in 1967, writing about the cultural Cold War displayed a strong revisionist impulse. The CIA was credited with having a heavy influence on the production of high culture in the United States and its distribution abroad. In particular, the postwar preeminence of certain modernist cultural movements, such as abstract expressionism in painting, was ascribed, in part at least, to covert official sponsorship. The culmination of this school of thought was British researcher Frances Stonor Saunders's 1999 book *Who Paid the Piper?* (or, to give it its less provocative American title, *The Cultural Cold War*), a widely reviewed history of the CCF and allied CIA cultural activities.[11] Somewhat opposed to this interpretation, and more pronounced in works about the cultural Cold War that have appeared since the publication of the Saunders book, is a tendency to play down both the CIA's affinity for modernism and the control the Agency exerted over the artists who received its secret subsidies. Which of these interpretations—the revisionist or the "post-revisionist"—is correct? What were the CIA's aesthetic tastes, and how much control did the Agency exert over American high culture?

"Suddenly, there were limousines, parties with lashings of smoked salmon, and so on," recalled Jason Epstein of the 1950s, when the Congress for

Cultural Freedom appeared on the U.S. literary scene. "People who couldn't normally afford the bus ticket to Newark were now flying first class to India for the summer."[12] American writers stood to benefit from the clandestine largesse of the CIA in several ways. First, there were travel expenses for attending international meetings of the CCF. The Agency wanted to show off the cream of American literary talent to European intellectuals and thereby forge a sense of Atlantic cultural community. For their part, novelists, poets, and critics such as Mary McCarthy, Robert Lowell, and Dwight Macdonald were happy to travel in comfort to glamorous destinations (but often privately scornful of the quality of intellectual discourse at the CCF's meetings).[13] Thanks to rising rents and the decline of old bohemian neighborhoods, the existence of the freelance writer was becoming increasingly precarious. Literary prizes and fellowships donated by such CIA pass-throughs as the Farfield Foundation made life for the writers a little bit easier. Also welcome were book contracts with one of the publishing houses in which the Agency had an interest, such as Frederick A. Praeger (another area of specialization for Howard Hunt).[14]

In addition—and, when the *New York Times* published details of the Agency's covert cultural operations in 1967, most controversial of all—there was secret support for literary magazines. Some of these, like the London-based, Anglo-American monthly *Encounter*, were creations of the CCF and, as such, received regular subventions (in *Encounter*'s case, from MI6 as well as the CIA: the latter funded the magazine's American editorship, the former its British). Other publications, whose existence predated that of the CCF, only received occasional help, often to stave off the threat of imminent financial collapse, a chronic threat in the permanently cash-strapped world of independent publishing.

One such publication was *Partisan Review*, the principal literary vehicle of the New York intellectuals and one of the most influential little magazines of the twentieth century. Born in the 1930s, and only recently deceased (in 2003), *Partisan Review* went to the grave with its editors insisting that it had never been subsidized by the CIA. William Phillips, who had helped found the publication in 1934 and was still editing it when he died in 2002, was especially sensitive on this point, threatening several writers who had suggested the possibility with legal action.[15] Yet there is now indisputable evidence that Agency money did find its way to *Partisan*

Review on a number of different occasions. In 1953, shortly after the magazine had been forced to retrench when its chief "angel," real estate speculator Allan D. Dowling, went through an expensive divorce, Phillips obtained a grant of $2,500 from the American Committee for Cultural Freedom, on whose Executive Committee he served throughout the 1950s. As already noted, further Agency funds percolated to *Partisan Review* later in the decade, when the ACCF suspended its active organizational life and bequeathed half of its remaining monies to the magazine. A Farfield "grant for expenses" and aid from the Congress for Cultural Freedom ($3,000 a year over a three-year period in the form of free foreign subscriptions) followed in the early 1960s. Meanwhile, well-placed admirers inside or close to government, such as C. D. Jackson and Sidney Hook, helped *Partisan Review* with other financial matters—the preservation of its tax-exempt status, for example, and bids for Rockefeller Foundation support.[16]

Despite his later protestations, *Partisan Review* founder William Phillips was fully witting of the covert official interest in his magazine. Indeed, documents among the Henry Luce papers at the Library of Congress (the publisher of *Time* bailed out *Partisan Review* during its funding crisis in the early 1950s with a gift of $10,000) indicate that "Luce's assistant" Allen Grover arranged direct personal contacts between Phillips and Walter Bedell Smith when the latter was Director of Central Intelligence. "Mr. William Phillips called," reads an undated office memorandum to Grover. "On that letter to General Smith, he asks if he should say he was writing at your suggestion—or would you suggest your name not be mentioned, or what?"[17] After the 1960s revelations, several New York intellectuals were surprised by the high-toned, moralistic stance Phillips took on the question of covert subsidies, particularly his condemnation of CCF magazines such as *Encounter*. "I can't forget how ardently Phillips wooed the CIA when he thought he could get money for *The Partisan Review*," Bertram Wolfe told *Encounter* editor Melvin Lasky.[18]

It is not hard to understand why the CIA should have been interested in *Partisan Review*. Having originated as a literary organ of the New York Communist Party, the magazine had rebelled against Stalinist domination in 1936 and, after its relaunch on an independent footing the following year, emerged as a major center for the American non-communist left. It also enjoyed immense cultural prestige, in Europe as well as the United

States, thanks to its association with such literary eminences as T. S. Eliot, Edmund Wilson, and George Orwell. Here, then, was a publication that commanded the respect of precisely the sort of foreign intellectual the Agency most wanted to influence and whose mere existence demonstrated that, contrary to Soviet propaganda, America did possess a high intellectual tradition. And if these qualities were not already evident to those charged with dispensing official patronage, boosters of the magazine were more than ready to point them out. "From direct experience, I know that those who have seen *Partisan Review* find it immensely interesting and stimulating," wrote Hook to John Thompson, Executive Director of the Farfield Foundation in 1959 (and himself a writer well known in New York intellectual circles). "I am convinced that its distribution abroad in certain selected institutions will prove to be very fruitful."[19]

Collaboration between the CIA and *Partisan Review*, however, had its limits. During a visit to the U.S. embassy in Paris in the winter of 1949, Phillips was asked by an intelligence officer if he would "pass money to friendly Europeans" he might encounter in his work as a writer and editor. Like the unionist Victor Reuther a few years later, Phillips refused, citing his "feeling of discomfort and of being compromised by anything having to do with secret agencies."[20] Still, this squeamishness did not prevent him from pursuing a plan for raising the international profile of his beloved *Partisan Review*: publishing a European edition of the magazine, secretly backed by the CIA. In January 1950, back in Paris, Phillips contacted an expatriate American author and UNESCO official, H. J. "Kappy" Kaplan, asking if Kaplan would be interested in managing the venture, "the object of which is to create proper conditions for a fruitful dialogue between European and American intellectuals."[21] Despite Phillips's dangling a pledge of $40,000 from the "AF of L" before Kaplan, the latter, doubtful that he would be allowed any editorial freedom by the magazine's New York office, turned down the invitation.[22] Back in the United States, Phillips continued to discuss the proposal with James Burnham, who was impressed by the potential of a Paris-based, anticommunist review to serve not only as a "rally-point for French intellectuals" but also as "a point of liaison and contact, and also of cover, with many potential uses." Nonetheless, Burnham was not convinced that Phillips had "a practically feasible plan" worthy of OPC "financial support," and the notion of a "French *Partisan Review*" was quietly dropped.[23] However, the idea of a highbrow

American literary review edited from Paris was not abandoned altogether. It is tempting to speculate that the *Paris Review*, taken over by Peter Matthiessen and George Plimpton in 1953, was descended in part from Phillips's proposal, especially given that we now know, thanks to research by Richard Cummings, that Matthiessen used the magazine as cover for his work as a CIA officer and that Plimpton served the Agency as an "agent of influence."[24]

In any case, what is clear is that the CIA's tastes in literature were predominantly highbrow and modernist. Much the same could be said, it seems, of the visual arts. The abstract expressionist movement (whose guiding aesthetic principles received their fullest expression in the writings of New York art critic and *Partisan Review* editor Clement Greenberg) has featured most prominently in accounts of the cultural Cold War.[25] Many of the artists in the movement had radical backgrounds (Jackson Pollock, for example, had worked in the studio of Marxist Mexican muralist David Alfaro Siqueiros) yet had renounced communism in favor of a belief in art for its own sake.[26] Their painting, with its gestural expression of the individual artist's consciousness and total rejection of representation, constituted a massive rebuke both to the banal illusionism of the official style of Soviet art (socialist realism) and the almost photographic mimesis of such middlebrow American painters as Norman Rockwell. Here was an artistic movement that, in all its formal difficulty and obscurity—attributes that help explain why professional explicators like New York intellectuals Greenberg and Harold Rosenberg featured so prominently in its ranks—would surely appeal to even the most refined of European sensibilities. Yet, for all the high modernist aesthetics, it could also be claimed that there was something peculiarly *American* about abstract expressionism, with its giant canvases, its virile daubings of paint, its foregrounding of the *act* of artistic creation. Pollock—western-born, taciturn, hard-drinking—was the artist as cowboy, shooting paint from the hip, an incontrovertibly American culture hero.

Of course, the CIA was not the first patron to spot these qualities. A number of private American citizens had already begun collecting and exhibiting the works of the abstract expressionists, emulating those European aristocrats whose patronage had earlier enabled the modernist avant-garde to evade the twin threats of totalitarianism and kitsch. Foremost of these American patrons was Nelson Rockefeller, the fabulously wealthy president of the Museum of Modern Art and admirer of what he liked to call "free enterprise painting."[27] Another influential booster of the so-called new American painting was John Hay Whitney, benefactor of New York's second great exhibitor of modern art after MoMA, the Whitney Museum. As well as holding positions of immense power within the New York art world, these men were profoundly connected to the U.S. intelligence community. Indeed, Rockefeller had pioneered many of the CIA's characteristic methods of psychological warfare while serving as Coordinator of Inter-American Affairs during World War II. He would later reprise this role when he took over from C. D. Jackson as President Eisenhower's Special Assistant for Foreign Affairs in 1954. Whitney likewise worked in Inter-American Affairs before joining the OSS. His secret service in the Cold War took the form of a berth on Harry Truman's "psywar" planning unit, the Psychological Strategy Board. He also allowed the CIA to use the Whitney Trust as one of its funding conduits. These and numerous other links between the worlds of intelligence and art—perhaps the most telling of which was Tom Braden's working as MoMA's executive secretary in the late 1940s—meant that the CIA did not always have to foot the bill in the Cold War promotion of American art. They also provided the Agency with a host of privately owned and internationally famous institutions behind which it could conceal its interest in artistic patronage.

The typical CIA operation in this theater of the cultural Cold War, then, was a joint public-private venture, usually involving Rockefeller's Museum of Modern Art and the Agency's Congress for Cultural Freedom. In 1952, MoMA provided the art exhibit for the CCF's spectacular "Masterpieces of the Twentieth Century" festival in Paris, the event that established the CCF as a major presence in European cultural life and the Farfield Foundation as a credible pass-through for the Agency. Although the new American painting was not on show at Paris—the exhibit took a mainly retrospective and Eurocentric view of modern art—the Cold War subtext was plain enough, with curator James Johnson Sweeney, an advisor to MoMA (and associate of *Partisan Review*), proudly proclaiming that the works he had chosen for display "could not have been created . . . by such totalitarian regimes as Nazi Germany or present-day Soviet Russia."[28] A second collaboration in 1954 resulted in the show "Young Painters," consisting almost entirely of new abstract works, with large cash prizes donated by the CIA's principal front man in the cultural Cold War, Julius Fleischmann. It was presumably efforts such as these that August Heckscher of MoMA had in mind when he declared that the museum's work was "related to the central struggle of the age—the struggle of freedom against tyranny."[29] Then, in 1960, came the opening of the "Antagonismes" show at the Louvre, with the U.S. participants chosen by MoMA and the costs met by the Farfield and another CIA conduit, the Hoblitzelle Foundation. Among the American artists represented were abstract expressionists Pollock, Mark Rothko, and Franz Kline.

By no means were all of MoMA's exhibits sponsored by the CIA—the Rockefeller Brothers Fund remained the museum's chief source of financial support throughout this period—nor were their organizers' tastes confined to abstract expressionism. Indeed, there was sufficient representational art featured in MoMA shows for one critic to complain that the museum was dedicated less to the "art of our time" than the "art of our grandfathers' time."[30] In his encyclopedic 2003 history of the cultural Cold War, *The Dancer Defects*, David Caute accuses Frances Stonor Saunders of confusing the actual importance of abstract expressionism in the 1950s American art scene with the claims for its supremacy made by such critic-boosters as Clement Greenberg.[31] A number of art historians have similarly claimed that the revisionist historical school exaggerated MoMA's support for the new American painting in the early Cold War period, dating the beginning of the museum's interest in promoting the abstract expressionists as a distinct avant-garde movement to as late as 1956.[32] Saunders has responded to such charges by arguing (not unpersuasively) that while the museum might have pandered to more conventional artistic tastes in many of its public exhibitions, its collection policies during the 1940s and 1950s were heavily slanted toward the acquisition of recent American abstraction. The evidence connecting abstract expressionism with MoMA—and, through MoMA, the CIA—remains, she insists, compelling.[33]

The post-revisionist argument that the CIA's aesthetic preference for modernism has been overstated seems most convincing when applied to the realm of music. Classical symphonies, Broadway musicals, even the jazz of Dizzy Gillespie, all were used by a large array of U.S. government bodies (the postwar military government in Germany, the State Department, President Eisenhower's Emergency Fund) in an attempt to persuade music lovers around the world that America was no less hospitable to the aural arts than the literary and visual.[34] Yet surprisingly, the CIA appeared reluctant to extend its patronage to America's musical avant-garde, experimental, "serialist" composers such as Milton Babbitt and John Cage, both of whom shared many of the same aesthetic ideas and indeed often collaborated with the abstract expressionists.

Instead, the music program of the CCF, as it developed under the guiding hand of the organization's flamboyant General Secretary, Nicolas Nabokov, seemed more concerned with presenting earlier European works that had either been banned or condemned as "formalist" by the Soviet authorities. The glittering 1952 "Masterpieces" festival in Paris opened with a performance of Igor Stravinsky's *The Rite of Spring*, with the composer himself sitting in the audience, flanked by the French president and his wife. Over the next thirty days, nine separate orchestras performed works by over seventy composers who had been dismissed by communist commissars as "degenerate" and "sterile," among them Dmitri Shostakovich and Claude Debussy.[35] Here indeed were "the abundant riches which the mind of free man has created in the first half of our century" promised in the festival program, except that the emphasis clearly was on the early 1900s, the Parisian "good old days," as one unimpressed spectator sniffed.[36]

If American avant-garde composers were overlooked by the CCF, American virtuoso musicians were very much in favor. The Paris performance of *The Rite of Spring* marked the first appearance in Europe by the Boston Symphony Orchestra (BSO). The huge expenses of transporting an orchestra across the Atlantic had been met by a grant from the CIA's International Organizations Division of $130,000, arranged by Tom Braden and BSO trustee C. D. Jackson (and recorded in CCF accounts as a donation from "prominent individuals and associations.")[37] "You know how much capital our enemies constantly make about the lack of culture in this country," Jackson explained to a colleague. "The Boston Symphony's music, played in Europe, with the attendant European publicity, would be a most startling and useful refutation of these charges." Was the outlay worth it? Some observers reckoned not. "I thought [the festival] was trivial," recalled one of the CCF's founders, Melvin Lasky. "It's unimportant whether foreigners think Americans can play music or not." Braden and Jackson, however, were delighted with the overwhelmingly positive responses of European audiences. "The Boston Symphony Orchestra won more acclaim for the U.S. in Paris," thought Braden, "than John Foster Dulles or Dwight D. Eisenhower could have brought with a hundred speeches."[38] Thus was launched a collaboration that would continue throughout the cultural Cold War. "The juggernaut of American culture," writes Saunders, "the Boston Symphony became the CIA's answer to the agitprop trains of old."[39]

This is not to say that the CCF completely ignored American composers or the "New Music." Samuel Barber, Aaron Copland, and Virgil Thomson were all on the program of the 1952 festival. (Thomson's adaptation of Gertrude Stein's *Four Saints in Three Acts* was sung by an "all-Negro" cast, pointing toward a subplot of the CIA's music program: the desire to feature African American performers wherever possible so as to dispel negative foreign perceptions of U.S. race relations.) Similarly, when two years later Nabokov arranged a follow-up event in Rome—a competition of twelve young composers with prize money adding up to $6,000 "donated" by Junkie Fleischmann, with the winners promised first American performances of their work by the Boston Symphony ("Now is that a prize or isn't it?," asked Nabokov)—he included in the lineup several representatives of the atonal, "twelve-tone" school.[40]

It would, however, be wrong to suppose that the 1954 Rome competition marked the conversion of the CCF to "serialist orthodoxy."[41] The twelve-tone school failed to dominate the event, and the likes of Babbitt and Cage continued to be ignored by the Congress. "As far as the New Music is concerned," writes Nicolas Nabokov's biographer, Ian Wellens, "there is no evidence to suggest that a 'hidden hand' was at work."[42] The reason for this state of affairs—a curious one, given the growing international stature of American experimentalists, Cage in particular, in this period—might simply be that Nabokov did not personally care for the new serial compositions, his tastes remaining rooted in the tonal tradition of Russian music. If so, the situation can hardly have been helped by the spectacularly abusive response he received when he invited Pierre Boulez, one of the New Music's best-known exponents, to take part in the Rome competition. "What do you expect to resolve by these murky undertakings, by the concentration of numerous jumping-jacks in one single location, stuck there in a pit of liquid manure?" Boulez demanded to know. "They will undoubtedly learn to appreciate the quality of each other's sweat but they are unlikely to produce anything more fruitful."[43]

Nabokov's aesthetic prejudices notwithstanding, there is documentary evidence that the CIA's own tastes in the realm of the performing arts were far from high modernist. Witness a letter written in 1955 by Frank Wisner in response to a request from Nelson Rockefeller for Wisner's reaction to a suggestion by Lincoln Kirstein that the New York City Ballet visit and perform in Moscow. This was not, Wisner felt, a good idea, because "it would place us at a comparative disadvantage in an area in which the Russians are most prominent." Former DCI Walter Bedell Smith was of the same view, so Wisner reported, in a passage remarkable not only for its martial metaphors but also for the image it conjures of the notoriously irascible general pondering the finer points of Cold War cultural diplomacy:

> In fact, Bedell was opposed to governmental encouragement for American ballet to appear in Western Europe on the ground that it might well be met and challenged by a Soviet troupe, and this would amount to our having elected to join battle with the opposition on grounds of his choosing and greatest strength.[44]

This attitude, combined perhaps with the fact that Nabokov was a composer rather than a choreographer, helps explain why dance did not feature prominently in the CCF's international program. Instead, American ballet tended to be promoted abroad by the overtly government-funded President's Emergency Fund (which echoed the CCF's approach to music by neglecting avant-garde dancers such as Merce Cunningham in favor of more traditional fare).[45]

Wisner then goes on in his letter to Rockefeller to make several suggestions for future cultural exchange with the Soviet Union. Regarding music, "our initial presentations to Soviet audiences should aim for mass appeal" and be "expressive of our folklore or unmistakably typical of the U.S." Musical shows such as *Oklahoma*, *Carousel*, or *Kiss Me Kate* would suit this purpose; even the Ice Capades might serve "as a good example of American showmanship in pageantry, skill, and precision." Another possibility, and a "pet theory of my own," Wisner professed, was to send "one of our top-flight 'name' jazz orchestras." It might be advisable to prepare the cultural ground in the Soviet Union by first exposing "their audiences to American symphonic organizations," such as, for example, the BSO. "A subsequent introduction of first-rate American jazz against this backdrop would serve to demonstrate the breadth and vitality of American musicianship in rather telling terms." Finally, having reasserted the desirability of using such productions to showcase the talents of "negro performers" in order to demonstrate simultaneously their "capacity" and "the opportunities they have in U.S. artistic life," Wisner closed by pronouncing on the place of the visual arts in possible Soviet-American exchanges. "In the realm of painting and sculpture, almost anything of quality that the U.S. could exhibit is likely to surpass conventionalized Soviet efforts," he confidently told Rockefeller. "However, in initial displays, extreme modern or experimental forms should be avoided."[46]

Wisner's letter is concerned specifically with U.S. cultural diplomacy in the Soviet Union, so it should not necessarily be read as a definitive statement of CIA aesthetics in the cultural Cold War generally. There is still much good evidence to support the revisionist argument that there was a basic sympathy between many intelligence officers and modernist artists, based on such shared values as formalism, internationalism (or "cosmopolitanism"), and elitism.[47] That said, Wisner's letter, combined with other proof that "extreme modern or experimental forms" were not always privileged over the middlebrow or popular, cautions us that pragmatism was an equally, if not more, decisive factor in shaping the CIA's cultural patronage. What mattered ultimately was a cultural activity's effectiveness in helping the U.S. cause in the Cold War. If an artist's work was considered unlikely to impress foreign opinion positively, it would be ignored. One project, for example, an international sculpture competition to design a monument to political prisoners staged by the London Institute of Contemporary Arts and funded by the CIA via John Hay Whitney, was abandoned halfway through in the face of unfavorable British press attention.[48]

There were also two prosaic, but nonetheless important, considerations. First, because the CIA patronized only those cultural practices that needed financial subsidy, its patronage is bound in retrospect to appear highbrow. The Agency clearly was also interested in such mass media as the Hollywood movie industry (as is discussed below), but its influence over them was restricted by their economic self-sufficiency. Second, it is possible that some intelligence officers, out of a desire to enhance their personal image and divert attention from some of their less benign covert activities in the Cold War, have since portrayed the CIA as a more enlightened cultural patron than it in fact was. In Agency legend, the cultural Cold War has come to perform something of a redemptive function.

If revisionism's account of the CIA's aesthetic preferences needs some modification, so too does its portrayal of the Agency's cultural influence. The implied claim in the British title of Saunders's book, *Who Paid the Piper?*—that America's Cold War spy establishment called the tune of western intellectual life—is problematic in several respects. To begin with, the CIA could not always predict or control the actions of the musicians, writers, and artists it secretly patronized. The history of the Congress for Cultural Freedom's involvement with America's avant-garde is littered with incidents of literary feuding, prima donna-ish tantrums, and various other forms of temperamental behavior, several of which are related by Saunders herself. A South American tour by Robert Lowell had to be curtailed when the poet threw away the pills prescribed for his manic depression, stripped naked, and mounted an equestrian statue in one of the main squares of Buenos Aires, declaring himself to be "Caesar of Argentina" and his CCF minder one of his generals. Ad Reinhardt denounced his fellow abstract expressionists for "selling out," calling Rothko a "*Vogue* magazine cold-water-flat-fauve," Pollock a "*Harpers Bazaar* bum," and Barnet Newman an "avant-garde huckster-handicraftsman."[49] Dwight Macdonald ended his brief spell as an editor of the London-based *Encounter* in 1956–57 by sending the magazine a blistering attack on U.S. culture entitled "America! America!" and then, when the CCF suppressed the piece, denouncing the organization in *Dissent*. True, this properly notorious incident shows that the editorial freedom supposedly enjoyed by the CCF's magazines was in fact mythical. Yet at the same time Macdonald's protests, and the negative publicity for the CCF that resulted, demonstrated that the Agency was by no means in control of Cold War intellectual discourse.[50]

The row over "America! America!" is reminiscent of the difficulties that the CIA experienced with the CCF's U.S. section, the American Committee for Cultural Freedom. On one wing of the organization were upper-class bohemian dissenters like Macdonald, individuals who were highly sensitive about their intellectual independence and just as likely to sound off about American "mass culture" as the threat of communism. On the other were New York Jewish intellectuals reared in the American communist movement but now so bitterly anticommunist that they even flirted with support for Joseph McCarthy, individuals like Macdonald's predecessor as the American editor of *Encounter* and founding father of the neoconservative movement, Irving Kristol. This situation was typical of the sort of difficulties that the Agency tended to experience with its earliest front organizations, which often contained personalities whose Cold War zeal exceeded that of the professional spies. That said, it is also possible to discern a larger political significance in the clash between the ACCF and the CIA, with the former embodying a kind of embryonic neoconservative consciousness that was at odds with the predominantly liberal politics of the Agency officers housed in the International Organizations Division. In any case, the history of the ACCF gives the lie to simplistic depictions of Cold War American intellectuals as so many ventriloquist's dummies and the CIA as their "animating performer."[51]

Nor was the CIA necessarily able to dictate how foreign intellectuals would respond to its cultural blandishments. While the Boston Symphony Orchestra might have won plaudits for its performance at Paris, the most common response of French intellectuals to the CCF's 1952 "Masterpieces" festival—"cette fête américaine"—was one of haughty disdain. "Dear sirs, you have made a big mistake," Serge Lifar, head of the ballet troupe at the Paris Opera, told the event's organizers. (He may have been piqued that his dancers had not been invited to perform.) "From the point of view of spirit, civilization, and culture, France does not have to ask for anybody's opinion; she is the one that gives advice to others."[52]

Inadvertently enflaming the cultural anti-Americanism of European elites was not the only trap awaiting the CIA. Forced to operate at one remove from the recipients of its patronage, the Agency often had to watch as foreign intellectuals spent CCF money on pet projects that had little or nothing to do with the Cold War. This tendency was especially pronounced in Britain where, as the philosopher Isaiah Berlin observed, there was no shortage of "English intellectuals with outstretched hands making eyes at affluent American widows."[53] Sometimes this kind of local appropriation could be quite subtle: *Encounter*'s British editor Stephen Spender, for example, tried constantly to reduce American influence over the magazine and turn it into a vehicle for Bloomsbury literati such as himself. At other times, it was more crude, with officers of the CCF's British national affiliate taking friends out to lunch at expensive Soho restaurants and joking that American taxpayers were paying the bill.[54]

But what about "blowback," the influence of CIA patronage on domestic American culture? In 1978 Allen Ginsberg wrote a sketch in which he imagined encountering T. S. Eliot on the fantail of a boat in Europe. "And yourself," the Beat poet asks the high priest of literary modernism. "What did you think of the domination of poetics by the CIA? After all, wasn't Angleton your friend? Didn't he tell you to revitalize the intellectual structure of the West against the so-to-speak Stalinists?" Eliot admits that he did know of Angleton's "literary conspiracies," but insists that they are "of no importance to Literature." Ginsberg disagrees.

> I thought they were of some importance since [they] secretly nourished the careers of too many square intellectuals, provided sustenance to thinkers in the Academy who influenced the intellectual tone of the West. . . . And the Government through foundations was supporting a whole field of "Scholars of War." . . . The subsidization of magazines like *Encounter* which held Eliotic style as a touchstone of sophistication and competence . . . failed to create an alternative free vital decentralized individualistic culture. Instead, we had the worst sort of Capitalist Imperialism.[55]

The picture Ginsberg paints is overdrawn. In fact, when *Encounter* began appearing in 1950s London, Eliot had thought it so "obviously published under American auspices" that he kept his distance from it.[56] Similarly, in New York, several intellectuals refused to join the American Committee for Cultural Freedom—Columbia University art historian Meyer Schapiro, for example, turned down his invitation on the grounds that the ACCF was not "a 'Committee for Cultural Freedom,' but an organization for fighting the world Communist movement."[57] Others quit when the ACCF took what they deemed to be too equivocal a position on McCarthyism. Even those who stayed behind failed to toe the CIA's line, pursuing a hard-line anticommunist political agenda that had more to do with their peculiar ideological evolution from anti-Stalinist Marxists into neoconservatives than the needs of the national security state. Their example reminds us that political conviction mattered more than secret financial inducements in shaping the ideas of the cultural Cold War, that intellectuals as well as government officials were capable of determining political outcomes (as shown in the eventual triumph of neoconservatism over liberal anticommunism), and that Angletonian conspiracies did not always work.

In addition, modernism and CIA patronage did not necessarily go hand in hand. Indeed, where the performing arts were concerned, the Agency appears to have been aesthetically blinkered, giving a wide berth to the most experimental (and, we can now see, the most promising) work of the period. The evidence linking abstract expressionism and the American secret service is also more ambiguous than many revisionist accounts would have us believe. To give Ginsberg his due, it is in the realm of literature that the link between modernism and the CIA appears clearest, not only in the tastes of officers like Angleton (whose famous description of the spying business as a "wilderness of mirrors" was culled from Eliot's *Gerontion*)[58] but also in the covert subsidies to little magazines such as *Partisan Review*. In the end, then, the most important blowback from the CIA's cultural operations abroad may have been to shore up the authority of the old, *Partisan Review*–led literary avant-garde at a time when it was being challenged by new movements that wanted to experiment with more traditional, "American" forms (such as Ginsberg's Beats). This is not to claim that the Agency can be credited with (or blamed for) the continuing dominance of modernism in American literary culture during the 1950s and 1960s. Still, it is worth wondering how writing might have developed in Cold War America without the "umbilical cord of gold" that united spy and artist.[59]

Of course, whether the literary highbrows of the International Organizations Division liked it or not, the truth was that the great majority of foreigners derived their main impressions of the United States not from *Partisan Review*, MoMA, or the BSO, but from American popular culture and, most of all, the slick, spectacular, mass entertainments of Hollywood. This presented the spies with a problem. Noncommercial cultural enterprises such as little magazines needed patronage and were therefore susceptible to (some) external control. The massively profitable U.S. movie industry offered no such point of entry, even though its products had great potential for influencing—negatively as well as positively—the international image of America. Fortunately for the CIA, two factors predisposed the major Hollywood studios that dominated the industry to take a "responsible" position in the cultural Cold War. One was a strong tendency toward self-censorship, the result of many years' experience avoiding the commercially disastrous effects of giving offense to either domestic pressure groups like the American Legion or foreign audiences. The other was the fact that the men who ran the studios were intensely patriotic and anticommunist—they saw it as their duty to help their government defeat the Soviet threat.

This spontaneous willingness of the moviemakers to cooperate with U.S. officialdom manifested itself in many ways. Some ways were overt (boosting the Army or Navy in war movies, for example, or helping the United States Information Agency make pro-American documentaries), others covert. The most dramatic instance of the latter was Militant Liberty, a multi-agency propaganda campaign devised in 1954 with the aim of embedding American-style democratic values in foreign cultures, especially in such new theaters of the Cold War as Central America, the Middle East, and Southeast Asia. (Secret planning documents identified "target" countries for "testing" the program, including Japan.)[60] Although the architects of Militant Liberty did not limit themselves to cinema—other "informational" techniques discussed included letter-writing and leader exchanges—they did attach particular importance to film production, reflecting the common assumption of Cold War western propagandists that the moving image was the most appropriate medium for "Third World" audiences. Among the several Hollywood personalities who volunteered their services for this program were eminent director and former OSS filmmaker John Ford; the cinematic embodiment of the American masculine ideal, actor John Wayne; and world-famous studio boss/director Cecil B. DeMille (who had already agreed to serve as film consultant to the recently created USIA).[61] Along with a few other key studio players, such as Twentieth Century–Fox boss Darryl Zanuck, this group composed what Frances Stonor Saunders has called the "Hollywood consortium," an informal but powerful group of movie artists and moguls who shared the belief that (in the words of foreign market specialist Eric Johnston), "We need to make certain our films are doing a good job for our nation and our industry."[62]

Not only did the CIA seek to influence the production of commercial films—"to insert in their scripts and in their action the right ideas with the proper subtlety," as C. D. Jackson put it;[63] the Agency also occasionally initiated film projects. The best documented instance of the latter practice is the animated version of George Orwell's celebrated 1945 novella *Animal Farm*, a satirical allegory about Stalinism that depicts an uprising against humans by a group of farmyard animals and the subsequent transformation of the animal revolution into a totalitarian state ruled by pigs and dogs. The Information Research Department, the secret anticommunist "publicity" unit in the British Foreign Office, had already exploited the Cold War propaganda potential of Orwell's fable, sponsoring the publication of several foreign-language translations and even producing a cartoon-strip version for dissemination in South America, Asia, and the Middle East (one official noted the happy coincidence that "both pigs and dogs are unclean animals to Muslims").[64] In 1950, the OPC went a step further, with Joe Bryan's Psychological Warfare Workshop recruiting anticommunist documentary-maker Louis de Rochemont to produce a movie version of the tale.[65] Having secured the appropriate rights from Orwell's widow, Sonia Blair, de Rochement turned to the British animation studio of husband and wife John Halas and Joy Batchelor to make the film.[66] Halas and Batchelor's undisputed brilliance as animators was no doubt one factor in this choice, but it is likely that de Rochemont and his backers in the OPC were also motivated by tactical and financial considerations: having the film produced in Britain would both save money (costs there would be lower than at a U.S. studio like, say, Disney) and disguise the American hand in the project.[67]

Scheduled to take only eighteen months to film, *Animal Farm* was not in fact completed until November 1954, at a total cost of over $500,000, of which a CIA shell corporation, Touchstone, Inc., provided about $300,000.[68] The highly labor-intensive nature of frame-by-frame animation was one reason for the film's extended production and cost: in all, 300,000 man-hours (and over two tons of paint) were required to produce 250,000 drawings and 1,000 colored backgrounds.[69] Another cause of the delay, according to the memoirs of Psychological Warfare Workshop officer Howard Hunt, was "the leaden weight of a bureaucracy which began spreading within OPC," with "accountants, budgeteers, and administrators" all demanding a say in the operation (a further manifestation, presumably, of the professionalizing drive that took place under "Beetle"

Smith).[70] Most problematic of all was a series of indirect interventions in the production by intelligence officers, who were concerned that socialist elements in Orwell's allegory, such as its satirical depiction of neighboring farms meant to represent the western powers, might blunt its value as anticommunist propaganda and invite hostile attention from McCarthyite vigilantes in the United States.[71] The most blatant interference occurred in February 1952, shortly after the Psychological Strategy Board had complained about a draft script that "the impact of the story [was] . . . somewhat nebulous." Lothar Wolff, de Rochemont's associate producer, sent John Halas a long list of proposed changes, including the addition of scenes showing the other farms in a more flattering light ("maybe a cat which laps up some cream and another animal being fed carrots by a farmer") and a new ending to Orwell's story, in which the pigs and dogs eventually face a liberation-style uprising of the other animals.[72] Although Wolff told Halas that the revisions had been suggested by the script department of a potential distributor, in fact they had originated during a meeting held two weeks earlier between de Rochemont's production company and Joe Bryan's staff.[73] "It is reasonable to expect that if Orwell were to write the book today, it would be considerably different," explained an anonymously authored review of the script, "and that the changes would tend to make it even more positively anti-Communist and possibly somewhat more favorable to the Western powers."[74] Such alterations continued right up to the end of the production process, often over the objections of the animation team (Batchelor in particular fought fiercely, although unsuccessfully, to preserve the original ending), with the script going through a total of nine different versions.[75] As well as showing how interfering the CIA could be as a cultural patron, this episode demonstrates that, despite the constant use of his fiction by British and American propaganda agencies, George Orwell's politics were not simply reducible to Cold War anticommunism.[76]

Considering the challenges faced by the makers of *Animal Farm*, the film itself proved to be a fine cinematic achievement, enjoying tremendous critical, and some commercial, success: proof, perhaps, of art's ability to transcend the historical conditions of its production.[77] The CIA, however, does not appear to have been moved to repeat the experiment of commissioning a feature film, at least not right away. On May 16, 1956, during a meeting of Agency deputy directors, Allen Dulles described a proposal for a covertly funded film production based on Khrushchev's revelations about the Stalin purges as an "excellent idea," announcing "that he would authorize funds for such a project but would withhold decision on whether to make a movie out of it as was done in the case of the *Animal Farm* program."[78] Whatever became of the plan, the implication of Dulles's comments is that, at least as of May 1956, the Orwell adaptation was unique.

A more usual approach was for government officials to intervene unobtrusively in commercial film productions, ensuring the insertion of material that displayed the United States in a favorable light, and deletion of what did not. A cache of anonymously written letters dating from early 1953 discovered among the C. D. Jackson records at the Eisenhower Presidential Library reveals a CIA agent based in Hollywood's Paramount Studios who is engaged in an astounding variety of clandestine activities on the Agency's behalf. In one letter, he reports having excised a gag involving "the manhandling of Moslem women," which might have had "potentially disastrous results in the Moslem world," from a Jerry Lewis and Dean Martin comedy, *Money from Home*. In another, he describes his success "in removing American drunks" (again, probably in deference to Moslem sensibilities) from five Paramount pictures, including *Houdini*, *Legend of the Incas*, *Elephant Walk*, *Leininger and the Ants*, and *Money from Home*. Some ideas, such as *Gringo*, a Bob Hope vehicle likely to prove "very offensive South of the Border," were "killed" before they even got off the ground. One lengthy letter records an attempt to persuade Billy Wilder ("a very, very liberal minded individual" whom "you have to handle . . . easy") that a movie he planned to direct about the illegitimate Japanese baby of a GI would prove "a wonderful piece of propaganda . . . for the Commies." Sometimes it was too late to prevent the making of films that might provide grist for the communist mill. The Gary Cooper western *High Noon*, for example, was doubly unfortunate in its unsympathetic portrayal of American townsfolk and its featuring a Mexican prostitute character. "I could write the French, Italian, [and] Belgian commie reviews for this picture right now," the agent reflected gloomily, before going on to recount his efforts to sabotage the film's chances in the 1953 Academy of Motion Picture Arts and Sciences awards. Not all of this agent's actions were destructive: another strong theme in the letters is the author's desire to counter adverse publicity about U.S. race relations by having films depict

African Americans mixing on equal terms with whites. One proposal to play up "the negro angle" involved planting black spectators in a crowd watching a golf game in the Martin and Lewis comedy *The Caddy* and showing others "using a nice up-to-date car."[79]

The secret Hollywood reports do indeed "make extraordinary reading," as Frances Stonor Saunders asserts.[80] However, it is possible to overestimate their significance. For one thing, they show that independent filmmakers, such as Billy Wilder, were able to elude the CIA agent's influence. "Since this is a picture which would be made outside the aegis of one of the major companies," he wrote of the Japanese baby idea, "it is difficult to keep track of it, and impossible to bring 'front office' pressure to bear on points in which we are interested."[81] For that matter, not all attempts to massage the content of Paramount movies succeeded: director Norman Taurog and studio head Y. Frank Freeman refused to plant black actors on the golf links in *The Caddy* for fear they might upset southern white moviegoers—an example of the limits of CIA manipulation in the face of commercial and domestic political pressure—while drunkenness crept back into a number of productions (in *Money from Home*, for example, in the shape of a red-nosed English jockey).[82]

Just who was this Hollywood CIA agent? It seems that Frances Stonor Saunders was mistaken in identifying the author of the reports as Carleton Alsop, an OPC officer with interests in Hollywood who worked on the production of *Animal Farm*. By piecing together clues in the letters, such as the author's membership in various Academy Awards committees, film historian David Eldridge has established that the CIA's man in Hollywood was in fact Luigi G. Luraschi, a longtime Paramount executive and, in 1953, head of foreign and domestic censorship at the studio, whose job it was (as he put it himself) "to iron out any political, moral or religious problems and get rid of the taboos that might keep the picture out of, say, France or India."[83] (Other studios, including MGM and RKO, had similar officers.)

As Eldridge shows, replacing Alsop with Luraschi, a veteran foe of the Hollywood communist movement as well as an expert on foreign film markets, causes the activities reported in the anonymous letters to appear in a different light, as less like external meddling and more an extension of existing studio self-regulation. In the early 1950s the studios evinced greatly increased sensitivity to foreign audience reactions because of domestic problems facing the industry, including threats to the major studios' oligopoly and the growth of television ownership. One response to these developments was the creation by the Motion Picture Association of America of an International Committee consisting of studio foreign specialists, which for much of the early 1950s was chaired by none other than Luraschi (a fact that helps explain why the letters' author has such good knowledge of the internal affairs of other studios besides Paramount). In other words, CIA operations in Hollywood, such as they were, originated in a shared set of assumptions and goals. Indeed, the irony was that the Agency enjoyed better relations with the movie industry than it did with several organizations it directly funded and controlled, such as the Congress for Cultural Freedom and the American Committee for Cultural Freedom.

SIX

The CIA on Campus

STUDENTS

On April 20, 1951, a Harvard student by the name of Henry A. Kissinger wrote a letter to the Georgetown address of H. Gates Lloyd, a Princeton graduate, Philadelphia investment banker, and intelligence officer in Joe Bryan's Psychological Warfare Workshop. "At our recent conversation you asked me to furnish you with a number of phase lines for our project," Kissinger began. He then proceeded to lay out a list of financial requirements, the most pressing of which was "the figure for the selection process," adding up to $20,300.[1] A follow-up letter of May 7 enclosed a copy of a report "from one of our contacts in Denmark," a leader of the "Danish youth movement," which, Kissinger hoped, Lloyd might find "interesting as a symptom of the need for United States efforts in the psychological realm."[2]

Kissinger had been put in touch with the Office of Policy Coordination by Harvard professor William Y. Elliott. An all-American tackle at Vanderbilt, poet of the southern Fugitive school, and Roosevelt brain-truster, Elliott had done his best academic work, on European political relations, in the 1920s, thereafter living off his reputation as the "grand seigneur" of Harvard's Government Department and trusted counselor of six U.S. presidents.[3] The 1950s found him slightly decrepit—"a glorious ruin" was how one Harvard colleague, Arthur Schlesinger, Jr., described him[4]—but still esteemed in Washington, where he commuted every week to consult with, among other parties, the Office of Defense Mobilization, the State Department, and the OPC. In addition to regularly advising Frank

Wisner, Elliott helped the CIA by sitting on the board of the émigré organization AMCOMLIB, overseeing student front groups, and steering promising Harvard graduates toward secret government service.

It was in his famous class "The Development of Constitutional Government" that Elliott first noticed the Jewish refugee with the thick Bavarian accent and profound grasp of political philosophy. Kissinger was brilliant and ambitious—he graduated summa cum laude, in the top 1 percent of his class, having written a 383-page senior thesis on no less a subject than the meaning of history—and had begun work at Harvard on a doctoral dissertation about nineteenth-century diplomacy. At this early stage of his career, however, the bookish U.S. Army veteran lacked the easy self-confidence and self-deprecating wit he would later employ to such renowned effect at international conference tables. Elliott helped Kissinger overcome these deficiencies by easing his path to acceptance by an academic community that was proving slow to embrace him (fellow graduate students jealously nicknamed him "Henry Ass-Kissinger").[5] It was Elliott who provided the future National Security Advisor and Secretary of State with his principal power base at Harvard—and launchpad for his rise to global celebrity—in the shape of the university's International Summer School.

The aim of this program, as described by Kissinger in an "Informal Memorandum for Professor Elliott," was to create "a spiritual link between a segment of the foreign youth and the U.S." Postwar assistance programs designed to aid European recovery had undoubtedly demonstrated the material superiority of the American way of life over the Soviet, but they had so far failed "to swing the spiritual balance in favor of the U.S." Indeed, Americans' generosity had if anything only served to confirm Europeans' suspicion that the United States was "bloated, materialistic, and culturally barbarian," a misperception that communist propagandists, already experienced in methods of appealing to "the souls of the young generation," were quick to exploit. The need therefore was to demonstrate to young foreigners that America possessed cultural traditions and values worthy of their affiliation and, in doing so, "create nuclei of understanding of the true values of a democracy and of spiritual resistance to Communism."[6]

Kissinger's plan took shape in the fall of 1950, as he met with Elliott and other Harvard professors. Starting the following summer, he and his fellow graduate students would invite a group of fifty young Europeans to take part in a ten-week course under the aegis of the university's Summer School (which was run by Elliott). The program would consist of regular Summer School courses on American history and literature; special seminars on various aspects of U.S. culture, to be addressed by a mixture of Harvard faculty and distinguished guest speakers; and a series of informal discussions, where the students would have the opportunity to present their own national viewpoints. Applications were welcomed from anywhere in Europe, with the exception of Britain, the Scandinavian countries, and Switzerland, because all these places possessed "a firm democratic tradition." Candidates must be in their twenties and already embarked on promising careers. A meticulous selection process, including the sifting of applications by a screening committee in Cambridge and interviews held in Europe by a university representative (a role to be performed by Kissinger himself), would ensure a careful balance between the "plasticity" of participants and "the possibility of a more immediate impact on the home countries." According to an invitation issued to possible applicants, all expenses connected with attending the program were to be paid by the Summer School.[7]

Where, though, to find this money? Although Elliott undertook to inquire how Harvard's Cambridge neighbor, MIT, raised the funding for its summer foreign student program, there is no evidence in the professor's papers to suggest that he approached genuinely private sources in the buildup to the 1951 pilot seminar. Instead, there is the correspondence between Kissinger and H. Gates Lloyd and an earlier letter from Elliott that suggests the OPC was informed of the Harvard project from its inception. "I very much hope that some progress may be made on the lines that we were discussing before I next come down to Washington," the professor wrote Lloyd in November 1950 (at precisely the time Kissinger began making arrangements for the following summer with his Harvard colleagues). "I think it is probably not very useful for me to come down until I have some word from you that matters have been arranged so that some actual organizational plans can be undertaken." Like several other OPC operations launched around this time, prior to the creation of the dummy foundations, seed money for the International Summer School came in the form of "one-year grants from individuals" (as Elliott told another correspondent). Later, money started to flow from conduits like the Farfield

Foundation—a Farfield grant arrived in late January 1953, a few weeks after Elliott had entertained Julius Fleischmann at Harvard's New York club—and front organizations such as the American Friends of the Middle East.[8]

The first seminars proved, by general agreement, a tremendous success. Through a mixture of flattery and cajolery, Kissinger attracted an impressive roster of guest lecturers, among them Eleanor Roosevelt, John Crowe Ransom, and Walter Reuther. He also laid on an exhausting program of social activities, including trips to baseball games, beach parties, and showings of Marx Brothers movies. Each seminar was accompanied by a cocktail party, and twice a week Kissinger and his wife, Ann Fleischer, hosted informal dinners for the students. Perhaps reflecting his own immigrant origins, the budding statesman took great care to avoid "the appearance of condescension and purposeful indoctrination," always emphasizing that the seminar was "a two-way process" (although the possibility of the foreign students giving public lectures to local audiences was ruled out for fear of the mutual offense they might cause).[9] Judging by the enthusiastic letters of thanks written to the school's organizers by participants after their return home, the Kissinger charm offensive worked. Even students "who were uncommitted and often a bit critical," so Elliott reported, were transformed into "friendly champions abroad who could refute, by personal experience, the misrepresentations of the United States."[10] Corporate America was similarly impressed. Although initial attempts to attract funding from such philanthropies as the Sloan and Carnegie Foundations were rebuffed, Elliott succeeded in obtaining a grant from the Ford Foundation in 1954. The Harvard International Summer School had joined the Fulbright exchange program and the Salzburg Seminar (whose origins can also be traced to Harvard) as a vital tool of Cold War U.S. cultural diplomacy.

The venture also proved highly profitable for Henry A. Kissinger. As well as bringing out the less pompous, ponderous side of his personality, it placed him in charge of a pot of patronage he could use to build and defend his position at Harvard. ("Academic politics are vicious precisely because the stakes are so small," he was reputedly fond of saying.) Elliott's wooing of the foundations also provided his graduate student, who was just embarking on his doctoral dissertation, with a further career opening. In 1954 *Confluence*, a Harvard-based journal of foreign affairs, was launched under Kissinger's editorship, with backing from the Rockefeller Foundation and contributions from various luminaries who had passed through the Summer School as lecturers or students (the project was devised, according to Elliott, "as a continuation of the Seminar"). Perhaps most important for Kissinger, his traveling abroad to interview applicants and inviting illustrious Americans to lecture at the seminar allowed him to collect "a repertoire of people," as one Harvard professor recalled, "who could turn out to be his host later." Among the future foreign leaders who passed through the Harvard program were Valéry Giscard D'Estaing of France, Yasuhiro Nakasone of Japan, and Bülent Ecevit of Turkey; Americans invited to speak included Richard M. Nixon. "I was very much embarrassed to hear myself described as the guiding genius of the Seminar," Kissinger coyly wrote his mentor Elliott at the conclusion of the pilot event in 1951. "I, for one, have no illusions on this score."[11] Most who took part in the Harvard International Summer School, however, remembered Kissinger rather than Elliott.

Inevitably the question arises: was the future Nobel Peace Prize winner "witting" about the CIA's bankrolling of the International Summer School? In 1967, when the *New York Times* reported that Harvard had acknowledged receiving some $456,000 in disguised subsidies from the CIA between 1960 and 1966, of which $135,000 went to the foreign seminar, Kissinger explicitly denied having known the true source of the money. This is a claim repeated by his biographers, one of whom describes him flying into a rage on learning that the American Friends of the Middle East was a front.[12] However, it is difficult to reconcile this display of unwittingness with the letters to H. Gates Lloyd, in which Kissinger carefully itemized the expenses of the Summer School. Indeed, other documents among William Elliott's papers suggest that the then graduate student might even have acted as a contract consultant for the OPC: Elliott's letter to Lloyd of November 15, 1950, urging progress with the Summer School proposal, enclosed "papers for Mr. Kissinger," which the professor had apparently "discussed" with Cleveland Cram, another senior intelligence officer.[13] Whether Kissinger's status with the CIA was ever "regularized" remains unclear. In July 1951, Elliott felt compelled to point out to Frank Wisner that his student's name had been "about a year in the mill," despite the necessary security clearance having been granted.[14] In any case, it does seem improbable that someone of Kissinger's political acumen could have dealt as extensively as he did with the CIA without having some inkling of just whom he was doing business with.

More important than the question of Henry Kissinger's wittingness is the broader pattern of CIA activity on Cold War American university campuses to which the Summer School episode points. Harvard was not unique in this respect. Yale, its campus adorned by a statue of alumnus and Revolutionary-era spy Nathan Hale (a replica of which stands in front of the CIA's Langley headquarters), was the single most fertile recruiting ground for the Agency in its first years, yielding among others Cord Meyer and two of the brightest stars of the "Golden Age" of covert operations, Richard Bissell and Tracy Barnes. The domination of American counterintelligence by Yalies James Angleton and Norman Holmes Pearson (who, after serving in the OSS, helped set up his alma mater's American Studies program) has already been noted. CIA research and analysis was presided over for much of the Agency's early existence by Sherman Kent, a Yale history professor and author of a widely read text, *Writing History*, of which it was said one could substitute the words "intelligence officer" for "historian" and the book would still make perfect sense.[15] Princeton, too, was an important "P-Source" (CIA code for academic intelligence), hosting the "Princeton Consultants," a panel of senior academic advisors that convened four times a year under the chairmanship of Allen Dulles (Class of 1914) in the university's Nassau Club.[16] Countless other less well-known institutions contributed to the secret Cold War effort: the *Ramparts* revelations began in 1966 with a report that the CIA had paid Michigan State University $25 million to hire five Agency employees to train South Vietnamese students in covert police methods.[17]

The CIA's backing of Kissinger's enterprise also points to the mobilization of yet another important citizen group in the superpower struggle for hearts and minds: young people and students. Long before the start of the Cold War, communist propagandists had recognized the importance of winning the loyalty of student leaders—the world leaders of tomorrow—and the peculiar susceptibility of young people to appeals cast in the idealistic language of peace and progress. There was even a separate Young Communist International (KIM) created by Willi Münzenberg for this purpose. As with so many other groups whose identity transcended territorial boundaries, labor being the most obvious example, the end of World War II saw youth organizations from all over the world coming together to create global bodies meant to overcome the destructive rivalries of traditional international relations. The World Federation of Democratic Youth (WFDY), like the World Federation of Trade Unions, was launched at a conference in London in 1945, and the International Union of Students (IUS) was formed the following year in Prague. Neither organization, though, was truly independent of old-fashioned power politics: both rapidly succumbed to domination by communist bureaucrats, who harnessed sincere youthful hopes for world peace to the cause of defending the Soviet Union against perceived American aggression. As in other theaters of the Cold War ideological confrontation, the U.S. government was relatively slow to respond to Soviet provocation, largely leaving it to the British and, in particular, the staff of the Foreign Office's little-heralded Cultural Relations Department, to formulate western strategy on the youth front. It was not until August 1948 that a counterorganization to the World Federation of Democratic Youth was created, at the founding Westminster congress of the World Assembly of Youth (WAY). An alternative to the International Union of Students would not come into existence until the following decade.[18]

This is not to say that the late 1940s found American youth altogether lacking in stomach for the Cold War. At Harvard, an International Affairs Committee (HIACOM), staffed predominantly by young veterans with wartime intelligence experience, hatched a variety of schemes to foil the communist bid for ideological hegemony (the Salzburg Seminar, for example, was in part a HIACOM invention). In December 1946, HIACOM officers helped organize a meeting in Chicago to discuss the possibility of creating a national body to represent American students at international events. This initiative, which grew out of discussions among the twenty-five U.S. delegates who had attended the founding congress of the International Union of Students in Prague earlier in the year, led in the summer of 1947 to the first meeting of the United States National Student Association at Madison, Wisconsin. In 1949 and again in 1950, Harvard students conducted surveys of international student opinion with the thinly disguised aim of identifying potential anticommunist allies abroad, especially ones who might be counted on to join the National

Student Association in a secession movement from the IUS. Funds for the second survey, which was administered by the NSA's national offices in Madison, were provided by the OPC via two ostensibly private patrons, an industrialist by the name of Thomas D. Brittingham of Wilmington, Delaware, and Chicago lawyer Laird Bell, each of whom provided checks for $6,000.[19] In November 1950, another "private donor" came up with the money for an International Student Information Service to coordinate preparations for a meeting of dissident western student leaders due to take place the following month in Stockholm (a not unprovocative choice of venue, given the city's prominent role in the Soviet peace offensive).[20]

It would be a mistake, however, to see the National Student Association of 1950 as utterly beholden to the OPC or, for that matter, as bent on bolting the International Union of Students. The dreams of international unity nursed so fondly in 1945 died very hard, even in the freezing atmosphere of the Cold War. No national union wanted the dubious distinction of being the one to split the ranks of the world student movement. Moreover, from the moment of its birth in 1947, the NSA was just as interested in domestic as foreign affairs, in particular liberal reform issues like race relations (the organization's second president, James T. "Ted" Harris, Jr., was black), and such commitments did not necessarily go hand in hand with Cold War anticommunism. Indeed, if anything, civil rights activism was still more closely associated with communist front groups than New Deal–style liberalism. Also, only a handful of the NSA's officers were witting about the true source of the 1950 international survey's funds, and the officers in general were reluctant to become too closely involved with the U.S. government. Erskine B. Childers, for example, the vice-president in charge of the NSA's international affairs in 1949–50, resisted attempts by the State Department to use American student delegations to international meetings for intelligence-gathering purposes.[21] He also asked some awkward questions about the two angels of the survey. "I never saw a written report of the solicitation, or a covering letter from them transmitting the funds, or anything else," he told a fellow officer in December 1950, the same month the NSA was preparing for the meeting at Stockholm. "I'm still a little peeved about this, as you can see."[22]

Enter NSA's newly elected national president, Allard K. Lowenstein. A contradictory, driven personality, made up of equal parts intense charisma and profound insecurity, Lowenstein would later acquire a reputation as the pied piper of 1960s American youth, whipping up protest against the apartheid regime in South Africa, organizing white support for voter registration drives in Mississippi, and eventually leading the opposition to President Lyndon B. Johnson's conduct of the war in Vietnam. In 1950, however, while already known for his outspoken attacks on racial segregation—as a student at the University of North Carolina in the late 1940s he had campaigned against Jim Crow in Chapel Hill's fraternity houses—Lowenstein was an ardent supporter of the U.S. crusade against communism in all its forms, writing Secretary of State Dean Acheson that the "Communist-dominated" IUS's monopoly of international student politics "must not continue" (before signing off with sophomoric grandiloquence, "With all the confidence of the Student in his Master and the Citizen in his Statesman, I await your reply").[23] The slowness of NSA officers like Childers and his successor as International Affairs Vice-President, Herbert Eisenberg, to sign up to the movement for a new student international greatly vexed Lowenstein, who traveled to Stockholm intent on forcing western student leaders to choose sides in the Cold War. "When the Communists say they want peace we know too well what peace they want, and why," the twenty-one-year-old firebrand told the conference in a widely reported speech. "It is about time that in our deliberations we took stock and faced facts."[24] His address was a bravura oratorical performance, the most impressive some in the audience could remember ever having witnessed at any international meeting, but it failed to carry the day. Indeed, as Eisenberg reported to the NSA's Executive Committee shortly after returning home, the other delegates adopted a resolution officially "regretting" Lowenstein's speech, an expression tantamount to formal censure. Lowenstein's insensitivity to the mood of the meeting was summed up by the fact that he read his speech from notes clearly written on U.S. Senate notepaper.[25]

The suspicion that Lowenstein was acting at the behest of the U.S. government in seeking to split the International Union of Students has clung to his reputation ever since. Critics of his legacy, noting his later association with such front operations as the Committee on Free Elections in the Dominican Republic, have speculated that he was already a CIA agent in 1950 and that his presidency of the NSA was crucial in bringing about closer relations between that organization and the Agency.[26] More sympathetic observers have pointed to evidence suggesting that, at least at this early date, Lowenstein was free from such ties. First, there was his own later denial of a relationship. "I am not now and have never been an agent of the CIA," he insisted in 1967. "I've never even visited Vienna, Stockholm, Peoria, Ill., or any place else on funds provided by the CIA."[27] There had, Lowenstein admitted, been a "suspicious offer" of money from an "unknown source" for him to attend the Stockholm meeting.[28] He turned down that funding, however, and paid his own passage to Sweden. Two CIA officers privy to details of the Agency's dealings with the NSA have explicitly backed up these claims. "There was no formal contact, there had never been any effort to recruit him," stated one. "He was too loud, too intent on holding forth," explained the other. The suggestion that Lowenstein was deliberately left out of the loop because he was "a loose cannon" (to quote the second officer again) is echoed in dispatches from the American Embassy in Sweden at the time of the Stockholm meeting. "If he impressed the other delegates by his extraordinary eloquence and the quality of his ideas, he was all the same perceived as immature and, in some way, as an abrasive element in the conference," reported Cultural Affairs Officer Robert Donhauser. "The officials at the embassy also thought him immature."[29] There are parallels here with Frank Wisner's displeasure at the exuberance of another young American anticommunist, Melvin Lasky, at the Congress for Cultural Freedom in June 1950.

A recently declassified OPC memorandum of February 1951 confirms the claim of Lowenstein's defenders that he was "unwitting" at the time of his presidency of the NSA, although the same document also shows that the OPC secretly supported his position within the student organization. A summary of a conversation between Kissinger's mentor William Elliott and the new head of covert operations, Allen Dulles, the memo begins by acknowledging that the student association, which derived its income principally from the dues of member unions, "is not receptive to accepting government subsidy, because it considers that such a course of action would run contrary to its basic principle of independent thought and action." This attitude "means that such a relation as is maintained is an extremely delicate one, particularly with reference to . . . plans involving the passing of funds." Complicating the picture further was the internal division in the NSA between "more idealistic, less militant" officers such as

Eisenberg, and those like Lowenstein, who favored "a forthright stand on the part of the organization concerning Communism." The latter viewpoint appeared to be the dominant one on the NSA's Executive Committee. Accordingly, OPC had arranged, "covertly and through the proper channels," for Lowenstein's military service to be deferred, "although he is completely unaware of this fact." (The possibility that the CIA orchestrated Lowenstein's draft deferment, which coincided with the outbreak of war in Korea, has been raised by at least one of his detractors, but the memorandum, while proving that such was indeed the case, also exonerates him of complicity in the arrangement.) The document concludes with the recommendation that the OPC refrain from subsidizing the NSA on a regular basis, as had apparently been suggested by Elliott, but rather continue to sponsor "individual projects by careful use of such means as will not offend or arouse . . . suspicion . . . that the government is at all interested."[30]

The question of what and when exactly Al Lowenstein knew about the CIA's interest in the NSA, however, is something of a side issue. More important is the broader significance of his presidency, which definitively established the NSA's characteristic combination of hard-line anticommunism in foreign affairs and dynamic liberalism on domestic issues. Lowenstein's success in equating engagement in the Cold War abroad with social activism at home helps explain why he played such a prominent role in the first stirrings of the U.S. youth movement during the late 1950s and early 1960s. It is also the reason why his later disillusionment with U.S. policy in Vietnam was interpreted by many as signifying the breakdown of the "liberal consensus" that had to that point masked some of the contradictions of the American postwar order, such as the emergence of educated white youth as a distinct political force for change. Given his function as a bridge figure between Cold War ideologies and generations, it is no wonder that Lowenstein has proved so controversial among historians and biographers, with radicals descended from the New Left seeing in his alleged links with the CIA further proof, if any were needed, of the fundamental rottenness of liberal anticommunism.[31]

Lowenstein's wittingness or lack thereof also seems of secondary importance next to the indications contained in the February 1951 memorandum that he was in any case leading the NSA in directions favored by the CIA. Despite the negative effects of his intemperate speech, the Stockholm meeting achieved two of the aims with which Lowenstein had set out to Sweden: a commitment by the national unions represented there to carry on meeting and cooperating, and approval of a proposal by the National Student Association that it launch a Student Mutual Assistance Program (SMAP) to assist young people from the "developing countries" (Lowenstein was much exercised by communist successes in appealing to Third World student leaders). Although NSA resistance to the notion of a new western union of students persisted—the Association's 1951 national congress supported Eisenberg against Lowenstein on this question—the momentum was now behind the splitters. A second meeting of the International Student Conference (ISC), held in a chilly Edinburgh in January 1952, not only endorsed NSA's ownership of such practical programs as the Student Mutual Assistance Program, it also agreed on the creation of a permanent Coordinating Secretariat (COSEC), to be based in the Dutch town of Leiden. The IUS at last had a serious contender for leadership of the world's students. Lowenstein's vision—and the secret wishes of the CIA—had been realized.

At the same time that these events were unfolding, the Agency was busy extending its control of American student affairs. The Cultural Affairs Officer in Sweden, Robert Donhauser, after observing the American delegation to the Stockholm meeting, had concluded "that the present leaders of the NSA are [not] of sufficient caliber to carry through their part of the program" and recommended that more "outstanding graduate students be found to run NSA's international program." This was precisely what happened. In August 1951, Avrea Ingram, a twenty-four-year old identified only as a Harvard graduate student (he had joined the Harvard International Affairs Committee just a few months earlier), appeared from nowhere to win the election for International Affairs Vice-President. It was, the outgoing president, Al Lowenstein, told a friend later, the "most curious" election he had ever seen.[32] (The fact that Ingram ran on a platform of continued cooperation with the IUS, defeating a hard-line anticommunist candidate backed by Lowenstein, suggests something of the CIA's subtlety in its handling of potentially useful private organizations.) The same congress also witnessed the election of William Dentzer, a graduate of Muskingum College in Ohio, as National President. Dentzer shared his predecessor's hostility toward the IUS but was less confrontational in the way he handled the issue.

With the NSA's leadership now in safer hands, the OPC reconsidered the question of the organization's long-term funding. Covert grants for specific field projects in Latin America and Southeast Asia had increased during the summer of 1951. The NSA's overall financial position, however, was perilously weak. In 1950–51, it had debts amounting to $25,000; its offices in Madison were in a condemned schoolhouse; and its staff was so poorly paid that Al Lowenstein later recalled one vice-president working nights at a pizza parlor to make ends meet.[33] Meanwhile, the communists had scored another propaganda victory with the successful staging in August of a World Youth and Student Festival in Berlin.[34] Late in September, the subject of the NSA came up in a conversation between a group of University of North Carolina students and the university's president, Gordon Gray, who had just become head of the new government psy-war coordinating unit, the Psychological Strategy Board.[35] Alerted to Gray's interest in the National Student Association, Ingram and Dentzer went to Washington the following month and pleaded with John Sherman, the PSB's Assistant Director of Policy Coordination, for funding. "After they left," Sherman told a board staff meeting, "it was possible to get in touch with a department of the Government and as a result I have just been advised that a private 'angel' has appeared on the doorstep of the National Student Association and has provided the necessary funds."[36]

The "angel" was John Simons, a founding officer of the NSA who had joined the CIA and now reappeared at the Association's offices claiming to be the intermediary for a private donor. In early November 1951, Ingram provided Simons with a prospectus for the Student Mutual Assistance Program and the forthcoming Edinburgh conference, both of which projects, so he reported to Dentzer, "had fascinated our angel." The following month, after meeting Simons in Cambridge, Ingram was further able to inform the NSA president "that there is a better than good chance that his sources will provide us money for the trip to Edinburgh," but that the prospects of "an open ended agreement" with "Santa Claus" to fund "the Secretariat which is to be set up (if we have our way)" were less favorable. Both officers consequently continued to petition such government agencies as the State Department and the Psychological Strategy Board for additional funding, but they met with little success. Indeed, in the case of the latter, the response "was downright curt," Ingram told Dentzer. "I was at a loss to understand the obvious change of attitude on the part of the Board." Both the NSA president and the vice-president obviously knew that Simons's money was official in origin, but it is not clear whether they, at this stage, were aware of its precise source. Dentzer has repeatedly insisted that he did not become witting until later, and his claims appear to be borne out by a letter of March 27, 1952, in which, having described to Ingram a visit by a "man from Central Intelligence" requesting copies of NSA reports, he felt obliged to explain that "CI [*sic*] is the overall coordinating intelligence agency." Dentzer, incidentally, provided the reports to the CIA without a moment's pause.[37]

The success of the Edinburgh meeting in establishing a coordinating secretariat for the International Student Conference removed any lingering doubts in the CIA's mind about subsidizing the NSA's international program. Grants for particular field projects multiplied, with the Asia Foundation's precursor, the Committee for Free Asia, joining Simons as a conduit of secret subventions. In February 1952, just after returning from an extended tour of Europe, Dentzer received a telephone call from Simons inviting him and Ingram to Washington "to touch moneybags" for the new coordinating secretariat, COSEC. "Ah, the bottomless pitcher," Dentzer mused, whimsically.[38] By the summer, Simons had been placed in charge of a more formal funding mechanism, the Foundation for Youth and Student Affairs (FYSA), which began channeling covert subsidies to the NSA's international office on a regular basis. Meanwhile Dentzer, having completed his presidential term and now fully witting of the true source of Simons's moneybags, was assigned to Leiden as an assistant secretary to COSEC, ostensibly supported by a floating fellowship from Princeton.[39] Ingram, who served an unprecedented two terms as NSA International Vice-President, succeeded Dentzer in this role the following year. Having ensured the NSA's financial future, the Foundation for Youth and Student Affairs now became the International Student Conference/COSEC's principal source of funding as well. An internal CIA memorandum summed up the arrangement with frank simplicity. "The ISC is controlled through one of our agents in a key position, through two leaders of the NSA, and through a foundation financed by the CIA which enables us to control its finances."[40]

The later 1950s were the heyday of the National Student Association. At its peak in 1960, over 400 U.S. institutions of higher education, among them Ivy League schools, big state universities, and liberal arts colleges, were affiliated with the organization, giving it a breadth of representation that later bodies, including the famous Students for a Democratic Society, never quite matched.[41] The international program included annual foreign relations seminars for American students, scholarships for students from the "developing world" to visit the United States, overseas leadership training projects, and extensive travel by International Commission staff members and their representatives abroad. The costs of these activities were covered by generous subsidies from the Foundation for Youth and Student Affairs, with other CIA front organizations and pass-through foundations occasionally granting smaller donations. In 1957–58, for example, according to the NSA's financial report for the year (which quite likely did not record all the money that reached the organization), the FYSA provided $55,000 for general operating expenses and supplemental grants of $76,842; other donors in the same year included the Asia Foundation, American Friends of the Middle East, and the Catherwood Foundation.[42] The International Student Conference thrived, too, so that by the middle of the decade, fifty-five national unions, more than half from the developing world, had signed up to COSEC, many attracted no doubt by the travel grants that, thanks to subsidies from the FYSA, the ISC was now able to offer.[43] Nor was CIA funding of the young confined to students. Covert subsidies found their way via various conduits to a bewildering assortment of groups, among them the United States Youth Council (the American member of the World Assembly of Youth), Pax Romana and the International Catholic Youth Federation, and even the Young Women's Christian Association.[44]

The defense of these operations given after 1967 by the CIA officers who dispensed the patronage and the youth leaders who wittingly accepted it consists of two main claims. The first is that U.S. government funding for a liberal organization such as the NSA had to be kept secret because of McCarthyism. "Back in the early 1950s, when the cold war was really hot," wrote Tom Braden in 1967, "the idea that Congress would have approved many of our projects was about as likely as the John Birch Society's approving Medicare."[45] There is a great deal of truth in this argument. As noted earlier, McCarthyism threatened other front operations involving ex-leftists and even damaged the careers of liberals within the CIA. The NSA too was the victim of red-baiting during the early 1950s, by a right-wing group called Students for America, who saw in the Association's stand against racial segregation evidence of communist subversion.[46] Nonetheless, the desire of enlightened liberals to circumvent conservative yahoos was only one, and probably not the most compelling, of the factors requiring secrecy. Equally if not more important was the perceived need to preserve for these organizations the appearance of private citizens acting voluntarily in the defense of world freedom—as enjoined by George Kennan in 1948—and to avoid stimulating the sort of foreign suspicion that an overtly U.S. government-sponsored initiative was likely to provoke. As a confidential White House report compiled immediately after the 1967 revelations ruefully observed, "We cannot expect to duplicate with overt funding the flexibility, responsiveness, and directly targeted results obtained by [the] CIA."[47]

The other main plank in the defense case—that the relationship between the CIA and the NSA was an entirely consensual one based on shared values and common objectives[48]—likewise has some substance to it, but just as many holes. To begin with, the consensus, if indeed such consensus existed, was to a great extent artificially manufactured by the CIA, beginning with the selection of the NSA's officers. Each year promising graduates would be invited to attend the student foreign relations seminars, held in the summer at Bryn Mawr. There they would be given a history of the NSA, published by the University of Pennsylvania's Foreign Policy Research Institute (another Agency beneficiary), and scrutinized by undercover CIA operatives, usually themselves former NSA staffers.[49] One ex–National President turned intelligence officer, Robert Kiley, later remembered, "The international student relations seminar, particularly during the 1950s–early '60s, was a fantastic mechanism, not just for attracting people but for really giving them a deep immersion and exposure to an awful lot of people."[50] If the individuals groomed in this fashion lacked a current educational affiliation—a necessary qualification for NSA office—credentials might be secured through some obliging institution, such as the Harvard University Graduate Student Council or Roosevelt University in Chicago.[51]

The next stage—democratic elections at the NSA's annual congress—was potentially the most difficult to manage. However, the support, both public and behind the scenes, of witting incumbent officers, combined with the political inexperience of the student delegates, most of whom were attending for the first time, usually ensured the victory of the favored candidates. In 1961, for example, the young civil rights activist Tom Hayden tried to win the support of the Congress for his candidacy as National Affairs Vice-President, but withdrew when he realized that the NSA "old guard" regarded him as "too militant" (earlier his application for a place at the international summer school had been rejected "on the strange grounds that I already was sufficiently knowledgeable about foreign policy"). On the final night of the meeting, Hayden obtained from the president's office a yellow notepad containing a chart of the political forces at work at the Congress: on one side was a box featuring the names Hayden and Haber (Al Haber was a University of Michigan undergraduate who the previous year had launched Students for a Democratic Society); on the other was the conservative youth organization Young Americans for Freedom (also only just founded, in 1960); and, in the middle, with lines leading to it from the boxes, was a circle containing the words "Control Group." "It was a diagram for preventing the election of a 'militant' like myself," Hayden surmised, "drawn by someone skilled in manipulating student movements abroad, now bringing his or her talents home." Having despaired of transforming the NSA into a vehicle for his growing political radicalism, Hayden turned instead, much to the delight of his friend Haber, to the fledgling SDS.[52]

The supposed consensus also contained elements of deception and coercion. When the CIA judged it necessary to have an unwitting officer made aware of the true source of the organization's funds, a meeting would be arranged between the individual concerned, a witting colleague, and a former NSA officer who had gone on to join the Agency. At a prearranged signal, the witting staffer would leave the room. The CIA operative (still identified only as ex-NSA) would explain that the unwitting officer had to swear a secrecy oath before being apprised of some vital secrets, and, after getting the officer to sign a formal pledge, the operative would then reveal the Agency's hand in the Association's affairs. "The signing of a secrecy agreement with one's own government seemed a reasonable price to pay for timely assistance in a common cause," reckoned one senior CIA official. Indeed, many NSA officers initiated in this manner do not appear to have nursed any sense of grievance about their treatment; several subsequently participated in the same ceremony as intelligence officers.[53] Others, however, especially later in the organization's history, did object, claiming that the secrecy agreements, which imposed a twenty-year prison sentence on violators, were tantamount to entrapment. "People were duped into this relationship with the CIA," alleged a head of the NSA's National Supervisory Policy Board, "a relationship from which there was no out."[54]

Part of the burden of being witting was keeping secrets from unwitting fellow officers. Office memoranda were produced in different versions—"Confidential," "Top Secret," and "Top Secret, Top Secret"—according to the security clearance of their recipient.[55] Financial statements had to be vetted so as not to draw attention to the NSA's overwhelming dependence on grants from the Foundation for Youth and Student Affairs.[56] Most demanding of all was "the everyday dishonesty, the need to clam up when in the presence of 'non-witty' [*sic*] staff members, to fudge, to make excuses and deflect embarrassing questions," as one regretful NSA officer put it at the time of the revelations.[57] The CIA offered witting NSA staff some limited training in spy tradecraft. International Affairs Vice-President Len Bebchick, for example, was taught "how to destroy documents: burn them in an ashtray, stir up the ashes, and flush them down the toilet."[58] There was also the psychological thrill of dealing clandestinely with professional spies—the "fellas," or "boys," as CIA case officers were called among witting NSA staff—as well as tangible rewards such as travel expenses and draft deferments.[59] Still, the constant subterfuge was trying, especially for young people used to more openness in their personal relations. "You learn to lie very well, even to your close friends," confessed one former NSA president, sounding old before his time. "This constant deception is very hard on some people."[60]

Although the separation was not hard and fast, the division between witting and unwitting tended to mirror the split between the NSA's domestic and international programs. The former was relatively democratic and spontaneous and, as the 1950s gave way to the 1960s, increasingly liberal, with congresses in the early 1960s voting to express their condemnation of the McCarthyite House Un-American Activities Committee and support for the antisegregationist Student Nonviolent Coordinating Committee. The NSA's international officers, in contrast, while sometimes taking positions on such questions as nuclear testing that were to the left of majority opinion (presumably in order to create the impression in foreign eyes of healthy dissent from U.S. government policy),[61] gradually took on the appearance of an aging hereditary elite, with the same ex-officers popping up at congresses year after year, unintentionally confirming the ironic adage that hung in NSA headquarters, "The student leader of today is the student leader of tomorrow."[62] The sense of there being a divide between the two programs of the NSA was exacerbated by the fact that until 1960 they were located in different places, the national offices in Philadelphia (where they had moved, to rent-free accommodation, in 1952), the International Commission in Cambridge (not coincidentally, near the headquarters of the Harvard International Affairs Committee). Perhaps even more than the age difference between the organization's national and international officers, this awkward fact of geography symbolized the provisional nature of the alliance between domestic reformism and Cold War anticommunism that underpinned the NSA—and much else of the CIA's Mighty Wurlitzer besides.

That said, it is partly the advantage of hindsight that makes this alliance now appear so fragile. At the end of the 1950s, on the eve of the election of John F. Kennedy, the prospect of combining patriotic service in the war against communism with the uplifting of the poor and oppressed, both at home and abroad, still seemed positively enchanting to many young Americans. Hence the undeniable dynamism of a major CIA-financed student enterprise launched in 1959 with the aim of rescuing Third World youth from the clutches of communist propagandists: the Independent Service for Information on the Vienna Youth Festival (ISI).

It was the fall of 1958 and, like many educated young women of her generation, Gloria Steinem was having difficulty finding a rewarding job. Dazzlingly bright and talented, just returned from a year-and-a-half-long scholarship trip to India, where she had befriended Indira Gandhi and the widow of revolutionary humanist M. N. Roy, the twenty-four-year-old Smith graduate was reduced to sleeping on the floors of friends' apartments as she hunted for work in New York. Then came a call from Clive S. Gray, a young man she had met in Delhi, where he was ostensibly working on a doctoral dissertation about the Indian higher education system. Some former officers of the NSA had just created an organization to encourage attendance by young, non-communist Americans at a youth festival being held the following summer by the communists in Vienna. Was she interested in running it?

The suggestion immediately appealed to Steinem, not just because it meant paid work but because it also offered an outlet for the political idealism awakened in her by her Indian experiences, and soon after the call from Gray she met in New York with another former NSA president turned CIA officer, Harry Lunn (who, like most other young men of her acquaintance, promptly fell in love with her). Next she traveled to Cambridge, there to be interviewed by two former NSA Vice-Presidents for International Affairs, Len Bebchick and Paul E. Sigmund, Jr., and Boston lawyer George Abrams. By January 1959, she had taken up the post of Director of the Independent Service for Information, with offices in Harvard Yard and a salary of $100 a week, plus $5 per diem "because Cambridge rents were so expensive" (a generous allowance fixed by the infatuated Lunn).[63]

The ISI was a CIA operation from beginning to end. Spectacularly staged festivals celebrating the themes of international peace and friendship were a crucial element in the communist campaign to capture young hearts and minds: witness the success of the 1951 Berlin rally, which had helped concentrate CIA minds on student affairs. The fact that the Vienna World Festival of Youth and Students was being planned personally by the new head of the KGB, former student leader Alexander Sheljepin, was some measure of the importance it was accorded in the Kremlin.[64] The CIA had attempted to disrupt an earlier festival, held in Moscow in 1957, by providing funding to the NSA delegation, briefing its members before they departed, and encouraging the use of crude wrecking tactics like stink bombs and fake invitations to nonexistent official receptions. The 1959 rally in Vienna was the first to be held outside the communist bloc, and this greatly increased the scope for such activities. The NSA, however, was officially boycotting Vienna—hence the need for other measures to ensure attendance by anticommunist American students. Lunn, Sigmund, and Bebchick were all working directly for the CIA when they organized the ISI. So too was Gray, whose real purpose in India was talent-spotting potential agents in the student movement. As for Steinem herself, she became witting when she began asking questions about the ISI's funding, and the undercover CIA officers explained that the Boston grandees and foundations apparently subsidizing the venture were in fact pass-throughs for secret official funds.

With staff, accommodation, and funding in place, the ISI now set about preparing the festival counteroffensive. A booklet-exposé entitled

"The Background of the Vienna Youth Festival" was sent to a mailing list of 6,000. Other pamphlets and fact sheets on subjects such as "negro segregation" were issued to young Americans traveling to Vienna to help them prepare for encounters with possibly hostile Third World students.[65] In the weeks immediately before the start of the festival, the ISI even staged "Meet the Critic" role-playing workshops in New York, with Steinem and Bebchick, dressed as "Mohini, an Indian girl, and Kofi, a Ghanaian," peppering departing students with awkward questions about U.S. foreign policy.[66] "We wanted to show that we were for self-determination and not for colonialism or imperialism," explained one ISI volunteer worker, "that the communists did not have a monopoly on the national liberation struggle."[67] Another important function of ISI publicity, at least as far as Steinem was concerned, was to let the American public know that not all students going to Vienna were communist sympathizers.

A key contact for Steinem in her ISI publicity work was the former psywar supremo, Time, Inc., executive C. D. Jackson, who had secretly volunteered to coordinate a massive antifestival propaganda campaign on the CIA's behalf, involving Radio Free Europe, *Time* reporters, and Austrian cabinet ministers. The two first met in late January at Jackson's Rockefeller Center office, but only after Steinem had been made to wait for several hours. "He was blustery, a name-dropper always talking about how he wrote speeches for Eisenhower," she recalled. "An asshole—no, a king-sized asshole."[68] Jackson, in contrast, was charmed by his young guest and offered to provide Steinem with *Time* photos of earlier festivals for free reproduction in ISI literature. He also came to her assistance when, three weeks before the festival was due to open, she learned that CBS had abandoned plans to produce a one-hour documentary on the subject. "The Vienna Youth Festival itself is an extremely important event in the Great Game," Jackson wrote the network's president, Frank Stanton, quoting Rudyard Kipling's *Kim*. "This is the first time commies have held one of these shindigs on our side of the iron curtain." Stanton then saw Steinem in his office and assured Jackson that CBS would endeavor to broadcast a half-hour documentary instead. "Gloria Steinem asked me to help out on this, and Frank Stanton came through handsomely," Jackson self-congratulatingly reported to Cord Meyer of the CIA.[69] In fact, as Steinem later pointed out, "What [Stanton's] letter really said was that the hour documentary had been canceled and would remain so."[70]

Rather more effective were Jackson's efforts to raise support for the other main part of the ISI's program, the actual recruitment of "informed" young Americans to attend the festival. Steinem and Bebchick were extremely successful at placing non-communists on the official U.S. delegation and obtaining credentials for others to travel independently. However, there were some outside participants who were too well known as anticommunists to be seen flying to Vienna on the plane chartered by the ISI. It was to fund the extra travel expenses of four such individuals that Jackson secured a donation from, as he put it to Steinem, "several business leaders of my acquaintance." In the event, the free berths proved surprisingly difficult to fill. Of the four original candidates, only one remained constant: Zbigniew Brzezinski, a Harvard graduate student who would later serve as President Jimmy Carter's National Security Advisor, described to Jackson by Steinem as "a star member of the Independent Service."[71]

Among those to drop out was Michael Harrington, a young socialist intellectual soon to grab national attention with his book *The Other America*, an exposé of the poverty of millions of U.S. citizens. The offer of free passage to Vienna had placed Harrington in a quandary. He strongly suspected State Department involvement in the ISI—"Had I dreamed that the CIA was involved," he wrote later, "there would have been no issue"—but, as a fervent anti-Stalinist, he badly wanted to get to Vienna in order to counter the machinations of the festival's organizers. The National Committee of the Young People's Socialist League, after a long debate in the course of which "inevitably, someone pointed out that Lenin had accepted railroad transportation from the Kaiser when he went from Switzerland to Russia in 1917," decreed that Harrington should accept the airline ticket, but only on the understanding that he was an independent delegate prepared to criticize capitalism and communism equally. "That did it," recalled Harrington. "The offer of help was withdrawn forthwith and I paid my own way, having nothing to do with what turned out to be the CIA's dirty games."[72]

The festival opened in the last week of July 1959, with a parade, motorcade, and huge fireworks display. Over the next ten days, thousands of young delegates from countries all over the world were treated to a lavish program of art exhibits and competitions, athletic games, an international fashion show, and a giant ferris wheel.[73] The staging was immaculate. "They had the Bolshoi ballet, gymnasts, and Chinese dancers with flags," recalled one young American. "You felt you were surrounded by perfection, that history was on their side, there was so much power and momentum."[74] Still, the organizers were taking no chances, such were the dangers of defection by, or "contamination" of, eastern-bloc delegates, many of whom were traveling outside the Iron Curtain for the first time. Young Soviets were chaperoned at all times and transported between events in buses with blacked-out windows; restaurant waiters were instructed to serve the Chinese delegation in silence. Austrians in Jackson's CIA-funded covert network responded by arranging bus trips to the Hungarian border so that delegates could see for themselves the watchtowers and barbed-wire fences.[75] Perhaps the greatest problem for the festival organizers was the atmosphere of Vienna itself. "The Soviets took a great risk in holding an obviously staged propaganda show in a charmingly free city," wrote Samuel S. Walker, Jr., director of the Free Europe Press, to Jackson, "and grimness, as usual, has given way to charm, artificiality to naturalness, regimentation to the Austrian spirit of casual rebellion."[76]

Meanwhile, Steinem and her ISI troops, who had taken up position in Vienna the week before the festivities commenced, launched a series of sorties against the communist foe. These began within the official U.S. delegation, with calls for democratic leadership elections. This precipitated a split between communists and non-communists, reckoned by one of Jackson's operatives to be "among the more effective anti-Festival occurrences."[77] Next came a fusillade of publicity intended to counteract the Moscow-produced festival newspaper and take advantage of an Austrian press boycott. Steinem presided over an International News Bureau, which became the most important source for western news coverage of the event and prompted a formal complaint from the Soviet ambassador to the Austrian government (a cause of immense gratification to ISI staff). "Gloria is all you said she was, and then some," Sam Walker reported to Jackson. "She's operating on sixteen synchronized cylinders and has charmed the natives. . . . I think you will be pleased with this (i.e. friends) aspect of things all the way up and down the line."[78] There were also efforts to sow dissension within the ranks of the communist delegations. Having sneaked into the Soviet encampment, Zbigniew Brzezinski (the son of a Polish diplomat) walked openly among its Russian residents deliberately bumping into them and saying in Russian, with a heavy Polish accent, "Out of my way, Russian pig!" in a deliberate attempt to stir ill feeling between the Russian and Polish contingents. Every day there were hotel-room meetings to discuss strategy and plan the next day's tactics. "I remember Gloria lying in bed in a sort of frilly robe while the rest of us sat around the bed strategizing," said Brzezinski later. "I thought it was kind of an amusing and slightly eccentric scene."[79]

The communists responded by tailing ISI staff, strong-arming anyone they found trying to enter delegates' quarters without proper documentation, and organizing events intended to divert American students from attending meetings of the U.S. delegation, such as swimming parties in the Danube. The Americans were not deterred so easily, however. On the final day of the festival, Brzezinski, one of his Harvard students, and Walter Pincus, later of the *Washington Post*, concealed themselves on a rooftop overlooking Vienna's Rathausplatz; then, as the closing ceremonies got underway in the square below, they unfurled an Algerian and a Hungarian flag with their centers cut out (an expression of solidarity with both Third World and communist-bloc liberation struggles) and a banner that read "Peace and Freedom" in German. The event's managers doused the square's floodlights and sent guards into the building to apprehend the protestors, but they had already made their getaway, scrambling across a plank to the adjoining rooftop, then melting away into the Viennese night.[80]

To be sure, there was a strong element of youthful high jinks about all this. Pincus later summed up his memories of the festival as like "a college weekend with Russians."[81] However, it would be a mistake to underestimate the impact of the ISI's activities. Combined with "Operation Dynamic Boycott," as Jackson called the antifestival Austrian media campaign he had orchestrated, they undoubtedly helped persuade the communists to think twice before venturing beyond the Iron Curtain again.[82] The next youth festival was held in the Finnish capital of Helsinki in 1962 and, as before, Steinem and the ISI (or Independent Research Service, as it had been renamed in late 1959) were on hand to foil the plot. Attorney General Bobby Kennedy took a personal interest this time, requiring a detailed review of the group's preparations for the event. After the festival, he was so pleased with the results that he invited the student activists to his office, along with Cord Meyer of the CIA, to congratulate them in person.[83]

It would also be unfair to ignore the powerful sense of liberal idealism that drove many of the Americans involved, especially Steinem. "It's a realization that, pretty often, the men who run Everything are just guys with gravy on their vests and not too much between the ears," she wrote her aunt and uncle with youthful exuberance (and perhaps a hint of her later feminism), "and that you (one) can do something toward putting monkey wrenches in the totalitarian works and convincing the uncommitted that it's smarter to stay that way than to trade Western colonialism for Communist imperialism. . . . I think it struck a lot of us the same way," she continued. "I suppose that this was my small world equivalent of going off to join the Spanish Revolution."[84]

It was the sense of an idealistic, dynamic, even noble cause that Steinem tried to articulate in 1967, when CIA funding of the Independent Research Service was revealed. Among the many individuals named in that year of revelations, Steinem was one of the most forthright in acknowledging her wittingness and explaining the reasons why she had become involved in a front operation. "I'm fine," she told George Abrams, when he asked if she was prepared to deal with questions about the Independent Research Service. "I'll take the heat on this."[85] By now a prominent journalist, she appeared on Walter Cronkite's evening news program and gave interviews to several newspapers. "Far from being shocked by this involvement," she told the *New York Times*, "I was happy to find some liberals in government in those days who were farsighted and cared enough to get Americans of all political views to the festival." To the *Washington Post*, she presented this picture of the CIA: "In my experience the Agency was completely different from its image; it was liberal, nonviolent, and honorable."[86]

It is not hard to see why Steinem should have taken this view of the CIA: her brush with the Mighty Wurlitzer took place when the alliance between Cold War anticommunism and liberal idealism still appeared natural and right. By 1967, however, the Cold War consensus had broken down irretrievably, and her comments proved ill-judged. Indeed, Steinem would live to regret her candor about this issue more perhaps than any other incident in her long and controversial career. Defenders of the CIA, including several former intelligence officers writing their memoirs, invoked her remarks as evidence of the Agency's liberalism and the basically consensual nature of Cold War front operations, in the process reminding their readers of Steinem's role in the ISI.[87] Even more distressing for Steinem personally was the resurrection of the episode within the women's movement during the 1970s, when radical feminists who objected to her relatively moderate position in the sex war seized on it as evidence that she was a secret agent of the patriarchal power structure. Steinem tried repeatedly to end discussion of the episode by painstakingly explaining the reasons for her involvement in the ISI, as she had in 1967, but all to no avail: the story simply would not die.[88] Others implicated in the revelations who were less honest about their wittingness were to get off much more lightly.

Allen Dulles, Director of Central Intelligence during the CIA's "Golden Age" of covert operations, dispensing orders. (Richard J. Aldrich)

Frank Wisner, as he appeared in the 1934 University of Virginia yearbook. (Special Collections, University of Virginia Library)

A propaganda balloon release by the National Committee for a Free Europe. (Radio Free Europe/Radio Liberty Corporate Records, Hoover Institution, Stanford University)

George Meany (left) and Jay Lovestone loom over international labor affairs. (Jay Lovestone Papers, Hoover Institution, Stanford University)

New York intellectual and zealous anti-Stalinist Sidney Hook in 1960. (Sidney Hook Papers, Hoover Institution, Stanford University)

Arthur Koestler (left), Irving Brown (center), and James Burnham caucus during the Congress for Cultural Freedom, Berlin, 1950. (International Association for Cultural Freedom/Congress for Cultural Freedom Papers, Special Collections Research Center, University of Chicago Library)

Napoleon salutes his fellow pigs in the CIA-financed film adaptation of George Orwell's anti-Stalinist fable, *Animal Farm*. (Halas and Batchelor Collection Ltd.)

Henry Kissinger, Director of the Harvard International Seminar, in 1957. (Corbis)

U.S. National Student Association delegates at the Third International Student Conference, Copenhagen, 1953. (U.S. National Student Association Papers, Hoover Institution, Stanford University)

Gloria Steinem in 1967, around the time that the Independent Research Service was revealed as a CIA front. (Corbis)

Wounded veteran and ardent advocate of world government Cord Meyer, shortly before he joined the CIA in 1951. (Cord Meyer Papers, Library of Congress)

Dorothy Bauman, front-line fighter in the Cold War struggle for women's hearts and minds. (Committee of Correspondence Papers, Sophia Smith Collection, Smith College)

Women of the Committee of Correspondence and Third World guests on the steps of the Lincoln Memorial. (Committee of Correspondence Papers, Sophia Smith Collection, Smith College)

Jungle doctor Tom Dooley helping Americans locate Vietnam. (Thomas Dooley Papers, Western Historical Manuscript Collection, University of Missouri, St. Louis)

Quiet American and Office of Policy Coordination operative Edward Lansdale under cover as U.S. Air Force officer in Honolulu, late 1940s. (Edward Lansdale Papers, Hoover Institution, Stanford University)

Bing Crosby and rosary priest Patrick Peyton on a Hollywood TV set in 1956. (Corbis)

J. Peter Grace, lay protector of Patrick Peyton's Family Rosary Crusade and CIA go-between. (Corbis)

Novelist Richard Wright, beneficiary and casualty of the covert Cold War. (Corbis)

John Davis sits between Kenyan politician J. Gikonyo Kiano and Senator John F. Kennedy at the Second Annual Conference of the American Society of African Culture, New York City, 1959. (American Society of African Culture Papers, Moorland-Spingarn Research Center, Howard University)

Nina Simone (third from left) and other African American jazz musicians arrive in Lagos, Nigeria, for the 1961 festival "Negro Culture in Africa and the Americas." (American Society of African Culture Papers, Moorland-Spingarn Research Center, Howard University)

Civil rights leader James Farmer (right) takes questions from the press during his 1965 African tour as James Baker of the American Society of African Culture listens closely. (American Society of African Culture Papers, Moorland-Spingarn Research Center, Howard University)

Joseph (left) and Stewart Alsop, journalistic avatars of the Cold War foreign policy establishment. (Corbis)

Ramparts editors Warren Hinckle (left) and Robert Scheer (right) flank Sol Stern, author of the 1967 exposé of the U.S. National Student Association's links with the CIA, at the magazine's San Francisco offices. *(New York Times)*

Director of Central Intelligence Richard Helms (far left) and other members of the Katzenbach Commission in an apparently relaxed meeting with LBJ, March 22, 1967. (Lyndon B. Johnson Library, Austin, Texas)

An unabashed Tom Braden, pictured just after implicating Victor Reuther and other leaders of the non-communist left in the CIA front scandal, May 1967. (Corbis)

SEVEN

The Truth Shall Make You Free

WOMEN

One evening in 1952, soon after Dorothy Bauman had returned to New York from one of her frequent trips to Europe, a dinner party was given in her honor. There the patrician, silver-haired journalist told fellow guests of how Soviet propagandists were specifically targeting European women, promising them respect and equality if they converted to communism, and portraying their American counterparts as "superficial," "just butterflies." At the end of the evening, one of the other guests, later described by Bauman as "a man from *Reader's Digest*," took her to one side and asked quietly, "Do you mind if I have someone call you?" Bauman, expecting an invitation to write an article about her European experiences, agreed. When the call came, though, it was not a journalistic commission. Instead, "this person . . . asked me if I would go into Washington" to meet with officers of the Central Intelligence Agency.[1]

Another surprise awaited Bauman in the nation's capital. Across the desk from her was a face she recognized. It belonged to Cord Meyer, "a young man I had known as an idealistic youth when he had returned from the war and had spoken on the subject of World Government at a meeting I had helped to sponsor."[2] A tall, pale man in his early thirties "with a preoccupied smile and wavy brown hair," Meyer literally bore the scars of the Second World War, having lost an eye when a Japanese grenade exploded in his foxhole on Guam (another grenade killed his twin brother on Okinawa).[3] In 1945, determined to help prevent a recurrence of the sort of global conflict in which he had suffered so grievously, Meyer served as an assistant to the American delegation at the founding conference of the United Nations in San Francisco and afterward helped launch a utopian world government organization, the United World Federalists. Later in the decade, however, following a struggle with communists for control of the American Veterans Committee (a liberal alternative to the American Legion), Meyer "became convinced that it took more than idealism and goodwill to have a chance in the Cold War."[4] He joined the CIA in 1951, assisting Tom Braden in the International Organizations Division (IOD). "Facing reality" was how he later described this move.[5]

Dorothy Bauman's ideological journey to CIA headquarters was in many ways similar to Meyer's, although it was also typical of a certain kind of American woman who lived between the first wave of feminism in the nineteenth century and the second in the late twentieth century: a wife and mother who engaged extensively in voluntary work for non-government organizations outside the home, and a patriotic U.S. citizen who believed that women had a potentially vital role to play in promoting international understanding between the warring nations of the world. Born Dorothy Sprague in a small town in southwestern Minnesota, Bauman had three children with her first husband, from whom she was divorced after he lost his job and turned to alcohol during the Depression. Happily married for a second time to businessman John Bauman, she worked for a variety of women's voluntary organizations and New Deal relief agencies during World War II. Then in 1946, still hopeful of a united world effort in postwar reconstruction, Bauman helped convene the First International Assembly of Women in New York. "We believed that women could be influential in building a better world," she later explained. In 1948, wanting to see for herself how the women she had met in New York were faring in their efforts to reconstruct civil society in their homelands, Bauman signed up with a lecture bureau and undertook a four-and-a-half month tour of Europe and the Middle East. Having witnessed the crucial spring elections in Italy and violent civil unrest in Greece, she visited Prague just as Czechoslovakia was being absorbed into the Soviet bloc, meeting a Czech women's leader who, she learned subsequently, was later shot and killed by the communists. On returning to the United States, she wrote a report on her tour for the State Department and gave a series of lectures about "the influential role women leaders were beginning to play in the reconstruction and in the ideological struggle in their countries." She entitled her talks "Patriots in Petticoats," cleverly evoking American women's long tradition of civic engagement in times of national crisis, dating from the Revolution.[6]

It was this tradition Meyer was hoping to harness in the Cold War when he summoned Bauman to Washington. After hearing her repeat her stories about communist propaganda aimed at women—the promises of sexual equality, the attacks on American womanhood, and the appeals to a supposedly feminine desire for "world peace"—the Deputy Chief of the International Organizations Division asked Bauman to carry out a survey of women's associations in the United States, "to see if they [were] doing anything about any of this."[7] Two weeks and fifty-five interviews later, Bauman reported back to Meyer. The picture she painted of U.S. attempts to win female hearts and minds was not a flattering one. Apart from "some hospitality to United Nations delegates' wives," American women's organizations were currently doing almost nothing to combat the communist peace offensive. Official activity in the field was similarly negligible. Foreign exchange programs, in particular, appeared systematically to ignore women. In contrast, communist women leaders were "competent and dynamic," "twice as disciplined and well-trained." What should the CIA do, Meyer asked. Bauman now resurrected a proposal she had originally made in her 1948 State Department report. The government must lend its support, secretly if necessary, to the creation of "an organization of a small number of intelligent and high-minded United States women leaders who would assist women leaders in other countries in building voluntary organizations using democratic methods." The group should have an executive director, secretary, and small office in New York, "with an appropriate cover."[8] Meyer's response was immediate. "Let's get started," he said.[9]

Almost immediately after her visit to Washington, Bauman learned of the emergence in New York of a group that bore an uncanny resemblance to the organization she had just outlined to Meyer. Led by her old friend Rose Parsons, a former chief of the Red Cross Volunteers and member of the blue-blooded Peabody clan, the "Anonymous Committee," as it called itself initially, was made up of prominent American women all of whom were experienced in the world of voluntary organizations, connected in one capacity or another with the United Nations, and fed up with communist attacks on the United States. At an organizing meeting, held in the elegant surroundings of the Women's University Club on April 16,

1952, Parsons reported on the "devious methods" employed by communist propagandists: "holding large conferences, organizing letter-writing campaigns, and using other mass-communication media which in many cases appeared above reproach on the surface, yet were in reality only clever disguises for the communist aims." Various ideas for counteracting this campaign were discussed, including the suggestion that members use Mother's Day as an opportunity to challenge communist efforts to appeal to women's "maternal" instincts—although it was also pointed out that, since its founding in the nineteenth century as a call for disarmament and peace, "Mother's Day in the U.S. had acquired a mawkish, sentimental aura." What was clear was that the "undertaking would be a big one, and that to do it well would require funds."[10] One member mentioned the Ford Foundation as a potential sponsor, another the Advertising Council. A third suggestion, recorded in a rough draft of the meeting's minutes but omitted from the final version, was "that maybe the Government could subsidize the enterprise (though this would have to be done secretly to achieve the desired results)."[11]

Whether or not this initiative was entirely spontaneous is unclear; but the fact that covert government subsidies were discussed as one among several funding possibilities seems to bear out committee members' later claims that, at this early stage, they were acting independently of the CIA. In any case, shortly after the founding meeting, Bauman met with Rose Parsons on Cape Cod and showed her the paper commissioned by Meyer. The impulsive Parsons "just grabbed my report, took it right out my hand," Bauman remembered. "She was not a disciplined person but she had all the contacts in the world, being a Peabody. She was all for going to Allen Dulles. I had to hold on to her. It was really delightful."[12] The two agreed that Parsons's group should serve the function of the government-sponsored body proposed by Bauman. The latter started attending meetings of the new group in October 1952 and renewed her contact with the International Organizations Division. In December, the committee prepared a seven-page prospectus laying out its purpose, plan of operation, and budgetary needs, ostensibly for submission to private foundations. On January 27, 1953, Parsons announced to a meeting at her Manhattan residence that, "thanks to the efforts of Mrs. Bauman," the group had just received a gift of $25,000 from a "donor, representing a group of people, [who] prefers to remain anonymous."[13] By this point, the organization had acquired a new name, the Committee of Correspondence, which deliberately conjured the memory of the colonial resistance organizations formed by American patriots before the Revolutionary War. Its motto, which was emblazoned across its letterhead, was taken from John 8:32: "The Truth Shall Make You Free." The choice would later strike some as unfortunate, not least because in 1961 Allen Dulles had the same words engraved on the lobby wall of the CIA's new headquarters in Langley, Virginia.

The first years of the Committee of Correspondence's existence coincided with some important changes in the CIA's Cold War effort. In 1954, Tom Braden quit the Agency to publish a newspaper in California ("I was kind of glad to get out of it because it was heavy—all these things going on," he later explained, "worrisome—the things that could go wrong, big things"), and Cord Meyer took over as Chief of the International Organizations Division.[14] Meyer's previous career as a world federalist, combined with the fact that in 1953 he had been suspended from active service while undergoing a security investigation (during which both Braden and Dulles had rallied valiantly in his defense),[15] meant that his promotion consolidated IOD's reputation as a relatively liberal and internationalist corner (the "Greenwich Village," as one intelligence officer put it) of the CIA.[16] Meanwhile, the stock of psychological warfare generally, and front operations in particular, was rising, thanks to both the personal support of new president Dwight Eisenhower, whose enthusiasm for psy-war dated back to World War II, and a series of high-level committee reports that urged ever bolder action in the superpower struggle.[17] "It is now clear that we are facing an implacable enemy whose avowed objective is world domination by whatever means, and at whatever cost," noted the presidential Doolittle Committee in 1955. "We must learn to subvert, sabotage, and destroy our enemies by more clever, more sophisticated, and more effective methods than those used against us."[18] Responding to this recommendation, the National Security Council issued NSC 5412, a series of directives that was intended to increase presidential control over the CIA by establishing a Planning Coordination Group (also known as the Special Group and, during Lyndon Johnson's administration, the 303 Group), but had the effect of removing the Agency further still from congressional oversight. Allen Dulles reveled in his new freedom, hatching yet more covert operations over Sunday lunches with his brother Foster.[19] Meanwhile, the focus of the Cold War continued to shift geographically, from Europe to the decolonizing "periphery," where conditions demanded new, more subtle propaganda methods.

Nowhere was the effect of these changes on the Mighty Wurlitzer more evident than in the program of the Committee of Correspondence. At first the organization's activities were straightforwardly, even crudely, anticommunist. A letter challenging communist claims that the United States was using biological weapons in the Korean War (charges of "germ warfare" were a staple of early Cold War Soviet propaganda) was addressed to the Cominform-controlled Women's International Democratic Federation (WIDF). Signed by many prominent American women, among them Parsons's friend and role model Eleanor Roosevelt, the "germ warfare letter" was distributed to the *New York Times* and other leading newspapers, U.S. Information Service Centers abroad, and Radio Free Asia (the CIA's Asian equivalent of Radio Free Europe), whose announcers read out sections on the air.[20] In November 1952, attention turned to the Congress of the Peoples for Peace, due to be held in Vienna in December. A second letter, denouncing the "Peace" campaign as a "hate" campaign and drawing attention to the communist backing of the conference organizers, was sent out over Parsons and Bauman's signatures.[21] The first of the Committee's regular monthly newsletters, issued in April 1953, countered communist exploitation of motherhood for propaganda purposes by accusing the Soviet government of forcing women out to work so that it could exert "absolute control over the child with the opportunity to mold him into the pattern of well-disciplined little robots."[22] The notion that communist totalitarianism had invaded even that most private area of everyday life, the home, became a perennial theme of Cold War western propaganda.

Gradually, however, as the Committee "learned though correspondence and personal interviews that 'negative' propaganda was unacceptable to many," the strident tone of these early pronouncements began to soften. The newsletters were restricted to "'positive,' non-controversial subjects," such as "International Friendship at Work" and "Progress in the Field of Labor," and more obviously anticommunist material was reserved "for special mailings to carefully selected lists."[23] Increasingly, the women of the Committee devoted themselves to the more constructive project of fostering democratic institution-building in the developing world. This tendency was best expressed in a series of "workshops" held in the United States between 1956 and 1963, to which were invited small groups of foreign women's leaders "to discuss the responsibilities of freedom, techniques of voluntary activity and civil leadership, and the contributions women can make to their community and nation."[24] These events were complemented by an extensive program of activities abroad, including numerous overseas trips by Committee members; the occasional Committee-organized conference on foreign soil, most notable of which was a 1963 seminar held in Iran; and the posting of field-workers to Africa and South America. Yet, throughout its existence, the fundamental activity of the Committee of Correspondence remained, as its name suggested, the exchange of personal letters between its American members and their correspondents abroad who, by the mid-1960s, numbered as many as 5,000 women in over 140 countries.

To a certain extent, this shift of emphasis signified a return to the sort of internationalist, proto-feminist work that Bauman had been carrying out before the Cold War took hold in the late 1940s. The Committee's activities appear to have given rise to a genuine feeling of community—of common values and interests based on a shared female identity—which transcended the international tensions of the period. "It is almost impossible to realize that two short months ago we had most of us never seen one another," wrote Gertrude Protain, a West Indian participant in a 1960 workshop, "and yet in such a short space of time about forty women of varied backgrounds and races could succeed in forming a chain of friendship around the world."[25] One reason for the emergence of this sense of sisterhood (not a word used at the time, but it accurately describes some of the emotions aroused by the Committee's work) was the extraordinary level of cultural sensitivity shown by the American women toward their foreign correspondents. Special sessions held prior to workshops and foreign trips trained members in discussion skills pioneered by such voluntary women's organizations as the League of Women Voters.[26] After the workshops had ended, participants were sent highly sophisticated questionnaires that evaluated every aspect of their experience; one even asked the foreign visitor what motives she thought lay behind the organizers' choice of program. "We always shared, we all participated, and we picked up what we felt was closest to us," recalled Zarina Fazelbhoy, an eminent

Pakistani physician who had taken part in the Committee's first workshop in 1956. "Never at any time did they tell us the 'best' way to do anything."[27] There was also the apparently inexhaustible good humor and openness to new experiences shown by Committee women, none of whom was in the first flush of youth, when on their foreign travels. Jean Picker, a former UN correspondent who joined the Committee in 1958, was particularly "game," rounding off a day spent traveling though East Africa along unpaved roads in scorching heat by dancing "with several chiefs."[28]

At the same time, it is important to realize that the change in the Committee's mission harmonized with the evolution of U.S. foreign policy. The Eisenhower administration had realized the formidable communist challenge in the Third World—the Soviet record of rapid modernization held obvious attractions for developing nations, as did offers by Moscow of favorable trading arrangements and technical assistance—and had responded in some ingenious ways. At the same time they encouraged modernization through democratic means, including the training of "leadership groups," U.S. officials tried to humanize their country's image by fostering bonds of personal sympathy between the citizens of the "new nations" and ordinary Americans. People-to-People, a United States Information Agency program created in 1956, was an example of this new kind of "grassroots diplomacy," as was the Peace Corps, an even bolder initiative launched in 1961 by the Kennedy administration.[29] In addition to their impact abroad, such measures had the advantage of binding U.S. citizens more tightly into the Cold War consensus at home.

More acute male observers in Washington were also beginning to appreciate the growing strategic significance of women in the shifting terrain of the Cold War. Women's traditional role as educators made them potentially powerful agents of development—"Educate a man and you educate an individual," so the saying went, "but educate a woman and you educate a family, a community, a nation." Modernization also promised to liberate women as a political force, to enable them to go "from Purdah to Parliament." The CIA understood this. "It is obvious that women are now a very important factor in the nation-building going on in a large part of the world," noted one intelligence officer. "The possibility of developing new techniques to help them find their own role in the hopefully growing democratic societies is becoming a greater factor all the time."[30] In other words, the Committee of Correspondence's engagement in network building, training, and letter writing, all of which may be interpreted as evidence of a nascent international feminist consciousness, might also be viewed as clever tactics in the Cold War.

Moreover, the outward appearance of the Committee's being disengaged from the superpower struggle helped conceal the fact that certain of its members were involved in activities that differed little in practice from the work of professional spies. Dorothy Bauman, for example, appears to have been assigned the role of the U.S. government's chief woman agent in the covert Cold War, carrying out a series of what she called "special jobs" during the 1950s and 1960s. These included observing and reporting on communist-backed international conferences, such as the 1952 peace rally in Vienna (where doves flew out of the audience and Korean mothers held aloft screaming babies who were alleged to be victims of American germ warfare) and a meeting of the Women's International Democratic Federation in Copenhagen the following year. Communist agents followed Bauman wherever she went. While going in search of opera in Vienna, she wandered by mistake into the Soviet-controlled zone and found herself seated in a box with three communist officials, who pursued her from the theater, demanding to know who she was and what she was doing there. During the Copenhagen conference, she reported every evening to the First Secretary at the American embassy, Lucius Battle. "Again I was followed," she recalled, and "my room in a perfectly good hotel was searched." Battle introduced Bauman to a British intelligence officer, who "was so impressed" by her reports that he invited her to London to brief his colleagues there, and she was "brought into their intelligence apparatus." Bauman's clandestine work was curtailed abruptly in 1956, when her husband, John, died of a heart attack in a taxicab just as she was returning home from a WIDF gathering in Brazil, and she was forced to find full-time work in order to support herself and her children. Even then, however, she still found time to help run various voluntary groups and consult regularly with the USIA. Like other ideologically driven members of the CIA's covert network, Bauman had a prodigious capacity for self-punishingly hard work.[31]

Meanwhile, the CIA improved its arrangements for supporting the Committee of Correspondence. As with other front operations, clandestine payments made via individual agents were replaced by more elaborate arrangements involving dummy charitable foundations. In October 1953, the Committee received a letter from its "sponsor" in which it "was congratulated upon its work thus far" and "advised that a decision will be made in January concerning support for . . . next year."[32] Clearly, the organization's activities were winning admirers in the intelligence world (Rose Parsons also received complimentary letters from William Donovan and C. D. Jackson).[33] Predictably, the CIA review board's ruling went in the women's favor. In February 1954, a letter arrived from the Dearborn Foundation of Chicago encouraging the Committee to apply for a grant. ("This letter should not be construed as a commitment of assistance on our part," it read. "I think I can assure you, however, that your application will receive our earnest consideration.")[34] An application was submitted, and an award of $25,000 (precisely the same amount as the first, direct payment from the CIA through Bauman) duly materialized, enabling the organization to carry on making, as another letter from the Dearborn put it, a "substantial contribution to the unity of the free world through international women's activities and organizations."[35] In 1955, the CIA subsidy increased to $30,000, and an additional grant of $23,000 was made for "expanded activity."[36] In all, the Dearborn Foundation contributed some $587,500 to the Committee of Correspondence between 1954 and 1966. Substantial grants earmarked for specific activities, such as the workshops, also arrived via other CIA conduits, including the Asia Foundation, the J. Frederick Brown Foundation, the Florence Foundation, the Hobby Foundation, and the Pappas Charitable Fund.[37]

Who on the Committee knew what was going on? Dorothy Bauman and Rose Parsons were, of course, in on the secret. So too were successive Executive Directors Anne Hester, Alison Raymond, and Anne Crolius (indeed, it seems likely that Hester, at least, was placed directly on the Committee by the CIA: she took up her post in 1953, just after the first, anonymous grant of $25,000 was made, having worked previously for another front group, the Committee for Free Asia).[38] The circle of early initiates also included two of the Committee's most eminent members: Anna Lord Strauss, former president of the League of Women Voters, UN delegate, and great-granddaughter of famous abolitionist and woman suffrage leader Lucretia Mott; and Constance Anderson, Vassar graduate, former president of the Young Women's Christian Association, and senior officer of numerous other women's voluntary organizations (all of which roles she combined with being "wife of a pediatrician, mother of two, and twice a grandmother," so noted a Committee publicity pamphlet).[39] Later, the group of the witting expanded to include Jean Picker and another former UN correspondent, Susan McKeever, brought in as "protégés" of, respectively, Strauss and Anderson.[40]

But not everyone knew. Early on, Bauman had agreed with Cord Meyer that the Committee's relationship with the CIA should be revealed only on a "need-to-know" basis. As intelligence officer Spencer Arnold explained, a "rule of thumb" of front operations was to "keep the circle of knowledgeability as small as you can as long as you can. . . . The chronology of Board members learning about this association is one that grew out of the Agency's technique."[41] Some, however, managed to defy this rule. The feisty Picker, for example, when told "by these men from Washington" that "you can't talk to anybody and you can't tell your husband," replied, "Forget it. At this point in our marriage, I'm not going to have a double life." The CIA subsequently vetted Harvey Picker's security status and cleared him to be made witting.[42] Alison Raymond, too, dug in her heels when the Agency vetted her Latvian secretary negatively. "Finally I said to Anne Crolius, 'I have to have her cleared. I can't have two things going all the time in my office.' And they did clear her finally."[43]

Such incidents, though, were rare: for the most part, the witting, often despite private misgivings, played along. Indeed, compared with most other CIA front organizations, the Committee of Correspondence was extremely conscientious in its approach to security matters. A topic of constant debate in its early meetings, for instance, was the question of publicity for its activities within the United States. "If the C of C is publicized may we not expect to be questioned about our financial support?" asked an internal report on the subject. "Would it not sound a bit queer if we 'cannot tell' or if, like most of us, we 'do not know'?"[44] The safest option, it was agreed, was to avoid publicity altogether. In 1954 members decided that the award by the USIA of a Certificate of Merit in honor of the group's work in "furthering understanding and friendship for the United States . . . throughout the world" should not be revealed to the press "because the Committee does not want to be identified with a Government agency."[45] The fear of exposure remained, however. Shortly after taking over as chair of the Committee in 1960, Anna Lord Strauss held a series of private meetings with other witting members to discuss possible breaches of security—"look out for 'governmental extravagance,' leatherette covers to reports, etc., [which were] not needed and show our hand," she was advised by Rose Parsons—and to draw up a "Blueprint for action if C of C [is] accused of being government subsidized."[46]

Then there was the need to keep the secret from other Committee members who, in most cases, were close friends and old colleagues. Successive Treasurers of the organization, for example, were deliberately kept in the dark about its chief source of income. Betka Papanek, the Committee's main fund-raiser in the early years, "worked like a dog to raise money," Alison Raymond recalled. "We would tell her to write this foundation or write that foundation. Then she would get some money, and she would be absolutely thrilled and everybody congratulated her. It was such a farce. It was a terrible thing to do to anybody."[47] Papanek's successor as Treasurer, Rosalind Harris, explained, evidently with some bitterness, "You'd get a list of foundations, and one of us would write this one, and another would write that one, and we always got the money. We'd have serious meetings, I as treasurer and three others, deciding how we were going to get this year's money. That was all a charade. It was all hype." Just why the post of treasurer appears not to have been included in the circle of the Committee's witting officers is not clear. The explanation offered later for Betka Papanek's unwitting status was that she was married to a Czech citizen and therefore failed the CIA's security clearance. However, the fact that Rosalind Harris was also excluded raises the possibility that the Agency found it useful for cover purposes to have unwitting Committee officers sincerely engaging in private fund-raising activities. "To put on an act like that," Harris suspected, "was carrying it beyond just not telling."[48]

It was this issue above all—the fact that some members knew while others did not—that caused controversy when the CIA's covert patronage was exposed by the *New York Times* in February 1967. Initially, the witting opted for a strategy of blanket denial. After a series of emergency meetings, Jean Picker sent a statement to members insisting that, "we, with other educational organizations, have evidently been caught up in a situation of which we were not aware. . . . The Committee of Correspondence has never sought or received direct support from the CIA nor has it knowingly received CIA support indirectly." (A covering note cautioned members that the statement was "only to be used when needed. It is still our understanding that the less attention we bring to ourselves, the better.")[49] Not everyone was persuaded, however. Unwitting members were asking awkward questions, and legitimate, non-CIA foundations refused to rescue the organization from the financial mess left by the collapse of the Agency's pass-throughs until the witting made some acknowledgment of their complicity.

Eventually, it was decided to make a clean breast of it. The CIA agreed to send an officer to a special July meeting of the Committee to explain to its members, unwitting as well as witting, the nature of the Agency's past interest in the organization. Susan McKeever, who, clearly unable to shake off old habits, coyly introduced the officer in question, Spencer Arnold, as "a representative of our past donors," hoped that his talk might persuade the unwitting that they had not been "used" and "weld us into a group—erase misunderstanding, build up trust in each other."[50] As the meeting unfolded, however, some members grew more, rather than less, restive. They demanded to know, for example, "how much reporting we did to the CIA—did reports from individual letters go to them?" Despite assurances from Arnold and the witting that the Agency had never exploited the Committee for intelligence purposes, the questioning continued.[51]

Beset by arguments and starved of funding, the Committee gradually gave up its various functions, sending its last correspondence in February 1969. Not even its dissolution, however, put an end to the protests of the unwitting. In 1970, Eleanor Coit, Elizabeth Jackson, and Alice Clark signed a statement that they demanded be placed with the Committee's papers, which were to be deposited at Smith College, Massachusetts. The signatories wanted "to have it on record" that they had not known about the CIA funding "until the closing months of the Committee's existence."

> We believe (to use Eduard Lindeman's words) that "the Democratic Way of Life rests firmly upon the assumption that means must be consonant with ends." The use of CIA funds for the Committee's work seems to us to have been contrary to this ideal, so basic to the democratic way of life.[52]

Later still, in a series of oral history interviews, several unwitting members of the Committee elaborated on the reasons they disapproved so strongly of secret official subsidies. All were troubled by the contradiction between the group's professed commitment to truth, as expressed in the motto on its letterhead, and the deception involved in CIA funding. "How could they have dared to put that on?" Rosalind Harris wanted to know. "Considering what some of these people were doing, that phrase was really chutzpah."[53] The other main concern was the damage that exposure of covert government involvement might do—indeed, already had done—to the credibility of not just the Committee but the whole voluntary sector in the United States, which depended precisely upon the perception that it was independent of officialdom (just as U.S. women had historically derived much of their moral authority in American society from their perceived independence of the venal, male-dominated world of politics and business). As another unwitting member, Elizabeth Wadsworth, pithily put it, "You cannot do everything to give the impression that you don't take government money and take it. . . . We did make an issue of it and then we took it. Dumb."[54]

The witting suspected that such protests were produced, in part at least, by the anger of the unwitting at having been left out of the loop. Alison Raymond, for example, wondered whether some women had not joined the organization principally "for social reasons"—"they wanted dinner conversation for tomorrow night's dinner party"—and were now disgruntled at finding out "there was a little inner group" from which they had been excluded. Raymond did not confront the "more pink-tea-ish" members with this suspicion, however.[55] Like other members of the inner group, she regretted having deceived colleagues and, in the wake of the revelations, tried hard to soothe their feelings.

The main line of self-defense employed by the witting was the argument that the CIA had not used its position as donor to manipulate the Committee. "There was no hanky-panky, no underhandedness," claimed Anne Crolius, "no influence on the committee to do anything other than it intended to do."[56] All the Agency had done was come to the aid of an organization that happened to share its aims and, in the absence of a public U.S. funding agency like the British Council, would otherwise have died through lack of resources. This was also the explanation favored by the CIA itself. "In working with groups like the Committee of Correspondence," stated Spencer Arnold, "it came down to the fact that [they] had the same goals, methods, techniques, and experience . . . [as] long-range

United States policy." Indeed, if anything, "as grantors the agency was probably a lot less closely reviewing than most foundations have to be."[57]

Yet evidence suggests that the CIA did try to shape the Committee's program. The Dearborn Foundation was one channel of influence. This pass-through not only insisted on receiving detailed quarterly reports of the organization's activities, including its accounts, copies of all its publications, and letters from correspondents (clearly viewed, despite Spencer Arnold's denials, as a valuable source of intelligence about women's issues overseas); it also nudged Committee members toward new fields of operation.[58] The initial offer of a grant for "expanded activity" in 1955, for instance, came with several suggestions as to how the additional money might be spent, such as on "foreign travel to ensure sound American representation at women's international meetings" or assistance to foreign women for the same purpose.[59] In addition, meetings were occasionally held between certain members of the Committee and individuals claiming to be foundation officers. One set of Committee minutes dated December 1955 notes a visit to New York by a "Mr. McDonogh, representative of the Dearborn Foundation," and expresses regret "that advance notice was so short" that only a "few of the Committee" were able to meet him.[60] One wonders if the lack of warning was not a ruse to ensure the presence at the meeting only of witting members.

Then there were direct contacts between the Committee and CIA officers that were explicitly identified as such. Connie Anderson, for example, met with two Agency operatives once a month in her apartment and handed over the organization's minutes and other documents. (Jean Picker, who attended some of these meetings, "found these men a little ridiculous . . . like cops-and-robbers kids.")[61] Later this function was taken over by Anne Crolius, when in 1962, fresh from Wellesley, she became Executive Director. According to Dorothy Bauman, "she worked more or less as a courier. When they wanted to get in touch with me it was through Anne because she was paid staff and was there full-time." Although Anderson maintained that such contacts were limited to the passing of information about the Committee, which was necessary in order for the officers concerned to be able "to persuade their higher-ups that we were worth supporting," she also admitted that the CIA did issue the occasional directive. "Well, they told us some people to see and some people not to see in other lands." This included instructions for Committee members who were traveling abroad about how to send reports to Washington via staff at American embassies. Alison Raymond once used this method to transmit a list of women invited to a communist-organized peace conference she had obtained from a contact in Egypt. (The woman concerned, "Lily," had at first resisted her overtures, but Raymond went to bed one night to find the list nestling on her pillow.) There was also the odd hint about what sort of public activities the Committee should be carrying out. "Sometimes they'd say, 'We hope this year you'll take a look at . . . ,' wherever, upheavals in Kenya one time," recalled Anne Crolius. "It was not clear to us at the time, one was able to understand later." The 1963 workshop held in Iran was, according to Anderson, the result of such gentle pressure. Evidently, then, despite repeated statements by both parties to the contrary, there was an ongoing effort by the CIA to intervene discreetly in the organization's affairs. As Crolius primly put it, "They hoped the Committee would follow the positions they thought were good."[62]

Still, the importance of such interference should not be overstated. Several factors protected the Committee from excessive official meddling, one of which was the male intelligence officers' lack of knowledge about women's affairs. When in 1955 the Committee sought more detailed guidance from the Dearborn Foundation about what precisely it meant by "expanded activity," the foundation grew surprisingly reticent. "We want to assist you in your program," its secretary and treasurer, John H. Jamison, told Rose Parsons, "but feel you have the specialized and detailed knowledge, not available to us, to provide the necessary leadership. . . . [T]he initiative can and must come from you."[63] When Dorothy Bauman began working with CIA men on other operations, she discovered that "none of them knew anything about this organization, either that or it was sort of a laughingstock. I think they thought Cord Meyer was probably out of his mind to underwrite me."[64] Even Meyer himself, one senses in Bauman's accounts of their meetings together, was relieved to be able to turn over to her responsibility for a field that was both unfamiliar and perhaps less interesting to him than were other areas of covert operation.

More significant still was the simple fact that the CIA did not have to impose terms on the Committee because the women involved tended to share many of its values anyway. This was partly a consequence of the natural ideological sympathy that existed between anticommunist internationalists like Bauman and Meyer, as evidenced by their shared reverence for the United Nations. Also important was the women's assumption that, like generations of female Americans before them, they had a patriotic duty to serve their country when it was at war. Hence, in the discussions that took place during the first days of the Committee's existence, there was very little sense of the rigid distinction between governmental and nongovernmental, official and voluntary, public and private that during the late 1960s would underlie much of the debate about the CIA's covert network. For example, no member protested when it was announced at an October 1952 meeting that Bauman proposed to consult with a senior State Department official.[65] Similarly, when an idea originally conceived by the Committee was adopted by the Psychological Strategy Board, it was reported in Committee papers as a matter for self-congratulation.[66] The war atmosphere of the early 1950s, similar in many ways to that of the early 1940s, both determined and sanctioned such behavior.

This is not to say that the women's loyalty was entirely unquestioning. One suggestion tentatively advanced by the Dearborn Foundation in 1955, that the Committee channel funds to foreign women wanting to set up similar organizations abroad, was dismissed by Committee members as being outside the group's frame of reference.[67] One also detects, very occasionally, glimmerings of anxiety among the witting about the Committee's "autonomy." During her meeting with Anna Lord Strauss in 1960, Constance Anderson wondered out loud whether "taking from them assignment of people" was not giving "too much power" to the CIA. Perhaps the Committee should find "another leg to stand [on] besides [the] Dearborn," suggested Susan McKeever.[68] Such moments were exceptional, though. For the most part, the witting members of the Committee of Correspondence appear to have found the notion of government service—even secret government service—entirely unobjectionable.

One aspect of the relationship between the CIA and the Committee, however, continued to trouble the witting long after the organization itself had ceased to exist. In a brief memoir entitled "Right or Wrong?" written in 1974, Dorothy Bauman, the principal link between the world of male intelligence officers and that of female voluntary workers, spoke with pride of the Committee's many achievements: its transcendence of negative anticommunism, its forging of links between women in the United States and abroad, and its efforts to build democratic institutions in decolonizing countries. "With today's questioning of all of the CIA's activities," wrote Bauman, "it seems to me only fair to tell of one operation that was highly constructive and successful and where no overt pressure from the CIA was ever used on a group of competent, individualistic women." Yet running throughout the piece is a palpable sense of guilt. Bauman's acceptance of the CIA's injunction that she conceal the true source of the Committee's funds from most of its members was, she later realized, a terrible mistake. "I was so new at anything of this kind," she explained, "that I concurred in what the agency said was vital—namely, to have as few people as possible know where the money came from." The fact that she "did not insist at the start that all members of the committee be informed, so that they would have had the opportunity to withdraw if they did not approve of taking funds," was a cause of "everlasting regret." On the larger question of the morality of secret subsidies, she did not offer a firm view. "Whether ethically it was wrong not to divulge the true source of funds," she told the reader, "I leave to your judgment."[69]

Another question remains: to use the imagery of much recent scholarship about American women in the early years of the Cold War, were members of the Committee of Correspondence "contained" or "liberated" by the covert patronage of the CIA?[70] Although it is clear that their work with the Committee enabled some women to escape the patriarchal constraints of postwar U.S. society and forge rewarding new relationships with their counterparts in the developing world (who themselves no doubt used the opportunity to advance their position within their own societies), these benefits came at a tremendous cost. The decision of the witting to hide the truth of the organization's funding from the unwitting, and the feelings of hurt and betrayal that resulted from the revelations of 1967, destroyed the unstated, yet powerful, sense of sisterhood that had for a time bound these women together. Similarly, the pressures to pursue particular national objectives that inevitably accompanied secret government subsidies contradicted the internationalist spirit that had originally inspired the Committee's founders, undermining the women's claim to embody a universal spirit that transcended male power politics. Finally, and perhaps most damaging of all, the acceptance of covert official patronage violated the principle of voluntary association on which so much public activity by American women, at home as well as abroad, was predicated. Ultimately, the women of the Committee of Correspondence had allowed themselves to be manipulated by men.

EIGHT

Saving the World

CATHOLICS

The early years of the Cold War were good ones for American Catholicism. Between 1940 and 1960, the nation's Catholic population doubled; church leaders, such as the charismatic Bishop Fulton Sheen, enjoyed unprecedented popularity; ordinary Catholics were better educated, wealthier, and more upwardly mobile socially than they had ever been before.[1] There were several reasons for this newfound acceptance and confidence, including a general easing of religious and ethnic intolerance on the part of native-stock Protestant Americans; but high on the list of contributory factors was the Cold War itself. With their frequent attacks on godless communism, Catholic clerics had long constituted "the backbone" of the anticommunist movement in America.[2] Now, with the whole of society mobilizing against Marxism-Leninism, pronouncements that might once have sounded fanatical or self-interested seemed instead prophetic and patriotic. To be sure, Cold War Catholic anticommunism retained a whiff of the lunatic fringe, a tendency personified by notorious red-baiter Joe McCarthy. However, as the 1950s wore on, the pantomime politics of McCarthyism gave way to the cooler Cold War engagement of another Irish-American politician, John F. Kennedy, whose victory in the 1960 presidential election signified that Catholics had finally arrived in the U.S. establishment.

On their own, these were reasons enough for Catholics to have featured in CIA front operations against communism, but there was an additional, tactical consideration that made their participation all but inevitable. Catholicism was a powerful ideological presence in two regions of the world where communism was threatening to expand: Southeast Asia and South America. U.S. Catholics were bound to their coreligionists in these new theaters of the Cold War not only by their common membership in a universal church, but also by historic ties of paternalistic sentiment, practical assistance, and missionary work. These links, similar in their way to the bonds that united American labor, youth, and women's organizations with their counterparts overseas, help explain why the CIA came to regard the American Catholic community as a valuable ally in its covert war with the Cominform—so valuable that, in addition to disregarding the prohibition against domestic operation it had already violated in its relations with several other citizen groups, the Agency was also prepared to ignore the separation between church and state ordained by the Establishment Clause of the First Amendment to the U.S. Constitution. The history of the CIA's secret alliance with U.S. Catholicism in the Cold War crusade against communism in Southeast Asia and Latin America is best told through the stories of two outstanding, charismatic, and, some would say, saintly individuals, Tom Dooley and Patrick Peyton.

Although little remembered today, Tom Dooley was during the final years of his tragically short life—he died in 1961 at the age of thirty-four—a true American celebrity. His boyish good looks adorned magazine covers; appearances on such television shows as *This Is Your Life* drew millions of viewers; there was even a hit song about him, recorded by the Kingston Trio (or so it seemed: in fact, "Tom Dooley" was a revival of a Civil War–era ballad about the execution of a young Confederate soldier for the murder of his mistress, but many listeners mistakenly associated it with the handsome "jungle doctor").[3] Explaining why Dooley inspired such admiration during his lifetime, and then—contrary to the fate of most other youth icons of the era who died young—sank into posthumous obscurity, requires a detailed accounting not only of his extraordinary life and career but also of the numerous CIA front operations in Southeast Asia into which he was unwittingly drawn.

Little in the early life of Thomas A. Dooley hinted at the heroic humanitarian he would become. A dandyish scion of an affluent midwestern family, the young Catholic drifted through Notre Dame and nearly flunked out of St. Louis University (SLU) medical school, graduating 109th out of a class of 116.[4] It was not until 1954, the year that France was forced to withdraw from Indochina in the face of the Vietminh insurgency led by the communist Ho Chi Minh, that Dooley revealed a side to himself other than that of St. Louis playboy. Having enlisted in the U.S. Navy, he volunteered for service in "Passage to Freedom," an emergency effort to transport non-communist Vietnamese to the south of the country as the north fell under communist domination.[5] His facility with languages (he already spoke French and soon acquired serviceable Vietnamese) and obvious sympathy for the predominantly Catholic refugees he treated as they boarded American vessels for the journey south so impressed his superiors that in October 1954 Dooley was assigned his own medical task unit in the port of Haiphong, the last neutral enclave in North Vietnam. There he distinguished himself further by managing to prevent any major outbreaks of epidemic disease in the teeming refugee camps and transporters bound for Saigon. In the process he attracted the attention of several Vietnam-based U.S. newsmen, who detected in the spectacle of this youthful Irish-American ministering to Catholic evacuees a human interest story that would tug the heartstrings of their audiences back home. Dooley's motivation was not entirely selfless: letters written from Haiphong to his mother hint at a growing appetite for publicity linked to the wounded pride he still felt about his poor performance at SLU.[6] That said, he was undeniably moved by the devotion he appeared to inspire in the refugees, especially the children, who flocked around him, calling "Bac Sy My" ("good American doctor"), as well as by the suffering of Catholic victims of torture at the hands of the Vietminh, whose injuries he described in the letters to his mother with palpable horror.[7] Dooley risked his own health caring for his Vietnamese patients, nearly dying of malarial fever, acquiring four different types of intestinal worm, and frequently hallucinating due to sleep deprivation.[8] It was in recognition of this self-sacrifice that the new Catholic premier of South Vietnam, Ngo Dinh Diem, decorated Dooley in May 1955 at a special award ceremony in the Saigon presidential palace. The doctor's "medicine and knowledge," so Diem's citation claimed, had demonstrated to ordinary Vietnamese "the true goodness and spirit of help and cooperation that America is showing in Viet Nam and in all the countries of the world."[9]

Not all was as it seemed, however. Behind Passage to Freedom and Diem's honoring of Dooley was the CIA—or, to be more precise, the shadowy figure of archetypal American Cold War secret agent Edward G. Lansdale. There has been so much myth-making about Lansdale that it is almost impossible to separate the facts of his career from the fictions about it. (In addition to a thinly veiled portrait of Lansdale appearing in William J. Lederer and Eugene Burdick's *The Ugly American*, a best-selling fictional critique of U.S. foreign policy in Southeast Asia, he is also widely, if mistakenly, believed to have inspired the character of American antihero Alden Pyle in the Vietnam of Graham Greene's novel *The Quiet American*.) Nonetheless, certain biographical details do seem to be incontrovertible. Born to a middle-class, Catholic father and Christian Scientist mother in Detroit, and educated at the University of California, Los Angeles, the soft-spoken Lansdale left a lucrative career in a San Francisco advertising agency to serve in the Pacific with military intelligence and the OSS during World War II. After the war, he returned to the Philippines as a psychological warfare and counterinsurgency expert in Frank Wisner's OPC, under cover as a U.S. Air Force Lieutenant Colonel (later Major General), despite the fact that he never learned how to fly a plane. During a tour of duty that lasted until 1953, Lansdale waged an ingenious psy-war campaign against the communist Hukbalahap insurgency and developed a Svengali-like relationship with the pro-U.S. Filipino Defense Minister, Ramón Magsaysay. In addition to employing American advertising techniques to promote the cause of his friend, the OPC operative cunningly exploited local superstitions to turn ordinary Filipinos against the Huks, on one occasion arranging for the body of an insurgent to be drained of blood, punctured twice in the neck, and laid out in a Luzon village street to create the impression that a local vampire was preying on communists.[10] In 1953, Magsaysay won a presidential election with an overwhelming majority and the following year drove the Huks into the Sierra Madre, earning Lansdale a reputation in Washington as a master practitioner of "unconventional" warfare and authority on all matters Asian.[11] It was no surprise, therefore, that in 1954, when the Dulles brothers were looking for ways of stabilizing the fragile regime of the Vietnamese anticommunist Diem, they turned to "Colonel Landslide." Lansdale left for Saigon in June of that year with instructions from Foster "to help the Vietnamese the way you helped the Filipinos" and a personal message from Allen: "God bless you."[12]

Within weeks of his arrival, Lansdale had assembled a crack team of American and Filipino covert operatives, the Saigon Military Mission (SMM), to carry out paramilitary and psychological operations intended to undermine the Vietminh and buttress the South Vietnamese government. These included contaminating oil in the tanks of Hanoi buses, winning Diem the support of powerful Vietnamese sect leaders by providing their mistresses with English classes, and artificially stimulating the migration of Catholics from the North whom Dooley was treating in Operation Passage to Freedom.[13] Lansdale was interested in the Catholic exodus for several reasons. It aroused domestic American support for the anticommunist cause in Vietnam and at the same time created an electoral constituency for Diem in the South. Refugee movements also functioned as cover for paramilitary activities—SMM had a branch in Haiphong under the command of Lansdale's right-hand man, Lucien Conein. The Lansdalian imagination ran riot generating psy-war materials for secret circulation in the North: an almanac in which notable Vietnamese astrologers predicted disaster for the Vietminh and prosperity for the South, handbills showing an aerial view of Hanoi on which was superimposed target sites purportedly representing American plans for a nuclear attack on the North, and posters of a Catholic cathedral being ransacked by the Vietminh while the congregation was forced to pray to a portrait of Ho Chi Minh.[14] Eventually, roughly 60 percent of the nation's 1.5 million Catholics journeyed south, many from the dioceses of Phat Diem and Bui Chu, both close to Haiphong. So convinced was Lansdale about the moral virtue of his anticommunist ends that the methods he used never gave him a moment's pause. "You can . . . get away with almost anything," he later told an interviewer, "so long . . . as you do it for the right reasons."[15]

Not that Lansdale's techniques for influencing Vietnamese public opinion were confined to dirty tricks: in line with the Eisenhower administration's new emphasis on containing communism by integrating the free world, he also believed that Americans needed to capture popular support from the communists by demonstrating empathy for local values and objectives. This involved U.S. officials distancing themselves from European-style colonialism and engaging in "nation-building"—helping to create democratic political structures, if necessary by economic means such as land reform, that would be capable of withstanding communist pressure. "Let's cut out the American self-delusion," Lansdale insisted, in the face of CIA colleagues concerned only with espionage ("the shoe clerk and librarian types," he called them) and cosseted State Department career diplomats who talked down to the Vietnamese.[16] One early application of this strategy was "Operation Brotherhood," a program ostensibly sponsored by the Junior Chamber of Commerce but in fact run by the Saigon Military Mission, which brought 100 Filipino doctors and nurses to South Vietnam, a country almost deserted by medics in the wake of the French withdrawal. "The presence of medical personnel," explained Lansdale in a secret report, "furnishes the ideal answer to meeting the initial suspicion that foreigners evoke."[17]

Dooley's role in Passage to Freedom might have been scripted by Lansdale. On the one hand, the young doctor perfectly embodied America's humanitarian, modernizing mission in Asia, bringing the benefits of western medical science to the victims of communist aggression with a smiling face. On the other, echoes in his performance of earlier Catholic missionary work in Asia stirred the emotions of American Catholics and fostered the impression, which the planners of Passage to Freedom were all too glad to see perpetuated, that the conflict in Vietnam was a war between atheists and Christians. (Although Dooley explicitly denied any evangelical intent, it was hard not to read some religious significance into his actions, such as the way he administered U.S.-manufactured drugs to Catholic refugees "almost as a surrogate Eucharist.")[18] The fact that other American officials thought Dooley an immature attention-seeker or "blowhard" did not bother Lansdale. "I said no," the maverick spy recalled in 1984. "I had seen him look at the Vietnamese that he's treating and there's a real affection in his emotions and the guy cares."[19] Documentary evidence linking the two men at this stage in Dooley's career is scant, but the fact that SMM had a base in Haiphong is suggestive, as is Lansdale's later claim that the decoration of the young doctor by Diem was his idea. (Apparently, when Dooley boasted that the honor was fitting recognition of his heroism in the refugee camps, Lansdale invited him to compare the text of Diem's citation with other documents produced on his U.S. government-issue typewriter: the script was identical.)[20] The irony is that Dooley already believed that he was on a secret mission in Haiphong—gathering medical intelligence about epidemiological conditions in North

Vietnam ahead of possible American troop deployments there—when his most valuable function, as far as SMM was concerned, was simply as a front man for Passage to Freedom.[21] His biographer, James T. Fisher, even speculates that Dooley had been "loaned" by the Navy to Lansdale and was stationed in the northern port for precisely this purpose.[22]

It also seems likely that Lansdale was behind the next twist in Dooley's improbable career: his debut as a best-selling author. There were already hints of the storyteller who would captivate American readers in the shipboard lectures about Passage to Freedom that Dooley periodically gave to U.S. Navy "white-caps" while stationed in Vietnam; according to one officer present, his descriptions of Catholic torture victims drew sobs from even the most "grizzled old bosuns."[23] Dooley's letters to his mother also sounded occasionally as if they were written with a larger audience in mind.[24] However, his first attempt to record his Vietnamese experiences, a manuscript drafted in late 1954 under the unimaginative title "Passage to Freedom," lacked the verve of his lectures, reading more like an official report to his commanding officers. It was at this point that William Lederer, a Navy public information officer and former submarine skipper, entered the picture, "to handle the polish and publication of the book" (as Dooley explained in a July 1955 letter home).[25] Again, it seems unlikely that this was mere coincidence. Lederer knew Lansdale and shared his views on U.S. Cold War diplomacy.[26] Indeed, the two men were good friends, having served together in the Philippines, where both displayed an attitude toward bureaucratic red tape that was "irreverent as hell."[27] (Lansdale's portrait in Lederer and Burdick's *Ugly American* as the motorcycle-riding, harmonica-playing, palm-reading "Ragtime Kid" Edwin B. Hillandale was wholly positive—unlike the Pyle character in Greene's *Quiet American*.) There is also evidence suggesting that Lederer was on loan from the Navy to the CIA in June 1955, when he made contact with Dooley: on May 11, 1955 (one day prior to the Lansdale-orchestrated award ceremony in Saigon), Allen Dulles wrote to Admiral Felix Stump, Commander-in-Chief of the Pacific Fleet, requesting that Lederer be made available for a "special assignment."[28]

Whatever its inspiration, Lederer's contribution to Dooley's publishing success was crucial. In a series of lengthy meetings, the two thrashed out a new draft of "Passage to Freedom" with the more symbolically charged title *Deliver Us from Evil*. The lifeless prose of the original was replaced with an overwrought but compelling first-person narrative emphasizing the author's moral growth from spoiled adolescent to selfless physician, the childlike gratitude of his patients, and the ghastliness of the injuries inflicted on the Vietminh's torture victims.[29] After helping rewrite the manuscript, Lederer then oversaw its publication, introducing Dooley to the owner of *Reader's Digest*, DeWitt Wallace, who immediately offered to carry an abridged version in his magazine, then passed it along to Roger Straus of Farrar, Straus, and Cudahy, who likewise accepted it on the spot.[30] Published in early 1956, *Deliver Us from Evil* enjoyed unanimous critical praise—*The New Yorker*, for example, described it as "a moving poem of the human spirit victorious"—and unprecedented sales, eventually going through twenty printings and translation into more languages than any previous book except for the Bible.[31] It also helped transform popular attitudes toward the Cold War in Asia, "quite literally locat[ing] Vietnam on the new world map for millions of Americans" and reducing the conflict there to a straightforward clash between good and evil.[32] One historian has described *Deliver Us from Evil* as "the *Uncle Tom's Cabin* of the Cold War."[33]

It was at just this moment, with the Junior Chamber of Commerce voting him one of the "ten outstanding men of 1956," that Dooley experienced the first major setback in his career. The young man's brashness had already aroused the hostility of senior officers in the Navy and the CIA. He also had a secret: in an age of institutionalized homophobia, when sexual "deviancy" was equated with political subversion, not only was he homosexual, he was also, in the words of James Fisher, "one of the great underground sex symbols of his era—a figure well-known in sophisticated gay circles as far-flung as Hollywood, Washington DC, and the capitals of Southeast Asia."[34] The Office of Naval Intelligence had launched an investigation of Dooley's private life in 1955. While he was on the road promoting his book early the following year, his telephone calls were bugged, his luggage opened, and his movements scrutinized by spy cameras. Eventually a Marine Corps colonel, William Corson, confronted Dooley with the ONI's evidence of "dishonorable conduct" (which was considerable). The Navy doctor, apparently relieved, agreed to resign on the spot, "for the good of the service." In July, he received a general discharge under less than honorable conditions (later changed to an honorable discharge), but without any of the usual attendant publicity.[35]

Dooley's departure from the Navy might have been hushed up successfully, but it still left him jobless. Enter another ostensibly private player in Cold War Asian politics with hidden official ties: the International Rescue Committee (IRC). The IRC was a very different organization from Dooley's previous employer. Created by prominent American left-liberals in the 1930s to aid socialists in Nazi Germany (Jay Lovestone was a founding member), by the 1950s it had grown into one of the largest and most prestigious refugee relief organizations in the western world, its attention now focused chiefly on anticommunist exiles from eastern Europe and the Soviet Union. At first, the IRC's involvement in Asia was tentative and halting: in 1951, for example, it resisted urging from U.S. government officials to assume responsibility for the relief of Chinese intellectuals stranded in Hong Kong and Macao.[36] In 1954, however, the IRC did heed calls from Harold Stassen of the Foreign Operations Administration (a successor agency to the Marshall Plan's Economic Cooperation Administration) to intervene in the Vietnamese refugee crisis, dispatching Joseph Buttinger, an émigré Austrian socialist, to Saigon. There Buttinger helped set up several relief programs, including popular cultural associations to host intellectuals displaced from the North, Operation Brotherhood (which the International Rescue Committee cosponsored with the Jaycees), and a local IRC office.

More important, though, was what Buttinger did on his return to the United States. Having become a devoted friend of Diem during his time in Vietnam, he now set about promoting the virtues of the Catholic premier to the American public, giving newspaper interviews, writing articles for such publications as the *New Leader*, and sending memos to influential allies in and outside government.[37] Next, along with other leaders of the IRC, namely businessman Leo Cherne, diplomat Angier Biddle Duke, and public relations expert Harold Oram, Buttinger launched the American Friends of Vietnam (AFV), a dynamic and high-profile organization that effectively functioned, as one of its own members admitted, as "uncritical spokesman for and defender of the Diem regime."[38] Indeed, one of the organization's earliest actions was to circulate a letter, drafted by Oram and signed by distinguished socialist Norman Thomas, defending Diem's decision not to hold nationwide elections mandated for 1956 by the Geneva Accords. (As Thomas's membership in the AFV suggests, the group was, like its progenitor, the International Rescue Committee, heavily slanted toward non-communist leftists, who appear mistakenly to have perceived Diem as a fellow liberal anticommunist.)[39] It would be an exaggeration to say that the "Vietnam Lobby," as it was christened in a later, hostile *Ramparts* exposé, was to blame for leading Americans into the Indochinese quagmire: the U.S. government was already irrevocably committed to an anticommunist foreign policy in Southeast Asia.[40] Nonetheless, the American Friends of Vietnam undeniably played a part in persuading the Eisenhower administration to support the haughty, repressive, and inflexible Diem as South Vietnamese head of state—to "sink or swim with Ngo Dinh Diem," as the saying had it—when there were several other, arguably better qualified candidates available for that role.[41]

Although both received grants via CIA proprietaries or fake foundations, neither the International Rescue Committee nor the American Friends of Vietnam were front organizations in the sense that the Agency regularly funded and controlled them.[42] That said, both were heavily implicated in the covert network that bound the U.S intelligence community to the émigré relief organizations of the early Cold War era. Some links were obvious, such as the presence of Wild Bill Donovan and future Director of Central Intelligence William J. Casey on the IRC's Board of Directors. Others were less apparent—for example, a secret agreement reached by Joseph Buttinger and Samuel Adams, a Vietnam-based CIA officer operating under cover of the Foreign Operations Administration, that the IRC would take responsibility for projects with which the U.S. government could not be openly associated; or Harold Oram's acting as a regular reporting channel between Buttinger and Allen Dulles.[43] Predictably, given his dominant role in Southeast Asian covert operations, the Vietnam Lobby also had ties to Edward Lansdale. He it was who first introduced Buttinger to Diem; he was in regular contact with the chair of the American Friends of Vietnam from March 1956, General John "Iron Mike" O'Daniel, with whom he had first visited Vietnam on a U.S. survey team in June 1953.[44] There is even evidence that Lansdale invented the AFV in the first place: while Buttinger was visiting Saigon in the fall of 1954 he met an "American officer," referred to in his diary only as "Mr. X," who advised him, "You must help get American public opinion on our side. Create a committee of friends of Vietnam."[45] Mr. X, historian Seth Jacobs writes, was "almost certainly" Colonel Lansdale.[46]

Perhaps the most remarkable instance of cooperation between

Lansdale and the American Friends of Vietnam involved a third party: movie director, producer, and screenwriter Joseph L. Mankiewicz. Early in 1956 Mankiewicz, whose filmography included such popular and critical successes as *The Philadelphia Story* and *All About Eve*, visited Saigon to research locations for a cinematic version of Greene's *The Quiet American*. During this trip, he met both with staff of the International Rescue Committee's Vietnam office and Lansdale himself, who followed up the encounter with a long letter offering various pieces of advice about the project, chief of which was the suggestion that Mankiewicz depict an incident portrayed in Greene's novel, the bombing of a Saigon square in 1952 by a Vietnamese associate of Lansdale's, General Trinh Minh Thé (and attributed by Greene to the baleful influence of the American, Pyle), as "actually having been a Communist action."[47] On his return home, Mankiewicz contacted the chair of the AFV, Iron Mike O'Daniel, telling him that he intended "completely chang[ing] the anti-American attitude" of Greene's book. The U.S. ambassador to South Vietnam, Frederick Reinhardt, was sympathetic but skeptical, telling the American Friends of Vietnam's Executive Committee: "If [the book] were to be edited into a state of complete unobjectionableness, there might be nothing left but the title and scenery."[48] This is, however, precisely what Mankiewicz proceeded to do, turning the American character into his hero and portraying Greene's fictional alter ego and Pyle's nemesis, the English journalist Fowler, as a communist stooge. Not only that, in an astonishing piece of casting apparently suggested by O'Daniel, the part of Pyle—in Greene's novel, a callow Ivy League brahmin—was given to the World War II hero Audie Murphy, a fine soldier but limited actor, who reportedly distressed his English costar, Michael Redgrave, by storing a .45 and 500 rounds of ammunition in his Saigon hotel room to protect himself from Vietminh agents. "I figured if they were going to get me," he explained, "I'd give them a good fight first."[49]

The resulting movie was a travesty of Greene's book, but Lansdale was delighted. After a premiere at Washington's Playhouse Theater, the proceeds of which were donated to the AFV, the spy wrote his friend Diem describing "Mr. Mankiewicz's 'treatment' of the story" as "an excellent change from Mr. Greene's novel of despair," and suggesting "that it will help win more friends for you and Vietnam in many places in the world where it is shown."[50] It was a brilliantly devious maneuver of postmodern literary complexity: by helping to rewrite a story featuring a character reputedly based on himself, Lansdale had transformed an anti-American tract into a cinematic apology for U.S. policy—and his own actions—in Vietnam. Greene himself was understandably furious. "Far was it from my mind, when I wrote *The Quiet American*," the Englishman raged, "that the book would become a source of spiritual profit to one of the most corrupt governments in Southeast Asia."[51]

In addition to salvaging Greene's novel for the western cause in the Cold War, the Vietnam Lobby helped Lansdale rehabilitate Tom Dooley, turning him from (in the words of his biographer) "potential sex criminal to secular saint."[52] This act was not entirely disinterested: as a well-known Catholic, Dooley was capable of giving the Jewish and "WASP-ish" liberal intellectuals of the IRC and AFV an appeal to heartland conservatives they would otherwise have lacked. Judging by the audiences who flocked to Dooley's speaking engagements during the promotional tour for *Deliver Us from Evil* in early 1956, he also had considerable potential as a fund-raiser. Hence, when the young doctor was cut loose from the Navy, the Vietnam Lobby was there to catch him. The IRC became the official sponsor of his new enterprise, a jungle hospital opened in Vang Vieng, a village in the mountains of Laos, near the Vietnamese border, in October 1956. It was also behind the launch in February 1958 of Medical International Cooperation (MEDICO), an ambitious scheme to create a chain of western-style medical clinics throughout the Third World. With the IRC as his new patron, Dooley now settled into a routine of long spells in the Laotian jungle treating hill tribespeople, most of whom had not seen a westerner, let alone a doctor, before, punctuated by frenetic fund-raising tours in the United States. So effective was he as a front man for the International Rescue Committee that, unlike the Navy, the IRC was prepared to turn a blind eye to his sexuality, even paying the bills for his assignations at the Waldorf-Astoria, his favorite New York hotel.[53]

It is clear now that Dooley's hospital operated in part as a military intelligence-gathering operation: whenever the doctor returned to the United States, he was debriefed by CIA officers eager for information about communist troop movements and popular attitudes in Laos.[54] However, as with Passage to Freedom, it would be simplistic to reduce Dooley's role to mere espionage. Lansdale was again in the background, helping the medic and his team of corpsmen get established in Vang Vieng, first by intervening in Saigon through Anne Miller, the wife of his friend, information officer Hank Miller, "to straighten out their personal affairs" (Dooley "had homosexual tendencies and his team got mad at him personally," Lansdale explained later, "and there were fights and I had to straighten that out"), then by delegating his deputy in charge of Operation Brotherhood, Rufus Phillips, to arrange strategic support for the new clinic.[55] "Operation Laos" had two main psy-war targets. One was ordinary Laotians: as Dooley explained in a frank and revealing prospectus for the IRC, his aim was not only to provide medical care but also to "illustrate to these people some of the nature, principles, and achievements of America, and especially to show them that we are anxious to help them on a person-to-person basis, at the grass-root level of diplomacy." Medicine was in this sense merely an "instrument" for demonstrating the benefits of "democratic ideals" to Asians, along with other American artifacts that Dooley intended to show the villagers, such as baseball, a Sears Roebuck catalog, and Disney cartoons (it was perhaps not coincidental that Lansdale had earlier made similar use of Disney in the Philippines).[56] The fact that Dooley became known in Laos as "Thanh Mo America," or "Dr. America," suggests that this objective was at least partly accomplished.

Although not stated in the prospectus, the other intended audience for Operation Laos was back home in the United States. Shortly after his arrival in Vang Vieng, Dooley began recording weekly commentaries that were shipped to St. Louis and broadcast by CBS radio station KMOX. Entitled *That Free Men May Live*, the programs consisted of anecdotes about events at Dooley's "hut-of-a-hospital," analysis of Laotian politics (Dooley naturally favored those anticommunist factions receiving secret backing from the Lansdale apparatus), and musings on the "Asian character." Combined with a second book, further personal appearances, and numerous accolades—in a 1959 *Life* article, "Salute to Deeds of Non-Ugly Americans," Lederer and Burdick celebrated "a doctor of democracy . . . who was ready to do a needed job in a foreign land for nothing more than prayerful thanks"—the radio series cemented Dooley's crossover reputation as both Catholic folk hero and exemplary young American.[57] The image was a carefully constructed one, but it drew energy from the same spontaneous sense of internationalist idealism that animated the student activists of Gloria Steinem's Independent Research Service. "The children were electrified!" recalled a Sacred Heart nun about Dooley's visit to his old St. Louis school. "I really felt he was like a Pied Piper, and they would all have followed him out of the front door if we had not directed them elsewhere!"[58]

Dazzling though public performances of the Dooley persona undoubtedly were, behind the scenes serious difficulties were emerging. Fears that the cause of his "resignation" from the Navy might be exposed, perhaps as a result of a deliberate leak by enemies in the CIA, constantly haunted Dooley. His health took a sudden turn for the worse in August 1959, when a lump in his chest was diagnosed as malignant melanoma, an especially aggressive form of cancer. Meanwhile, organizational problems threatened to wreck Dooley's plans to extend his overseas medical empire. A personal rift between him and Peter Comanduras, the man brought in to run MEDICO while Dr. America was in the field practicing, drained the venture of valuable energy and goodwill. The IRC, too, was proving a less than ideal sponsor, partly because it demanded constant public endorsement from Dooley in return for its patronage, and partly because the Vietnam Lobby had begun to argue internally over the question of support for the increasingly autocratic Diem, with leftists such as Norman Thomas quitting the American Friends of Vietnam in protest and even true believers such as Buttinger starting to entertain doubts.[59] Edward Lansdale was disgusted by this wavering, describing the non-communist left intellectuals around the AFV (and, by implication, the IRC) as "a group of dilettantes" and "Madison Avenue eggheads."[60] By 1960, the IRC had severed its ties with MEDICO and withdrawn from its other Asian commitments, which were now turned over to the care of the Asia Foundation.[61]

At this point, there appeared in Dooley's life the last in a line of patrons with covert connections to the CIA. Paul Hellmuth was a Catholic lawyer from Boston who acted as sole trustee of the J. Frederick Brown Foundation, and was cotrustee of the Independence Foundation, two of the Agency's main conduits to the National Student Association. He also helped create, and later ran, Anderson Security, a CIA front company with ties to the Nixon administration that specialized in debugging offices and shredding sensitive documents. It was in the fall of 1959 that Hellmuth became Dooley's attorney and, in short order, most trusted confidant. While it seems reasonable to assume that, in doing so, he was acting at the behest of the CIA, it is only fair to note also that he was sincerely impressed by his new charge's ability to inspire humanitarianism in others, even proposing a program he called "The Transmigration of

Dooleyites" to send young American aid workers abroad in a scheme similar to the Peace Corps created by the Kennedy administration.[62] Whatever his motivation, Hellmuth proved a most dedicated manager of the young medic's affairs, arranging everything from the supply of office furniture for MEDICO to the purchase of personal gifts on his behalf.[63] "All we had to do was indicate a need, and somehow he found a way to fill it," remembered one of Dooley's assistants, Teresa Gallagher.[64] A sort of lay priest in his private life, Hellmuth also brought about a closer relationship between the jungle doctor and the influential president of Notre Dame, Father Theodore Hesburgh, who in June 1960 presided over a graduation ceremony at which Dooley received a honorary doctorate from his alma mater, stealing the show from other honorees such as President Eisenhower and Cardinal Montini, the future Pope Paul VI.

Hellmuth, though, was powerless in the face of Dooley's cancer, which by December 1960 had spread to every part of his body. The doctor confronted his illness with typical bravado, continuing to work furiously hard and even agreeing to the filming of a CBS documentary, *Biography of a Cancer*, to help educate fellow sufferers and promote MEDICO. It was a losing battle, however. Dooley died in his sleep in January 1961, a day after his thirty-fourth birthday, and was laid to rest at the Calvary Cemetery in St. Louis following a funeral attended, despite freezing midwinter weather, by thousands of mourners. A Gallup poll taken just days after his death ranked him as third in the list of "Most Esteemed Men" in the world, after only President Eisenhower and the Pope.[65]

Given the multifaceted nature of his short career, it is difficult to tell how Dooley's reputation would have developed had he lived. What is clear, though, is that his untimely death did not enhance his image. In 1963, the threat of financial extinction forced MEDICO, his major concrete legacy, to merge with another relief organization, CARE. Shortly afterward, stories began to appear about his intelligence-gathering activities for the CIA (ironically, the most detailed information emerged in the course of an unsuccessful campaign to have him canonized) and, later, about his sexuality. Where Americans had previously seen a selfless Christian patriot, now they beheld a morally compromised and ethnocentric egotist whose grossly distorted portrayals of Southeast Asia had helped create (to quote journalist Nicholas von Hoffman) "a climate of public misunderstanding that made the war in Vietnam possible."[66]

Meanwhile, the Vietnam Lobby that had sponsored Dooley also became the target of growing suspicion and criticism. Although the International Rescue Committee survived the U.S. disaster in Indochina intact, the American Friends of Vietnam, already weakened by the resignations of Joseph Buttinger and Iron Mike O'Daniel (the latter quit in 1963 after the organization eventually decided to renounce Diem, only weeks before the Vietnamese premier was murdered, with Kennedy administration connivance, in a palace coup), collapsed in 1965, thanks to hostile publicity resulting from the *Ramparts* exposé. At the same time, Edward Lansdale, having failed to work the same magic on Diem as he had on Magsaysay, found himself increasingly sidelined as an influence on U.S. policy-making in Vietnam, although his image as the diabolically cunning genius of Cold War covert operations lived on through such barely disguised portrayals as "General Y" in filmmaker Oliver Stone's conspiracy-theory interpretation of the Kennedy assassination, *JFK*.

As for Dooley himself, he remains too complex and ambiguous a figure on which to pronounce any final judgment, although with the sting having gone from the earliest revisionist denunciations of him, it would seem unjust not to acknowledge his extraordinary talents, the hardships he endured helping others, and the unforeseen nature of the massive attitudinal changes that occurred after his death, making actions that once seemed admirable (such as cooperating with the CIA) questionable, if not downright reprehensible.

Patrick J. Peyton had several things in common with Tom Dooley: both were Irish-American Catholics whose overseas missions attracted the secret patronage of the CIA. In other respects, however, the two men were very different. To begin with, Peyton's upbringing in County Mayo, Ireland, was worlds removed from lace-curtain St. Louis, Missouri. Born the sixth of nine children into a deeply religious but poverty-stricken family, Peyton emigrated to the United States in 1928, at the age of nineteen, settling in Scranton, Pennsylvania, where he worked as a janitor in St Joseph's Cathedral. His interrupted schooling seemed to have wrecked childhood dreams of becoming a priest, but in 1929 that ambition was rekindled when a mission band from the Holy Cross Congregation, a missionary and educational order whose roots could be traced to revolutionary France, came to Scranton. After returning to school and graduating magna cum laude from Notre Dame in 1937, Peyton entered Holy Cross College, a theologate of the Holy Cross Congregation associated with Catholic University in Washington, D.C. Shortly afterward, his hopes appeared to have been dashed again when he was diagnosed with an advanced case of tuberculosis and told that he would likely die unless he underwent radical surgery. Challenged by one of his Notre Dame professors to demonstrate his faith, Peyton prayed to the Virgin Mary—and his lungs began to clear. Having made a full recovery, which he later called "a miraculous healing," he returned to his studies and became a priest in June 1941.[67]

If not as dramatic as Paul's conversion on his way to Damascas, Peyton's illness was certainly the turning point in his career, similar to the effect that Dooley's experience in Haiphong had on the Catholic doctor. "Mary, I hope I will never disgrace you" were Peyton's first words on regaining his health, and from that moment he dedicated his life, with a single-mindedness that verged on obsession, to Marian devotion.[68] Casting around for ways to promote his cause, he remembered how during his childhood his parents had gathered their children together at the end of each day to say the rosary. To Peyton, this act was not only "the greatest tribute that could possibly be given," it also made their humble home into "a cradle, a school, a university, a library and, most of all, a little church."[69] In 1942, he wrote his Holy Cross superiors, asking their permission to devote himself to the mission of bringing the rosary back to ten million American homes. Impressed by his zeal, they granted him the rare favor of an independent apostolate. After a massive letter-writing campaign, Peyton established a Family Rosary Crusade office in Albany, New York. Next, following a trail blazed by Fulton Sheen (as well as the notoriously racist "radio priest," Charles Coughlin), Peyton took to the airwaves on Mother's Day 1945 with a half-hour broadcast that included a blessing from Francis Spellman; a guest spot by Bing Crosby; and the nation's most "loved and revered family," the Sullivans of Iowa, who had lost five sons on a battleship sunk in the Pacific, leading the rosary.[70]

Peyton's radio show, which was followed by the launch two years later of the star-studded weekly broadcast *Family Theater of the Air*, fit the postwar mood of many American Catholics. As well as seeing an upsurge of popular religiosity, the 1940s and 1950s witnessed the emergence of widespread anxiety about the strength of the nuclear family, an institution believed to be under threat from such scourges of modernity as divorce, birth control, and juvenile delinquency.[71] With his rosy-hued invocations of his rustic Irish childhood, stern admonitions that family disunity was "the deadly sin of our age," and memorable slogan "The family that prays together stays together," Peyton captured the spirit of the times perfectly.[72] Not all Catholic clerics approved of his brand of populist pietism, however; indeed, several of his superiors in Holy Cross came to regret the independence they had allowed him, not least because Peyton was prone to stating that he owed his obedience to Mary, not them. "We really didn't like that," recalled a fellow religious.[73] Still, it was difficult to argue with Peyton's dedication to the Virgin—colleagues later remembered that he would appear detached, even sullen, during mealtimes, until the conversation turned to Mary, at which point he would suddenly become animated, as if a lightbulb had been switched on[74]—just as it was impossible not to admire his ingenuity in using mass entertainment media to spread his message. Not content with the success of the Family Theater on radio, during the 1950s the rosary priest branched out into television, making devotional dramas such as *That I May See* and *Hill Number One* (the latter notable for the acting debut of James Dean), and then into film, organizing the production of fifteen half-hour films about the mysteries of the rosary, shot in Spain in 1956 under the direction of Joseph Breen, Jr., son of the famous movie censor, with the assistance of Generalísimo Francisco Franco.

Most remarkable, however, was Peyton's success in utilizing a form of worship usually associated with Protestant evangelizing: the open-air prayer meeting. Starting in London, Ontario, in 1948, the Family Rosary Crusade staged a series of rallies at which crowds, often more than a hundred thousand strong, heard the priest reminisce about his upbringing in Ireland, describe his miraculous recovery, and recite the rosary. The diocesan crusades all followed the same basic pattern, which Peyton likened to a military campaign. First there was an aerial bombardment, with mass media being used to soften the ground. Next came the crusade itself, with religious and lay assistants moving into localities like so many troops seeking to capture territory from the enemy, the climactic battle being the rally itself. Following the Family Rosary's inevitable victory, there was an occupation, a follow-up campaign designed to maintain the devotional intensity aroused by Peyton.[75] He was, by all accounts, an extraordinarily effective preacher. While far from eloquent—Bishop Thomas Flynn of Lancaster, England, described him as "quite artless, unstudied, [and] simple"—he nonetheless succeeded in conveying, with his massive, six-foot, four-inch frame, broad countenance, and Irish brogue, "a different kind of eloquence that captured you, that made you hang on to what he was saying."[76] The contrast between the Elmer Gantry–like razzmatazz of the buildup to the rallies and the painfully obvious sincerity and humility of Peyton in person made his appearances all the more poignant and affecting. By 1958, the Family Rosary Crusade had traveled to Europe, the Middle and Far East, Australasia, and Africa, winning literally millions of new devotees for the Virgin. One prize still eluded Peyton, however, a continent that was home to a quarter of the world's Catholic population, South America.

Of course, the Family Rosary Crusade was not the only U.S. organization interested in influencing the beliefs of South Americans. In addition to blatant interventions of the sort that took place in Guatemala in 1954, Cuba in 1961, and Chile in 1973, the CIA was constantly involved in more subtle ideological actions intended to secure U.S. hegemony in the western hemisphere. American labor organizations were one important instrument in this effort, with the U.S. sections of international trade secretariats—transnational bodies supposedly representing all the workers in a particular industry—often doubling as fronts for Agency operations. Hence, in 1963 CIA agents in the American Federation of State, County, and Municipal Employees (AFSCME), the U.S. affiliate of the Public Service International (PSI), incited a strike by civil servants in British Guiana that led to the unseating of the leftist prime minister, Cheddi Jagan.[77]

Supplementing these industry-specific activities were a host of labor education and research projects, the most wide-ranging of which was the American Institute of Free Labor Development (AIFLD), a trade unionist training program established in 1962 with headquarters near Washington and local centers dotted around South America. Ostensibly funded by the AFL-CIO, American business leaders, and the U.S. Agency for International Development (AID) (another descendant of the Marshall Plan's Economic Cooperation Administration), the AIFLD was heavily connected, through its Executive Director Serafino Romualdi (once labor counsel for Nelson Rockefeller's Office of Inter-American Affairs) and Social Projects Director William C. Doherty, Jr., to the Lovestone apparatus and the International Organizations Division.[78] Performing similar work, although on a smaller scale, was the New York–based Institute of International Labor Research, Inc., a program for "strengthening democratic forces" in central America and the Caribbean headed by Norman Thomas, administered by former Rumanian émigré and Radio Free Europe officer Sacha Volman, and covertly funded, via the foundation of grape juice magnate J. M. Kaplan, by the IOD.[79] Along with other NCL leaders such as Victor Reuther, Allard Lowenstein, and civil rights activist Bayard Rustin, Volman and Thomas also participated in the Committee on Free Elections in the Dominican Republic, a CIA-inspired effort to lend international credibility to a 1966 ballot effectively rigged against the socialist former president, Juan Bosch, with Thomas reprising the role he had performed in Vietnam in 1956 by declaring the elections fair before the results had been announced.[80]

In the Cold War struggle for South American hearts and minds, Christian evangelists were potentially more useful even than U.S. labor leaders. The employment of missionaries by intelligence agencies was nothing new. During World War II, the Baptist John Birch worked for the OSS in China before being killed (or "martyred," as many American conservatives believed) by communist soldiers when leading a patrol of Chinese Nationalists.[81] Meanwhile, William Cameron ("Cam") Townsend, founder of the Summer Institute of Linguistics and the Wycliffe Bible Translators, provided extensive intelligence to Nelson Rockefeller in return for logistical support as Townsend and his followers proselytized the bibleless tribes of the Amazon (he later worked with Edward Lansdale in the Philippines and Vietnam).[82] Catholic missionaries, however, offered the CIA the most tactical advantage in South America. Although Catholicism was clearly the greatest ideological counterweight to communism on the politically turbulent continent, the church there was widely perceived to be in a state of crisis, with a shortage of religious ordinations, doctrinal and liturgical ignorance rampant among the poor, and a commonly held view that clergy had failed to address the need for social action in many countries. It was against this background that "concerned" American missionaries from such Catholic societies as Maryknoll and the Jesuits traveled south with the twin aims of containing communism and promoting development—and they willingly collaborated with intelligence officers in local CIA stations. The best personification of this alliance was Belgian Jesuit Roger Vekemans, a former resistance fighter and liberal anticommunist who accepted covert CIA subsidies via the New York–based International Development Foundation to finance various social reform programs in Chile.[83]

Although it lacked the liberal aspect of much postwar Catholic missionary work in South America—indeed, its social implications were distinctly conservative—Patrick Peyton's Family Rosary Crusade fit the CIA's bill in several important respects. The intense piety it aroused in working-class Catholics was an extremely effective antidote against the contagion of communism. Peyton himself was deeply conscious of the political dimension of his mission, proudly proclaiming in a 1946 radio broadcast, "The rosary is the offensive weapon that will destroy Communism—the great evil that seeks to destroy the faith." Above all, the Crusade was very well planned and executed. It used a "proven technique of infiltration, employing indigenous organizations, communications, and peoples to penetrate Communist strongholds in depth . . . with a weapon Communists cannot fight on equal ground," noted a confidential 1962 report entitled "United States Security and the Power of Prayer." The same report concluded, "There is no other organization available which can mobilize local forces in Latin America on such a mass basis to accomplish these objectives."[84]

Peyton's anticommunist credentials notwithstanding, he might well never have featured in the CIA's plans for South America had it not been for the offices of a figure who came to perform a role in his life similar to that played in Tom Dooley's by Edward Lansdale. J. Peter Grace was president of a multimillion-dollar international corporation created by his great-grandfather, W. R. Grace, with interests in transport, sugar, and mining in South America. A hard-driven man, he always wore two watches, one showing the local time of wherever he happened to be, the other the hour back at his New York headquarters. He also carried a pistol tucked into his belt, which he would casually display "when showing off a thirty-four-inch waist—one of his many vanities."[85] A fierce believer in free enterprise and the "American way," Grace was an officer in a number of CIA front organizations, including AMCOMLIB, Aid Refugee Chinese Intellectuals, Inc., and—perhaps not surprisingly, given his company's stake in various South American industries—the American Institute of Free Labor Development. Grace was also a devout Catholic who wielded immense power within the American church through his position as president of the eastern chapter of the U.S. Knights of Malta (other members of this secretive chivalric order included two Directors of Central Intelligence, William Casey and John A. McCone).[86] His self-image as a kind of religious knight or protector of the faith appears to have earned him equal measures of gratitude and suspicion from the Catholic hierarchy.

Grace and Peyton first met on board ship in 1946 when the latter was returning to Ireland after his ordination, and the two immediately became ardent mutual devotees. The businessman was not only struck by the priest's holiness, he also quickly grasped the potency of his message as a defense against the various forces threatening the American way of life.[87] As well as soliciting donations from business acquaintances, Grace set up permanent financial structures for Crusade operations and arranged loans to Peyton of thousands of dollars (none of which was ever repaid) through his family's New York bank. For his part, Peyton was greatly relieved to be released from the temporal concerns of his mission and placed his trust in his lay champion entirely. "Of all men in the entire world Peter is the one, and the only one to whom we can look for the financial protection, defense, and security of the Crusade," he told a fellow religious.[88] Hence, in 1958, when Peyton resolved to take his crusade south of the border, it was no surprise that he should have sought assistance from Grace, who, equally predictably, "pledged that he would spare no effort in order to get financial help for us to cover Latin America" (as the priest told his superiors).[89]

Grace was as good as his word. In July 1958, he wrote his friend John Moore, chairman of the influential Business Advisory Council, asking "how we can get a movement similar to that described by Father Peyton financed—whether it be through the CIA, through Franco, or through some foundation."[90] Several months later, in mid-November, the two men approached Allen Dulles, who requested a formal, written project proposal from Grace. The businessman duly sent the Director of Central Intelligence a twelve-page letter on November 24 summarizing the rosary priest's achievements to date, pointing out the political potential of his message in South America, and estimating the Crusade's financial requirements at $500,000.

> When one considers, Mr. Dulles, that this priest came here from Ireland at age nineteen and went to Hollywood in 1945 with nothing but his

> faith and a dedicated will to win the world to family prayer and unity, with no previous experience or education in the entertainment field, I think it is pretty clear that when one gets behind this man, one is backing a proven winner.[91]

Dulles was favorably impressed and in early December summoned Grace to Washington, where they met in the White House office of Richard Nixon. The Vice President, who earlier in the year had hosted a meeting between Grace and other U.S. business giants with South American interests (among them David Rockefeller and Juan T. Trippe of Pan American Airways), was similarly taken with the proposal, exclaiming about Peyton, "Bring him by the office—must be fantastic."[92] Further meetings at Grace's home in Manhasset, New York, took place early in 1959, leading to the project's approval "on a pilot basis" and a payment of $20,000 in seed money.[93] Dulles's main proviso, that the money not be passed through "an individual or ostensibly a church organization" but rather via "a front organization," appears to have been satisfied by Grace's proposal that an entity called The Crusade for Family Prayer, incorporated in New York in 1954, act as the "intermediate group."[94] This measure was intended, presumably, to circumvent "our traditional and sound doctrine of separation of Church and state," which even Grace admitted was a problem.[95] Peyton, who had been kept informed of the negotiations' progress, was delighted by this outcome, hastening to tell his Holy Cross superiors "that if this proving goes through there will be more help forthcoming . . . to advance the wishes and will and person of Our Blessed Mother."[96]

Peyton did not have to wait long for "this proving." The pilot crusade, which took place in the Chilean town of La Serena (the CIA's choice—Peyton had originally favored Bolivia as his point of entry into South America), was considered so successful that in late April 1960, at a meeting with Grace and "another great friend of the Family Rosary Crusade" at Washington's Carlton hotel, the priest learned that he would be granted "five times what we received for entrance into Chile, for the entrance into another Latin American country."[97] The next target was soon revealed as Caracas, Venezuela, a city described by Peyton as "ready for revolution, very restless and disturbed."[98] Supported by U.S. Steel executive Walter Donnelly (who had attended Nixon's 1958 summit on South America), the Crusade delivered "a tremendous blow to the Communists and the Castroites," overcoming such acts of sabotage as the defacement of posters and even bomb threats to draw a crowd of 600,000 to the final rally on July 16.[99] After Caracas, it was off to Colombia, where a rally held in Bogotá in March 1962 was attended by some 1 million worshippers.[100]

No doubt U.S. officials were gratified by the Crusade's popularity in South America, just as Peyton clearly reveled in the opportunity to win new acolytes for the Virgin. Still, there were strains in this covert partnership of the sort that have always affected church-state relations, as well as more specific tensions typical of collaborations between the CIA and front organizations it had not created from scratch (such as, for example, the Free Trade Union Committee). Whereas Peyton measured a crusade's success by the number of religious pledges it gathered, intelligence officers looked for evidence of political impact, scrutinizing election results to see if communist candidates were suffering at the polls and comparing the attendance at rosary rallies with that at Party meetings. This kind of assessment took time, and often led to delays in the payment of subsidies, which understandably irritated Peyton. Why, he asked Grace, were "our friends . . . so demanding on the Family Rosary Crusade" when they "do not have a one hundred percent batting average" themselves?[101] Then there was the CIA's habit of suddenly shifting country targets according to the exigencies of South American politics, often undoing months of preparation by the Crusade (again reminiscent of the OPC's dealings with the Lovestoneites). One such "abrupt change in our plans took place at the end of the Bogotá crusade," Peyton informed Grace, "when it was decided that all plans had to be postponed and the Crusade effort should be immediately concentrated in Recife and Rio de Janeiro." The resulting Brazilian campaign, which lasted from 1962 to 1964, was constantly troubled by operational glitches, necessitating a series of high-level meetings between Grace, Donnelly, and "our benefactor" to "iron out some of the past communication difficulties" (not unlike the summits between the AFL and CIA in 1950 and 1951).[102]

For all these problems, Peyton's impact in Brazil was arguably greater than in any other South American country. The Crusade had by 1962 perfected an evangelical technique it called the "Popular Mission," which involved locally recruited technicians using mobile projection equipment to show the Spanish-made devotional films at open-air venues, with commentaries provided by lay catechists. To this were now added other spectacular effects designed to appeal to the massive populations of urban centers such as Rio de Janeiro, where the famous statue of the Cristo do Corcovado was adorned with a thirty-meter-long illuminated rosary and an eight-meter-high cross. When Peyton preached in the city on December 16, 1962, 1.5 million Brazilians came to listen. A year later, on the Feast of the Immaculate Conception (December 8, 1963), also declared Family Day by President João Goulart, the Crusade sponsored an hour-long television broadcast from Rio that featured, among others, Bing Crosby, soccer superstar Pele, and Agostinho dos Santos, the self-styled "bossa nova king of Brazil," who performed a Samba version of "Ave Maria." The program, which was also shown in other South American countries, reached the single greatest viewing audience in the Family Rosary's history.[103]

These astonishing feats were accomplished against a background of growing political unrest in Brazil, which culminated in March 1964 with the overthrow of President Goulart in a military coup led by the Army's Chief of Staff, General Humberto Castello Branco. Goulart had incurred the displeasure of Washington by pursuing such policies as appointing socialists to his cabinet, and the CIA was deeply implicated in the events that led to his unseating, through links both to local right-wing groups and U.S. organizations such as the AIFLD.[104] It is, of course, impossible to say for certain what effect the Catholic traditionalism of the Family Rosary Crusade had on the popular political mood in Brazil, but various well-placed observers reckoned it was considerable. According to one ecclesiastical authority, "the Rosary . . . consolidated the ties which existed between the people's aspirations and the patriotic vigilance of the Armed Forces."[105] "I admire the Crusade," General Branco himself announced, shortly after the coup. "Since the Great Meeting in Rio de Janeiro, I give it credit . . . for the formation of the public opinion of the Brazilian people in order to have the valor to bring about the revolution of March 31."[106] Patrick Peyton was, therefore, only telling the truth when he reported to his Holy Cross superiors, "much credit is given by great leaders in the Church and State in Brazil to the Family Rosary Crusade in the overthrow of the Goulart Government."[107]

As it turned out, Peyton's pleasure at events in Brazil was not shared by his Holy Cross colleagues. The Catholic church of 1964 was a very different institution from the one that had approved the rosary priest's entry into South America in 1958. The death that year of the unbending anticommunist Pope Pius XII and election of the reforming John XXIII opened a new era of dialogue between Catholics and communists. John's first major encyclical, *Mater et Magistra*, in July 1961, even proposed that it was colonialism, not communism, that was the main cause of Third World problems.[108] Meanwhile, the Second Vatican Council, which met in four sessions between 1962 and 1965, wrought a profound transformation in Catholic doctrine and observance, downgrading rote catechisms and ritualistic devotion in favor of an emphasis on the immanence of God and the church as a community of equals. Combined with local factors (among them the influence of liberal evangelists from the United States), these developments changed many South American clerics from defenders of the established order into advocates of the oppressed—and leading critics of the wave of militarism then appearing to engulf the continent. This religious movement, later known as "liberation theology," was especially strong in Brazil, where Catholic prelates such as Dom Hélder Câmara proclaimed the "Church of the Poor."[109] Although Peyton attempted to revise his ministry of family prayer in line with Vatican II, his theological conservatism and unquestioning anticommunism set him at odds with the spirit of the postconciliar hierarchy. His religious superiors, already peeved by his assertiveness, were therefore dismayed by the reports linking him to the Branco coup. Noting that some Brazilian bishops reckoned the new regime "extremely reactionary and conservative," the Superior General, Germain-Marie Lalande, instructed Peyton's Provincial Superior, Richard H. Sullivan, to tell the rosary priest and his associates to make sure "that nothing in their work is interpreted as smacking of politics." Sullivan thought that this "would be the last thing that Father Peyton would grant," but agreed that it should be "the goal for the Crusade that he avoid the possibility that politics use him."[110]

Lalande's misgivings about Peyton increased suddenly in October 1964 when he found out about the Crusade's secret financing by the CIA. His informer was Theodore Hesburgh, who had himself learned of the arrangement directly from the chairman of Notre Dame's board of trustees, Peter Grace. "I cannot alter my opinion that this situation is extremely dangerous," Hesburgh wrote Lalande, clearly in some dismay. "This is not to deny the good work that has been done by the Family Rosary, but I believe that all of the good would be destroyed, as well as many other innocent works, if the facts of this matter ever came to light. I am also reasonably sure that many of the American hierarchy would be horrified at the thought."[111] Evidently of the same mind, Lalande immediately called Peyton to the Holy Cross Generalate in Rome, where the two met, along with Assistant General Bernard Mullahy, on October 24. Apparently undaunted, the rosary priest related the history of his relationship with Peter Grace, emphasizing the businessman's religiosity and devotion to the Family Rosary. He then launched into a spirited defense of the secret subsidies, pointing out that other groups and individuals also received such payments (among those mentioned by name were Maryknoll, Vekemans, and Billy Graham), predicting dire consequences for both the Crusade and its U.S. base, the Holy Cross's eastern province, if the funding were terminated, and claiming that the chances of being found out were extremely slim, probably in the region of 5 percent. Lalande, however, was unswayed, commanding "that the Crusade slowly become free of this source of revenue and that it only undertake the work that is possible from other sources . . . that are more normal." The meeting ended with an agreement that, while Peyton could continue to accept support from the CIA for the moment, he "must break away when it is provided from another source."[112]

Lalande remained apprehensive, however, telling Sullivan in February 1965 that he had communicated with a former CIA officer who reckoned that there was "a much higher than 5% chance that the recipients of funds from the CIA will become known." Eventually, after lengthy consultations with his assistants, the Superior General decided to seek an audience with the Holy Father himself and, on July 9, 1965, met privately in the Vatican with Paul VI (John had died two years previously). In a report on the meeting to Sullivan, Lalande insisted that he had put both sides of the argument to the Pope, presenting Peyton's viewpoint as well as his own, but a follow-up letter to Paul suggests otherwise. "The CIA is the ultra-secret spy organization of the United States," the Holy Cross superior told the pontiff. "If the CIA has agreed to furnish money to the Rosary Crusade for its work in Latin America, it is surely not because of any religious motivation, but because it believes that the Crusade, in its work, is a way to promote the American policy of appeasing the popular masses." Although Peyton and Grace believed that the secret was safe "because of the ultra-secret character of the CIA," Lalande continued, other well-placed Americans, such as Hesburgh, thought that exposure was quite likely. The Pope sided with Lalande, ruling that "the Family Rosary . . . should absolutely not accept funds or help from the source you are acquainted with." When Lalande remarked that Peyton would probably want to come to Rome to plead his case in person, Paul responded, "Please tell Father Peyton that it is the Holy Father who wants the question settled in this way and that the Holy Father has understood the problem very well." He then added, "Tell Father Peyton that I shall say a special Hail Mary for him."[113]

Despite this unequivocal backing from the Holy See, Lalande still did not find it easy to disentangle the Family Rosary from the CIA. In September he learned that, only a few days before his audience with the Pope, Peyton had accepted an offer of $200,000 for follow-up work in Chile, Colombia, and Venezuela, and a new crusade in Ecuador. As Sullivan pointed out, it would be impossible to find replacement support for these ventures at such short notice, and hard to explain their sudden cancellation, so Lalande reluctantly authorized the money's expenditure, on the understanding that this was the final time he would do so.[114] The Vatican, meanwhile, was breathing down the Superior General's neck, demanding a full accounting of the monies the Family Rosary had received from Grace for its South American mission and instructing him to keep a close eye on Peyton.[115] Apart from the potentially disastrous consequences of the CIA subsidies becoming public knowledge, high-placed officials in Rome, such as Secretary of State Amleto Cardinal Cicognani, were concerned about the Crusade's identification with right-wing regimes in Brazil and Spain, as well as about its lack of "pastoral or theological foundation." This last complaint was echoed in Lalande's demand, also reflecting the influence of Vatican II, that the Family Rosary embark on a "renewal in its methods and its work in a post-conciliar Church."[116]

Neither Peyton nor his secretive patrons in the CIA were squelched so easily. Throughout the fall of 1965, Lalande received intimations that, despite the Vatican's injunction, "the company which has given him assistance . . . might consider that there are ways of 'getting around' the prohibition."[117] On December 20 the exasperated Holy Cross Superior General (by all accounts, usually a cheerful and even-tempered man) instructed Sullivan to make it clear to Peyton that "if he does not carry out the wish of the Holy See," he, Lalande, would recall all "religious engaged in the apostolate of the Crusade" and "acquaint the bishops of South America with the situation of the Family Rosary Crusade."[118]

Still, the Crusade's relationship with the CIA was not ended, with the Agency delaying payment of the subsidies it had promised in July and questions arising about the financing of postcrusade work in Ecuador.[119] In April 1966, at a meeting of eastern province priests in Montreal, Lalande was horrified to learn how thoroughly the Family Rosary had been controlled not only by the CIA, which has "decided for several years now the places where the crusades should take place," but also by "large American capitalist enterprises that have interests in Latin America." As a result of his "blind and exaggerated confidence in Peter Grace," the Superior General realized, Peyton did "not see very clearly in all of this." At the close of the meeting, Lalande set specific deadlines in June and September, after which no official funds could be received by the Crusade. Nonetheless, Grace and Peyton persisted, proposing that Francis Spellman take over as the principal conduit of CIA support for the Family Rosary. Lalande countered by warning Sullivan that he would inform Rome if he ever discovered any evidence of Spellman's performing such a role. Finally, by October, the last of the secret funds had changed hands, and Lalande breathed a sigh of relief. "Not a day passes when we do not read in the papers . . . harsh criticisms about the organization which was procuring this aid," he remarked to Sullivan. But even then the Superior General was not entirely released from his anxiety about the Family Rosary Crusade. Some surplus funds, it appeared, remained locked in a strongbox in the Immigrants Bank in New York, and the only two with keys were Patrick Peyton and Peter Grace.[120]

Despite suffering recurrent poor health as a result of the huge demands he made on himself, Peyton lived to a ripe old age, dying at the age of eighty-three in 1992. His reputation, which had suffered in the wake of Vatican II and the accompanying liberalization of American Catholicism, was largely restored by the time of his death, thanks in no small part to the revival of Catholic traditionalism and anticommunism that occurred during the papacy of John Paul II. It remains to be seen whether a campaign to have him canonized, launched in 2001, will be derailed by revelations about his links to the CIA, as happened in the case of Tom Dooley. Any assessment of this episode in his life would have to take account of the fact that, unlike Dooley, Peyton was fully witting of the Agency's role in the Family Rosary Crusade. At the same time, it should also acknowledge the complete trust Peyton placed in his Edward Lansdale, J. Peter Grace, and his utter conviction that all other considerations were secondary to the cause of Marian devotion.

As for the larger pattern of secret CIA funding for Catholic missionaries to which Peyton's example points, several conclusions seem possible, apart from the perhaps obvious point that the story of Peyton and his Family Rosary Crusade was symptomatic of the blurring between religion and politics that has been a dominant theme in recent American history. One is that, like many of the unnatural institutional alliances conjured into existence by the covert Cold War, the partnership was beset by various tensions and disagreements, strongly echoing earlier church-state conflicts involving perceived secular usurpations of ecclesiastical authority. Another is that, while in the short term the secret subsidies appear to have served the CIA's interests well, as shown in Peyton's impact on Brazilian politics, their eventual exposure badly damaged the United States's image, turning even anticommunist missionaries against the American government.[121]

Finally, the CIA's use of the Family Rosary Crusade in South America throws a revealing light on the Agency's internal politics. It is generally assumed that the International Organizations Division was predominantly liberal and internationalist in its political sympathies, an image personified by the world-federalist, UN-supporting target of McCarthyism Cord Meyer. The examples of the National Student Association, the Committee of Correspondence, and even the Kennedyesque, "crossover" Catholic Tom Dooley, with his links to the Ugly American Edward Lansdale and NCL-dominated Vietnam Lobby, would seem to confirm this impression. However, the pre–Vatican II Catholicism of Patrick Peyton and the aggressive Americanism of Peter Grace complicate the picture, suggesting that, as in the realm of cultural patronage and aesthetic taste, the CIA was rather more flexible and pragmatic in its choice of front groups than has previously been supposed. Defeating communism and advancing American power were the primary objectives; the promotion of social progress and international understanding came second.

NINE

Into Africa

AFRICAN AMERICANS

On a cold night in early November 1960 an audience gathered at the American Church on the Quai D'Orsay in Paris to hear a lecture entitled "The Situation of the Black Artist and Intellectual in the United States." The speaker, Richard Wright, was the son of an illiterate Mississippi sharecropper who had won literary fame and fortune during the 1940s as the creator of one of the great characters in African American fiction, Bigger Thomas, the antihero of Wright's debut novel, *Native Son*. Now, however, living the life of the exiled American writer in Paris, Wright was plagued by illness, self-doubt, and financial hardship. Disheveled and visibly ailing, he stunned his listeners by launching into a furious tirade against his country of birth. Black American artists lived in "a nightmarish jungle" under a government that systematically silenced those who tried to speak out against the racial status quo.[1] Overseas, the same government not only spied on expatriate U.S. citizens in cities such as Paris, including Wright himself, it also secretly funded apparently radical groups in an effort to defuse challenges to its growing global power. "I'd say that most revolutionary movements in the Western world are government-sponsored," Wright claimed. "They are launched by *agents provocateurs* to organize the discontented so that the Government can keep an eye on them." The writer concluded his long, rambling speech with an implied promise of more revelations to come. "I think that mental health urges us to bring all of these hidden things into the open where they can be publicly dealt with," he said.[2]

A few weeks later, Wright lay dead in a Parisian clinic. He was only fifty-two years old.

The aim of this chapter is not to investigate the mysterious circumstances of Wright's death (there have been recurrent rumors that he was murdered).[3] Rather it is to explore his claim that the U.S. government was involved in the covert funding of black nationalist groups. In particular, the chapter will tell the story of the CIA's principal front organization in the African American community, the American Society of African Culture (AMSAC)—a group that, ironically, Richard Wright himself had helped to create.

The suggestion that the CIA fielded an African American front group is less implausible than it might at first sound. The U.S. Communist Party had a long tradition of front activities among American blacks, a group historically neglected by more mainstream white reformers. (Wright himself had been a communist during the 1930s, before breaking with the party in the early 1940s, then contributing to the confessional classic, *The God That Failed.*) In the post-1945 period, this tradition merged with the exigencies of the Cold War to produce a series of protest actions that seriously embarrassed American officialdom in its confrontation with the Soviet Union, such as the presentation to the United Nations by the communist-controlled Civil Rights Congress of a petition alleging that the United States was engaged in a campaign of genocide against its black citizens.[4]

By the mid-1950s, two developments had occurred that made the need for a response to such provocations all the more urgent. One was an escalation in the racial violence endemic in the American South, as the Supreme Court's 1954 *Brown* decision and the emergence of the civil rights movement threatened the survival of the region's segregationist order, and southern white supremacists resorted to any means necessary to preserve it. The other was the continuing retreat of the European powers from their colonial dominion in the Third World and the ensuing contest between the superpowers for the political allegiance of the "emerging nations." Images of southern police turning dogs and fire hoses on nonviolent black protestors played particularly badly in postcolonial Africa, a region of growing strategic and economic importance where Cold War propagandists had to compete for ideological influence with new currents of black cultural nationalism. It was against this background that U.S. government agencies, including the CIA, began casting around for black American leaders who might be called on to paint a positive picture of their country's race relations and help steer newly independent African nations away from the communist camp.[5]

Where, though, to find such leaders? What recent tradition of engagement with Africa there was among black Americans belonged mainly to the left and such organizations as the Council on African Affairs (CAA), which espoused a mixture of socialist economic ideals and a diasporic cultural consciousness known as pan-Africanism.[6] The CAA boasted two of the most eminent African Americans of the day, singer and actor Paul Robeson, and W. E. B. Du Bois, distinguished scholar and founding father of the powerful African American civil rights group, the National Association for the Advancement of Colored People (NAACP). As the organizer of a series of pan-African congresses in Europe (the first of which, held in Paris in 1919, coincided with the Versailles Peace Conference), Du Bois was very well connected with African and African diaspora intellectuals. Nonetheless, by 1950 the rise of Cold War anticommunism had pushed the CAA beyond the political pale (just as it helped move the NAACP toward the Truman administration) and made political pariahs of Du Bois and, especially, Robeson, who in that year was denied a passport by the State Department. Clearly, U.S. government officers would have to look elsewhere for their black allies.[7]

Fortunately for them, the same developments that had suddenly made winning the battle for African hearts and minds so crucial—decolonization and the rise of the civil rights movement—were also producing a new generation of more moderate black American leaders who shared the CAA's interest in Africa but not its radicalism. Typical of this breed was a Columbia University–educated social scientist and CCNY professor of government, John A. Davis, a self-confessed member of Du Bois's "talented tenth" (the great writer's explicitly elitist plan for creating an African American intelligentsia) who had later rebelled against his mentor's influence.[8] In 1954, following a meeting at the Connecticut home of former Executive Secretary of the NAACP Walter White, attended by the likes of Eleanor Roosevelt and Victor Reuther, Davis was placed in charge of a two-year research project investigating foreign attitudes toward civil rights and race problems in the United States. With funds provided by Orin Lehman, a great-nephew of New York governor Herbert Lehman, and attorney Bethuel M. Webster, the American Information Committee on Race and Caste also lobbied the federal government to increase black representation in the American foreign service and began laying the foundations of a permanent organization for promoting cultural exchange between the United States and the new nations.[9] Davis's project thus embodied a new approach to African affairs that was very different from that of the Council on African Affairs, one that served the interests of black Americans as much as the welfare of Africans and downplayed socialist anticolonialism in favor of liberal anticommunism.[10]

As yet, though, this tendency lacked any ideological purchase beyond elite black circles in the United States. This was where Richard Wright came in. Having moved to Paris in 1947, mainly in order to escape white racism in the United States, the novelist had befriended a group of French African intellectuals dedicated to the principles of "Negritude"—a movement started by Senegalese poet-politician Léopold Senghor during the 1930s in "celebration of African cultural heritage in the Francophone world."[11] Wright was too much of a western modernizer to feel entirely comfortable with Negritude's mystical invocations of a precolonial African past, but he did share the French-speaking intellectuals' desire to cast off white cultural domination and explore new forms of black literary expression.[12] When in 1947 the group began publishing a literary journal, *Présence Africaine*, under the editorship of Senegal-born Alioune Diop, Wright persuaded Jean-Paul Sartre and Albert Camus to lend their names to the venture, thereby protecting it from possible harassment by the Ministère des Colonies.[13] In 1956, Wright was again ready to help Diop when the latter called an international Congress of Negro Writers and Artists in Paris. Seeking to attract the participation of black American intellectuals, Wright contacted Roy Wilkins, Executive Director of the NAACP, who delegated responsibility for organizing a U.S. delegation to John Davis and the American Information Committee on Race and Caste.

Just how spontaneous was this sequence of events is hard to gauge. The mid-1950s were a crucial period in the developing relationship between the Cold War and the struggle for black freedom, witnessing not only the first serious challenges to segregation in the U.S. South, such as the launch of the Montgomery bus boycott in late 1955, but also, earlier that year, the Bandung conference, an epoch-making gathering in Indonesia of representatives from nonaligned nations in the Third World. Bandung was viewed by John Foster and Allen Dulles as marking the start of a new communist offensive in the postcolonial countries, and the 1956 Paris conference, which clearly owed some of its inspiration to the previous year's event (Diop called it a "second Bandung"), likely stirred similar misgivings in Washington.[14] Certainly Richard Wright, who had attended and reported on Bandung (with a grant from the Congress for Cultural Freedom), feared the possibility of the communists hijacking Diop's initiative, just as he believed they had exploited the suffering of African Americans during the 1930s. In May 1956, with the conference scheduled for September, Wright called at the U.S. embassy in Paris, on the pretext of renewing his passport, and expressed "certain concerns over the leftist tendencies of the Executive Committee for the Congress," an embassy officer reported to Washington. "To counteract such a tendency," the report continued, "Mr. Wright wondered if the Embassy could assist him in suggesting possible American negro delegates who are relatively well known for their cultural achievements and who could combat the leftist tendencies of the Congress." Wright returned to the embassy on several occasions to discuss how officials there might "offset Communist influence."[15]

Precisely what happened next is unclear, but the delegation organized by John Davis, at the prompting of Wright and Wilkins, had all the hallmarks of a CIA front operation like earlier initiatives among intellectuals, students, and women. Shortly after the meetings in the Paris embassy, Davis approached Orin Lehman, "who agreed to underwrite the trip."[16] By the beginning of August, Wright had learned from Wilkins of Davis's interest in coming to Paris, and arranged for Diop to issue formal invitations to the American Information Committee on Race and Caste. "I'm sure glad that we have at long last got some response from the States," Wright wrote Davis. "The influence of other countries and other ideas have flooded the preparation for this congress and other points of view will be welcome."[17] In the weeks that followed, Davis corresponded with such eminent African American intellectuals as Horace Mann Bond, president of Lincoln University (and father of future civil rights activist Julian Bond), informing them that his organization would pay their passage to Paris and a $20 per diem on condition that they all provided reports on the Congress after their return to the United States.[18] By September 5, Davis was able to confirm with Wright that a five-man American delegation would be coming to Paris.[19] The other members beside himself would be Bond, James Ivy (editor of the NAACP's magazine, *Crisis*), William Fontaine (a philosophy professor from the University of Pennsylvania), and Mercer Cook (a professor of romance languages at Howard University, former director of the Congress for Cultural Freedom's African program, and later U.S. ambassador to Nigeria).

Suspicions that the U.S. delegation was not all that it seemed abounded during the Paris Congress itself, which opened on the morning of Wednesday, September 19, in a hot, cramped lecture theater at the Sorbonne. Shortly after Alioune Diop had given a welcoming address, a message from W. E. B. Du Bois was read aloud. The American father of pan-Africanism apologized for his absence, explaining, "I am not present at your meeting because the U.S. government will not give me a passport." This statement was greeted "by great waves of laughter, by no means good-natured," reported African American novelist James Baldwin in the CCF magazine *Encounter*, "and by a roar of applause, which, as it clearly could not have been intended for the State Department, was intended to express admiration for Du Bois' plain speaking." If the U.S. delegates were discomfited by this response, they must have been appalled by the next sentence of the message, which drew even more applause. "Any American Negro traveling abroad today," it read, "must either not care about Negroes, or say what the State Department wishes him to say." In Baldwin's view, Du Bois's remarks "very neatly destroyed whatever effectiveness the five-man American delegation then sitting in the hall might have hoped to have." From that point on, the African Americans sat through the conference "uncomfortably aware that they might have at any moment to rise and leave the hall."[20]

For their part, Davis and his party regarded many of the non-American delegates with an equal measure of mistrust, as their postconference reports make clear. Horace Mann Bond, for example, suspected (with good reason) that the British delegation, led by a white woman, Dorothy Brooks, was communist-dominated and financed. He also believed that the audience for a speech by a founding member of the Negritude movement, the Martinique-born Aimé Césaire, was stacked with communists, who cheered the anti-American remarks of the leftist deputy and poet "to the rafters."[21] Another, anonymous report echoed Bond by describing the conference session featuring Césaire's lecture as "obviously stacked" and went on to recount how the same audience howled down an inoffensive speech by a Protestant pastor from Cameroon. Generally, though, the communists were surprisingly reticent and self-effacing, the report continued—"very calm, very sweet to everybody. Everything is rosy, peaches and cream."[22] Bond wondered whether the conference organizers themselves were not subject to communist control. "While speculating on where they found the financial resources (e.g., to pay for simultaneous translation)," he reported, "I could not but hope that their earnest efforts would not be 'captured' by agencies and interests hostile to American democracy."[23] Interestingly, neither report made much of the presence at the Congress of the young theoretician of Third World revolution, Frantz Fanon, whose paper included the charge, "Racism haunts and vitiates American culture."[24]

Interwoven with these political divisions were unexpected racial tensions, which constantly threatened to undermine the Congress's appeals to pan-Africanism and Negritude. Encounters with different diasporic cultures could be rewarding and pleasurable—the American delegates, for example, clearly enjoyed the African dishes and Haitian rum on offer at a Parisian café during one conference mealtime. Such meetings, however, were often beset with mutual misunderstanding and prejudice. In particular, many Francophone Africans and Haitians felt, as an officer of the American Society of African Culture put it a few years later, "that the American delegation was far more American than Negro," an attitude expressed in insensitive and sometimes chauvinistic remarks about skin color.[25] The very light-skinned John Davis, for example, was asked "just why he considered himself a Negro—he certainly did not look like one" (as Baldwin recalled). Davis responded to this question by trying to explain that "he was a Negro by choice and by depth of involvement—by experience." This statement was met with blank stares.[26] One Haitian even suggested that "mulattoes" were unreliable as allies in the black freedom struggle, a barb clearly aimed at the U.S. delegates (although, ironically, it was the communist-controlled British contingent that took offense at the remark).[27] For their part, "the Americans were struck by the fact that the Africans were exceedingly French or British."[28]

Caught in between the two camps was the "liaison man," Richard

Wright, a literary lion whom (Baldwin reported) "both factions tended to claim . . . as their spokesman."[29] Wright's natural position was a combination of the American and African viewpoints. On the one hand, he was fiercely anticommunist. "We start neck and neck with the Communists in bidding for the loyalty of Africa," he wrote privately. "I'm certain that the Communists will be swiftly overhauling their concepts and if we don't they will have the advantage in terms of being much freer to act effectively." On the other hand, Wright was deeply sensitive to the new currents of black nationalism sweeping postcolonial Africa—Americans must engage with Africans "in terms of sympathy and identification," he insisted[30]—and he was horrified by the possibility of being perceived along with the other American blacks present as "agents of some kind." "We had a message today that hurt me," he told the Congress's organizers during a closed session on the evening of the first day, in obvious reference to Du Bois's greeting.[31] Small wonder, given these conflicting impulses and pressures, that by the end of the event Wright should have begun to show signs of emotional and mental strain. "The consciousness of his peculiar and . . . rather grueling position weighed on him, I think, rather heavily," observed Baldwin.[32] A few days after the Congress closed, Wright told a friend that it had left him "terribly depressed." All the same, he was prepared to acknowledge that it had been "a success of a sort."[33]

This perhaps surprising judgment reflected the fact that, despite its many internal divisions, the Congress did manage to agree on certain things. One of these was the necessity for Africans to free themselves from white colonialism, exploitation, and racial discrimination if they were fully to come into possession of their common heritage and achieve "integration into the active cultural life of the world." Another was the need to draw up an "inventory" of the various black cultures that had been "systematically misunderstood, underestimated, sometimes destroyed" by colonialism, so that peoples of African descent everywhere could gain an accurate appreciation of the values they all shared and begin to define themselves "instead of always being defined by others." Finally, as announced by Alioune Diop to a restive audience on the sweltering afternoon of the conference's closing day, the Congress resolved to create a permanent organization, "an international association for the dissemination of black culture."[34]

The creation of the Société Africaine de Culture (SAC) only weeks after the Congress's conclusion was greeted with universal acclaim. It was not long, however, before the political and cultural tensions within the African diaspora resurfaced. In January 1957, Diop wrote to John Davis informing him that international members were being sought for SAC's executive council—and that the individuals he had in mind to represent the United States were none other than Paul Robeson and W. E. B. Du Bois.[35] Davis, who had himself begun to organize the American delegation into a permanent entity, was aghast at this suggestion, immediately cabling Wright, "Cannot go along. Welcome your intercession. Please inform."[36] It was not that he did not respect Du Bois's many accomplishments, Davis explained to Diop the following month: "We are all, in fact, a product of his 'better tenth' movement." Rather, the problem was that Du Bois and Robeson "are now completely dedicated to a political doctrine," and "uncritical acceptance of any political dogma destroys any man as a cultural being." In any case, he and his American colleagues could not accept the principle that French Africans sitting in Paris had the right to select the U.S. members of the new movement's governing body. Indeed, the Americans' continued participation depended on their being able to nominate their own representatives.[37]

Confronted with this ultimatum, Diop opted for a conciliatory response. It had never been his intention to impose candidates on the U.S. delegation, he reassured Davis. "We [were] unaware of the extent to which the names of these two cultured men, whom we admire, can arouse the anxiety of other Negro Americans," he carried on. Of course, Davis and his friends should choose their own representation.[38] Suitably mollified, the Americans proceeded to do just that, replacing Du Bois and Robeson with Duke Ellington (Davis's "favorite of jazz musicians") and the NAACP's counsel in the *Brown* case and future Supreme Court Justice, Thurgood Marshall, neither of whom were well known for their leftist convictions.[39] The new ascendancy among leading black Americans of a liberal, anticommunist approach to African affairs, as opposed to the earlier form of leftist engagement personified by Du Bois, could not have been clearer.

Encouraged by this victory, John Davis set about cementing his plans for a U.S. affiliate of the international society. The American Society of African Culture came into existence in June 1957, although active operations did not begin until November. The intervening months, it seems, were spent in working out the arrangements by which the organization would be funded and governed, with Orin Lehman, Bethuel Webster, and a new white "angel," Philadelphia construction magnate, Matthew H. McCloskey, all prominently involved in the discussions.[40] The most important of these occurred on September 24, 1957, when it was decided that, in addition to carrying on its research function, the American Information Committee on Race and Caste would "serve as directing and coordinating agency for related groups and functions," including the newly formed AMSAC. The only problem with this proposal, it was agreed, was the committee's name. "The word 'information' had very unpleasant connotations," a minute of the discussion noted in a rare moment of frankness, "and was a sure indicator to certain groups of the nature of sponsorship."[41] The possibility of such embarrassment was averted the following month, when a special meeting of the committee's directors in the Wall Street office of Webster's law firm agreed to rename the organization the Council on Race and Caste in World Affairs (CORAC). At that meeting Davis reported that the American Society of African Culture had acquired office space on East Fortieth Street (the same midtown territory occupied by such front organizations as the Committee of Correspondence and the American Committee for Cultural Freedom) and an apartment on Fifth Avenue for use as guest quarters; it had also taken on staff, including James T. "Ted" Harris, Jr., a former president of the National Student Association and director of the NSA's Foreign Student Leadership Program, who would assist Davis in his role as Executive Director. These measures, Davis explained, would "provide an excellent means of disseminating accurate information concerning the progress of Negroes under American democracy."[42] This remark, the involvement of such well-connected whites as Webster (who earlier in the 1950s had helped set up the American Fund for Free Jurists as a conduit for CIA funds to the International Commission of Jurists), the change of name, the lavishness of AMSAC's accommodation, and the appearance of Harris: all these circumstances point to the hidden hand of the CIA's International Organizations Division.

Something else AMSAC shared in common with other Agency fronts was the ambivalent response it provoked abroad, a peculiar mixture of suspicion and opportunism. Within days of becoming operational, the American Society of African Culture received a letter from Diop begging for a loan to bale SAC and *Présence Africaine* out of an impending financial crisis caused by a delay of subsidies from donors in Africa. Davis was reluctant to approve this request, reasoning that a loan might endanger CORAC's tax-exempt status.[43] Nonetheless, he could see the tactical advantages that might accrue from AMSAC's making regular grants to its cash-strapped parent body. "This raises the possibility of some American who might serve as a member of the editorial board in Paris for us," he explained to Richard Wright, an arrangement that "from our point of view is highly desirable anyway. . . . We find ourselves rather seriously handicapped by the lack of a medium of communication and contact between our French-speaking African colleagues and their American associates." Would Wright investigate the likely reception of such a proposal at *Présence Africaine*'s editorial offices? Indeed, would he consider taking on the role himself?[44]

Davis's proposal found Wright more torn between his various intellectual allegiances than ever. He agreed with Davis that there was a "real and urgent" need for more dialogue between American and French African intellectuals. "The tide of black nationalism rolls strongly on, gathering in its momentum more and more blacks from every point of the intellectual compass," he observed. "The movement will forge ahead and I think it is better for them to obtain money from an American source than from behind the Iron Curtain." Still, he could not think of any individual capable of meeting the "stupendous" challenges that the role envisioned by Davis would pose. Moreover, it was "indelicate" for the suggestion to be made at the same time that a possible loan was being mooted, not least because Alioune Diop had just returned from a trip to the United States in an anti-American frame of mind. "With the exception of a few . . . intellectuals, which he counted on the fingers of his two hands, he found that the American Negro seems to have been caught in some stagnant intellectual eddy in the stream of life," Wright bluntly told Davis.[45]

By April 1958, Wright's objections to AMSAC's tactics had multiplied. Diop and his brother, Thomas, were "scared stiff that the American section is out to grab control of SAC," he reported to Ted Harris. "If they are made to feel that the Americans are out to control the organization, they will then mobilize Communist support in order to stay in power! This is the danger." What "you fellows there in New York" must do,

Wright advised, is "sit down and devise another method of working with these African boys." In part, this was a matter of "approach," which should be "modest [and] slow," not unlike the manner in which he himself had won the confidence of the Diops. "There are delicate techniques which we must learn to master if we would influence other people," he elaborated. "We simply cannot go in like a salesman." But it was not just a matter of technique: AMSAC also needed a more "constructive outlook and program" than it had come up with so far. "The aim should be not only to defeat Communism in Africa; that is a negative aim," Wright explained. "A healthy, free Africa bent upon industrialization is about all that anybody can honestly ask for." One other thing was crucial: African Americans must avoid any hint of apologizing for the U.S. government. "If our actions carry the faintest overtones of American official policy, we are licked before we start."[46] The irony was that all of Wright's recommendations for winning hearts and minds in Africa were remarkably similar to the secret tactics of the Eisenhower administration.

AMSAC did come to regret its "Uncle Moneybags" image and backed away from the American-in-Paris proposal.[47] Still, Wright's qualms about the organization were not assuaged; indeed, if anything, they seem to have deepened. Despite pleading from Harris that he participate, Wright turned down an invitation to a second Congress of Negro Writers and Artists taking place in Rome in 1959, after hearing rumors that the event was to be underwritten by the Italian government.[48] "I'm for all governments except those of African or black nationalist origins being kept out of this organization," he told John Davis, with possibly deliberate ambiguity.[49] "My political experience has taught me that one should never conduct a fight on grounds chosen by others and for ends that are not one's own."[50] In May 1959, with his financial affairs at rock bottom, Wright halfheartedly approached Davis, asking for $10,000 to enable him to undertake a seven-country tour of West Africa so that he could research a book about the "highly fragile and tragic Black Elite."[51] This time, it was AMSAC's turn to hang back. "While I personally . . . feel it would do the French Africans a whole lot of good," Davis responded, "there is still the question of our sponsorship doing us harm or good in the work in which we are interested. . . . After you have finished the book, it may turn out that we may feel that we ought not to associate ourselves with it from purely organizational reasons."[52] Wright accepted this judgment without demur. "I'd not like to go there with the feeling that I'd have to inhibit myself in whatever I'd write," he told Davis. "I think that the wiser course for me would be to seek some more disinterested sponsorship."[53]

This exchange was the last act in Richard Wright's association with AMSAC. Although the documentary record is sparse, it seems clear that by the time of his death on November 28, 1960, the writer was thoroughly disillusioned with the American effort in the Cold War struggle for hearts and minds, which in his own case involved the CIA's vacillating between secretly sponsoring and spying on him. "My attitude to Communism has not altered but my position toward those who are fighting Communism has," he told one correspondent. "I lift my hand to fight Communism and I find that the hand of the Western world is sticking knives into my back. The Western world must make up its mind as to whether it hates colored people more than it hates Communists or . . . Communists more than . . . colored people."[54]

Soon after its launch in the fall of 1957, AMSAC embarked on an extraordinarily ambitious program of events and activities, all intended, as a handsomely produced publicity pamphlet explained, "to spread understanding of the validity of African and Negro cultural contributions" and thereby "provide a basis for mutual respect between Americans and Africans."[55] Starting with a three-day planning meeting in June 1958, the organization sponsored a series of annual conferences featuring a glittering array of black intellectuals, artists, and performers. The 1959 event, staged (like so many other important engagements in the cultural Cold War) at the Waldorf-Astoria, was addressed by Massachusetts senator John F. Kennedy (who arrived late, via the servant's entrance, having given his bodyguards the slip earlier in the evening).[56] Other high-profile events were held in New York, such as "The Negro Writer and His Relationship to His Roots," a winter 1959 conference graced by the dean of African American poetry, Langston Hughes; regional meetings; and regular lectures at AMSAC's New York offices.[57] The printed word was not neglected. Among AMSAC publications were a monthly six-page newsletter, printed in English and French; a special collaborative issue of *Présence Africaine* (the influential "Africa Seen by American Negroes"); and several volumes of proceedings from its conferences.[58] AMSAC also provided a host of cultural services to Africans visiting the United States, including an information service, student exchange grants, and English-language education for UN delegates from former French colonies. African guests of honor were entertained at annual holiday parties, where they danced to the music of Count Basie and his jazz orchestra.[59]

The event that really put AMSAC on the map in Africa took place in December 1961. Timed to coincide with Nigerian independence celebrations, "Negro Culture in Africa and the Americas" was a festival of the performing arts that brought together the cream of black creative talent from both sides of the Atlantic for two days and nights of music, dance, and theater under open skies in Lagos's King George V Stadium. Yvonne O. Walker, the AMSAC officer charged with assembling, transporting, and managing the American contingent, faced her share of difficulties. The famous jazz bandleader Lionel "Hamp" Hampton, who traveled separately from the main party, did not arrive until 11:00 at night on the event's first day, then demanded a tour of Lagos nightspots, which lasted well into the following morning. He also overran badly on stage, causing the next act, Nina Simone, to refuse to come on until Walker threatened her with "a long, cold swim back to the United States." Artistic temperaments notwithstanding, the festival was judged a spectacular success, with audiences of up to 5,000 "going wild" for Hampton, Simone, and the other U.S. performers.[60] Shortly afterward, Ben Enwonwu, a noted Nigerian painter and sculptor, cut the ribbon on the West African Cultural Center, a local branch of AMSAC housed in a downtown Lagos office building, inaugurating a new program of art exhibits, receptions, and performing arts exchanges.[61] With Ted Harris having quit the organization earlier in the year to run the Institute of Law and Administration in Leopoldville (later Kinshasa) in the Congo, management of the African office was entrusted to his successor as Associate Executive Director, Calvin H. "Hank" Raullerson, who was accompanied to Lagos by his wife, Olive, and their three children.[62] Raullerson was replaced in New York by another Lincoln University graduate, lawyer James K. Baker.

It was, perhaps, predictable that AMSAC's expansion into Africa, which had taken place without consultation with the Société Africaine de Culture and violated the territorial jurisdiction of the international movement's Nigerian affiliate, NIGERIASAC, should have been greeted by protests from Paris. Granted, Alioune Diop admitted, in a frosty letter to

John Davis, AMSAC was "the most important section of SAC at present because of the number of its writers and artists and because of the financial and political means which support it," but this did not give it the right to trample on NIGERIASAC. "We have suffered enough from the cultural oppression of Europe to hope that our Black brothers of America will not . . . give rebirth to cultural colonialism," Diop continued.[63] As in earlier disputes with SAC, Davis attempted "to smooth the ruffled feelings of Mr. Diop," paying for him to travel to New York for talks about the future of the Lagos office, and himself journeying to Paris.[64] The ill feeling carried on, however. AMSAC refused to concede control of the West African Cultural Center to NIGERIASAC, as Diop demanded, and Davis reminded Diop, somewhat tactlessly, that the American Society was "representative of some 20 million Negroes in the nation which is one of the world's great powers."[65] Underlying the clash about Lagos was the division between English and French-speaking Africans that had been highlighted by the 1956 Congress. "We wish that the Negro Americans, instead of being assimilated into the Western culture of America, would to the contrary assign greater importance to the originality of their African heritage," Diop revealingly told Davis.[66]

What was less to be expected was that members of AMSAC's own circle in the United States would share some of SAC's misgivings. In part, their reasons were pragmatic. "The fact that we have started under 'the auspices' of a well-known stable group of Africans is an advantage not to be taken lightly [nor] easily recovered if lost," the outspoken Adelaide Cromwell Hill told fellow members of AMSAC's Executive Council before urging them to compromise with Diop's demands.[67] Others objected in principle. "I am somewhat sensitive about educated Negro Americans overexposing themselves in Africa at this stage," Davis was told by Martin Kilson, a member of Harvard University's Center for International Affairs (and later head of Harvard's black studies program), in April 1962. African students at Harvard did not like AMSAC's "assertive features," Kilson reported, viewing the organization as an "'Uncle Tom agent'" of "'American imperialism.'" These young Africans preferred to identify with black Americans who addressed the economic and social problems of Africa, rather than "pointing at a few doctors, lawyers, artists, etc., as if they were representative of the Negro community at large—which they obviously are not." AMSAC must get off its "phony high horse," Kilson urged, and concentrate on what he "thought was supposed to be its original aim and purpose," that is, educating the mass of ordinary American blacks about their African roots, something that had become "lost in an attempt to project America (and I'm not really sure it is NEGRO AMERICA) into Africa."[68] These remarks, which strongly echoed Alioune Diop's earlier assertion that the "mission of AMSAC . . . [was] the work of integrating into the national American culture . . . the special qualities which constitute the African cultural heritage," clearly upset the normally equable Davis, who devoted much of a lengthy response to an impassioned defense of his own record as a civil rights activist, one he compared favorably with Kilson's and that of his mentor, W. E. B. Du Bois.[69]

Fuelling African apprehension about the Lagos office were recurrent rumors "of a liaison between AMSAC and government," as one confidential internal report delicately put it.[70] Such suspicions were, of course, entirely justified. In the first years of its existence, AMSAC received almost all of its funds directly from the Council on Race and Caste in World Affairs, an arrangement reminiscent of the relationship between the National Student Association and the Foundation for Youth and Student Affairs. Between June 1958 and May 1959, for example, out of a recorded total income of $32,985, the amount of $30,500, or 92 percent, was listed as "Grants from CORAC," the remainder being made up of membership dues and individual donations.[71] In March 1959, however, Orin Lehman signaled a move away from this state of near complete dependence by telling an annual meeting of CORAC directors that "some foundations and also some additional individuals" had expressed an interest in sponsoring AMSAC. (The same meeting approved AMSAC's program "on the understanding that activities that might possibly be considered of a political nature should be avoided.")[72] Matthew McCloskey resigned from CORAC in April (later going into overt government service as John Kennedy's ambassador to Ireland, then resigning this position in the wake of a financial scandal involving his construction empire), and in February 1960 AMSAC received its own certificate of incorporation (predictably, perhaps, in Delaware), the legal paperwork having been filed by Frederick "Rusty" Van Vechten of Bethuel Webster's law firm.[73] Federal tax exemption followed in May and, after a separate bank account was opened at the Park Avenue office of the Chemical Bank New York Trust Company in June, the organization was ready to start receiving subsidies from pass-through foundations.[74] Henceforth, financial assistance from CORAC would be limited to routine operating costs, such as officers' salaries.[75] Grants for specific projects, which was by far the largest part of AMSAC's annual budget, would come from elsewhere, so that in 1964–65, for example, CORAC supplied $12,500 and foundations $87,500.[76] That said, CORAC maintained a say in AMSAC's affairs, with its annual meeting of directors providing an opportunity for Lehman and Webster to steer the organization toward particular activities.[77] Meanwhile, money flowed into AMSAC's coffers from such CIA conduits as the Colt and Cleveland Dodge foundations.[78]

Like the majority of organizations exposed as CIA fronts in 1967, AMSAC denied all knowledge of secret government funding, posing as a victim of successful official deception. At first sight, this claim appears to be borne out by the organization's records and, for that matter, the personal papers of many of the prominent individuals involved, all of which are conspicuously free of any of the coded references to covert dealings usually detectable in such documents. There is, however, one striking exception to this rule, a memorandum entitled "Disclosures in the *New York Times* of CIA Support of AMSAC" written by Boston University sociologist Adelaide Cromwell Hill to other members of AMSAC's Executive Council in February 1967. "First of all, the possibility of CIA involvement is not new information to me," Hill stated. "I remember the exact time and place almost eight years ago when such a possibility was first confided in me and by whom. Several years later further and more detailed confirmation was given me by another friend. Around the edges were frequent innuendoes and asides. None of this was documented, understandably so."[79] In addition to suggesting a widespread state of wittingness within AMSAC, Hill's memo provides an explanation of the strange absence from the archival record of any trace of such knowledge: the statement "None of this was documented" indicates that the organization was unusually conscientious about observing front group security protocols. In short, far from being dupes of the CIA, AMSAC's African Americans were among the Agency's most effective secret agents.

Given that members of AMSAC's Executive Council were in on the secret, it does not come as a surprise to learn that the organization's officers were fully witting too—indeed, had sworn secrecy oaths in the same manner as had the NSA's international staff. Interviewed many years later, Yvonne Walker recalled how, shortly after she was appointed Managing Director, friends began calling to find out what she was involved in "because [she] was being checked on by the FBI." "I didn't know what was going on either, and then finally one day two members of the CIA showed up for an appointment with Dr. Davis. I didn't know who they were at the time, but they . . . called me into the office and explained to me what was going down, and that they would require me to take an oath."

Subsequently, Walker and other officers of the organization would meet with their CIA case officers in hotel rooms, usually in New York but, on at least one occasion, in Washington, D.C., as well. "They [the CIA officers] were kept fully informed . . . by Dr. Davis on everything that was going on," Walker remembered, "and I'm sure that they helped to steer some of the plans."[80] These briefings probably also involved a certain amount of foreign intelligence gathering on the part of the Agency. Although Davis later advised against "such an organization being used for intelligence purposes," the reports on their travels overseas submitted by such AMSAC officers as Ted Harris to the New York office give the strong impression of having been written with a readership in Washington or Langley also in mind.[81] Harris's move from New York to the Congo in 1961 is suggestive of his importance to CIA operations in Africa: the murder of Congolese Prime Minister Patrice Lumumba in January of that year had cleared the way for the creation of a U.S.-friendly government in the central African republic, and the purpose of Harris's new institute in Leopoldville was to train local politicians in western administrative techniques (and, probably, channel CIA subsidies to them).

When asked which elements of the AMSAC program had been shaped by the CIA, Walker became a little vague, referring to "the festival, the cultural exchange programs, and what have you."[82] In her 1967 memo, Hill was more specific, citing three examples of "the harm done to AMSAC and its goals by having decision-making occur beyond the control of the Executive Board": the opening of the Lagos office, an initiative that seemed to her "designed to suit some unexplained and not unanimously approved ends"; the organization's "inability to develop the fullest rapprochement with SAC," a consequence of "the long history of rumor that associated our financing with the CIA or some other non-obvious source"; and, finally, "the unpredictability or almost capricious nature" of the Agency's funding, which made impossible "intelligent long-range program planning." In other words, Hill's quarrel was not with the ethical propriety of secret subsidies—"I felt that, as AMSAC was a weak and new organization, it perhaps could, or should, take help from any source, provided we were left free to pursue our own goals"—rather it was the group's resulting lack of control over its own affairs.[83]

No matter how tightly the CIA controlled AMSAC, it did not have a stranglehold on contact between black U.S. citizens and Africans. Although the old form of leftist engagement with African affairs epitomized by W. E. B. Du Bois was by now more or less squelched, a new kind of cultural nationalism was stirring among young African Americans, one that celebrated black identity not to achieve integration into western culture, but rather as a rejection of it. Identified after the mid-1960s by the slogan "Black Power," this new mood was most powerfully expressed during the early years of the decade by the radical nationalist Malcolm X, who preached a doctrine of racial separatism and dared to criticize the nonviolent tactics of civil rights leader Martin Luther King, Jr. Twice in 1964, Malcolm visited Africa, the second time on an eighteen-week tour, meeting government representatives, speaking on the radio, and addressing the Organization of African Unity in Cairo.[84] Concerned American officials wondered how to counter his charismatic presence and the threat to U.S. African policy it posed.

Enter the towering figure of African American leader James Farmer. A founder of the Congress of Racial Equality (CORE), a prominent civil rights organization, Farmer had risked his life taking part in the 1961 Freedom Rides on segregated interstate buses in the Deep South, but he was no racial radical in the mold of Malcolm X. He shared Martin Luther King's belief in integration and nonviolence; indeed, he was a pioneer in the application of Gandhian protest techniques to the African American struggle for freedom. Moreover, Farmer had a proven interest in African affairs, having participated in November 1962, along with King and other representatives of the "Big Six" African American organizations, in the launch of the American Negro Leadership Conference on Africa (ANLCA), an initiative to build links between the civil rights movement and the new African states, as well as to strengthen black representation in official U.S. foreign policy.[85]

Farmer had already taken part in a tour of Africa, in late 1958, as a representative of the American Federation of State, County, and Municipal Employees, in a five-member delegation of the Public Service International (the same organization that collaborated with the CIA in 1963 to unseat Cheddi Jagan in British Guiana).[86] This experience had stirred unexpectedly powerful feelings of cultural solidarity in both Farmer and his African hosts. "When I landed in Africa, I felt quite literally like falling on my knees and kissing the earth," he remembered later. When the time came for him to leave, "Nigerian trade-unionists gathered at the airport to see me off, and they threw their arms around me and kissed me."[87] The PSI report on the trip noted the same phenomenon, but in more dispassionate terms, describing Farmer as a "colored trade unionist—a fact which naturally proved of considerable advantage to the delegation in its approach to the Africans."[88]

Farmer, then, was the obvious choice to counter Malcolm X. How, though, to get him to Africa without undermining his credibility as an independent spokesman for black America? In December 1964, only a couple of weeks after Malcolm had returned from his second African trip, AMSAC approached the American Negro Leadership Conference on Africa (not difficult, given that the two organizations shared the same offices), offering to finance "an extended trip to Africa." ANCLA immediately asked Farmer to represent the organization, giving him twenty-four hours to reply; he "accepted eagerly," despite some protest from CORE, which was going through an organizational crisis at the time.[89]

The next few weeks were a rush of frantic planning in AMSAC's New York headquarters. Hank Raullerson, returned from Lagos and back in his old position as John Davis's assistant director, sorted out Farmer's travel arrangements, put him in touch with African acquaintances, and smoothed his path with American officialdom.[90] Carl T. Rowan, director of USIA (and the first African American to sit on the National Security Council), looked forward to Farmer's "voicing the true aspirations of most Negro Americans as compared with what has been said in Africa by such 'spokesmen' as Malcolm X" and offered to brief him before his departure.[91] Meanwhile, John Davis alerted Raullerson's replacement in Lagos, James Baker, to Farmer's imminent arrival, explaining the purpose of the trip in words almost identical to those used by Rowan.[92] Baker was instructed to accompany Farmer throughout the tour in his capacity as a member of the

ANLCA's planning committee, rather than as an officer of AMSAC.[93] This reticence about the latter organization's role in conceiving, funding, and planning the trip was presumably related to its reputation in Africa as a U.S. government front.

James Farmer arrived in Africa on January 7, 1965, and stayed five weeks, visiting nine countries: Tanzania, Kenya, Uganda, Zambia, Southern Rhodesia, Ethiopia, Nigeria, the Congo, and Ghana. His personal reputation, combined with the good offices of AMSAC, ensured him access to an extraordinary range of African leaders. As he recalled in his memoirs,

> I saw the heads of state of practically every country: Julius Nyerere and two vice-presidents, Karume and Kawawa, in Tanzania; President Kenneth Kaunda in Zambia; President Jomo Kenyatta in Kenya; His Imperial Majesty Haile Selassie I in Ethiopia; President Nnamde Azikiwe in Nigeria; Moise Tshombe and Joseph Kasavubu in the Congo; President Kwame Nkrumah in Ghana. In every country I met with cabinet ministers, members of parliament, and university students. I lectured at universities in several countries and spoke at meetings sponsored by social and civic organizations. And I met with trade unionists.[94]

Farmer returned to the United States very pleased with the tour, reckoning that he had been able to view Africa with greater objectivity than had been possible on his previous trip and had therefore performed his role as a representative of black Americans all the more effectively. This positive assessment was shared by official America. "From [a] public relations point [of] view [the tour was a] great success," the U.S. embassy in Lusaka reported to Washington. "Farmer attracted favorable comment from almost everyone who met him."[95] AMSAC too was delighted with the fruits of its patronage, Baker describing the tour as "easily the most significant happening in the last five or six years insofar as relations between Africans and American Negroes are concerned."[96] Farmer was the "perfect speaker for the forensic-minded African," AMSAC's man in Lagos explained to Raullerson, echoing earlier comments by Richard Wright about the need for a "rational" approach to a continent still supposedly mired in tribal superstition.[97]

Not everything about the trip went according to plan, however. To start with, U.S. diplomats in Africa displayed a "heavy hand" at a number of Farmer's public engagements, stirring suspicions that his tour was in fact officially sponsored. "In Dar [Es Salaam] and Addis [Ababa], I was aggressively asked [about official sponsorship]," Baker told Raullerson, "the interrogator stating that he received his information from persons in the respective Embassies."[98] According to Bill Sutherland, an old colleague and friend of Farmer's who provided an important point of private contact and support during his time in Africa, the source of such rumors was a Tanzania–based official named Barney Coleman, who "was using this as a wedge to get more credit and involvement for the Embassy in Dar." The effect of Coleman's machinations was disastrous. As well as jeopardizing Sutherland's own relationship with the Tanzanian government, they caused the cancellation of a potentially momentous meeting between Farmer and the African Liberation Committee and cast "an air of suspicion" over the whole tour. From now on, AMSAC officials decided, they would have to watch "the eagerness of the Embassy to get in on a free ride."[99]

In addition to this crossing of wires between the overt and covert agencies of U.S. diplomacy, AMSAC faced another potential problem: Farmer's tendency to criticize American foreign policy. One complaint voiced several times by the civil rights leader, concerning the lack of African American representation in the nation's foreign service, was predictable enough; AMSAC itself had made it on a number of occasions.[100] Harder to handle were Farmer's frequent and unequivocal condemnations of U.S. policy in South Africa, the Portuguese colonies, and especially the Congo.[101] These remarks were usually made within a Cold War frame of reference: if American officials continued to support repressive regimes in these regions, they would not only drive Africans "into the arms of Peking and the Soviets," Farmer claimed, they would also help forge a domestic alliance between white communists and black nationalists. Still, there came a point when such comments ceased being supportive of the wider American Cold War effort and became merely embarrassing, as when Farmer described sharing a ride on a U.S. transport plane in the Congo with "a sleazy bunch" of white mercenaries, "every one with a pistol on his hip," who were only able to carry out their campaigns of "nigger-killing" because of "the support we gave them."[102] As has been seen in earlier chapters, covert CIA sponsorship of individual American citizens had its share of unintended consequences, and this incident, which clearly deepened Farmer's alienation from aspects of U.S. African policy and increased his militancy as a civil rights leader, must surely be counted as one of them.

The tour had one other major unintended consequence. AMSAC had sent Farmer to Africa as a living rebuttal to Malcolm X, and he performed this part well enough, drawing laughter and applause from African audiences when he described the black Muslim's message of racial separatism as "apartheid and . . . worse." The two men had clashed publicly on a number of occasions in the United States, and by 1965 Farmer feared that Malcolm, who was searching for a new role after his recent break with the Nation of Islam, might become a bridge figure between the forces of black nationalism in America and international Maoism, making him "a really serious problem for the civil rights organizations, [an] almost terrifying problem." On a personal level, however, the relationship between Farmer and Malcolm was very different. A mutual respect, even affection, had developed in the course of their public encounters, and the black Muslim sent the civil rights leader a postcard every week while he was on his second African tour in 1964. On the eve of Farmer's departure for Africa in January 1965, Malcolm, having heard the trip announced by a New York radio station, visited Farmer in his apartment, asking that he not say anything that might damage his (Malcolm's) reputation in Egypt, a major source of his funding. "I said, 'I'm not going there,'" Farmer recounted later. "He said, 'fine.' We're good friends."[103]

Then, shortly after he arrived in Ghana, Farmer met with a young woman he had known in the United States, who suddenly announced, in the course of a conversation about Malcolm's recent trip to Africa, "He is going to be killed, you know." When pressed by Farmer, the woman (unidentified in his later account of the meeting) went on to state that the assassination would take place before April 1, 1965, and would be carried out by a mysterious group "far more dangerous" than the Black Muslims. On February 21, back in his New York apartment, Farmer learned that Malcolm had been shot to death during an appearance at the Audubon Ballroom in Harlem, reportedly by gunmen from the Nation of Islam. "The Black Muslims did not kill him," he told a news conference immediately afterward. "Malcolm's murder was a political killing with international implications." Later, Farmer tried unsuccessfully to locate the woman he had met in Ghana. "The last line I got on her," he recorded sadly, "was that she was doing a striptease act in a Sicilian nightclub."[104] Still, this did not prevent Farmer from speculating publicly that Malcolm's assassination was the work of Harlem drug racketeers (who were known to resent his preaching against narcotics) in league with the CIA.[105]

Whether justified or not, Farmer's suspicions about the CIA were obviously not in AMSAC's plans for his African trip. As well as demonstrating (once again) the practical hazards of "arm's length" operations, Farmer's statements against U.S. foreign policy and the CIA show that, although his African agenda was similar to that of his sponsors, it was not identical, and that while he might have served as an unwitting agent of the Agency, he was not its stooge. Still, the episode evidently did not put AMSAC off the idea of sponsoring civil rights leaders to undertake similar trips in the future. In April 1965, Calvin Raullerson wrote Martin Luther King expressing his "interest in having you make a tour of Africa under the auspices of the American Negro Leadership Conference on Africa through a grant provided by the American Society of African Culture." The initial response was encouraging. "He is very interested in doing this kind of trip and thinks it is something he ought to do," Raullerson reported to John Davis. "He is specially interested in going to East Africa where he has never been."[106] King's schedule, however, ruled out such a tour before late 1966, by which time the likelihood of the CIA's subsidizing him via AMSAC had become extremely remote, partly because of King's growing dissatisfaction with Cold War American foreign policy in Vietnam and partly because of other developments affecting AMSAC.

The Farmer tour was AMSAC's last really successful venture. The growth of radicalism among young African Americans was reflected by the emergence in New York of a new generation of black artists who rejected the vanguardist leadership of the "Negro intellectual establishment," a move symbolized by the staging of a dissident American Festival of Negro Arts at Fairleigh Dickinson University in 1965.[107] The following year, these tensions spilled over into the First World Festival of Negro Arts, an event held in Dakar, Senegal, under the joint sponsorship of Léopold Senghor's Senegalese government, UNESCO, and AMSAC. While the Soviets moored a cruise ship offshore and tried to lure delegates aboard with vodka and an exhibit about the slave trade, the Americans at the festival argued among themselves about the cultural politics of Negritude, the racial politics of federal funding for the arts, and the Cold War politics of events such as the festival itself. Ralph Ellison, Harry Belafonte, and James Baldwin, the latter having been a friendly observer at the Paris Congress of Negro Writers and Artists a decade earlier, stayed away in protest.[108]

Whether it was because of this spectacle, fears of imminent exposure, or changes within the CIA is not known, but throughout 1966 signs were clear that the Agency intended withdrawing its patronage from AMSAC. First came the news that the Council on Race and Caste in World Affairs grant for the coming financial year would be its last. As Hank Raullerson explained to the Executive Council, "The CORAC board feels that it has given AMSAC a start, a generous one, and [AMSAC] now should develop sources of funds apart from those provided by it (CORAC), the foundations and individuals CORAC and AMSAC have appealed to in the past."[109] The blow was softened by the news that the terminal grant would be for $100,000 and that Rusty Van Vechten would be on hand to offer free investment advice.[110] Then it was announced that AMSAC-Lagos was to be closed and James Baker recalled home. The official line was that the African office cost too much to run and that its functions could largely be duplicated in New York, but later oral testimony suggests that the real reason for the closure was that AMSAC's reputation in Nigeria had become so bad that Baker's personal safety could no longer be guaranteed.[111] Finally, AMSAC suffered a slew of resignations by its officers, including the highly capable and well-liked Hank Raullerson, who left in October 1966 to become head of the East African division of the Peace Corps.[112]

Hence, by February 1967, when the *New York Times* exposed its CIA funding, AMSAC was a shadow of its former self. The exposé resulted in some internal recriminations, with Adelaide Cromwell Hill in particular demanding from Davis a complete disclosure of the organization's dealings with the Agency, but there was nothing on the same scale as the controversy that engulfed the Committee of Correspondence in the wake of the revelations, perhaps reflecting the relatively higher proportion of witting members in AMSAC.[113] Predictably, the loudest complaints came from Paris, with the Société Africaine de Culture's Administrative Secretary, Kala-Lobe, demanding that Alioune Diop's name be removed from the editorial board of *African Forum* (a quarterly journal of African affairs launched by Davis in summer 1965) and speculating darkly about the motives of past AMSAC actions, such as the controversial opening of the Lagos office.[114] There was some debate about relaunching the organization as a domestic venture (ironically, the preferred strategy of earlier critics such as Diop and Martin Kilson) that would be geared toward checking the worst excesses of the young black nationalists "and those who excite the rage of the Negro poor by referring to the African and slave past" (as Davis put it in a begging letter to Assistant Secretary of State for Educational and Cultural Affairs Charles Frankel).[115] The discussion proved academic, however, as pleas for replacement funding addressed to the State Department, the Ford Foundation, Chase Manhattan Bank's African Section, and the Carnegie Foundation all fell on deaf ears.[116] Not even James Farmer, now serving Richard Nixon as Assistant Secretary of Health, Education, and Welfare, answered AMSAC's distress calls.[117] The organization eventually went into suspended animation in the summer of 1969.[118]

What are we to make of the African Americans who belonged to AMSAC? A "combination of careerists, slick articulate operators with little conviction, and leaders of the integrationist Negro intellectual establishment" was how black radical Harold Cruse described them. "They were liberals without a base whose legitimacy came entirely from their association with established groups like AMSAC," Cruse continued. "I even doubt they were capable of thinking this kind of operation up themselves."[119] Certainly, John Davis's many references to the "talented tenth" and (initial) rejection of proposals that AMSAC concentrate on educating U.S. citizens about African culture demonstrate the basic elitism of the organization's self-conception and its lack of an organic relationship with ordinary African Americans. Moreover, AMSAC's attitude toward Africa and Africans tended to the paternalistic or "redemptionist"—that is, the notion that diaspora and, in particular, American blacks had a duty to save the "dark continent" from the forces of atavistic mysticism on the one hand and communist manipulation on the other. In both these respects, the "AMSAC Afros" (as Cruse contemptuously referred to them) fit the bill perfectly for the CIA, which viewed African cultural nationalism as a vehicle for modernization and anticommunism rather than black self-emancipation.

Still, Cruse's blanket indictment ignores certain complexities and nuances. The suggestion that there was something insincere and opportunistic about participation in AMSAC is unfair. Wright and Davis were second to none in their opposition to communism, which they perceived as supporting the black freedom struggle for ulterior purposes, and they were equally passionate in their dedication to the concept of cultural freedom—or, as Horace Mann Bond put it, "the ideal of the free man—the independent man—who owes no allegiance to any power that would . . . trammel the free expression of the individual artistic genius."[120]

That said, there clearly was an element of self-interest about a common complaint of the "AMSAC Afros": the lack of black faces in the U.S. foreign service. The organization's constant agitation of this issue—in May 1961, it even called a special meeting of black leaders to discuss the failure of government, foundations, and other institutions to utilize African American expertise in foreign affairs[121]—might be interpreted as part of what historian Penny Von Eschen has called "a middle-class politics of symbolism and federal patronage," but it could also be counted as (yet another) instance of a CIA front group using covert patronage to enhance its own status and legitimacy in American society.[122] There were even hints that some of the events staged on American soil by AMSAC were used by elements of the old, anticolonial African American left for cultural purposes that had little to do, and even conflicted with, the official U.S. mission in Africa.[123]

Similarly, the AMSAC encounter with African culture was not an entirely one-way street. In 1959, for example, the arrival at Atlanta's airport of Kenyan trade unionist Tom Mboya (a darling of the American noncommunist left and target of a number of CIA front activities) not only excited true feelings of African identity in Horace Mann Bond, it also gave him a fine opportunity to thumb his nose at southern segregation. Dressed in a dashiki and clutching a huge banner in red, gold, and green emblazoned with the legend "Uhuru" ("Freedom" in Swahili), Bond paraded around the arrival hall "curiously . . . observed by the crowds of travelers" before entering a whites-only toilet where "a big cop" could only stand and stare, "absolutely dumbstruck at the intrusion."[124] Jazz pianist and composer Randy Weston, another black American who wore the dashiki as a gesture of cultural solidarity with Africa, returned from an AMSAC-sponsored trip to Nigeria reportedly "enthusiastic about tapping the rich variety of African music in his own compositions."[125] CIA patronage did not always reinforce American "cultural imperialism"; sometimes it "helped to nurture the development of oppositional transnational and Afro-diasporic sensibilities" (to borrow again from Von Eschen's insightful discussion of overt U.S. cultural diplomacy in Africa).[126]

To a certain extent, then, the "AMSAC Afros" were doing the same thing African American leaders had always tended to do with white patronage—that is, apparently accepting it on one set of terms, then actually using it according to another, turning it to the limited advantage of their own race. They were, in other words, "putting on"—a skill that perhaps helps explain why they were so much better than other front groups at maintaining the appearance of unwittingness. Still, it is very much open to question whether the advantages to AMSAC of its covert contract with the CIA outweighed the disadvantages: the loss of organizational independence, the suspicion of many Africans, and the allegations of race betrayal from other African Americans after the secret had been revealed. "It's a nasty deal and I don't like it myself," says college principal Dr. A. Herbert Bledsoe (a character clearly based on famous integrationist black leader Booker T. Washington, whose enormous personal success was largely derived from his ingenious courting of white patrons) in Ralph Ellison's novel *Invisible Man*. "But I didn't make it and I know that I can't change it. . . . After you win the game you take the prize and keep it and protect it: there's nothing else to do."[127]

TEN

Things Fall Apart

JOURNALISTS

In 1977, a few years after breaking open the story of the Watergate cover-up with his *Washington Post* colleague Bob Woodward, Carl Bernstein interviewed retired columnist Joseph W. Alsop for a piece on the CIA and the American news media he was researching for *Rolling Stone* magazine. Although Alsop did not care much for the kind of adversarial investigative journalism Bernstein practiced—his relations with younger colleagues had soured during the Vietnam War, a cause he supported passionately long after most of the U.S. press corps had turned against it—he proved surprisingly expansive on the subject of his own dealings with the American intelligence community. Yes, he had performed certain "tasks" for the Agency, such as a trip to Laos in 1952 at the request of Frank Wisner, who suspected that existing U.S. coverage of political unrest there was based on anti-American sources, and a visit the following year to the Philippines, whence he filed reports praising Edward Lansdale's protégé Ramón Magsaysay. No, his actions were not the result of bribery or cajolery. "I never received a dollar, I never signed a secrecy agreement," he explained. "I didn't have to." Senior CIA officials such as Wisner and his successor as Deputy Director/Plans, Richard M. Bissell, Jr.—the "Founding Fathers," Alsop called them—"were close personal friends." Indeed, he had known Bissell since childhood: the two had grown up near each other in Connecticut, and both attended Groton. "It was a social thing, my dear fellow," Alsop told Bernstein, in his famously patrician drawl. Moreover, in a time of national emergency—a struggle to the death with communist totalitarianism—it was "the right thing to do, . . . my duty as a citizen." True, attitudes might have changed since the 1950s, Alsop conceded, meaning that journalists now "would be outraged by the kinds of suggestions that were made to me." Nevertheless, he was still proud to have been asked to cooperate with the CIA, "and proud to have done it. . . . The notion that a newspaperman doesn't have a duty to his country is perfect balls."[1]

Although the intimacy of his bonds with the Washington foreign policy establishment was unique, Alsop was by no means the only U.S. journalist of the early Cold War era to work closely with the CIA. After initially shying away from press contacts, the Agency under the directorship of Allen Dulles positively cultivated the news media. With their unrivaled ability to circulate overseas, journalists were excellent sources of intelligence, so much so that senior Agency officials, "flashing ID cards and looking like they belonged at the Yale Club" (as one reporter recalled), would greet returning foreign correspondents directly off the boat to debrief them about their travels.[2] Moreover, friendly newspapermen like Alsop could be "tasked" for propaganda purposes, reporting stories that showed the United States—and sometimes the Agency itself—in a flattering light while keeping to themselves information Dulles did not want leaked. Although less image-conscious than his publicity-hungry Director, Frank Wisner was especially interested in this kind of news management. He would constantly confer with the likes of Alsop (not coincidentally, a prominent member of his Georgetown social set) and consult the wire-service tickers kept in a room across the hall from his office. "A story would come over and he'd get on the phone," William Colby remembered. "Get something out! The Mighty Wurlitzer!"[3] Many reporters shared the sense of insider status and civic obligation that motivated Alsop, while others were simply grateful for the scoops that privileged access to classified information could bring them. "We had formed a partnership over secrets," Bob Woodward wrote of his relationship with 1980s DCI William Casey. "In entirely different ways, we were both obsessed with secrets."[4]

Estimates of the number of U.S. reporters who carried out secret assignments for the CIA vary: in 1973, the Agency itself conceded, in the face of questioning from newspaper publishers, a figure of "some three dozen"; a congressional inquiry conducted in 1976 concluded that the total was more like fifty; a year later, Carl Bernstein calculated that as many as four hundred American journalists had worked for the CIA since 1952.[5] Whichever reckoning is most accurate, the incidence of individual reporters performing covert tasks was less significant than the larger pattern of institutional collaboration between the Agency and major news media that Bernstein and other investigators uncovered during the 1970s.[6] Many of the United States's best-known newspapers cooperated with the CIA as a matter of policy. Arthur Hays Sulzberger, publisher of the *New York Times*, was a good friend of Allen Dulles and signed a secrecy agreement with the Agency, although he delegated liaison duties to subordinates so as to give himself plausible deniability. Under the terms of this arrangement, the *Times* provided at least ten CIA officers with cover as reporters or clerical staff in its foreign bureaus, while genuine employees of the paper were encouraged to pass on information to the Agency about, for example, potential foreign agents.[7] Another eminent news executive on friendly terms with Dulles was William Paley of the Columbia Broadcasting System, whose news president, Sig Mickelson (later chief of Radio Free Europe), was in such constant telephone contact with CIA headquarters that, tired of leaving his offices to use a pay phone, he installed a private line that bypassed the CBS switchboard. Among the services provided the Agency by Paley and Mickelson was a "recruiting-and-cover capability" like that offered by the *New York Times*, the laundering of CIA funds by the William S. Paley Foundation, and the loan of the CBS broadcast booth at the United Nations to intelligence officers so that they could lip-read the whispered conversation of Soviet delegates during Nikita Khrushchev's visit in 1959.[8] The relationship was cemented by an annual New Year's Day dinner at Washington's exclusive Alibi Club, paid for by Dulles, and remembered by Mickelson for "top newsmen, top agency men, good talk and cigars, each side out for what it could get."[9] A third mechanism for disseminating CIA-approved stories was the syndicated news service, with the Agency using existing organizations such as Associated Press and United Press International for this purpose, as well as creating its own: Forum World Features.[10]

One organization not mentioned by Bernstein was the journalists' trade union, the American Newspaper Guild (ANG), whose international staff served the CIA in ways reminiscent of the Lovestoneites in the AFL's Free Trade Union Committee. The ANG was a founder member of the International Federation of Journalists, a society of anticommunist newspapermen established in Brussels in 1952 in opposition to the Prague-based, communist-dominated International Organization of Journalists.[11] Following a major expansion of the ANG's international program in 1960, funded by seed money from the AFL-CIO and a grant from "a private philanthropy," an ANG staffer, Ronald Watts, was dispatched to Brussels to oversee the development of free trade unionism and "professional journalism" in Africa and, with occasional assistance from the Asia Foundation, the Far East.[12] Meanwhile, another ANG international affairs representative (Richard P. Davis, later succeeded by John K. Sloan) took up residence in Panama City to run the Inter-American Federation of Working Newspapermen's Organizations (IAFWNO), a hemispheric trade union secretariat with close links to the CIA's South American labor front, the American Institute of Free Labor Development. Overseen by Charles A. Perlik, the American Newspaper Guild's energetic Secretary-Treasurer, Watts, Davis, and Sloan offered journalists from the Third World a host of free services, including technical assistance, educational and training seminars, and "leadership development." These activities were financed from the ANG's International Affairs Fund, which in turn was subsidized by an assortment of foundations all later identified as CIA pass-throughs: the Granary Fund, the Andrew Hamilton Fund, the Broad High Foundation, the Chesapeake Foundation, and the Warden Trust. Grants received from these sources between 1960 and 1967 added up to a total of just under a million dollars.[13]

As with other citizen groups allied with the CIA in the early Cold War, it would be simplistic to depict the U.S. press corps as merely parroting the "Company" line. Some publishers and reporters politely declined invitations to double as secret agents. Despite being another of Allen Dulles's many friends in journalistic circles, David Lawrence, founding editor of *U.S. News and World Report*, threatened to fire any employees of the magazine who entered into a formal relationship with the Agency. Sam Jaffe of CBS was similarly firm in rejecting CIA requests that he take advantage of an assignment in Moscow to engage in espionage.[14] Even the most biddable of newsmen could occasionally present problems. In his determination to get the inside story, Joe Alsop sometimes pushed government officials too far: Charles Bohlen, C. D. Jackson, Paul Nitze, and eventually even Frank Wisner grew fed up with his constant wheedling.[15] During the

1960s, both Joe and his co-columnist, younger brother Stewart (an OSS-er and early CIA booster), became increasingly critical of what they perceived as a loss of nerve within the Agency. Stewart complained that "Bold Easterners," Old Grotonian swashbucklers like himself, were being forced out by intelligence technocrats with slide-rule minds, the "Prudent Professionals"—and the brothers grew correspondingly less cooperative.[16] "The analytical side of the Agency [was] dead wrong about the war in Vietnam—they thought it couldn't be won," Joe told Carl Bernstein in 1977. "I stopped talking to them."[17]

Even allowing for such fallings out, the basic mood of CIA-press relations during the 1950s and early 1960s—the so-called Golden Age of covert operations—was one of harmony. The pervasiveness of the Cold War consensus that supported the Mighty Wurlitzer is perhaps best illustrated by the example of a journalistic medium not mentioned so far: the news magazine. Three publications in particular spanned the spectrum from political left to right as well as from small to mass circulation. The *New Leader* was a long-established, New York–based journal that mixed leftist politics in the domestic sphere with unbending anti-Stalinism in the foreign—a sort of political equivalent to the New York intellectuals' literary flagship, *Partisan Review*. Presided over by Russian social democrat Sol Levitas, who fled the Soviet Union in 1923 disguised in a Red Army colonel's uniform, the magazine also served as an American mouthpiece for the Menshevik émigrés who had proved such a thorn in the side of AMCOMLIB. Although never commanding a large audience—its readership was heavily concentrated in the New York labor movement and similar circles in western Europe—the *New Leader* did enjoy a reputation as an important center of anti-Soviet expertise and activism. Its editors and chief contributors were consulted frequently by government officials such as George Kennan, Allen Dulles, and C. D. Jackson.[18] The publication was also valued as a propaganda counterweight to McCarthyism, its mere existence giving lie to European perceptions that American anti-communism was necessarily uninformed and reactionary. As Jackson explained to Dulles, "The particular tone of voice with which Levitas speaks to a particular group of people here and abroad is unique and uniquely important."[19]

Combined with its chronic financial difficulties—Levitas spent much of his time as the magazine's business manager writing begging letters to potential private patrons—these attributes were enough to put the *New Leader* in line for covert subsidies from the CIA. During the early 1950s, Irving Brown generated extra revenue for the magazine by the simple expedient of arranging for thousands of new European subscriptions to be taken out free of charge.[20] On at least three separate occasions during the same period, Tom Braden resorted to the more direct method of personally handing sums of about $10,000 to Levitas.[21] Meanwhile, the National Committee for a Free Europe provided the publication with an annual grant of $25,000.[22] Although this subsidy was cancelled in 1955, additional covert funding was secured thanks to a "Save the *New Leader*" drive launched by former OPC officer Franklin Lindsay, which by the end of 1956 had netted the magazine donations totaling $45,000.[23] These various ploys were intended, as C. D. Jackson put it, "for all of us to have our Levitas and let him eat, too."[24] The *New Leader* was no mere functionary of the CIA: its coverage of the Cold War actively shaped official attitudes as much as it was shaped by them, while its Menshevik blend of social democracy and zealous anticommunism put it at odds with such Agency fronts as AMCOMLIB (whose association with Russian monarchists it deplored) and the Congress for Cultural Freedom (which it deemed insufficiently resolute in the Cold War struggle for hearts and minds—the hard-line stance of the unruly American Committee for Cultural Freedom was more to its liking). Still, the magazine survived the 1950s only because the CIA wanted it kept alive, for intelligence and propaganda purposes.

Moving from the left wing of the Cold War consensus to its center, one encounters another news magazine with intimate ties to the U.S. intelligence community. Like the *New Leader*, *The Reporter* was strongly identified with the personality of a political refugee, in this case its founder and chief editor, domineering Italian antifascist Max Ascoli. In other respects, however, the two magazines were very different. *The Reporter* was not launched until 1949, and therefore lacked the factional, socialist pre–Cold War history of the *New Leader*. The younger publication consciously styled itself as a mouthpiece for the liberal anticommunist politics of the postwar Washington foreign policy establishment—what Arthur Schlesinger, Jr., "a charter member of the *Reporter* family," had dubbed the "Vital Center." As such, it managed to achieve a respectable readership of 200,000 (the circulation of the *New Leader* hovered around a mere 30,000).[25] Possibly because of its relative fiscal health, there is no evidence to suggest that Ascoli ever received covert payments in the same manner as Levitas, although this is perhaps not surprising, given the apparent destruction of *The Reporter*'s financial records. It also no doubt helped that the Italian had what Frank Wisner would have called "conspicuous access to wealth" in the shape of his wife, Sears Roebuck heiress Marion Rosenwald.[26]

That said, there is abundant proof of other links between *The Reporter* and the Cold War secret state. During World War II, Ascoli worked alongside Nelson Rockefeller, John Hay Whitney, and C. D. Jackson (although the latter never warmed to him personally, thinking him "outstanding—as a difficult character").[27] More significantly, the two most influential members of the magazine's staff beside Ascoli, Philip Horton and Douglass Cater, were ex-OSS-ers who maintained their intelligence connections—what Horton called "the old school tie"—after the war.[28] Indeed, Horton served briefly as the CIA's first station chief in Paris before moving to Henry Luce's *Time* and thence to *The Reporter,* where he acted as Ascoli's second-in command. Described by the Italian as an "extraordinarily industrious intelligence officer," Horton used his "Old Boy" contacts with the likes of William Donovan, Allen Dulles, and James Jesus Angleton to enhance *The Reporter*'s foreign coverage.[29] Cater had helped found the U.S. National Student Association before taking up the position of the magazine's chief Washington correspondent; a widely acknowledged expert on psychological warfare, he would later serve as a special assistant in the Johnson White House. In addition to Cater's NSA associations, *The Reporter* had ties to such Agency fronts as the CCF, the American Committee on United Europe, the NCFE, and the Vietnam Lobby.[30] Perhaps it is telling that Ascoli suspended publication in 1968: *The Reporter*'s life span nearly exactly matched that of the Mighty Wurlitzer.

The right wing of the CIA's covert network in the news magazine world was occupied by the mass-circulation *Time*. Like the *New York Times*, Henry Luce's weekly provided CIA officers with journalistic credentials (Philip Horton's brief spell on the magazine before his move to *The Reporter* was probably designed for cover purposes); Dulles laid on regular dinners for *Time* foreign correspondents similar to those he gave for CBS, receiving in return postassignment debriefings and favorable publicity; and the Luce organization would come to the assistance of other magazines whose circulation figures did not match its own yet were considered worthy causes by the Agency, such as *Partisan Review* and the *New Leader*.[31] Again, there was a healthy amount of self-interest in these actions—both of these publications were useful sources of cultural and political research data for *Time*'s own files—and the relationship with the Agency was not without its occasional strain. Overall, though, the collaboration was extraordinarily successful, so much so it was difficult to tell precisely where the Luce empire's overseas intelligence network ended and the CIA's began. A good case in point was the western response to the communist-controlled 1959 youth festival in Vienna, coordinated by C. D. Jackson and Cord Meyer and largely implemented on the ground by Sam Walker, who was both a *Time* reporter and an officer of the NCFE.

If the Alsop brothers personified the Cold War consensus in journalism, Warren Hinckle and Robert Scheer were its antithesis. At first sight, the two men made a strange partnership. Hinckle was a rambunctious, eye-patch-wearing Irish American from San Francisco whose disrespect for authority, including the traditional ideals of the American left, was matched only by his fondness for hard drinking, fine dining, and his pet monkey, "Henry Luce."[32] Scheer was a Bronx-raised, City College–educated intellectual who had won a reputation in the nascent Free Speech Movement at Berkeley as a formidable, perhaps arrogant, radical ideologue. "If a cartoonist were to draw him," Hinckle wrote later, "Scheer would be just a pair of eyeglasses and a beard."[33] What united the two men, apart from the attraction of opposite personalities and their youth—neither was yet out of his twenties in the early 1960s—was a common desire to awaken the nation from what Hinckle called the "Big Sleep of Journalism."[34]

The unlikely instrument Hinckle and Scheer selected to achieve this ambition was *Ramparts*, a literary journal founded in Menlo Park, California, in 1962, by Catholic convert and millionaire Edward Keating (another man who owed much of his wealth to a good marriage, in his case to Helen English, a gypsum heiress). Brought in by Keating as his promotional director, then fired and hired back again, all in the space of the first year of publication, Hinckle set about trying to expand the magazine's base of appeal beyond Catholic literati by covering such burning political issues of the day as the civil rights movement and the war in Vietnam.[35] Scheer joined *Ramparts'* editorial board in 1964, after signing a contract written on a brown paper bag in a crowded New York bar, as part of this process of reinvention.

In addition to challenging what Hinckle saw as the "don't rock the boat" attitude of the previous journalistic generation, the young editors of *Ramparts* thumbed their noses at other conventional wisdom of the news magazine publishing world. Although they eventually quit suburban Menlo Park for offices in a seedy neighborhood of San Francisco, they remained firmly rooted in the Bay Area, providing them with "a natural, relatively unspoiled talent pool," as Hinckle described it, and enabling them to defy "the shibboleth that a national magazine need be produced from New York." Moreover, whereas most previous left-wing publications had eschewed commercial ambitions and concentrated on minimizing their overhead by, for example, using "butcher paper," Hinckle aimed to make *Ramparts* a well-produced, glossy title that would not only cover its costs but even make a profit. This he never achieved, inheriting as he did an operating deficit of about $100,000 from Keating—although *Ramparts* managed, at the height of its popularity, a laudable readership of 250,000. Still, through a combination of attention-grabbing stunts and muckraking scoops, Hinckle succeeded in getting his magazine noticed well beyond the normal confines of the left, even being credited with inventing a new kind of journalism, "radical slick."[36]

The noisy arrival on the national scene of the "new journalism" coincided with a sudden reversal in the fortunes of the CIA. Even during the late 1950s, there had been warning signs—most conspicuously, a botched attempt to unseat President Sukarno of Indonesia in 1958—that covert operations were not all that they were cracked up to be. However, it was not until April 1961, and the disastrous failure of an effort to topple Fidel Castro by landing a small army of Cuban émigrés at the Bay of Pigs, that the CIA's Golden Age truly came to an end. The Kennedy administration, initially as enthralled by the Agency's mystique as its predecessor, decided that the time had come "to take the CIA away from the Club" (as Arthur Schlesinger, now a White House aide, advised the president on April 21, 1961).[37] "If this were the British government, I would resign, and you, being a senior civil servant, would remain," JFK told DD/P Richard Bissell, the planner of the abortive operation. "But it isn't. In our government, you and Allen have to go."[38] Dulles stepped down in November 1961, his publicly brave face concealing a profound inner sense of humiliation and betrayal; Bissell followed in February 1962. Their replacements, John McCone and Richard M. Helms respectively, both clearly conformed more to the Prudent Professional type than the Bold Easterner, stressing as they did "the need to develop more professional espionage and counterespionage operations" (a policy rapidly vindicated by the Agency's detection of nuclear missile emplacements on Cuba in October 1962) "and to tighten the discipline in the covert-action arena."[39] The advantage in the struggle between covert operations and intelligence, as old as the Agency itself, appeared at long last to be tilting in favor of the latter.

The Bay of Pigs also badly tarnished the once golden public image of the CIA. "Suddenly, the Agency appeared to be, not an elite corps of slick, daring James Bond operatives," remembered William Colby, "but rather a collection of bunglers, launching harebrained escapades and leading men uselessly to their death."[40] Congressmen who had expressed their complete confidence in secret executive measures to prosecute the Cold War now demanded greater legislative oversight; even as establishmentarian a voice as Senator J. William Fulbright's was among those raised in criticism of the Agency. Newspapers that had formerly printed nothing but praise for the CIA began lobbing brickbats instead (a notable exception being the conservative *Chicago Tribune*, transformed from its earlier role as a leading skeptic about the need for a peacetime intelligence agency into one of its most passionate advocates). Publishing houses that had once accepted Agency commissions now started putting out distinctly hostile books, such as David Wise and Thomas B. Ross's memorably titled *The Invisible Government*. The CIA fought back, leaking a document blaming adverse press comment about it on a Soviet-inspired campaign of defamation, but the response lacked conviction. As intelligence historian Rhodri Jeffreys-Jones has written, "the supportive consensus in government, the media, and Congress which had seen Dulles through thick and thin in the 1950s had lost its former strength."[41]

The new, dissident mood also spread into the Agency itself. True, many of the liberals in charge of covert operations responded to questioning of their activities by hardening their anticommunist stance. Cord Meyer, for example, once the golden boy of world federalism, now described by one observer as "a gray man with a gray suit and gray hair," was so dogmatic in his Cold War orthodoxy that he would harass fellow guests at Georgetown dinner parties who failed to display the same degree of ideological fervor. (A variety of factors have been blamed for this transformation in Meyer's personality, among them the trauma of his 1953 loyalty investigation, the paranoid influence of James Angleton, and a series of ghastly personal tragedies that included the murder in mysterious circumstances of his former wife, Mary Eno Pinchot.)[42] Others, however, dismayed by the excesses that were being committed in the name of democracy, broke away from the Cold War consensus and became whistle-blowers, thereby establishing a precedent for the sensational exposés by former intelligence officers that would dominate headlines about the CIA during the early 1970s.

One such dissident was Paul Sakwa, the IOD officer who had dared to challenge Jay Lovestone and Irving Brown's conduct of covert labor operations in the late 1950s. In 1959, Sakwa was transferred to the Vietnam desk of the Far East Division, where he rapidly realized that the United States was "locked into a disaster of our making" which would only "become worse."[43] Shortly after the launch of the Kennedy administration in 1961, Sakwa began communicating his concerns to sympathetic liberals in the White House, including his friend from Americans for Democratic Action, Arthur Schlesinger. When Schlesinger encouraged him to commit his thoughts to paper, Sakwa produced a long memorandum for the president under the title "CIA: Problems of a Clandestine Agency." "Inter-agency struggles, internal political conflicts, and an over-extended involvement in foreign policy operations . . . have made some men giddy with power and imbued with self-righteousness," reads this document, now filed among Schlesinger's White House papers at the Kennedy Library in Boston. "About half the present operations are useless if not counter-productive, or just plain not worth the expense."[44] When Meyer, the likely inspiration of the jibe about self-righteousness, learned of Sakwa's actions, he was furious. Not only had a junior officer gone over a superior's head outside the Agency, Sakwa had also usurped Meyer's function as CIA liaison with the White House. (Meyer's links with JFK went back to 1945 when they had attended the UN's founding meeting at San Francisco together. The two men's relationship had soured by the early 1960s, however, possibly as a result of an affair between the president and Meyer's wife, Mary Pinchot. In March 1963, Meyer recorded in his diary his puzzlement about JFK's "strange competitiveness" combined with "a curiosity and interest in my private life that I find un-explainable."[45] According to Sakwa, Kennedy would complain to his aides after visits from Meyer, "Why does CIA send that shit to see me?")[46] Shortly after the delivery of the memo to Schlesinger, Sakwa was effectively hounded out of the Agency, and his attempt to find other government employment at the State Department was blocked by Meyer. The whistle-blower was still seeking reinstatement and compensation for unfair dismissal in 1979.[47]

Given that the CIA's own covert action divisions were no longer water-tight, it was hardly surprising that the Agency's front organizations were also beginning to spring leaks. Rumors about secret official subsidies had circulated in émigré, intellectual, and labor circles ever since the early 1950s. "It was meant to be a cover, but actually it was transparent," one intelligence officer admitted of the Farfield Foundation, the Agency's main conduit to the cultural world. "We all laughed about it, and called it the 'Far-fetched Foundation.'"[48] Extra security measures were adopted, including the use of genuine philanthropies, such as the J. M. Kaplan Foundation of New York and the Hobby Foundation of Houston, Texas, to piggyback covert subsidies between the CIA's dummy donors and front organizations. ("We have for a period of several years cooperated with [the CIA] on several projects," William P. Hobby, a trustee of the Hobby Foundation and editor of the *Houston Post*, later told the *New York Times*. "We are proud . . . to have been of service to the Federal Government.")[49] There was even talk between Richard Helms and Frank Wisner "of phasing out CIA support . . . in favor of . . . open funding from private organizations and perhaps some semi-official government sources," a course of action also strongly recommended in 1960 by the Sprague Committee (another of President Eisenhower's several reviews of overseas information programs).[50] However, the secret funding continued, probably as a result of bureaucratic territoriality and inertia; indeed, judging by the example of the American Newspaper Guild, the CIA appears, if anything, to have expanded into new fields of front operation during the early 1960s. ("So much for the adage against fixing things that aren't yet 'broke,'" Helms later reflected wryly.)[51] The loose talk carried on as well. To cite just one example, the American Friends of the Middle East (AFME), an organization created in 1951 to facilitate U.S. contacts with pro-western Arabs, was the target of repeated allegations by American Zionists that it was secretly funded by the U.S. government. The charge later turned out to be accurate: AFME's main source of funding was the Dearborn Foundation, the same pass-through philanthropy that supported the Committee of Correspondence.[52]

In April 1966, when *Ramparts* published its exposé of the CIA's hand in the Vietnam Project at Michigan State University (MSU), the Agency's covert network truly began to unravel. Hinckle and Scheer had earlier provided glimpses of the Mighty Wurlitzer at work in their coverage of the war in Indochina, including *Ramparts* pieces on Tom Dooley and the Vietnam Lobby.[53] The Michigan story was, however, the magazine's first thoroughgoing investigation of an Agency front operation, based, like the others that followed, on firsthand testimony from a disillusioned "witting asset"—in this instance, former project director Stanley K. Sheinbaum.[54] The article caused consternation at an apparently unprepared CIA headquarters in Langley, where the new DCI, William F. Raborn, Jr., urgently instructed Security Director Howard J. Osborn to provide him with a "run down" on *Ramparts* on a "high priority basis."[55] As Osborn's deputies scrambled to assemble information about the magazine and its staff, another internal task force set about investigating, in the words of Richard Helms, "all of our relationships with academic institutions and academicians," with the aim, presumably, of plugging possible future leaks of the sort that had just happened at MSU.[56] After Raborn had been briefed, Osborn's team turned its attention to digging up material on *Ramparts* "of a derogatory nature," Raborn recalled, concentrating in particular on the magazine's sources of funding. They hoped to find evidence showing Hinckle and his colleagues to be "a subversive unit."[57] The goal clearly was to find a legal way of shutting down the publication, thereby preventing further revelations about the CIA's front operations.

By then, however, the genie was out of the bottle. The *Ramparts* scoop on the MSU project provided the "adequate news peg" that the *New York Times* had been waiting for before publishing a series of critical articles about the CIA compiled by a Washington-based team of reporters led by Tom Wicker. Intelligence officers were appalled by this display of assertiveness on the part of the previously pliable newspaper. "Radio Moscow is quoting you by name these days," one official told Wicker at a party. "You really helped your country, didn't you?"[58] A few weeks after the appearance of the *Times* articles, in May 1966, Irish intellectual Conor Cruise

O'Brien, delivering a lecture entitled "The Writer and the Power Structure" to an audience of New York University alumni, implied that the Congress for Cultural Freedom's English-language organ, *Encounter,* had received secret U.S. government subsidies.[59] A vituperative response in the magazine's pages provoked the Irishman to sue for libel, earning his original comments more publicity and eventually an apology from the editors. Also in May 1966, Victor Reuther gave the *Los Angeles Times* a long interview hinting at CIA involvement in U.S. labor foreign operations. Cord Meyer was horrified. "Something has got to be done to stop this," he told an AFL-CIO official. "It's doing a lot of damage."[60] Eventually, Victor gave into pressure from his brother Walter to pipe down. The issue would not go away, however. Victor was profoundly disenchanted with the drift of American foreign policy in the 1960s, and the ancient rivalry between the Reuthers of the CIO and the Lovestoneites of the AFL provided the potential for further confrontations and indiscretions.

In the end, though, it was not the CIA's traditionally troublesome labor and intellectual front groups that caused the house of cards to collapse. The coup de grâce came from a more unexpected quarter. Law student Phil Sherburne, described in the alumni magazine of his alma mater, the University of Oregon, as an ingenuous-looking twenty-four-year-old with "a lock of brown hair that forever spills over his forehead," became witting of the NSA's clandestine relationship with the CIA shortly before his election as the organization's president in 1965, having served the previous year as an unwitting National Affairs Vice-President.[61] At first Sherburne appeared to toe the line, agreeing to give a speech opposing a proposal for an East-West student conference and continuing to accept Agency subsidies, via the Foundation for Youth and Student Affairs, on the NSA's behalf. Simultaneously, however, he busied himself raising funds from other sources, an activity in which he had excelled while National Affairs Vice-President, and working quietly to assert ownership of the NSA's overseas program, by, for example, appointing only unwitting students to international office. In March 1966, Sherburne revealed to his case officers what had been his secret intention all along: as of 1966–67, the NSA would no longer accept money or direction from the CIA. The spies, not surprisingly, were taken aback and tried a variety of measures to dissuade him, including withholding $70,000 of promised funds, a measure that forced the NSA president to sack two conscientious and unsuspecting staff members.[62] The unassuming but steely Sherburne refused to be daunted, retaliating by preventing the CIA from using the NSA as a conduit for subsidies to the International Student Conference in Leiden.[63] "Some of the fights with the Agency were really hair-raising," he later told his successor, Eugene Groves.[64] By the end of his presidency, with the organization nearly self-sufficient financially and Groves equally determined to end the relationship, Sherburne felt confident that he had broken the CIA's grip on the NSA, and that he had done so without the covert subsidies becoming public knowledge.

Sherburne had, however, made one mistake. Shortly before leaving office, he told an unwitting NSA fund-raiser, who had developed suspicions about the organization's finances when he was instructed not to approach a CIA dummy foundation from which Sherburne would no longer accept subsidies, about the Agency link. Initially, the fund-raiser, a Pomona College graduate by the name of Michael Wood, agreed to remain silent, but by January 1967 his conscience had got the better of him. During a mid-afternoon meeting in the dining room of New York's Algonquin Hotel that had been arranged by public relations executive Marc Stone (brother of radical journalist I. F. Stone), a "fidgety and run-down" Wood told Warren Hinckle all about the NSA's covert funding: the case officers, conduits, and code-names. Although the *Ramparts* editor was mystified as to "what the CIA would want with a bunch of left-wing longhairs," he knew a good news story when he saw one, and directed a team of reporters to start looking into the student organization's finances, using records that Wood had provided him.[65]

Almost immediately the researchers found evidence confirming Wood's claims. A few years earlier, in August 1964, a maverick Texan congressman, Wright Patman, had accidentally stumbled across eight CIA funding pass-throughs while conducting an investigation into foundation tax loopholes. After a closed meeting with CIA and Internal Revenue Service officials, Patman hurriedly turned his attention elsewhere, but the names of the "Patman Eight" had already found their way onto the back page of the *New York Times*.[66] The *Ramparts* investigators cross-checked the names in the *Times* with the donors listed in the pilfered files Wood had given them and found that they matched. Wood had told the truth—the CIA was funding the NSA.

The Agency, meanwhile, having accepted that there was no legal way of closing *Ramparts* down, was experimenting with new methods of curbing the magazine's investigations. Richard Helms, who had just replaced Raborn as Director of Central Intelligence, transferred responsibility for the operation from Howard Osborn to Richard Ober, a counterintelligence specialist in the Directorate of Plans. Ober, who had early knowledge of *Ramparts*' interest in the NSA—the magazine "leaked like a bad kidney," Hinckle admitted later—opted for a strategy of "damage control," proposing that NSA officers hold a press conference shortly before the results of the investigation were due to be published, admitting to the relationship and declaring it was now over, at their insistence.[67] "The plan was to steal the thunder from the *Ramparts* story," explains journalist Angus Mackenzie, "limiting its impact by making it old news."[68] Hinckle, however, who had his own spies in the NSA, got wind of the plot and decided that, rather than be scooped by the CIA, he would scoop himself. Resorting to a tactic he had used to publicize earlier *Ramparts* exposés, he purchased full-page advertisements announcing the story in both the *New York Times* and the *Washington Post* due to appear on Tuesday, February 14, the same day the NSA press conference was scheduled to take place. The stratagem worked better than Hinckle dared hope. When Neil Sheehan of the *Times* phoned NSA headquarters on Monday, February 13, with questions about the advertisement, Eugene Groves, after hasty consultation with the CIA, read a statement confirming the truth of the charges.[69] Hinckle was jubilant, writing later, "It is a rare thing in this business when you say bang and somebody says I'm dead."[70] When *Ramparts* eventually brought out its March issue containing an article by Sol Stern entitled "A Short Account of International Student Politics with Particular Reference to the NSA, CIA, Etc.," it was already an international news story.[71]

In the days that followed the *Ramparts* scoop, reporters from the *New York Times* and the *Washington Post*, until recently such good friends of the CIA, filed story after story exposing Agency front organizations, generating "a drumfire of editorial denunciation . . . that swept across the country" (as a rueful Cord Meyer recorded in his memoirs).[72] The frenzy of revelation climaxed on March 13, when CBS reporter and future *60 Minutes* host Mike Wallace stood in front of a large, three-dimensional diagram depicting the flow of covert subsidies to front organizations, in an hour-long CBS documentary entitled "In the Pay of the CIA: An American Dilemma," which featured interviews with, among others, Gloria Steinem, Norman Thomas, and Phil Sherburne.[73]

These reports brought forth universal political condemnation. Eight Democratic congressmen sent a letter to President Lyndon Johnson accusing the CIA of having "compromised and corrupted the largest student organization in the largest democracy in the world," while Vice President Hubert H. Humphrey told an audience at Stanford University that he was "not at all happy about what the CIA has been doing."[74] The right, too, was up in arms. Republican presidential contender Barry Goldwater asked "why all of this money went to left-wing organizations . . . instead of conservative groups such as Young Americans for Freedom." (Dave Jones, the Executive Director of YAF, wrote a brilliantly sarcastic letter to DCI Helms, explaining why "we feel we might also qualify for aid from the Central Intelligence Agency, and would appreciate an application form for such a request.")[75]

Abroad, while the general reaction in Europe to the CIA's embarrassment appears to have been one of cynical amusement or even sneaking admiration for the ingenuity of some of the operations that had been exposed—"Les Américains sont formidables," one French diplomat told a U.S. official at a Paris reception[76]—the response in the Third World countries that the Agency was most anxious to influence was predictably negative. In India, the journal *Seminar* accused the United States of engaging in "academic colonialism," while Indira Gandhi depicted the CIA as an international pariah.[77] Just as the furore appeared to be dying down in the subcontinent, John Kenneth Galbraith "raised unshirted hell" when he wrote a piece for the *Washington Post* describing his experiences with the Agency while serving as U.S. ambassador in New Delhi. After a frosty phone conversation with Richard Helms, the distinguished economist "agreed to remain silent and refrain from further public revelations."[78]

Meanwhile, the front organizations themselves imploded in a welter of protests and recriminations. Within the world of journalism, the sharpest barbs were reserved for the CIA-financed international operations of the American Newspaper Guild. While representatives of the International Federation of Journalists in Brussels and the Inter-American Federation of Working Newspapermen's Organizations in Panama rallied round, American reporters fell over themselves in their haste to denounce the ANG leadership.[79] Guild members in local units, including 127 who worked in the *New York Times* newsroom, signed petitions denouncing the organization's relationship with the Agency. "Whoever participated in this money grabbing has stained us all," declared the staff of *Look* magazine.[80] Despite protestations of unwittingness from ANG leaders, the attacks continued, with leading newspapers joining in the outcry. According to the *Washington Post* in a February 19 editorial entitled "The Eager Victim," the ANG had been "hungrily taking covert Government money" and, by doing so, had evinced "moral imbecility." The most colorful denunciation came from outspoken New York columnist Jimmy Breslin, who telephoned Chuck Perlik on the morning of the *Post* editorial to tell him that "You made us look like a bunch of whores up here . . . and we're f—— going to look into it."[81] Judging by his column of the following day, Breslin's main complaint about the ANG was the lack of "verve" of its response to the revelations. "All the people who run the guild can do," he chuntered, "is stand around with the imagination of the fat old madames who used to wring their hands and tell police, 'I don't know why all these men kept coming here.'"[82] Stung by Breslin's comments, the ANG leadership fought back, insisting that regardless of the ultimate source of its funds, the union's international program had been entirely independent (a common self-defense of blown front organizations).[83] The argument fell on deaf ears. By September 1967, the ANG's international representatives had been called home and reassigned to domestic duties.[84]

Media attention also focused on a White House evidently caught unawares by the scandal. (The first the Johnson administration had heard of the *Ramparts* article about the NSA was when Eugene Groves telephoned Douglass Cater seeking an appointment the week before it was due to appear.)[85] Much responsibility fell on the shoulders of the Acting Secretary of State, Nicholas B. Katzenbach, whose first instinct was to make only a "bare bones admission," putting the CIA's program of secret subsidies "in the most favorable light it could be put."[86] When it became clear that this approach would not placate the press, President Johnson announced the formation of a committee of inquiry into covert government funding of U.S. voluntary organizations, to be composed of Katzenbach, Secretary of Health, Education, and Welfare John Gardner, and DCI Helms. Although more robust than previous presidential responses to CIA "flaps," this initiative still smacked strongly of damage control. When Senator Mike

Mansfield, a longtime advocate of greater congressional control over the Agency (and, ironically, a former member of the Vietnam Lobby), wrote LBJ recommending a greatly expanded brief for the Katzenbach Commission, the president (in a reply drafted by Katzenbach) politely turned down the suggestion, citing the need for a quick report to help dispel the cloud of suspicion now surrounding American volunteer workers overseas.[87] Other CIA critics were discomfited by the participation in the inquiry of the DCI (whose principal assistant was to be none other than Cord Meyer). "I must say . . . that it is a little strange for one to ask Mr. Helms to investigate CIA," said William Fulbright. "It would be like asking Mr. Fowler (Treasury Secretary) to investigate [the] affairs of Fort Knox."[88]

Meanwhile, the CIA stepped up its investigation into *Ramparts*, hoping to turn up some information that would retrospectively discredit the magazine's reporting of the NSA story and head off future exposés.[89] By April 4, Richard Ober, his team now expanded to twelve, had inquired into the backgrounds of 127 *Ramparts* staff and contributors, as well as those of 200 other U.S. citizens associated with the publication.[90] Although the FBI had never investigated *Ramparts* per se, it had compiled numerous dossiers on individual members of its circle with past or current ties to the American communist movement. In addition to looking for evidence of political radicalism, Ober focused on the magazine's financial affairs, using IRS tax records to identify the angels who subsidized its considerable operating deficit and drawing up a list of advertisers who might be pressured into dropping their accounts.[91] The resulting report, which was filed on April 5, has never been declassified, but former intelligence officers have since stated that it contained a number of operational recommendations for measures to counteract *Ramparts*, variously described as "awful things" and "heady shit," including the planting of hostile news stories in other media.[92]

Such articles began appearing a few days later, in publications ranging from the daily *Washington Star* to the conservative weekly *Human Events*.[93] The latter, in a piece written by one M. M. Morton ("the pen name of an expert on internal security affairs"), documented *Ramparts*' political and financial history in impressive detail.[94] However, apart from the fact that Robert Scheer had visited Prague to meet officers of the communist-controlled International Union of Students around the time of the NSA flap, very little of the material unearthed by Ober's research team suggested any political motive on the part of the magazine's editors other than homegrown, New Left–style dissent.[95] The section on *Ramparts'* angels was particularly disappointing, listing as it did a few obviously non-communist American left-liberals. Something of the investigators' desperation can be sensed in an unintentionally humorous attempt to red-bait the magazine by mentioning an advertisement for Inch Kenneth, a Scottish island "which afforded a sweeping view of low-lying fog" belonging to a contributing editor, émigré British aristocrat and former communist Jessica "Decca" Mitford. According to Warren Hinckle's later recollection, the Communist Party of Great Britain had already turned down Mitford's free offer of the island, and "Decca had to deal with any number of imbeciles and wayfarers . . . before she found a real person to buy the island—a doctor of sorts, if memory serves."[96] Despite this failure, Ober's investigatory powers were expanded in the months that followed, with the launch in August 1967 of the CIA's domestic surveillance program, Operation MHCHAOS. Indeed, an important if ironic consequence of the *Ramparts* revelations about covert front operations was to increase the Agency's tendency to spy on American citizens. (Operation MHCHAOS would eventually be exposed too, by *New York Times* reporter Seymour Hersh in 1974.)

Several weeks after the appearance of the planted articles, on May 20, 1967, the Mighty Wurlitzer received another stunning blow in the shape of a brief but revelatory piece in the *Saturday Evening Post* by none other than Allen Dulles's lieutenant and the man charged with carrying out the Agency's non-communist left strategy in the early 1950s—Tom Braden. Having left government employment in 1954, Braden had spent the intervening years publishing a newspaper in Oceanside, California, and serving as president of the State Board of Education, in which role he courted controversy as an outspoken liberal and hate-figure of the west coast right.[97] His article, provocatively entitled "Why I'm Glad the CIA Is 'Immoral,'" was couched as a defense of the Agency's citizen group operations, listing as it did the front organizations created by the Soviet Union after World War II and making the argument, repeated so often in later discussions of the subject, that the subsidies were secret only because of the McCarthyite political atmosphere of early Cold War America. However, it was not so much these statements that attracted attention as the passages in which Braden disclosed operational details of a sort that the CIA is reluctant to reveal even today. In particular, the former chief of IOD referred to the placing of "agents" in the Congress for Cultural Freedom and *Encounter*, and to specific financial transactions with the Lovestoneites of the AFL and the Reuther brothers.[98]

Not surprisingly, these revelations triggered another flurry of condemnations and recriminations, with the editors of *Encounter* quarreling bitterly about who among them was the witting asset (the finger clearly pointed at Melvin Lasky) and Victor Reuther trying to salvage his reputation by describing the occasion on which he had rejected Braden's attempts to recruit him as an agent.[99] (The most robust response came from the redoubtable George Meany who, after implausibly protesting his unwittingness, proclaimed his "pride in the work that we have done overseas" and resentment "that the CIA is trying to horn in on it.")[100] The article also caused further dismay within the Agency itself. "I think Tom meant well but obviously it is going to be very damaging," Cord Meyer wrote Allen Dulles on May 1, enclosing an advance copy of Braden's piece. "I really can't understand why he did it." Braden's former boss was appalled by what he viewed as a violation of both personal loyalty and professional commitments. When Joan Braden, Tom's wife, tried to mend bridges between the two men a month later, the now frail Dulles regretfully told her that he could no longer have any dealings with his former deputy. "If he felt he could do this, how could he expect to be trusted in the future with work requiring discretion and confidence? He has hurt many of us and my feelings for Tom have been deeply affected."[101] Dulles died in January 1969, the rift with Braden still unrepaired.

Braden's article had all the appearances of an unauthorized action by a famously maverick operator, even to those who had once managed him at the CIA. However, some clues point to a different interpretation of the *Saturday Evening Post* piece. Meyer's intimation to Dulles that Braden was acting independently of, and even contrary to, the wishes of the Agency is implicitly contradicted by an apparently insignificant document held at the Lyndon Johnson Library in Texas, a memorandum from National Security Advisor Walt W. Rostow to President Johnson dated April 19, 1967. "I assume you know of the forthcoming Braden article on the CIA in the *Saturday Evening Post*," the note reads. "Here is the story from Dick Helms."[102] Although the attached report by the DCI is missing,

Rostow's covering memo suggests that the Agency not only had sufficient advance warning of the article's appearance for it to invoke Braden's secrecy oath and thereby prevent publication, it might even have played a part in the piece's planning, along with a knowledgeable and supportive White House. Two other pieces of circumstantial evidence point to the same tentative conclusion. One is the fact that the CIA had planted stories in the *Saturday Evening Post* before, with the help of one of its editors, Stewart Alsop.[103] According to Braden's later recollection, Alsop also collaborated in the drafting of his article (the two men had a history of writing together, going back to their coauthored 1947 celebration of the OSS, *Sub Rosa*).[104] Second, much press coverage of the article's impact dwelled disproportionately on the embarrassment of the non-communist leftists identified as witting assets by Braden, especially Victor Reuther. For example, reports of the affair by labor columnist Victor Riesel, who had cooperated secretly with the Agency since the early 1950s, reveled in the irony that the charges of accepting covert subsidies that Reuther had previously leveled against Jay Lovestone and Irving Brown "will reverse—perhaps boomerang."[105]

It was a well-worn technique of the CIA to blow the cover of covert operations when they were no longer considered desirable or viable, and there were a number of reasons why, by April 1967, the Agency might have tired of its alliance with the non-communist left. For one, the NCL had become a far less reliable instrument of U.S. foreign policy than it had been a decade earlier. With their propensity for criticizing the war in Vietnam, ADA-style left-liberals such as the Reuther brothers were increasingly perceived in Washington as a hindrance rather a help in the prosecution of the Cold War. This view had, of course, long been held by conservatives such as James Burnham, but it had now come to be shared by the Johnson White House, with the president himself deeply resentful of liberal anticommunists who had once supported U.S. policy in Vietnam and now opposed it. (Compared with his predecessors, LBJ had never been very enthusiastic about front group operations, nor for that matter about the CIA itself, which he suspected vaguely of having played some role in the Kennedy assassination.) The fact that Victor Reuther had also made several hostile, public statements about covert CIA involvement in American labor organizations would no doubt have been noticed in Langley. (An internal White House memorandum, written in the immediate wake of *Ramparts*' NSA story, noted that "the UAW boys are getting set to unload a chapter and verse indictment of Jay Lovestone's various operations.")[106] Certainly the *Saturday Evening Post* article, with its details about Braden's contacts with the Reuthers, was interpreted by Walter Reuther "as a warning shot over the bow," and the UAW boss again reprimanded his younger brother for putting them so far out on a political limb.[107] Even Braden himself, while still denying that he was put up to writing the piece, later told an interviewer that there were "those in the Agency who wanted to get rid of things like this that were virtually blown already. . . . I always had it in the back of my mind that they wanted it killed, but I can't prove it."[108]

While Braden helped wreck the CIA's front operations on the noncommunist left, the Agency's leaders fought to retain the right to subsidize voluntary organizations. The Katzenbach Commission had acknowledged the possibility of the federal government's creating a new, semiautonomous agency that would openly administer public funding to deserving private groups—the example of the British Council was cited on several occasions—and an interim report, issued on March 17, hinted at genuine internal debate, with Gardner (who already nursed misgivings about CIA activities in the academic world) urging a complete ban on all covert funding, and Helms opposing him.[109] The final report, issued on March 29, represented a compromise brokered by Katzenbach, recommending that all secret subsidies cease, yet acknowledging in a footnote that "overriding national security interests" might sometimes necessitate such an arrangement. As Katzenbach explained to LBJ, "we ought to *try* to achieve a flat ban, but without handcuffing the Administration or the United States Government, whatever the future danger."[110] Hence, although the report set December 31, 1967, as the final date by which all funding to private organizations should end, in fact covert subsidies for Radio Free Europe and Radio Liberty carried on, leading to a fresh round of revelations in 1972.[111] Meanwhile, a follow-up committee created to examine possible mechanisms for overt government funding and chaired by Secretary of State Dean Rusk failed to make any concrete practical recommendations. "It seems to me far better to let the CIA matter wither away and let a new Administration take a fresh look at the possibilities," Rusk told President Johnson in June 1968.[112]

For all the obvious limitations of LBJ's response to the *Ramparts* revelations, the events of 1967 did represent a turning point of sorts. The exposure of the Mighty Wurlitzer constituted "one of the worst operational catastrophes in CIA history," reckons a historian on the Agency's own staff. "Officials were forced to dismantle dozens of compromised operations with a combined budget of millions of dollars."[113] Moreover, while the Katzenbach Commission's main purpose was clearly to deflect further hostile publicity, its report, by recognizing the principle of restraint on the CIA's field of operation, established a precedent for the far more thoroughgoing congressional investigations of the Agency that would follow in the 1970s, including the famous Pike and Church Committees. Most importantly, the investigations of the *Ramparts* reporters symbolized the disintegration of the Cold War consensus on which the Mighty Wurlitzer had been built. Without that foundation, the edifice, a teetering, haphazard construction at best, was bound to come crashing down.

Conclusion

The CIA's relationship with its front organizations has often been depicted in the imagery of musical recitation or theatrical performance. The Agency has variously been portrayed as playing the keys of a giant organ, pulling the strings of marionettes, or calling the tune of a piper. Whatever the metaphor, the implication is the same: from behind the scenes, the spies exercised complete control over the recipients of their covert largesse.

The group-by-group analysis undertaken here suggests a more complex reality. To be sure, the CIA tried its utmost to dictate the terms of the patronage relationship, keeping the circle of knowledgeability in front organizations as small as possible, disciplining the witting with secrecy oaths, and gradually excluding those likely to make trouble (hence the common pattern of doctrinaire anticommunists losing influence to more subtle, tactically adept Cold Warriors). However, this was not the whole story. Few of the CIA's fronts were "innocents' clubs," to resurrect Willi Münzenberg's contemptuous description of "fellow travelers" in the Popular Front era. Genuine unwittingness was a rare condition. Many supposed innocents had a pretty good idea what was going on, and allowed it to continue because they naturally supported the U.S. cause in the Cold War. Others were simply grateful for money, whatever its source, so they could advance their own collective or individual agendas. And some, convinced that they were better equipped to fight the Cold War than government officials, actually tried to get the upper hand in the relationship. In every case, some metaphor specific to the particular group involved seems more appropriate than the conventional musical or dramatic imagery: industrial relations, for example, or church-state conflict.

The evidence presented here has also placed question marks next to other widely held assumptions about U.S. front operations (most of which, it is important to note, originated in publicity generated by CIA boosters such as Tom Braden). One of these is that covert funding of voluntary organizations was forced upon government officials by the McCarthyite atmosphere of the early Cold War era. There is some truth to this claim, but it disregards the fact that the first front groups predated the worst of the postwar Red Scare, as well as the great tactical advantages that the CIA gained from secrecy, at least in the short term. These included, as an expert witness before the Rusk Committee noted in May 1967, "considerable flexibility" in determining levels of support, "a minimum of red tape," and, most importantly, the appearance of independence in the eyes of target populations suspicious of American assistance "where the source of the funding is an identified U.S. Government agency."[1]

Similarly, the notion that the covert action divisions of the Agency were ideologically predisposed to favor groups on the non-communist left, while again having much to recommend it, fails to account for the tensions that existed between intelligence officers and such leftists as the Lovestoneites, the New York intellectuals, and the Mensheviks, not to mention the spies' readiness to sponsor right-wing émigré and religious groups when it served their purposes to do so. The corresponding claim that, in the cultural sphere, the CIA was particularly inclined to patronize modernist artists is undermined by evidence suggesting that, when circumstances demanded, it was also prepared to promote middle- and low-brow culture. Both politically and aesthetically, then, it seems that the Agency's choice of clients was dictated by pragmatism rather than principle. It is surely telling that the archetypal CIA liberal, Braden, was willing to help his former employer kill off its blown NCL fronts in 1967.

What do we now know about the Mighty Wurlitzer? Modeled on the communist front, and powered by the natural energy of American associationalism, the CIA's covert network was constructed by a group of elite men whose innate dislike of big government and official secrecy was offset by their hatred of communism and unquestioning belief in the moral righteousness of their own actions. Having failed in one of its original purposes, the mobilization of eastern-bloc émigrés to liberate the "captive nations," the network was increasingly employed instead to prevent the communization of, first, western Europe, then such regions of the developing world as Southeast Asia, South America, and Africa. As this shift took place, the early influence on front operations of ex-communist ideologues gave way to a liberal, internationalist emphasis on development and modernization, with many of the citizen groups involved also active in social movements and minority struggles on the home front. The CIA, however, was never able to resolve the fundamental contradiction between Cold War anticommunism and domestic reform at the heart of its front program; nor did the groups themselves ever succeed in reconciling their claims to representativeness at home and internationalism abroad with their covert purpose as state-funded weapons of political warfare. Eventually, when the Cold War consensus fragmented along racial, generational, and gender lines in the late 1960s, the difficulties not only of maintaining this unlikely alliance but also of keeping its existence secret became insurmountable, and the Wurlitzer collapsed. Its fate is symbolized most poignantly in the lives of the CIA officers who tried to "play" it: the suicide Wisner, the disillusioned Meyer, and the disgraced Dulles. Only Tom Braden emerged unscathed, and he had gotten out early.

The cost of the Wurlitzer to Americans was immense, both literally and figuratively. (One Rusk Committee witness put the total annual expense of "CIA support for private, voluntary organizations," excluding the proprietary radio stations, at about $15 million.)[2] Quite apart from the personal crises that enveloped many private individuals who had participated in front operations, whether wittingly or unwittingly, when these operations were exposed in 1967 (the example of student leader Eugene Groves springs to mind), there was the miasma of suspicion that attached itself to all U.S. citizens—students, journalists, clergy, and aid workers—who were working abroad for genuine nongovernment organizations or official agencies that had resisted covert penetration, such as the Peace Corps.[3]

At home, the revelations of 1967 damaged popular trust in government. Coming as they did several years before Watergate and the other political scandals of the mid-1970s, they constituted the first occasion in the postwar period when Americans learned en masse that they were being systematically deceived by federal officials. The news of covert CIA involvement also sullied the image of that most cherished of American institutions, the citizen association, arguably contributing to the decline of associational activity, which a number of observers have identified as one of the distinguishing features of late twentieth-century American life.[4] Finally, the cult of covert action that gave rise to the Mighty Wurlitzer in the first place—and the incapacitating, demoralizing bouts of hostile external scrutiny that ensued when operations were exposed—distracted the CIA from its founding mission, the gathering and analysis of intelligence about threats to national security, the prevention of another Peal Harbor. Combined with other factors, such as presidential inattention and intelligence manipulation, this failing has had unfortunate and sometimes tragic consequences, the brunt of which has been born by ordinary Americans.

Was the cost worth it? The United States eventually won the Cold War struggle for hearts and minds, but how much this victory had to do with government-funded psychological warfare measures, as opposed to the spontaneous appeal of consumer capitalism or factors internal to the communist bloc, is very much open to question. The impact of propaganda on target populations is notoriously hard to measure, and in the case of CIA front operations the researcher lacks access even to the results of the public opinion surveys conducted by overt information agencies such as the USIA. The handful of country studies undertaken by scholars to date suggests an uneven impact, with some front organizations enjoying an enthusiastic reception, others meeting with resistance or opportunistic acts of appropriation, and all prone to the vagaries of local conditions over which the CIA had little or no control. That said, one generalization does seem possible: front operations were most effective when they succeeded in attracting the support of national elites who shared a positive vision of American power in the world. Thus, for example, the internationalist, modernizing, social democratic-tinged politics of the Reutherite CIO played far better with overseas labor movements than the hectoring anticommunism and business unionism of the AFL's Lovestoneite foreign policy apparatus. There is perhaps a lesson to be learned here by those currently concerned about improving the United States's image abroad.

Indeed, a number of the issues raised by the history of the Mighty Wurlitzer are very much alive today, at a time when the CIA still holds a large stake in areas of American civil society. Take U.S. universities, for example. In 1976, the Church Committee reported that it was "disturbed" by the Agency's "operational use" of individual academics, which included "providing leads and making introductions for intelligence purposes, collaboration in research and analysis, intelligence collection abroad, and preparation of books and other propaganda materials."[5] In the years that immediately followed, American academic leaders, most notably the president of Harvard University, Derek Bok, attempted to impose some control over CIA activities on campus, drawing up codes of professional conduct to govern dealings between individual academics and intelligence officers. This campaign had little effect.[6] The Agency refused to abide by the guidelines and continued to employ professors for recruitment, research, and intelligence-gathering purposes, even at Bok's own university, where in 1986 Professor Nadav Safran, director of the Center for Middle Eastern Studies, was censured for using CIA money to organize an international conference without informing the attendees.[7] If anything, these practices have intensified in recent years, with the "war on terror" recreating the conditions of total mobilization that prevailed in the first years of the Cold War. A few intractable individuals still speak out, alleging a fundamental conflict between the values of scholarly inquiry and secret intelligence; but the CIA is, according to the *Wall Street Journal*, "a growing force on campus," even offering special scholarships to graduate students willing and able to obtain security clearances.[8]

The front group also has in recent years undergone a revival of sorts. Neoconservative intellectuals—the ideological and, in several cases, biological descendants of the New York intellectuals of an earlier generation—have employed tactics and techniques first used on American soil by the Old Left during the 1930s, which were then resurrected by a CIA front, the American Committee for Cultural Freedom, during the 1950s. Ventures such as the Project for a New American Century (the invention of William Kristol, son of ACCF officer and neocon intellectual "godfather," Irving Kristol) prosecute the neoconservatives' notion of a "global democratic revolution" in the Middle East.[9] There have even been reports linking Azar Nafisi's *Reading Lolita in Tehran: A Memoir in Books*, a hugely popular account of the author's experience introducing fellow Iranian women to forbidden works of western literature, with the neoconservative project of preparing American opinion for a U.S. invasion of Iran, in a scenario reminiscent of earlier deployments of literary texts in the cultural

Cold War.[10] Meanwhile, in an ironic and ghastly symmetry, radical Islamic groups posing as community welfare organizations have used the front tactic in an effort to recruit young British Muslims for further terrorist attacks on western targets. (It is not clear at this stage to what extent this practice has spread to the United States.)[11] Far from dying out after the end of the Cold War, the front group is alive and well, and living in Bradford, England.

Should western intelligence services use the tactic themselves in the war on terror? The example of the U.S. front groups created in the early years of the Cold War suggests that such operations do not necessarily entail cynical manipulation and passive obedience. Indeed, the CIA's state-private network was built to a great extent on shared values and involved a surprising amount of self-assertion on the part of the private citizens who belonged to it. Nevertheless, no matter how much one dwells on the consensual and voluntarist aspects of the relationship, the fact remains that the front tactic was based on secrecy and deception, making it all the more problematic when undertaken in a nation avowedly dedicated to the principles of freedom and openness. "Operations of this nature are not in character for this country," concluded George Kennan, who had been perhaps the most influential advocate of communist-style propaganda methods at the beginning of the Cold War, in 1985. "I regret today, in light of the experience of the intervening years, that the decision was taken."[12]

CIA front operations in the Cold War blighted individual careers and lives; their eventual exposure stained the reputation of the nation itself. Public diplomacy, the winning of hearts and minds, should be left to overt government agencies and genuine, nongovernment organizations. This is the most valuable lesson to be drawn from the history of the Mighty Wurlitzer.

Notes

Acknowledgments

Index

Notes

Introduction

1. Anon., "'Warm, Open' Scholar," *New York Times*, 16 February 1967, 26.
2. Ibid.
3. W. Eugene Groves, "President's Report to the Twentieth National Student Congress," 1967, box 62, folder President's Report, U.S. National Students Association Papers, Hoover Institution, Stanford University.
4. Ibid.
5. Ibid.
6. For more on the revelations and their aftermath, see chap. 10.
7. Anon., "Students to Cut Last Tie to CIA," *New York Times*, 12 August 1967, 1, 10.
8. Groves, "President's Report."
9. Arthur M. Schlesinger, Sr., "Biography of a Nation of Joiners," *American Historical Review* 50 (1944): 1–25; Alexis de Tocqueville, *Democracy in America*, ed. Harvey C. Mansfield and Delba Winthrop (Chicago: University of Chicago Press, 2000), p. 489.
10. Policy Planning Staff, "The Inauguration of Organized Political Warfare," 4 May 1948, in C. Thomas Thorne, Jr., and David S. Patterson, eds., *Foreign Relations of the United States, 1945–1950: Emergence of the Intelligence Establishment* (Washington, D.C.: U.S. Government Printing Office, 1996), p. 670.
11. Quoted in Scott Lucas, *Freedom's War: The U.S. Crusade against the Soviet Union, 1945–1956* (Manchester: Manchester University Press, 1999), p. 108.
12. Quoted in Evan Thomas, *The Very Best Men—Four Who Dared: The Early Years of the CIA* (New York: Simon and Schuster, 1995), p. 60.

13. Groves, "President's Report."
14. Recent publications that touch on CIA front operations include Eric Thomas Chester, *Covert Network: Progressives, the International Rescue Committee, and the CIA* (New York: M. E. Sharpe, 1995); Peter Grose, *Operation Rollback: America's Secret War behind the Iron Curtain* (Boston: Houghton Mifflin, 2000); Jöel Kotek, *Students and the Cold War* (Basingstoke: Palgrave Macmillan, 1996); Helen Laville, *Cold War Women: The International Activities of American Women's Organizations* (Manchester: Manchester University Press, 2002); Lucas, *Freedom's War*; Ted Morgan, *A Covert Life: Jay Lovestone, Communist, Anti-Communist, and Spymaster* (New York: Random House, 1999); and Robin Winks, *Cloak and Gown: Scholars in the Secret War, 1939–1961*, 2nd ed. (New Haven, Conn.: Yale University Press, 1996).
15. Frances Stonor Saunders, *The Cultural Cold War: The CIA and the World of Arts and Letters* (New York: New Press, 2000), published in the U.K. as *Who Paid the Piper? The CIA and the Cultural Cold War* (London: Granta, 1999).
16. Hugh Wilford, *The CIA, the British Left, and the Cold War: Calling the Tune?* (London: Frank Cass, 2003).
17. Examples of such operations include the American Committee on United Europe (ACUE), the CIA's principal front in the field of European federalism (the promotion of which was a major U.S. strategic aim in the postwar era), which dealt directly with federalist leaders in Europe. Similarly, the American Fund for Free Jurists (AFFJ) tended to function merely as a conduit by which CIA susbidies were channeled to the International Commission of Jurists (ICJ), a Europe-based organization that the Agency hoped would protest human rights abuses in the eastern bloc. For more on the ACUE, see Richard J. Aldrich, *The Hidden Hand: Britain, America, and Cold War Secret Intelligence* (London: John Murray, 2001), chap. 16, and Wilford, *CIA, British Left, and Cold War*, chap. 7. On the AFFJ and ICJ, see Howard B. Tolley, Jr., *The International Commission of Jurists: Global Advocates for Human Rights* (Philadelphia: University of Pennsylvania Press, 1994), chap. 1.

1. Innocents' Clubs

1. See Stephen Koch, *Double Lives: Spies and Writers in the Secret Soviet War of Ideas against the West* (New York: Free Press, 1995), pp. 3–4, 320; Sean McMeekin, *The Red Millionaire: A Political Biography of Willi Münzenberg, Moscow's Secret Propaganda Tsar in the West* (New Haven, Conn.: Yale University Press, 2003), pp. 304–305.
2. Quoted in Koch, *Double Lives*, p. 8.
3. McMeekin, *Red Millionaire*, pp. 113–114.
4. Ibid., p. 1; Koch, *Double Lives*, p. 27.

5. "Every business he touched . . . hemorrhaged red ink." McMeekin, *Red Millionaire*, p. 2.
6. Quoted in Koch, *Double Lives*, p. 14.
7. Quoted in McMeekin, *Red Millionaire*, p. 197.
8. Quoted in Albert Fried, *Communism in America: A History in Documents* (New York: Columbia University Press, 1997), p. 286.
9. For an overview of the Popular Front, see Michael Denning, *The Cultural Front: The Laboring of American Culture in the Twentieth Century* (London: Verso, 1996), chap. 1.
10. See Harvey Klehr, John Earl Haynes, and Fridrikh Igorevich Firsov, *The Secret World of American Communism* (New Haven, Conn.: Yale University Press, 1995); and Harvey Klehr, John Earl Haynes, and Kyrill M. Anderson, *The Soviet World of American Communism* (New Haven, Conn.: Yale University Press, 1998).
11. See Harvey Klehr and John Earl Haynes, *Venona: Decoding Soviet Espionage in America* (New Haven, Conn.: Yale University Press, 1999).
12. See Ellen Schrecker and Maurice Isserman, "'Papers of a Dangerous Tendency': From Major Andre's Boot to the VENONA Files," in Schrecker, ed., *Cold War Triumphalism: The Misuse of History after the Fall of Communism* (New York: Free Press, 2004), pp. 149–173.
13. Quoted in Koch, *Double Lives*, p. 15.
14. See Rhodri Jeffreys-Jones, *Cloak and Dollar: A History of American Secret Intelligence*, 2nd ed. (New Haven, Conn.: Yale University Press, 2003), chap. 9; and Thomas Powers, *Intelligence Wars: American Secret History from Hitler to al-Qaeda* (New York: New York Review Books, 2002), chap. 1.
15. Burton Hersh, *The Old Boys: The American Elite and the Origins of the CIA* (St. Petersburg, Fla.: Tree Farm Books, 2002), p. 52.
16. Quoted in Patrick K. O'Donnell, *Operatives, Spies, and Saboteurs: The Unknown Story of the Men and Women of World War II's OSS* (New York: Free Press, 2004), p. xi.
17. See Thomas F. Troy, *Wild Bill and Intrepid: Donovan, Stephenson, and the Origin of the CIA* (New Haven, Conn.: Yale University Press, 1996).
18. Hersh, *Old Boys*, p. 12.
19. Powers, *Intelligence Wars*, p. 46.
20. Hersh, *Old Boys*, p. 12.
21. Powers, *Intelligence Wars*, p. 48.
22. Atherton Richards, quoted in Hersh, *Old Boys*, p. 77.
23. On the Jedburghs, see the lively, semifictionalized portrait, clearly based on the authors' personal experiences, in Stewart Alsop and Thomas Braden, *Sub Rosa: The OSS and American Espionage* (New York: Reynal and Hitchcock, 1946). For more on university professors' service in the OSS, see Robin Winks, *Cloak and*

Gown: Scholars in the Secret War, 1939–1961, 2nd ed. (New Haven, Conn.: Yale University Press, 1996).

24. See Peter Grose, *Gentleman Spy: The Life of Allen Dulles* (Boston: Houghton Mifflin, 1994), chap. 9.
25. Alsop and Braden, *Sub Rosa*, p. 21.
26. Quoted in O'Donnell, *Operatives*, p. xv.
27. For more on the OSS's MO branch, see Clayton D. Laurie, *The Propaganda Warriors: America's Crusade against Nazi Germany* (Lawrence: University Press of Kansas, 1996), esp. chap. 7.
28. See Bradley F. Smith, *The Shadow Warriors: OSS and the Origins of the CIA* (New York: Basic Books, 1983), chap. 7.
29. Quoted in Peter Grose, *Operation Rollback: America's Secret War behind the Iron Curtain* (Boston: Houghton Mifflin, 2000), p. 37.
30. Quoted in Hersh, *Old Boys*, p. 194.
31. Ibid., p. 147.
32. Quoted in Grose, *Operation Rollback*, p. 89.
33. Quoted in Hersh, *Old Boys*, p. 154.
34. Quoted in ibid., p. 154.
35. Ibid., p. 160.
36. George F. Kennan, *Memoirs, 1925–1950* (Boston: Little, Brown, 1967), p. 293.
37. Ibid., pp. 557, 555, 557. For a highly suggestive analysis of Kennan's rhetoric, see Frank Costigliola, "Demonizing the Soviets: George F. Kennan's Long Telegram," in Robert J. McMahon and Thomas G. Paterson, eds., *The Origins of the Cold War*, 4th ed. (Boston: Houghton Mifflin, 1999), pp. 157–174.
38. Quoted in Rhodri Jeffreys-Jones, *The CIA and American Democracy*, 3rd ed. (New Haven, Conn.: Yale University Press, 2003), p. 35.
39. Grose, *Operation Rollback*, p. 88.
40. The text of the relevant section of the National Security Act is reproduced in William M. Leary, *The Central Intelligence Agency: History and Documents* (Tuscaloosa: University of Alabama Press, 1984), pp. 128–130.
41. See Frances Stonor Saunders, *Who Paid the Piper? The CIA and the Cultural Cold War* (London: Granta, 1999), pp. 36–37.
42. The helpful phrase "determined interventionists" can be found in Sallie Pisani, *The CIA and the Marshall Plan* (Lawrence: University Press of Kansas, 1991).
43. See, for example, Walter Hixson, *George F. Kennan: Cold War Iconoclast* (New York: Columbia University Press, 1989), p. xi.
44. Grose, *Operation Rollback*, p. 96. The text of NSC 4-A can be found in C. Thomas Thorne, Jr., and David S. Patterson, eds., *Foreign Relations of the United States, 1945–1950: Emergence of the Intelligence Establishment* (Washington, D.C.: U.S. Government Printing Office, 1996), pp. 650–651. It was so secret that only

three copies were made—one for the Agency, one for the White House files, and one for Kennan.

45. See Scott Lucas, *Freedom's War: The U.S. Crusade against the Soviet Union, 1945–1956* (Manchester: Manchester University Press, 1999), pp. 43–47.
46. Policy Planning Staff, "The Inauguration of Organized Political Warfare," 4 May 1948, Thorne and Patterson, *Foreign Relations*, pp. 668, 671.
47. Ibid., pp. 668–672. A fourth type of "specific project" is discussed in the memorandum, but the relevant passages have been redacted in the declassified version. In the absence of any clues as to the contents of the missing section, it is tempting to speculate that it deals with covert operations intended to expedite western European union, such as the American Committee on United Europe.
48. Quoted in Thorne and Patterson, *Foreign Relations*, p. 713.
49. For Kennan's list of nominees, which also included the "Lovestoneite" American Federation of Labor official Irving Brown, see Thorne and Patterson, *Foreign Relations*, p. 716.
50. William Colby and Peter Forbath, *Honorable Men: My Life in the CIA* (New York: Simon and Schuster, 1978), p. 73.
51. Frank Wisner to Roscoe Hillenkoetter, 29 October 1948, quoted in Thorne and Patterson, *Foreign Relations*, pp. 730–731.
52. See Pisani, *CIA and Marshall Plan*, pp. 72–78.
53. See Evan Thomas, *The Very Best Men—Four Who Dared: The Early Years of the CIA* (New York: Simon and Schuster, 1995), p. 40; Hersh, *Old Boys*, p. 220.
54. Hersh, *Old Boys*, p. 6.

2. Secret Army

1. See Christopher Simpson, *Blowback: America's Recruitment of Nazis and Its Effects on the Cold War* (New York: Weidenfeld and Nicolson, 1988), pp. 34–39.
2. For "secret army" phrase, see Evan Thomas, *The Very Best Men—Four Who Dared: The Early Years of the CIA* (New York: Simon and Schuster, 1995), p. 25. Kennan and Lindsay and Thayer quoted in Peter Grose, *Operation Rollback: America's Secret War behind the Iron Curtain* (Boston: Houghton Mifflin, 2000), p. 94. May 1948 report quoted in Burton Hersh, *The Old Boys: The American Elite and the Origins of the CIA* (St. Petersburg, Fla.: Tree Farm Books, 2002), p. 211. For Operation Bloodstone, see Simpson, *Blowback*, pp. 112–124. Rositzke quoted in Thomas, *Best Men*, p. 35.
3. Quoted in C. Thomas Thorne, Jr., and David S. Patterson, eds., *Foreign Relations of the United States, 1945–1950: Emergence of the Intelligence Establishment* (Washington, D.C.: U.S. Government Printing Office, 1996), p. 670.
4. Quoted in Michael Nelson, *War of the Black Heavens: The Battles of Western Broadcasting in the Cold War* (Syracuse, N.Y.: Syracuse University Press, 1997), p. 40.

5. Frances Stonor Saunders, *Who Paid the Piper? The CIA and the Cultural Cold War* (London: Granta, 1999), p. 131.
6. Quoted in NCFE press release, March 1950, box 43, folder 1, Allen W. Dulles Papers, Seeley G. Mudd Manuscript Library, Princeton University. (Hereafter, for box and folder numbers, e.g., 43.1.)
7. Nelson, *War of the Black Heavens*, p. 49.
8. See, for example, Lewis Galantiere, "Memorandum for the Record," 25 July 1956, 191.1, Radio Free Europe/Radio Liberty Corporate Records, Hoover Institution, Stanford University (hereafter RFE/RL Papers).
9. Sig Mickelson, *America's Other Voice: The Story of Radio Free Europe and Radio Liberty* (New York: Praeger, 1983), p. 21.
10. Abbot Washburn, quoted in Grose, *Operation Rollback*, p. 127.
11. "Free Europe, Inc., Operating Expenses by Divisions for the Year Ended June 30, 1952," 189.5, RFE/RL Papers.
12. According to Spencer Phenix, a CIA "watchdog" on the Crusade board, Washburn was released only after the Agency had applied pressure on senior executives at General Mills. Spencer Phenix to Allen Dulles, 29 January 1951, 167.1, RFE/RL Papers.
13. Larry Tye, *The Father of Spin: Edward L. Bernays and the Birth of Public Relations* (New York: Henry Holt, 1998), p. 35. For an excellent analysis of Bernays's influence on U.S. government psychological warfare, see Kenneth Osgood, *Total Cold War: Eisenhower's Secret Propaganda Battle at Home and Abroad* (Lawrence: University Press of Kansas, 2006), pp. 19–22.
14. See Daniel L. Lykins, *From Total War to Total Diplomacy: The Advertising Council and the Construction of the Cold War Consensus* (Westport, Conn.: Praeger, 2003).
15. The influence on CIA front operations of public relations theory and advertising techniques would remain—indeed, Edward Bernays himself played an important role on behalf of his client the United Fruit Company in the Agency-engineered coup that took place in Guatemala in 1954—but it would never be as strong again as it had been in the case of the Crusade for Freedom, due to the relatively lower domestic profile of subsequent front organizations.
16. Mickelson, *America's Other Voice*, p. 54; Walter L. Hixson, *Parting the Curtain: Propaganda, Culture, and the Cold War, 1945–1961* (New York: St Martin's Press, 1997), p. 60.
17. Quoted in Nelson, *War of the Black Heavens*, p. 48.
18. Scott Lucas, *Freedom's War: The U.S. Crusade against the Soviet Union, 1945–1956* (Manchester: Manchester University Press, 1999), p. 103.
19. Arch Puddington, *Broadcasting Freedom: The Cold War Triumph of Radio Free Europe and Radio Liberty* (Lexington: University Press of Kentucky, 2000), pp. 22, 23 (quotation on p. 22).

20. NCFE press release, March 1950, 43.1, Dulles Papers. In December 1954, for example, NCFE officers met with representatives of the "Sponsor" in Washington to discuss, among other matters, membership of the Romanian National Council. The intelligence officers provided a list of nominees, carefully balanced so as to reflect all elements of political opinion in the Rumanian emigration. Lewis Galantiere, "Washington Meetings, December 9 and 10," 13 December 1954, 190.12, RFE/RL Papers.
21. See Robert E. Terhaar to Brutus Coste, 1 September 1949, 26.1, Brutus Coste Papers, Hoover Institution, Stanford University.
22. For a lively insider's account of the Free Europe Press's efforts to infiltrate western publications behind the Iron Curtain, see John P. C. Matthew, "The West's Secret Marshall Plan for the Mind," *International Journal of Intelligence and Counterintelligence* 16 (2003): 409–427.
23. Thomas, *Best Men*, p. 33.
24. See Mickelson, *America's Other Voice*, pp. 56–57.
25. Hixson, *Parting the Curtain*, p. 66.
26. For Lenin example, see Nelson, *War of the Black Heavens*, p. 1; for Finland, Puddington, *Broadcasting Freedom*, p. 6.
27. Quoted in Lucas, *Freedom's War*, p. 67.
28. Hersh, *Old Boys*, p. 242.
29. Hixson, *Parting the Curtain*, p. 63.
30. Quoted in Lucas, *Freedom's War*, p. 101.
31. See Nelson, *War of the Black Heavens*, pp. 69–70, and Puddington, *Broadcasting Freedom*, pp. 33–35.
32. Puddington, *Broadcasting Freedom*, p. ix.
33. James Burnham to Levering Tyson, 27 February 1952, 9.2, James Burnham Papers, Hoover Institution, Stanford University. See also James Burnham to Levering Tyson, 17 August 1951, 9.2, Burnham Papers; C. D. Jackson to Levering Tyson, 20 September 1951, 9.2, Burnham Papers; James Burnham to A. A. Berle, Jr., 23 January 1952, 9.2, Burnham Papers.
34. National Committee for a Free Europe, Inc., Progress Report, January 1950, 26.5, Coste Papers.
35. Anon., "An NCFE Approach to the European Refugee Situation," 15 July 1952 (revised 20 July 1952), box 31, folder Bu-By-Misc.1, C. D. Jackson Papers, Dwight D. Eisenhower Library, Abilene, Kansas.
36. The report of the President's Committee on International Information Activities (known as the "Jackson Committee" after its chair, William H. Jackson), quoted in Hixson, *Parting the Curtain*, p. 66.
37. Quoted in Nelson, *War of the Black Heavens*, p. 39.
38. Anon. [probably James Burnham], "Polish Social-Democrats in relation to

Czeslaw Milosz, Kultura, and the Congress for Cultural Freedom," 5 February 1952, 11.7, Burnham Papers. The social democrats also alleged that Milosz was homosexual.

39. Willis D. Crittenberger to Committee members, "Opposition to European Advisory Group," 21 April 1958, box 54, folder Free Europe Committee, Jackson Papers. See Puddington, *Broadcasting Freedom*, chap. 5.
40. Puddington, *Broadcasting Freedom*, pp. 29, 43; Cord Meyer, *Facing Reality: From World Federalism to the CIA* (New York: Harper and Row, 1980), pp. 117–118.
41. Quoted in Nelson, *War of the Black Heavens*, p. 52.
42. Frank Altschul to Allen Dulles, 20 May 1955, box 54, folder Free Europe Committee, Jackson Papers.
43. Carmel Offie to Jay Lovestone, 4 April 1951, box 381, folder "Monk," Jay Lovestone Papers, Hoover Institution, Stanford University.
44. Robert H. McDowell, memorandum for the record, "Friction between Committee Free Europe and Émigré Organizations," 13 October 1952, 4.080, Psychological Strategy Board Files, 1951–1953, Harry S. Truman Library, Independence, Missouri.
45. Robert E. Lang to Executive Committee, NCFE, 4 March 1955, box 54, folder Free Europe Committee, Jackson Papers.
46. Anon. [probably DeWitt C. Poole], memorandum, 2 October 1950, F-1985-00856, www.foia.cia.gov (accessed 27 May 2006).
47. Altschul and Lang quoted in Puddington, *Broadcasting Freedom*, pp. 25, 28.
48. Ibid., p. 27.
49. C. D. Jackson to John C. Hughes, 15 March 1954, box 3, folder Hughes, John C., C. D. Jackson Records, Dwight D. Eisenhower Library, Abilene, Kansas.
50. C. D. Jackson, log, 23 June 1953, box 68, Log 1953.2, Jackson Papers.
51. Victor Marchetti and John D. Marks, *The CIA and the Cult of Intelligence* (New York: Alfred A. Knopf, 1974), p. 135.
52. See Mickelson, *America's Other Voice*, pp. 61–62; Nelson, *War of the Black Heavens*, p. 56.
53. Mickelson, *America's Other Voice*, p. 62.
54. For a helpful explanation of the divisions within the Soviet emigration, see Eric Thomas Chester, *Covert Network: Progressives, the International Rescue Committee, and the CIA* (New York: M. E. Sharpe, 1995), chap. 5. On the Mensheviks, see André Liebich, *From the Other Shore: Russian Social Democracy after 1921* (Cambridge, Mass.: Harvard University Press, 1997).
55. Grose, *Operation Rollback*, p. 131.
56. Anon. [probably James Burnham], "The American Committee for the Liberation of the Peoples of Russia," 27 February 1952, 11.7, Burnham Papers.
57. Boris Nicolaevsky to Carmel Offie, 28 March 1950, 495.18, Boris Nicolaevsky

Papers, Hoover Institution, Stanford University. Dallin quoted in Grose, *Operation Rollback*, p. 131. The Mensheviks also often used the *New Leader* as a launching pad for attacks on conservative Russians and those Americans they perceived as sympathetic to the émigré right. See anon. [probably James Burnham], "A Campaign by the Russian Menshevik Émigrées [*sic*]," n.d., 9.1, Burnham Papers.

58. See, for example, Eugene Lyons to Raphael Abramovitch, 17 July 1951, 421.8, Nicolaevsky Papers.
59. Eugene Lyons to Committee Members, 13 August 1951, box 3, folder Russia—American Committee for Liberation of Russia, William Y. Elliott Papers, Hoover Institution, Stanford University.
60. Grose, *Operation Rollback*, pp. 133–134; *Economist* quote on p. 132.
61. Quoted in Mickelson, *America's Other Voice*, p. 64.
62. Boris Sergievsky to Leslie C. Stevens, 7 January 1954, box 68, folder Logidensky, Alexis A.2, Jackson Papers. "This eight million American dollars were spent without achieving anything but scandal and confusion," reckoned Sergievsky.
63. C. D. Jackson to Tom Braden, 13 May 1954, box 31, folder Br-Misc.1, Jackson Papers; C. D. Jackson, log, 18 May 1953, box 68, Log 1953.2, Jackson Papers; C. D. Jackson, log, 15 May 1953, box 68, Log 1953.1, Jackson Papers.
64. Gene Sosin, *Sparks of Liberty: An Insider's Memoir of Radio Liberty* (Philadelphia: University Press of Pennsylvania, 1999), p. 9.
65. Quoted in Nelson, *War of the Black Heavens*, p. 58.
66. James Critchlow, *Radio-Hole-in-the-Head / Radio Liberty: An Insider's Story of Cold War Broadcasting* (Washington, D.C.: American University Press, 1995), p. 15.
67. Sosin, *Sparks of Liberty*, p. 33.
68. Puddington, *Broadcasting Freedom*, p. ix.
69. Quoted in Rhodri Jeffreys-Jones, *The CIA and American Democracy*, 3rd ed. (New Haven, Conn.: Yale University Press, 2003), p. 61.
70. Quoted in Nelson, *War of the Black Heavens*, p. 42. Philby, who disliked Wisner's "orotund style of conversation," went on to describe an OPC-MI6 meeting in London attended by British Foreign Office representative Tony Rumbold, where the American "expatiated on one of his favourite themes: the need for camouflaging the source of secret funds supplied to apparently respectable bodies in which we were interested. 'It is essential,' said Wisner in his usual informal style, 'to secure the overt cooperation of people with conspicuous access to wealth in their own right.' Rumbold started scribbling. I looked over his shoulder and saw what he had written: 'people with conspicuous access to wealth in their own right = rich people'." Quoted in Nelson, *War of the Black Heavens*, p. 43.
71. Thomas, *Best Men*, p. 42.

72. Quoted in Lucas, *Freedom's War*, p. 130.
73. Thomas, *Best Men*, p. 43.
74. Hersh, *Old Boys*, p. 271.
75. Quoted in ibid., p. 282.
76. In fact, the Psychological Strategy Board largely failed to assert any control over Wisner's OPC. See John Prados, *Safe for Democracy: The Secret Wars of the CIA* (Chicago: Ivan R. Dee, 2006), pp. 80–82.
77. Jeffreys-Jones, *CIA and American Democracy*, p. 74.
78. Hersh, *Old Boys*, p. 306.
79. Thomas, *Best Men*, p. 138.
80. See ibid., and Hersh, *Old Boys*, for more on Wisner's deterioration.
81. Grose, *Operation Rollback*, p. 188.
82. Quoted in Hersh, *Old Boys*, p. 298.
83. Quoted in Thomas, *Best Men*, p. 71.
84. Ibid., p. 107.
85. Hixson, *Parting the Curtain*, p. 83.
86. Ibid., p. 81.
87. For more detail on RFE's role in Hungary, see ibid., pp. 83–86; Lucas, *Freedom's War*, pp. 254–262; Puddington, *Broadcasting Freedom*, chap. 6; and Prados, *Safe for Democracy*, pp. 153–159.
88. Nelson, *War of the Black Heavens*, p. 75; Meyer, *Facing Reality*, p. 129. For the text of the review itself, see George R. Urban, *Radio Free Europe and the Pursuit of Democracy* (New Haven, Conn.: Yale University Press, 1997), pp. 281–291.
89. Richard Bissell, quoted in Hersh, *Old Boys*, p. 372.
90. William Colby, quoted in Grose, *Operation Rollback*, p. 218.
91. Quoted in Lucas, *Freedom's War*, p. 267.
92. Hersh, *Old Boys*, p. 412.

3. AFL-CIA

1. Quoted in Ted Morgan, *A Covert Life: Jay Lovestone, Communist, Anti-Communist, and Spymaster* (New York: Random House, 1999), p. 229.
2. Quoted in ibid., p. 99.
3. Ibid., p. 141.
4. Quoted in Quenby Olmsted Hughes, "'In the Interest of Democracy': The Rise and Fall of the Early Cold War Alliance between the American Federation of Labor and the Central Intelligence Agency" (Ph.D. diss., Harvard University, 2003), p. 45.
5. See Ben Rathbun, *The Point Man: Irving Brown and the Deadly Post-1945 Struggle for Europe and Africa* (London: Minerva, 1996), pp. 91–93.

6. Quoted in Morgan, *Covert Life*, p. 192.
7. *Reader's Digest* quoted in ibid., p. 177; Brown quoted in Peter Weiler, *British Labour and the Cold War* (Palo Alto, Calif.: Stanford University Press, 1988), p. 91. For more on Brown's European activities in the late 1940s, see Morgan, *Covert Life*, chap. 11. On the breakup of the WFTU and launch of the ICFTU, see Anthony Carew, *Labour under the Marshall Plan: The Politics of Productivity and the Marketing of Management Science* (Manchester: Manchester University Press, 1987), chap. 5.
8. Quoted in Morgan, *Covert Life*, pp. 186, 191.
9. Ibid., p. 197.
10. Anthony Carew, "The American Labor Movement in Fizzland: The Free Trade Union Committee and the CIA," *Labor History* 39 (1998): 26.
11. Morgan, *Covert Life*, p. 198.
12. See, for example, Jay Lovestone to Irving Brown, 15 January 1951, box 29, folder 10, International Affairs Department, Irving Brown Papers (RG18–004), George Meany Memorial Archives, Silver Spring, Maryland; Jay Lovestone to Lillie Brown, 27 March 1951, 29.11, Brown Papers; Jay Lovestone to Irving Brown, 13 March 1951, 29.11, Brown Papers.
13. Carew, "American Labor in Fizzland," 27, 37.
14. Quoted in Morgan, *Covert Life*, p. 301.
15. Ibid., p. 203. For more on Lovestone's agent network, see ibid., chap. 15. Carew provides a useful summary of FTUC operations in "American Labor in Fizzland," 26–27. Hughes, "Interest of Democracy," concentrates on the FTUC's French and exile activities as well as its efforts to publicize the existence of slave labor camps in the Soviet Union.
16. Morgan, *Covert Life*, p. 154.
17. See, for example, Philip Taft, *The AF of L from the Death of Gompers to the Merger* (New York: Harper and Brothers, 1959).
18. See, for example, Ronald Radosh, *American Labor and United States Foreign Policy* (New York: Random House, 1969).
19. See, for example, Carew, "American Labor in Fizzland." This article is a pioneering exploration of the relationship between the FTUC and the CIA based on the newly available Lovestone papers, which are divided between the George Meany Memorial Archives, Silver Spring, Maryland, and the Hoover Institution, Stanford University.
20. Quoted in Carew, "American Labor in Fizzland," 28.
21. See, for example, Jay Lovestone to Irving Brown, 4 January 1951, box 283, folder Irving Brown, Lovestone Papers, Stanford.
22. Quoted in Morgan, *Covert Life*, p. 205.
23. Irving Brown to Jay Lovestone, 1 April 1951, box 283, folder Irving Brown,

Lovestone Papers, Stanford; Irving Brown to Jay Lovestone, 9 January 1951, box 283, folder Irving Brown, Lovestone Papers, Stanford; Jay Lovestone to Lillie Brown, 27 March 1951, 29.11, Brown Papers.

24. Carew, "American Labor in Fizzland," 28.
25. Jay Lovestone to Irving Brown, 2 April 1951, box 283, folder Irving Brown, Lovestone Papers, Stanford; Jay Lovestone to Irving Brown, 4 April 1951, 29.11, Brown Papers.
26. Jay Lovestone to Samuel Berger, 4 April 1951, box 283, folder Sam Berger, Lovestone Papers, Stanford.
27. Jay Lovestone to Carmel Offie, 1 May 1950, box 310, folder Offie, Lovestone Papers, Stanford.
28. Irving Brown to Jay Lovestone, 21 May 1951, 29.11, Brown Papers.
29. Carew, "American Labor in Fizzland," 28–29.
30. Jay Lovestone to Lillie Brown, 27 March 1951, 29.11, Brown Papers.
31. Thomas W. Braden, interview with author, Woodbridge, Virginia, 18 June 2001.
32. Peter Grose, *Operation Rollback: America's Secret War behind the Iron Curtain* (Boston: Houghton Mifflin, 2000), p. 112; Burton Hersh, *The Old Boys: The American Elite and the Origins of the CIA* (St. Petersburg, Fla.: Tree Farm Books, 2002), pp. 56–57; Evan Thomas, *The Very Best Men—Four Who Dared: The Early Years of the CIA* (New York: Simon and Schuster, 1995), p. 34.
33. Thomas, *Best Men*, p. 34.
34. For further details of Offie's persecution due to his sexuality, see Morgan, *Covert Life*, pp. 210–213, and Robert D. Dean, *Imperial Brotherhood: Gender and the Making of Cold War Foreign Policy* (Amherst: University of Massachusetts Press, 2001), pp. 104–105.
35. Quoted in Hersh, *Old Boys*, p. 237.
36. Jay Lovestone to Irving Brown, 26 March 1951, 29.11, Brown Papers.
37. Anon., "Notes on Conversation with Joseph Czapski," 4 June 1951, 9.3, James Burnham Papers, Hoover Institution, Stanford University.
38. Quoted in Morgan, *Covert Life*, p. 218.
39. Ibid., p. 218.
40. Carew, "American Labor in Fizzland," 29. For an excellent account of the Reuthers' foreign activities, see Nelson Lichtenstein, *The Most Dangerous Man in Detroit: Walter Reuther and the Fate of American Labor* (New York: Basic Books, 1995), chap. 15.
41. Jay Lovestone to Samuel Berger, 18 May 1951, box 283, folder Sam Berger, Lovestone Papers, Stanford.
42. Carmel Offie, "Memorandum," 24 November 1950, box 528, folder Carmel Offie, Lovestone Papers, Stanford. Quenby Olmsted Hughes quotes extensively from a document in the Lovestone Papers, Stanford, entitled "Proposed Agree-

ment between KMLAPPER and BGLEADER (TPLODGER)," which was possibly intended to serve as a draft of the proposed Charter of Operations. See Hughes, "Interest of Democracy," pp. 87–93.

43. Quoted in John Ranelagh, *The Agency: The Rise and Decline of the CIA* (New York: Simon and Schuster, 1987), p. 247.
44. Quoted in Rathbun, *Point Man*, pp. 116–117. This high opinion of Brown appears to have been widely shared in U.S. government circles. His name was on the list drawn up by George Kennan in 1948 of possible candidates for the role of chief of the Office of Policy Coordination. Kennan thought him "a very able and active citizen." See George F. Kennan, "Memorandum from the Director of the Policy Planning Staff (Kennan) to the Under Secretary of State (Lovett)," 30 June 1948, in C. Thomas Thorne, Jr., and David S. Patterson, eds., *Foreign Relations of the United States, 1945–1950: Emergence of the Intelligence Establishment* (Washington, D.C.: U.S. Government Printing Office, 1996), p. 716.
45. Braden interview.
46. Quoted in Ranelagh, *Agency*, p. 247.
47. Thomas W. Braden, "I'm Glad the CIA Is 'Immoral,'" *Saturday Evening Post*, 20 May 1967, 10.
48. Victor Reuther, statement, enclosed with Victor Reuther to Joseph Walsh, 4 May 1967, 17.30, Victor G. Reuther Papers, Archives of Labor and Urban Affairs, Wayne State University, Detroit.
49. Quoted in Morgan, *Covert Life*, p. 222.
50. "T" to Michael Ross, 21 June 1951, 1.7, International Affairs Department, Michael Ross Papers (RG18–002), George Meany Memorial Archives, Silver Spring, Maryland; Jay Lovestone to Irving Brown, 29.14, 26 May 1952, Brown Papers.
51. Jay Lovestone to Irving Brown, 30 April 1951, 29.11, Brown Papers.
52. Jay Lovestone to Irving Brown, 26 May 1952, 29.14, Brown Papers.
53. Quoted in Carew, "American Labor in Fizzland," 32; Jay Lovestone to Irving Brown, 26 March 1951, 29.11, Brown Papers.
54. Jay Lovestone to Irving Brown, 4 April 1951, 29.11, Brown Papers.
55. Jay Lovestone to Irving Brown, 26 March 1951, 29.11, Brown Papers; "Monk" to Jay Lovestone, 6 April 1951, box 381, folder Monk, Lovestone Papers, Stanford.
56. "Monk" to Jay Lovestone, 6 April 1951, box 381, folder Monk, Lovestone Papers, Stanford.
57. Carew, "American Labor in Fizzland," 35.
58. Quoted in ibid.
59. Frances Stonor Saunders, *Who Paid the Piper? The CIA and the Cultural Cold War* (London: Granta, 1999), p. 95.
60. It is unclear whether or not Wisner personally supported Dulles's decision. In his

earliest account of the incident, Braden suggested that the OPC chief asked to be overruled; later, however, in an interview with Frances Stonor Saunders, Braden described Dulles as "all over Wisner." See Braden, "I'm Glad the CIA Is 'Immoral,'" 12; Braden quoted in Saunders, *Who Paid the Piper?* p. 97.

61. Quoted in Saunders, *Who Paid the Piper?* p. 97.
62. Quoted in Hughes, "Interest of Democracy," p. 205; anon., "Notes on Conversation with Joseph Czapski," 4 June 1951, 9.3, Burnham Papers; Jay Lovestone to Irving Brown, 21 December 1951, box 283, folder Irving Brown, Lovestone Papers, Stanford. The NCFE was, Lovestone concluded in this last letter, a "gang of fakers."
63. See Jay Lovestone to Irving Brown, 9 November 1951, box 283, folder Irving Brown, Lovestone Papers, Stanford; Irving Brown to Jay Lovestone, 15 November 1951, box 283, folder Irving Brown, Lovestone Papers, Stanford.
64. Jay Lovestone to Irving Brown, 9 November 1951, box 283, folder Irving Brown, Lovestone Papers, Stanford.
65. Quoted in Hughes, "Interest of Democracy," pp. 177, 178.
66. C. D. Jackson, log, 1954, box 68, Log 1954.3, C. D. Jackson Papers, Dwight D. Eisenhower Library, Abilene, Kansas. Like Braden, Jackson had an altogether better opinion of Brown.
67. Quoted in Carew, "American Labor in Fizzland," 37.
68. Quoted in Hughes, "Interest of Democracy," p. 184.
69. Carmel Offie to Irving Brown, 23 January 1953, 32.1, Brown Papers.
70. Quoted in Morgan, *Covert Life*, p. 236.
71. Quoted in Carew, "American Labor in Fizzland," 39.
72. Quoted in Morgan, *Covert Life*, p. 231.
73. Ibid., p. 222.
74. See Hugh Wilford, *The CIA, the British Left, and the Cold War: Calling the Tune?* (London: Frank Cass, 2003), chap. 5.
75. Paul Sakwa, "Chief/Covert Action/Vietnam," 2 August/11 December 1976, 63.5, Victor Reuther Papers.
76. Carew, "American Labor in Fizzland," 40.
77. Morgan, *Covert Life*, chap. 13.
78. Anon., memorandum, n.d., box 381, folder Monk, Lovestone Papers, Stanford.

4. A Deep Sickness in New York

1. Quoted in François Bondy, "Berlin Congress for Freedom: A New Resistance in the Making," *Commentary* 10 (1950): 245.
2. Quoted in Frances Stonor Saunders, *Who Paid the Piper? The CIA and the Cultural Cold War* (London: Granta, 1999), p. 53. Saunders, chap. 3, gives a lively account of the Waldorf conference.

3. Irving Howe later recalled that this circle owed more to the "jungle of Hobbes than a commune of Kropotkin." Irving Howe, *A Margin of Hope: An Intellectual Autobiography* (London: Secker and Warburg, 1983), p. 120.
4. Irving Howe, "How *Partisan Review* Goes to War," *New International* 13 (1947): 109.
5. The principal works on the New York intellectuals are Alexander Bloom, *Prodigal Sons: The New York Intellectuals and Their World* (New York: Oxford University Press, 1986); Terry A. Cooney, *The Rise of the New York Intellectuals:* Partisan Review *and Its Circle* (Madison: University of Wisconsin Press, 1986); Neil Jumonville, *Critical Crossings: The New York Intellectuals in Postwar America* (Berkeley: University of California Press, 1991); Harvey M. Teres, *Renewing the Left: Politics, Imagination, and the New York Intellectuals* (New York: Oxford University Press, 1996); Alan M. Wald, *The New York Intellectuals: The Rise and Decline of the Anti-Stalinist Left from the 1930s to the 1980s* (Chapel Hill: University of North Carolina Press, 1987); and Hugh Wilford, *The New York Intellectuals: From Vanguard to Institution* (Manchester: Manchester University Press, 1995).
6. For further biographical detail, see Sidney Hook, *Out of Step: An Unquiet Life in the Twentieth Century* (New York: Harper and Row, 1987); and Christopher Phelps, *Young Sidney Hook: Marxist and Pragmatist* (Ithaca, N.Y.: Cornell University Press, 1997).
7. See Judy Kutulas, *The Long War: The Intellectual People's Front and Anti-Stalinism, 1930–1940* (Durham, N.C.: Duke University Press, 1995), pp. 157–163.
8. For more information, see Daniel Kelly, *James Burnham and the Struggle for the World: A Life* (Wilmington, Del.: ISI Books, 2002).
9. Ibid., p. 99.
10. Quoted in Kevin J. Smant, *How Great the Triumph: James Burnham, Anticommunism, and the Conservative Movement* (Lanham, Md.: University Press of America, 1992), p. 28.
11. Joseph Bryan to James Burnham, n.d., box 5, folder 22, James Burnham Papers, Hoover Institution, Stanford University. On Bryan and the OPC's Psychological Warfare Workshop, see Evan Thomas, *The Very Best Men—Four Who Dared: The Early Years of the CIA* (New York: Simon and Schuster, 1995), p. 33.
12. Joseph Bryan to James Burnham, 30 June 1949, 5.22, Burnham Papers.
13. Frederick W. Williams to James Burnham, 21 July 1949, 5.22, Burnham Papers.
14. Kelly, *James Burnham*, p. 152.
15. James Burnham, memorandum, 16 February 1951, 11.4, Burnham Papers. Burnham was regularly reimbursed by the OPC the additional costs of using his house for these purposes.
16. James Burnham, "A Trip to Boston and New York," 1 November 1950, 11.2, Burnham Papers.

17. E. Howard Hunt, *Undercover: Memoirs of a Secret Agent* ([New York]: Berkley Publishing Co., 1974), p. 69.
18. See, for example, James Burnham, "Kultura," March 1950, 9.3, Burnham Papers. According to *Washington Post* columnist Mary McGrory, Burnham's Washington residence was "a mecca for iron curtain refugees." Quoted in Kelly, *James Burnham*, p. 155.
19. James Burnham, "A Discussion with Officials of the International Rescue Committee, 17 July 1951," 20 July 1951, 11.5, Burnham Papers; James Burnham, "Czeslaw Milosz," 26 November 1951, 11.6, Burnham Papers.
20. James Burnham, "A Sour Taste in the Friends of Fighters For Russian Freedom," 7 March 1951, 11.5, Burnham Papers.
21. James Burnham "Stalin's Health," 14 December 1949, 11.1, Burnham Papers; James Burnham, "Cartoons," 8 December 1949, 11.1, Burnham Papers; James Burnham, "A Desirable Semantic Change," 1 November 1950, 11.3, Burnham Papers.
22. Miles Copeland, "James Burnham," *National Review*, 11 September 1987, 37–38.
23. Warren G. Fugitt to James Burnham, 23 March 1983, 9.1, Burnham Papers.
24. James Burnham to Sidney Hook, 3 December 1948, 8.5, Sidney Hook Papers, Hoover Institution, Stanford University.
25. James Burnham to Sidney Hook, 22 December 1948, 8.5, Hook Papers; James Burnham to Arthur Koestler, 14 September 1950, 6.49, Burnham Papers.
26. James Burnham, "The Strategy of the Politburo, and the Problem of American Counter-Strategy," n.d. [probably 1950], 2.13, Burnham Papers.
27. Walter Bedell Smith to Edward Barrett, 28 July 1950, 27.26, Hook Papers.
28. Saunders, *Who Paid the Piper?* p. 158; Sidney Hook to Raymond Allen, 26 November 1951, 29.23, Hook Papers.
29. James Burnham to Sidney Hook, 11 January 49, 8.5, Hook Papers. In April 1950, Burnham wrote Hook from Washington, informing Hook that he had "been discussing several of your admirable ideas with persons here," which suggests that Hook had still not been directly approached by the OPC. James Burnham to Sidney Hook, 5 April 1950, 6.38, Burnham Papers.
30. J. Edgar Hoover to "SAC, New York," 5 January 1943, Sidney Hook FBI file. The resulting file, no. 100-176573, was placed in a "closed status" after a Special Agent submitted a singularly unsensational report on Hook's Trotskyist activities in October 1944. Hoover requested the file be reviewed in March 1949 so that a "recommendation" could be made. This suggests that the OPC might have been investigating Hook after Burnham had recommended him for consultancy work. J. Edgar Hoover to "SAC, New York," 18 March 1949, Hook FBI file.
31. Sidney Hook to Harold M. Janis, 2 April 1948, 29.12, Hook Papers.
32. Sidney Hook to James Burnham, 15 September 1948, 8.5, Hook Papers.

33. There are several detailed accounts of the launch of the CCF. See Peter Coleman, *The Liberal Conspiracy: The Congress for Cultural Freedom and the Struggle for the Mind of Postwar Europe* (New York: Free Press, 1989), chaps. 1–2; Pierre Grémion, *Intelligence de L'Anticommunisme: Le Congrès pour la liberté de la culture à Paris (1950–1975)* (Paris: Fayard, 1995), chap. 1; Saunders, *Who Paid the Piper?* chaps. 1–5.
34. Quoted in Michael Warner, "Origins of the Congress for Cultural Freedom, 1949–50," *Studies in Intelligence* 38 (1995): 92. This is an immensely useful article written by a member of the CIA's History Staff on the basis of still classified Agency documents.
35. Quoted in Saunders, *Who Paid the Piper?* p. 54.
36. James Burnham, "Berlin Congress for Cultural Freedom," 17 May 1950, 11.2, Burnham Papers.
37. James Burnham, "New York Operations of the Congress for Cultural Freedom," 16 August 1950, 11.2, Burnham Papers.
38. Coleman, *Liberal Conspiracy*, p. 27.
39. Anon., "Report on Congress for Cultural Freedom," box 278, folder Congress for Cultural Freedom, Jay Lovestone Papers, Hoover Institution, Stanford University; Arthur Koestler, "Berlin Diary," 25 June 1950, MSS2395/3, Arthur Koestler Papers, Edinburgh University Library.
40. Saunders, *Who Paid the Piper?* p. 89. James Burnham, "The Strategy of the Politburo, and the Problem of American Counter-Strategy," n.d. [probably 1950], 2.13, Burnham Papers. Fischer quoted in Smant, *How Great the Triumph*, p. 34.
41. Wisner quoted in Warner, "Origins of Congress for Cultural Freedom," 92. Truman and Wisner quoted in ibid., 97. Josselson quoted in ibid., 94. "Well-earned vacation": Melvin J. Lasky, interview with author, Rusper, Sussex, 13 August 1997. In addition to displeasing Wisner, Lasky's actions during the Berlin Congress angered Burnham, who suspected that the young New York intellectual, a member of Sol Levitas's *New Leader* circle, was promoting the factional interests of the Mensheviks over other Russian and minority nationality groups. See Burnham, "A Campaign by the Russian Menshevik Émigrées [*sic*]," n.d., 9.1, Burnham Papers.
42. Arthur Koestler to Bertrand Russell, 22 September 1950, MSS2345/1, Koestler Papers.
43. Irving Brown to Arthur Koestler, 2 November 1950, 13.10, International Affairs Department, Irving Brown Papers (RG18-004), George Meany Memorial Archives, Silver Spring, Maryland.
44. Quoted in David Cesarani, *Arthur Koestler: The Homeless Mind* (London: William Heinemann, 1998), pp. 382–383.
45. Despite this coincidence of strategic vision, Burnham felt little personal sympa-

thy for Koestler, whom he described to the OPC as "neurotic in the strict pathological sense." In a lengthy memorandum of May 1951, in which he detailed Koestler's personality defects, Burnham advised the OPC against involving the Hungarian too closely in its front operations. James Burnham, "Arthur Koestler," 31 May 1951, 11.5, Burnham Papers.

46. James Burnham to François Bondy, 6 February 1951, 8.6, Burnham Papers.
47. The ex-communist Gibarti's recommendations for CCF activities sounded even more Leninist than Koestler's. "The organizational strategy must always consist of efforts to provide broad cadres by means which profoundly touch the masses," he told Burnham. Louis Gibarti to James Burnham, 8 September 1950, 6.32, Burnham Papers.
48. James Burnham to Howard Phillips, "Bureaucracy," 13 December 1949, 11.1, Burnham Papers. James Burnham, "Joseph Czapski," 28 February 1950, 11.2, Burnham Papers. In May 1950 Burnham protested OPC's failure to honor its pledge to support Czapski's journal, *Kultura:* James Burnham, "Kultura," 17 May 1950, 11.2, Burnham Papers. James Burnham, "The New Leader," 12 January 1950, 11.2, Burnham Papers.
49. Kenneth B. Hambley to Assistant Director for Policy Coordination, "An Act of Idiocy," 15 October 1951, 11.6, Burnham Papers.
50. Quoted in Kelly, *James Burnham*, p. 177.
51. Ibid., pp. 192, 193.
52. Minutes, 14 December 1950, 7.3, American Committee for Cultural Freedom Papers, Tamiment Institute Library, New York University Library; Certificate of Incorporation, 5 January 1951, 6.1, ACCF Papers.
53. Quoted in Saunders, *Who Paid the Piper?* p. 203.
54. James Burnham, "Certain Sums Transmitted to Sidney Hook by Kenneth B. Hambley," 21 September 1951, 11.4, Burnham Papers.
55. In December 1951, Burnham noted that "most of the Committee contributions are now coming to it through the National Committee for a Free Europe, and specifically through Mr. Spencer Phenix of that Committee." James Burnham, "Financial Statement—American Committee for Cultural Freedom," 21 December 1951, 11.7, Burnham Papers.
56. Anon., "Cable Received from Josselson," 14 February 1951, 8.5, Burnham Papers; James Burnham to Herbert Passin, 9 July 1951, 8.5, Burnham Papers; James Burnham, "Conversation with Pearl Kluger," 19 July 1951, 8.3, Burnham Papers.
57. James Burnham, "Conversation with Pearl Kluger," 17 July 1951, 8.3, Burnham Papers.
58. Pearl Kluger to James Burnham, 9 March 1951, 8.3, Burnham Papers.

59. Anon., "Telephone Conversation with Pearl Kluger," 6 July 1951, 8.3, Burnham Papers. This incident possibly explains why soon afterward Burnham instructed one of the CCF's Asian experts, Herbert Passin, to monitor the fate of the ACCF's Japanese grant. James Burnham to Herbert Passin, 9 July 1951, 8.5, Burnham Papers.
60. James Burnham, "Conversation with Pearl Kluger," 17 July 1951, 8.3, Burnham Papers.
61. Anon., "Requested of Pearl Kluger," n.d., 8.6, Burnham Papers.
62. Pearl Kluger to James Burnham, 27 February 1951, 8.3, Burnham Papers.
63. James Burnham, "Conversation with Pearl Kluger," 19 July 1951, 8.3, Burnham Papers.
64. James Burnham to Sidney Hook, 17 August 1951, 8.5, Burnham Papers; James Burnham, "The Financial Control of the Paris Arts Festival," 15 August 1951, 11.5, Burnham Papers.
65. Festival account deposit book, 1951–52, 6.10, ACCF Papers.
66. Anon., "Requested of Pearl Kluger," n.d., 8.6, Burnham Papers.
67. Braden and Josselson quoted in Saunders, *Who Paid the Piper?* pp. 127, 26.
68. Anon., "Requested of Pearl Kluger," n.d., 8.6, Burnham Papers.
69. On the ACCF, see Coleman, *Liberal Conspiracy*, chap. 9; Hook, *Out of Step*, chap. 26; Guenter Lewy, *The Cause That Failed: Communism in American Political Life* (New York: Oxford University Press, 1990), pp. 108–114.
70. Diana Trilling to Arnold Beichman, 4 January 1985, 124.5, Hook Papers.
71. Arnold Beichman to Diana Trilling, 13 January 1985, 124.5, Hook Papers.
72. James Burnham, "American Committee for Cultural Freedom," 29 October 1951, 11.5, Burnham Papers.
73. See Coleman, *Liberal Conspiracy*, pp. 163–164.
74. See, for example, Elliot Cohen to Sidney Hook, 5 October 1951, 8.3, Burnham Papers.
75. James Burnham to Sidney Hook, 20 October 1950, 6.38, Burnham Papers. William L. O'Neill, *A Better World: The Great Schism—Stalinism and the American Intellectuals* (New York: Simon and Schuster, 1982), p. 298.
76. Radical literary critic Irving Howe was one of those deliberately excluded.
77. Max Eastman, "Who Threatens Cultural Freedom in America?" March 1952, 9.11, ACCF Papers. See Saunders, *Who Paid the Piper?* pp. 198–208. James Farrell to Arthur Schlesinger, Jr., 6 March 1952, box 13, folder Farrell, James, Arthur M. Schlesinger, Jr., Papers, John F. Kennedy Library, Boston. Schlesinger's *Vital Center* quoted in Saunders, *Who Paid the Piper?* p. 63. Arthur Schlesinger, Jr., to Dwight Macdonald, 29 April 1952, 1.45, Dwight Macdonald Papers, Sterling Memorial Library, Yale University. Arthur Schlesinger, Jr., to

Nicolas Nabokov, 18 June 1951, box 2, folder Schlesinger, Arthur, Jr., Nicolas Nabokov Papers, Harry Ransom Humanities Research Center, University of Texas, Austin.

78. Quoted in Kelly, *James Burnham*, pp. 190–191.
79. Frank Wisner to Deputy Assistant Director for Policy Coordination, "Reported Crisis in the American Committee for Cultural Freedom," 7 April 1952, in Michael Warner, ed., *The CIA under Harry Truman* (Washington, D.C.: Center for the Study of Intelligence, 1994), p. 455.
80. Saunders, *Who Paid the Piper?* p. 205.
81. "In view of the deep internal disagreements and lack of restraint which were evident in some of the violent exchanges at the March 29 meeting," reported the PSB staffer, A. P. Toner, "any government association with the Committee at this time seems undesirable." A. P. Toner, "American Committee for Cultural Freedom," 9 April 1952, box 4, folder American Committee for Cultural Freedom, PSB Files, Harry S. Truman Library, Independence, Missouri.
82. Cord Meyer to Arthur Schlesinger, Jr., 16 February 1954, box 20, folder Meyer, Cord, Schlesinger Papers; Michael Josselson to Daniel Bell, 27 April 1956, 282.10, International Association for Cultural Freedom/Congress for Cultural Freedom Papers, Special Collections Research Center, University of Chicago Library.
83. James Burnham to Robert Gorham Davis, 15 September 1954, 3.4, ACCF Papers.
84. Michael Josselson to Sol Stein, 22 September 1954, 7.12, ACCF Papers. The CCF, Josselson explained, was ending assistance to all "areas which are not 'critical' or where possibilities for local fund raising exist." Stein, a former Voice of America advisor, later founded the publishing house Stein and Day.
85. Sidney Hook to John F. Dailey, Jr., 25 June 1952, 6.16, ACCF Papers.
86. John F. Dailey, Jr., to ACCF, 15 December 1952, 6.16, ACCF Papers.
87. Sol Stein to Edward Lilly, 23 February 1955, 16.8, ACCF Papers; E. C. K. Finch to Irving Kristol, 25 November 1952, 6.12, ACCF Papers. Among the cultural Cold War projects Stein initiated was a series of foreign productions of Sidney Kingsley's play *Darkness at Noon*, a dramatic adaptation of Koestler's novel. See 8.9, ACCF Papers. He was also heavily involved in promoting the film version of George Orwell's *Animal Farm*, discussed in the next chapter.
88. Sol Stein to Harold L. Oram, 4 October 1954, 6.13, ACCF Papers.
89. See contents of 3.12, ACCF Papers.
90. Sol Stein to Michael Josselson, 1 March 1955, 7.12, ACCF Papers; Sol Stein to Edward Lilly, 23 February 1955, 16.8, ACCF Papers; Sol Stein to Edward Lilly, 4 March 1955, 16.8, ACCF Papers.
91. See, for example, James T. Farrell to Julius Fleischmann, 25 March 1955, 6.16, ACCF Papers.

92. Diana Trilling, *We Must March, My Darlings* (New York: Harcourt Brace Jovanovich, 1977), p. 61. Sol Stein to Norman Thomas, 27 April 1955, 4.22, ACCF Papers. Norman Thomas to Sol Stein, 28 April 1955, 4.22, ACCF Papers. For Hook's approaching Meyer: Cord Meyer to Arthur Schlesinger, Jr., 16 May 1955, box 20, folder Meyer, Cord, Schlesinger Papers.
93. ACCF to Michael Josselson, 9 May 1955, 7.12, ACCF Papers; Robert Blum to James T. Farrell, 9 May 1955, 3.2, ACCF Papers.
94. Norman Thomas to Sol Stein, 10 May 1955, 4.22, ACCF Papers.
95. Jeal V. Peltier to Sol Stein, 11 May 1955, 6.16, ACCF Papers.
96. Cord Meyer to Arthur Schlesinger, Jr., 16 May 1955, box 20, folder Meyer, Cord, Schlesinger Papers.
97. Henry Schwarzschild to Norman Thomas, 15 November 1954, 13.16, ACCF Papers.
98. See 13.15, ACCF Papers.
99. Arthur Miller to ACCF, AMCOMLIB, and Union of Soviet Writers, 7 February 1956, 14.11, ACCF Papers.
100. James Farrell to Arthur Schlesinger, Jr., 6 May 1955, box 13, folder Farrell, James, Schlesinger Papers. Bertrand Russell to editor, *Manchester Guardian*, 26 March 1956, 282.10, CCF Papers.
101. James Farrell to Bertrand Russell, 5 April 1956, 282.10, CCF Papers.
102. The Emergency Civil Liberties Committee's officers informed Russell that the source of the ACCF's funds "is a mystery but there appears very good reason to believe that a part of them come from the State Department." Quoted in Barry Feinberg and Ronald Kasrils, eds., *Bertrand Russell's America, vol. 2: 1945–1970* (London: Allen and Unwin, 1983), p. 65.
103. Minutes of Nicolas Nabokov's visit to Bertrand Russell, n.d., 4.3, CCF Papers. Michael Josselson to Sidney Hook, 20 April 1956, 135.6, CCF Papers. For more on the Russell controversy, see Hugh Wilford, *The CIA, the British Left, and the Cold War: Calling the Tune?* (London: Frank Cass, 2003), pp. 210–217. Hook was an old friend of Russell's, although their relationship was sorely tested by the Cold War.
104. Hook, *Out of Step*, p. 424.
105. Diana Trilling to Sidney Hook, 15 October 1955, 3.15, ACCF Papers.
106. Sidney Hook to Michael Josselson, 23 September 1956, 124.5, Hook Papers.
107. James Farrell to Arthur Schlesinger, Jr., 15 April 1955, box 13, folder Farrell, James, Schlesinger Papers; James Farrell to Arthur Schlesinger, Jr., 6 May 1955, box 13, folder Farrell, James, Schlesinger Papers.
108. James Farrell to Radio Free Europe, 22 June 1956, 3.9, ACCF Papers; Norman Jacobs to James Farrell, 3.9, ACCF Papers; James Farrell to Meyer Schapiro, 10 September 1956, box 3, folder Farrell, James T., Meyer Schapiro Papers, Colum-

bia University; quoted in Christopher Lasch, *The Agony of the American Left* (New York: Vintage, 1968), p. 79.

109. James Farrell to Norman Jacobs, 28 August 1956, 3.9, ACCF Papers.
110. Norman Jacobs to H. William Fitelson, 5 September 1956, 3.8, ACCF Papers.
111. Quoted in Coleman, *Liberal Conspiracy*, p. 169.
112. ACCF Board of Directors minutes, 13 December 1960, 78.1, Bertram D. Wolfe Papers, Hoover Institution, Stanford University.
113. Hook, *Out of Step*, p. 449.

5. The Cultural Cold War

1. See Malcolm Muggeridge, *Like It Was: The Diaries of Malcolm Muggeridge*, ed. John Bright-Holmes (London: Collins, 1981), p. 363.
2. Quoted in John L. Cobbs, *Understanding John Le Carré* (Columbia: University of South Carolina Press, 1998), p. 5.
3. Norman Mailer, *Harlot's Ghost* (New York: Random House, 1991), p. 1287. See the descriptions of Pearson and Angleton in Robin W. Winks, *Cloak and Gown: Scholars in the Secret War, 1939–1961*, 2nd ed. (New Haven, Conn.: Yale University Press, 1996), chaps. 5 and 6.
4. Cord Meyer, *Facing Reality: From World Federalism to the* CIA (New York: Harper and Row, 1980), pp. 2–3.
5. Frances Stonor Saunders, *Who Paid the Piper? The CIA and the Cultural Cold War* (London: Granta, 1999), pp. 240–243. Later, when one of Meyer's recruits, Robie Macauley, became fiction editor of *Playboy*, the CIA officer wrote congratulating him and offering to send him a story "under an appropriate pseudonym." Cord Meyer to Robie Macauley, 19 September 1966, box 1, folder 8, Cord Meyer Papers, Library of Congress, Washington, D.C.
6. Rhodri Jeffreys-Jones, *Cloak and Dollar: A History of American Secret Intelligence*, 2nd ed. (New Haven, Conn.: Yale University Press, 2003), p. 162. Under the pen name David St. John, Hunt wrote several novels featuring Peter Ward, a would-be American James Bond.
7. Quoted in David Caute, *The Dancer Defects: The Struggle for Cultural Supremacy during the Cold War* (Oxford: Oxford University Press, 2003), pp. 545, 544.
8. Ibid., p. 544.
9. In a valuable corrective to prevailing interpretations of the "cultural Cold War," Michael Krenn has recently pointed out that, even during the height of McCarthyism in the early 1950s, some overt U.S. government patronage of modern American art did carry on, with the State Department and the United States Information Agency sponsoring traveling exhibits through the American Federation of Arts. See Michael L. Krenn, *Fall-Out Shelters for the Human Spirit:*

American Art and the Cold War (Chapel Hill: University of North Carolina Press, 2005).

10. Quoted in Evan Thomas, *The Very Best Men—Four Who Dared: The Early Years of the CIA* (New York: Simon and Schuster, 1995), p. 61.
11. Saunders, *Who Paid the Piper?*, published in the United States as *The Cultural Cold War: The CIA and the World of Arts and Letters* (New York: New Press, 2000). Three other important histories of the CCF are Christopher Lasch, *The Agony of the American Left* (New York: Vintage, 1968), pp. 63–114 (the first and highly influential statement of the revisionist thesis); Peter Coleman, *The Liberal Conspiracy: The Congress for Cultural Freedom and the Struggle for the Mind of Postwar Europe* (New York: Free Press, 1989) (a semiofficial and laudatory account, which nonetheless remains useful); and Giles Scott-Smith, *The Politics of Apolitical Culture: The Congress for Cultural Freedom, the CIA, and Postwar American Hegemony* (London: Routledge, 2002) (which effectively employs the Gramscian concept of hegemony to theorize the CCF's impact on western intellectual life).
12. Quoted in Saunders, *Who Paid the Piper?* p. 220.
13. Macdonald mischievously entitled a report on a 1955 CCF conference in Milan he had been commissioned to write for *Encounter* "No Miracle in Milan." See Hugh Wilford, *The New York Intellectuals: From Vanguard to Institution* (Manchester: Manchester University Press, 1995), p. 230.
14. See Saunders, *Who Paid the Piper?* pp. 244–247; and Kenneth Osgood, *Total Cold War: Eisenhower's Secret Propaganda Battle at Home and Abroad* (Lawrence: University Press of Kansas, 2006), pp. 294–304. One estimate puts the number of books financed or produced by the CIA during the early Cold War period at 250. John M. Crewdson and Joseph B. Treaster, "The CIA's Three-Decade Effort to Mold the World's Views," *New York Times*, 25 December 1977, 1.
15. See, for example, the exchange between Phillips and Carol and Richard Ohmann in *Critical Inquiry* 3 (1977): 817–820.
16. Saunders, *Who Paid the Piper?* pp. 162–163, 335–338.
17. "L" to Allen Grover, n.d., 51.4, Henry Luce Papers, Library of Congress, Washington, D.C.
18. Bertram Wolfe to Melvin Lasky, 22 January 1973, 9.44, Bertram D. Wolfe Papers, Hoover Institution, Stanford University.
19. Sidney Hook to John Thompson, n.d., 12.20, Sidney Hook Papers, Hoover Institution, Stanford University.
20. William Phillips, *A Partisan View: Five Decades of the Literary Life* (New York: Stein and Day, 1983), pp. 104–105.
21. Excerpt from H. J. Kaplan to J. M., 3 January 1950, 401.3464, Rockefeller Foundation Archives, Rockefeller Archive Center, Sleepy Hollow, New York.

22. "Excerpt from interview, E. F. D. with H. J. Kaplan," 14 February 1950, 401.3464, Rockefeller Foundation Archives.
23. James Burnham, "Mr. William Phillips' proposed French *Partisan Review*," 9 March 1950, 11.2, James Burnham Papers, Hoover Institution, Stanford University.
24. Richard Cummings, "An American in Paris," *American Conservative*, 16 February 2004, 21–22.
25. For revisionist studies of links between abstract expressionism and the Cold War American state, see Francis Frascina, ed., *Pollock and After: The Critical Debate* (London: Harper and Row, 1985), which contains essays by Max Kozloff, Eva Cockroft, and David and Cecile Shapiro; Serge Guilbaut, *How New York Stole the Idea of Modern Art: Abstract Expressionism, Freedom, and the Cold War*, trans. Arthur Goldhammer (Chicago: University of Chicago Press, 1983); and Saunders, *Who Paid the Piper?* chap. 16. Saunders's documentary film, "Art and the CIA," screened in the 1995 Channel 4 series *Hidden Hands: A Different History of Modernism*, also concentrates on abstract expressionism.
26. Caute, *Dancer Defects*, p. 547.
27. Quoted in Saunders, *Who Paid the Piper?* p. 258.
28. Quoted in ibid., p. 268.
29. Quoted in ibid., p. 272.
30. Clement Greenberg, quoted in ibid., p. 267.
31. Caute, *Dancer Defects*, pp. 550–556.
32. See, for example, Michael Kimmelman, "Revisiting the Revisionists: The Modern, Its Critics, and the Cold War," in *The Museum of Modern Art at Mid-Century: At Home and Abroad, Studies in Modern Art 4* (New York: MoMA, 1994). Nancy Jachec, in *The Philosophy and Politics of Abstract Expressionism* (Cambridge: Cambridge University Press, 2000), makes much the same point about MoMA's exhibition policies but still argues that the U.S. government deliberately promoted abstract expressionism because Marxist and existentialist influences on the movement's aesthetics rendered it attractive to non-communist left audiences in western Europe. Finally, see also Robin Burstow's excellent article, "The Limits of Modernist Art as a 'Weapon of the Cold War': Reassessing the Unknown Patron of the Monument to the Unknown Political Prisoner," *Oxford Art Journal* 20 (1997): 68–80.
33. Saunders, *Who Paid the Piper?* pp. 264–275.
34. See Kris Russman, "The Coca-Colonization of Music: Cultural Strategies of the American State Department and the CIA Regarding the Performance of Music during the Cold War" (D.Phil. diss., University of Cambridge, 2002).
35. See Saunders, *Who Paid the Piper?* chap. 8.
36. Herbert Luethy, quoted in Ian Wellens, *Music on the Frontline: Nicolas Nabokov's*

Struggle against Communist and Middlebrow Culture (Aldershot: Ashgate, 2002), p. 58.

37. Saunders, *Who Paid the Piper?* p. 117.
38. C. D. Jackson to Henry Cabot, 14 August 1951, box 38, folder BSO-1951, C. D. Jackson Papers, Dwight D. Eisenhower Library, Abilene, Kansas. Lasky quoted in Saunders, *Who Paid the Piper?* p. 124. Braden quoted in ibid., p. 125.
39. Saunders, *Who Paid the Piper?* p. 125.
40. Quoted in ibid., p. 221.
41. Ibid., p. 223.
42. Wellens, *Music on Frontline*, p. 125.
43. See Russman, "Coca-Colonization of Music," app. 5.
44. Frank Wisner to Nelson Rockefeller, "Cultural Exchange with the Soviet Union," 14 September 1955, 80.615, Nelson A. Rockefeller Papers, Washington, D.C., Files, Special Assistant to the President for Foreign Affairs, 1954–55, Rockefeller Archive Center, Sleepy Hollow, New York.
45. See Naima Prevots, *Dance for Export: Cultural Diplomacy and the Cold War* (Hanover, N.H.: Wesleyan University Press, 1998).
46. Frank Wisner to Nelson Rockefeller, "Cultural Exchange with the Soviet Union," 14 September 1955, 80.615, Nelson Rockefeller Papers. This letter of Wisner's to Rockefeller is the only contemporaneous written record of the CIA's tastes in the early Cold War period available to researchers. Rockefeller's papers also contain correspondence suggesting that Wisner not only closely monitored the reception of Robert Breen's production of George Gershwin's opera *Porgy and Bess* when it toured Europe with State Department backing (a venture generally considered one of the United States's most successful attempts at Cold War cultural diplomacy), but also that he might have been behind the official decision to sponsor the tour in the first place. In a letter of April 1955, Rockefeller tells Wisner, "You rendered a great service to our country in getting this started." Nelson Rockefeller to Frank Wisner, 12 April 1955, 89.674, Nelson Rockefeller Papers.
47. For a highly suggestive analysis of the ideological correspondences between modernism and Cold War American cultural power, see Alan Sinfield, *Literature, Politics, and Culture in Postwar Britain* (Oxford: Blackwell, 1989).
48. See Burstow, "Limits of Modernist Art."
49. Lowell incident recounted in Saunders, *Who Paid the Piper?* pp. 347–349, 277; Reinhardt quoted in ibid., p. 277.
50. For more on the Macdonald incident, see ibid., pp. 315–324; and Hugh Wilford, *The CIA, the British Left, and the Cold War: Calling the Tune?* (London: Frank Cass, 2003), pp. 279–281.
51. Michael Holzman, "Café CIA Roma: Mary McCarthy's Cold War," *Prospects* 25 (2000): 685.

52. Quoted in Saunders, *Who Paid the Piper?* pp. 122–123.
53. Isaiah Berlin to Arthur Schlesinger, Jr., 6 June 1952, box 9, folder Berlin, Sir Isaiah, Arthur M. Schlesinger, Jr., Papers, John F. Kennedy Library, Boston.
54. See Wilford, CIA, *British Left, and Cold War,* chaps. 6 and 8. A number of other recent studies of CCF activities focus on particular countries. See, for example, Pierre Grémion, *Intelligence de L'Anticommunisme: Le Congrès pour la liberté de la culture à Paris (1950–75)* (Paris: Fayard, 1995); Michael Hochgeschwender, *Freiheit in der Offensive? Der Kongress für kulturelle Beziehungen und die Deutschen* (Munich: Oldenbourg, 1998); John D. McLaren, *Writing in Hope and Fear: Literature as Politics in Postwar Australia* (Cambridge: Cambridge University Press, 1996); Ingeborg Philipsen, "Out of Tune: The Congress for Cultural Freedom in Denmark, 1953–1960," in Giles Scott-Smith and Hans Krabbendam, eds., *The Cultural Cold War in Western Europe, 1945–1960* (London: Frank Cass, 2003), pp. 237–253; Margery Sabin, "The Politics of Cultural Freedom: India in the 1950s," *Raritan* 14 (1995): 45–65; and Tity de Vries, "The Absent Dutch: Dutch Intellectuals and the Congress for Cultural Freedom," in Scott-Smith and Krabbendam, eds., *Cultural Cold War,* pp. 254–266.
55. Quoted in Saunders, *Who Paid the Piper?* pp. 248–249.
56. Stephen Spender to Michael Josselson, 22 October 1953, 94.7, International Association for Cultural Freedom/Congress for Cultural Freedom Papers, Special Collections Research Center, University of Chicago Library.
57. Meyer Schapiro to Irving Kristol, 22 October 1952, 7.35, American Committee for Cultural Freedom Papers, Tamiment Institute Library, New York University.
58. Winks, *Cloak and Gown,* p. 327.
59. The phrase is Clement Greenberg's, quoted in Saunders, *Who Paid the Piper?* p. 259.
60. See contents of 58.599, Nelson Rockefeller Papers.
61. For more on Militant Liberty, see Osgood, *Total Cold War,* pp. 314–321.
62. Saunders, *Who Paid the Piper?* p. 286; Eric Johnston, "What They Say About Us," April 1961, box 9, folder Johnston, Eric, "What They Say About Us," Association of Motion Picture and Television Producers' Collection, Margaret Herrick Library, Academy of Motion Picture Arts and Sciences, Beverly Hills, California.
63. C. D. Jackson to Governor Sherman Adams, 19 January 1954, 1.A, C. D. Jackson Records, Dwight D. Eisenhower Library, Abilene, Kansas.
64. Quoted in Wilford, CIA, *British Left, and Cold War,* p. 58.
65. For more on the backgrounds of de Rochemont and the Psychological Warfare Workshop officers involved in the project, see Daniel J. Leab, "The American Government and the Filming of George Orwell's *Animal Farm* in the 1950s," *Media History* 12 (2006): 133–155.

66. A number of books have made the claim that, for granting the rights to the film, Sonia Blair was rewarded with an introduction to one of her favorite Hollywood stars, Clark Gable. See, for example, Thomas, *Best Men*, p. 33. However, a letter among the personal papers of Louis de Rochemont suggests that in fact Orwell's widow wanted to meet Bob Hope. Louis de Rochemont to E. H. "Dutch" Ellis, 25 April 1951, 8.4, Louis de Rochemont Papers, American Heritage Center, University of Wyoming.
67. For further reflection on the reasons why de Rochemont hired Halas and Batchelor, see Tony Shaw, *British Cinema and the Cold War* (London: I. B. Tauris, 2001), pp. 95–96.
68. The figure of $300,000 is repeated in several documents in the de Rochemont collection, including Louis de Rochemont to Joseph Bryan and Finis Farr, 28 July 1951, 8.5, de Rochemont Papers.
69. Shaw, *British Cinema*, p. 96; Daniel J. Leab, "Animators and Animals: John Halas, Joy Batchelor, and George Orwell's *Animal Farm*," *Historical Journal of Film, Radio, and Television* 25 (2005): 238–239.
70. E. Howard Hunt, *Undercover: Memoirs of a Secret Agent* ([New York]: Berkley Publishing Co., 1974), p. 70.
71. See Louis de Rochemont to anon., 21 January 1952, 8.5, de Rochemont Papers. "We might as well face up to the fact that our financial backers are more than worried about the picture's editorial content," de Rochemont wrote a colleague in his production company. "This stems from the fact that some friends of theirs who are supposed to be experts in psychological warfare are convinced that in its present form the picture will not only be misunderstood but all of us will be accused of propagandizing for socialism."
72. Quoted in Saunders, *Who Paid the Piper?* p. 294; Lothar Wolff to John Halas, 28 February 1952, 8.5, de Rochemont Papers.
73. See Lothar Wolff to Louis de Rochemont and Joseph Bryan, 13 February 1952, 8.5, de Rochemont Papers. This memorandum summarizes the main points agreed at a meeting held the previous day. Wolff's letter to Halas of February 28 reproduces these points almost verbatim.
74. Anonymous review of *Animal Farm* script, n.d., 8.5, de Rochemont Papers.
75. Shaw, *British Cinema*, p. 101. Joe Bryan and other officers of the Psychological Warfare Workshop visited the studio in person on several different occasions. See Leab, "Animators and Animals," 244.
76. See Shaw, *British Cinema*, pp. 104–113, for information about the 1956 cinematic version of *Nineteen Eighty-Four*, including the involvement of the USIA and American Committee for Cultural Freedom.
77. One reason for the film's acclaim was its energetic promotion by other U.S. government agencies and front organizations, including the ACCF, which obtained

favorable coverage in New York newspapers, dispensed discount coupons to young moviegoers, and reminded exhibitors that Orwell's novel was "one of the most important anti-communist documents of our time." Sol Stein to Manager, Paris Theatre, 5 January 1955, 8.2, ACCF Papers.

78. Deputies' Meeting minutes, 16 May 1956, CIA Records Search Tool (CREST), National Archives, Washington, D.C. In 1953, CIA officer Tracy Barnes felt the need to scotch rumors circulating in the Pentagon that he had "MGM people making a movie out on the West Coast." The facts of the matter, Barnes wrote, were that "one of our people" had shown "certain MGM representatives an unclassified version of the film about the American fliers" on the understanding "that no use would be made of any portion of this film without first getting a clearance for the desired use. We are therefore not having MGM make a film." Tracy Barnes to William H. Godel, "Meeting in Pentagon on 29 September 1953," 1 October 1953, CREST.
79. Anon. to "Owen," 24 January, 6 February, 26 January, 7 February, 9 March, and 24 January 1953, box 5, folder Movies, Jackson Records.
80. Saunders, *Who Paid the Piper?* p. 290.
81. Anon. to "Owen," 7 February 1953, box 5, folder Movies, Jackson Records.
82. Tony Shaw, "Ambassadors of the Screen: Film and the State-Private Network in Cold War America," in Helen Laville and Hugh Wilford, eds., *The U.S. Government, Citizen Groups, and the Cold War: The State-Private Network* (London: Routledge, 2006), p. 167; David Eldridge, "'Dear Owen': The CIA, Luigi Luraschi, and Hollywood, 1953," *Historical Journal of Film, Radio, and Television* 20 (2000): 156, 185n69.
83. Quoted in Eldridge, "Dear Owen," 152. Saunders's misattribution is probably the result of the letters in the Jackson records being cross-referenced to "Carlton Alsop" (*sic*). Eldridge was unable to identify the author's correspondent, whom is addressed simply as "Dear Owen." The letters are reproduced in full in the Eldridge article.

6. The CIA on Campus

1. Henry Kissinger to H. Gates Lloyd, 20 April 1951, box 110, folder Central Intelligence Agency, 1949–1951 (hereafter CIA), William Y. Elliott Papers, Hoover Institution, Stanford University.
2. Henry Kissinger to H. Gates Lloyd, 7 May 1951, box 110, folder CIA, Elliott Papers.
3. Walter Isaacson, *Kissinger: A Biography* (New York: Simon and Schuster, 1992), p. 62.
4. Quoted in ibid., p. 63.
5. Quoted in ibid., p. 79.

6. Henry Kissinger, "Informal Memorandum for Professor Elliott," n.d., box 2, folder International Seminar—Harvard, 1951–1959 (hereafter IS—H), Elliott Papers.
7. Steering Committee minutes, Summer School Foreign Student Project, 14 November 1950, box 2, folder IS—H, Elliott Papers. For invitation: anon., "Harvard Summer School Foreign Student Program," n.d., box 2, folder IS—H, Elliott Papers.
8. William Elliott to H. Gates Lloyd, 15 November 1950; William Elliott to Julius Fleischmann, 7 January 1953; William Elliott to Julius Fleischmann, 21 January 1953, all box 110, folder CIA, Elliott Papers.
9. Henry Kissinger, "Informal Memorandum for Professor Elliott," n.d.; Steering Committee minutes, Summer School Foreign Student Project, 14 November 1950, both in box 2, folder IS—H, Elliott Papers.
10. William Elliott to Alfred P. Sloan, n.d., box 2, folder IS—H, Elliott Papers.
11. William Elliott to Don K. Price, 13 February 1954, box 2, folder IS—H, Elliott Papers. Harvard professor quoted in Isaacson, *Kissinger*, p. 71. Henry Kissinger to William Elliott, 22 August 1951, box 2, folder IS—H, Elliott Papers.
12. "Harvard Programs Received CIA Help," *New York Times*, 16 April 1967, 53. Isaacson, *Kissinger*, p. 70. A biography published in 2004 states that the CIA's hand in funding the Summer School was "unknown to Kissinger at the time." Jussi Hanhimaki, *The Flawed Architect: Henry Kissinger and American Foreign Policy* (Oxford: Oxford University Press, 2004), p. 6.
13. "I have not had them made out in triplicate," Elliott went on to inform Lloyd in his letter of November 15, referring to the "papers for Mr. Kissinger." "If that is necessary, I suggest that they be typed there and I will have him sign the extra copies. May I ask that all possible expedition should be given to these papers." William Elliott to H. Gates Lloyd, 15 November 1950, box 110, folder CIA, Elliott Papers.
14. William Elliott to Frank Wisner, 16 July 1951, box 110, folder CIA, Elliott Papers. There is also evidence to suggest that Kissinger was an FBI contact at Harvard. See Isaacson, *Kissinger*, pp. 70–71.
15. For details of Yale's multifarious intelligence connections, see Robin W. Winks, *Cloak and Gown: Scholars in the Secret War, 1939–1961*, 2nd ed. (New Haven, Conn.: Yale University Press, 1996).
16. John Cavanagh, "Dulles Papers Reveal CIA Consulting Network," *Forerunner*, 29 April 1980.
17. Rhodri Jeffreys-Jones, *The CIA and American Democracy*, 3rd ed. (New Haven, Conn.: Yale University Press, 2003), p. 153.
18. On the communist student campaign and the first stirrings of western opposition to it, see Jöel Kotek, *Students and the Cold War* (Basingstoke: Macmillan, 1996). On British measures, see Richard J. Aldrich, "Putting Culture into the Cold War:

The Cultural Relations Department (CRD) and British Covert Information Warfare," in Giles Scott-Smith and Hans Krabbendam, eds., *The Cultural Cold War in Western Europe, 1945–1960* (London: Frank Cass, 2003), pp. 109–133.

19. See contents of box 127, folder International Team, Miscellaneous, United States National Student Association Papers, Hoover Institution, Stanford University. In 1967, lawyer Frederic Delano Houghteling, a cousin of President Franklin Delano Roosevelt and former NSA officer, described to the *New York Times* how in 1950, following a late-night assignation with CIA officers on a country road outside Madison, he had visited two "wealthy citizens" in Chicago (one of whom he recognized as an acquaintance of his father's) who passed him several thousand dollars to finance a trip by twelve U.S. students to an international meeting in Europe. It seems reasonable to assume that the two citizens, not identified by Houghteling, were Brittingham and Bell. Roy Reed, "Ex-Student Describes Intrigue in Getting CIA Loan in '50," *New York Times*, 17 February 1967, 16.
20. Quoted in Karen Paget, "From Stockholm to Leiden: The CIA's Role in the Formation of the International Student Conference," in Scott-Smith and Krabbendam, eds., *Cultural Cold War in Europe*, p. 144. Paget generally is a source of excellent detail on HIACOM and the buildup to the Stockholm conference.
21. Paget, "Stockholm to Leiden," p. 143.
22. Erskine B. Childers to Shirley Neizer, 11 December 1950, box 127, folder International Team, Miscellaneous, NSA Papers.
23. Allard Lowenstein to Dean Acheson, n.d. [probably September 1950], 28.174, Allard K. Lowenstein Papers, Southern Historical Collection, Wilson Library, University of North Carolina at Chapel Hill.
24. Quoted in NSA pamphlet "A New Role for the American Student: Reports from Stockholm, Southeast Asia, United States," 1951, 28.183, Lowenstein Papers.
25. Herbert Eisenberg to Executive Committee, NSA, "Results of Conference in Brief/Effect of Lowenstein's Speech," 24 December 1950, box 1, folder ISC Conference, Stockholm 1950, NSA Papers.
26. For more on the Dominican Committee, see below, chap. 8, and William H. Chafe, *Never Stop Running: Allard Lowenstein and the Struggle to Save American Liberalism* (New York: Basic Books, 1993), pp. 256–259. See also ibid., chap. 6, for a discussion of charges that Lowenstein's activities in South Africa were financed by the CIA. Chafe's biography is generally sympathetic toward its subject. Richard Cummings, *The Pied Piper: Allard K. Lowenstein and the Liberal Dream* (New York: Grove Press, 1985) is more hostile.
27. Allard Lowenstein, statement on the NSA and CIA, 1967, 133.51, Lowenstein Papers.
28. Quoted in Cummings, *Pied Piper*, p. 67, and Chafe, *Never Stop Running*, p. 254.
29. Robert Kiley, Columbia University Oral History Project, 1990, addition 3.1,

folder 198, Lowenstein Papers; William Dentzer, Columbia University Oral History Project, 1989, addition 3.1, folder 165, Lowenstein Papers. Donhauser quoted in Cummings, *Pied Piper*, pp. 179–180.

30. Milton W. Buffington to Lewis S. Thompson, "United States National Student Association," 17 February 1951, in Michael Warner, ed., *The CIA under Harry Truman* (Washington, D.C.: Center for the Study of Intelligence, 1994), pp. 383–384.
31. For an impassioned defense of Lowenstein against Cummings's critical biography, *Pied Piper*, see Hendrik Hertzberg, "The Second Assassination of Al Lowenstein," *New York Review of Books*, 10 October 1985, 34–41.
32. Donhauser and Lowenstein quoted in Paget, "From Stockholm to Leiden," pp. 146, 149.
33. Allard Lowenstein, statement on the NSA and CIA, 1967, 133.51, Lowenstein Papers.
34. See Kotek, *Students and the Cold War*, chap. 11.
35. Avrea Ingram to Gordon Gray, 13 October 1951, box 4, folder 080 National Student Association, PSB Files, Harry S. Truman Library, Independence, Missouri.
36. Minutes, PSB Staff Meeting, 7 November 1951, 28.337, PSB Files.
37. Avrea Ingram to William Dentzer, 6 November 1951, box 72, folder NSA IC Office Correspondence, 1951–52, NSA Papers. Avrea Ingram to William Dentzer, 8 December 1951 and 19 December 1951, box 29, folder Correspondence with International, 1950–1954, NSA Papers. William Dentzer to Avrea Ingram, 27 March 1952, box 29, folder Correspondence with International, 1950–1954, NSA Papers.
38. William Dentzer to Avrea Ingram, 17 February 1952, box 72, folder NSA IC Office Correspondence, 1951–52, NSA Papers.
39. Writing to Ingram in late May 1952, Dentzer evinced his wittingness by including the following in a list of reasons why European officers of COSEC should accept his assignment to Leiden: "The money argument. You know what cannot be said about the fact that Americans will not be able to contribute unless someone they know is there." William Dentzer to Avrea Ingram, 26 May 1952, box 29, folder Correspondence with International, 1950–1954, NSA Papers.
40. Quoted in Kotek, *Students and the Cold War*, p. 209. For more details on the setting up of COSEC, see Paget, "From Stockholm to Leiden," pp. 152–157.
41. Sol Stern, "A Short Account of International Student Politics with Particular Reference to the NSA, CIA, Etc.," *Ramparts* 5, no. 9 (March 1967): 30.
42. Financial Report, 1957–58, box 314, folder Financial Reports, 1951–1965, NSA Papers.

43. Sol Stern, "Short Account," 30.
44. See Kotek, *Students and Cold War*, p. 210.
45. Thomas W. Braden, "I'm Glad the CIA Is 'Immoral,'" *Saturday Evening Post*, 20 May 1967, 10.
46. Robert Kernish, "A History of the United States National Student Association," p. 7, box 58, NSA Papers.
47. Anon., "Presentation to the Rusk Committee: The Problem and the Alternatives," 6 May 1967, box 192, folder CF Oversize Attachments, Packet 1, White House Central File, Confidential File, Lyndon B. Johnson Library, Austin, Texas.
48. See, for example, Cord Meyer, *Facing Reality: From World Federalism to the CIA* (New York: Harper and Row, 1980), pp. 94–109. This argument is echoed in Kotek, *Students and the Cold War*.
49. Editorial, "Playing It Straight," *New Republic*, 4 March 1967, 6.
50. Kiley, Columbia Oral History Project.
51. Todd Gitlin and Bob Ross, "The CIA at College: Into Twilight and Black," *Village Voice*, 6 July 1967.
52. Tom Hayden, *Reunion: A Memoir* (New York: Random House, 1988), pp. 50, 51.
53. Meyer, *Facing Reality*, p. 101.
54. Sam Brown, quoted in Victor Marchetti and John D. Marks, *The CIA and the Cult of Intelligence* (New York: Knopf, 1974), p. 48.
55. Quoted in Paget, "Stockholm to Leiden," p. 151.
56. See Len to Jim [presumably Leonard Bebchick to James Edwards], 2 March 1954, box 29, folder Correspondence with International, 1950–1954, NSA Papers.
57. Michael Wood, "An Epilogue," *Ramparts* 5, no. 9 (March 1967): 39.
58. Quoted in Sydney Ladensohn Stern, *Gloria Steinem: Her Passions, Politics, and Mystique* (Secaucus, N.J.: Birch Lane Press, 1997), pp. 110–111.
59. Quoted in Sol Stern, "Short Account," 34.
60. Phil Sherburne quoted in Ken Metzler, "Campaign against Covert Action Division No. 5," *Old Oregon*, May–June 1967, 6–11, 29.208, Lowenstein Papers.
61. See W. Eugene Groves, "NSA and the CIA: On People and Power (Second Thoughts after the Storm)," box 62, folder President's Report, NSA Papers.
62. Quoted in Sol Stern, "Short Account," 33.
63. Quoted in Sydney Stern, *Gloria Steinem*, p. 115. All other information in this paragraph is derived from Stern's well-researched biography.
64. Kotek, *Students and the Cold War*, p. 213.
65. Gloria Steinem, "Organization and Activities of the Independent Service for Information on the Vienna Youth Festival," n.d., box 115, folder Youth Festival, Vienna, General Correspondence 1959 1, C. D. Jackson Papers, Dwight D. Eisenhower Library, Abilene, Kansas.
66. Sydney Stern, *Gloria Steinem*, p. 116.

67. Zbigniew Brzezinski, quoted in ibid., p. 112.
68. Quoted in ibid., p. 116.
69. C. D. Jackson to Gloria Steinem, 4 March 1959, box 115, folder Youth Festival, 4, Jackson Papers. C. D. Jackson to Frank Stanton, 13 July 1959, and C. D. Jackson to Cord Meyer, 15 July 1959, both box 115, folder Youth Festival, Vienna, General Correspondence 1959 3, Jackson Papers.
70. Quoted in Sydney Stern, *Gloria Steinem*, p. 117.
71. C. D. Jackson to Gloria Steinem, 8 July 1959, and Gloria Steinem to C. D. Jackson, 12 June 1959, both box 115, folder Youth Festival, Vienna, General Correspondence 1959 3, Jackson Papers.
72. Michael Harrington, *Fragments of the Century* (New York: Saturday Review Press, 1973), pp. 138–139.
73. Anon., "Program of the Vienna Youth Festival," n.d., box 115, folder Youth Festival, Vienna, General Correspondence 1959 3, Jackson Papers.
74. Emory Bundy, quoted in Cummings, *Pied Piper*, pp. 63–64.
75. Sydney Stern, *Gloria Steinem*, p. 119.
76. Sam Walker to C. D. Jackson, 31 July 1959, box 115, folder Youth Festival, Vienna, General Correspondence 1959 2, Jackson Papers.
77. Anon., "Notes on U.S. Delegation," 5 October 1959, box 115, folder Youth Festival, Vienna, General Correspondence 1959 2, Jackson Papers.
78. Sam Walker to C. D. Jackson, 24 July 1959, box 115, folder Youth Festival, Vienna, General Correspondence 1959 2, Jackson Papers.
79. Brzezinski quoted in Sydney Stern, *Gloria Steinem*, pp. 120, 119.
80. Ibid., p. 120.
81. Quoted in ibid., p. 118.
82. C. D. Jackson to Fritz Molden, 11 November 1959, box 115, folder Youth Festival, Vienna, General Correspondence 1959 1, Jackson Papers.
83. Meyer, *Facing Reality*, p. 103.
84. Quoted in Carolyn G. Heilbrun, *The Education of a Woman: The Life of Gloria Steinem* (New York: Dial Press, 1995), pp. 88–89.
85. Quoted in Sydney Stern, *Gloria Steinem*, p. 291.
86. Quoted in ibid., p. 292.
87. See, for example, William Colby and Peter Forbath, *Honorable Men: My Life in the CIA* (New York: Simon and Schuster, 1978), p. 106.
88. See Sydney Stern, *Gloria Steinem*, pp. 293–306.

7. The Truth Shall Make You Free

1. Dorothy Bauman, oral history, box 54, folder 888, Committee of Correspondence Papers, Sophia Smith Collection, Smith College, Northampton, Mass.

Like the other oral histories cited in this chapter, the interview with Bauman was recorded in 1987 by Jacqueline Van Voris. I am indebted to Van Voris's *The Committee of Correspondence: Women with a World Vision* (Northampton, Mass.: Sophia Smith Collection, Smith College, 1989), and to the excellent account in Helen Laville, *Cold War Women: The International Activities of American Women's Organizations* (Manchester: Manchester University Press, 2002), chap. 7.

2. Dorothy Bauman, "Right or Wrong?" 29 October 1974, 54.888, Committee of Correspondence Papers.
3. "In a Drawing Room," *Time*, 16 February 1948, http://www.time.com/time/archive/ (accessed 21 December 2006).
4. Dorothy Bauman, "Right or Wrong?" 29 October 1974, 54.888, Committee of Correspondence Papers.
5. Cord Meyer, *Facing Reality: From World Federalism to the* CIA (New York: Harper and Row, 1980).
6. Dorothy Bauman, "Right or Wrong?" 29 October 1974, 54.888, Committee of Correspondence Papers.
7. Bauman, oral history.
8. Dorothy Bauman, "Right or Wrong?" 29 October 1974, 54.888, Committee of Correspondence Papers.
9. Bauman, oral history.
10. "What Steps Should Be Taken to Rally the Women of the Free World to Counteract Communist Propaganda?" 16 April 1952, 2.18, Committee of Correspondence Papers.
11. "Report of Meeting Held April 16, 1952," n.d., 7.213, Lena M. Phillips Papers, Schlesinger Library, Radcliffe Institute, Harvard University.
12. Bauman, oral history.
13. Minutes of meeting, 27 January 1953, 2.18, Committee of Correspondence Papers.
14. Thomas W. Braden, interview with author, Woodbridge, Virginia, 18 June 2001.
15. See Meyer, *Facing Reality*, chap. 4.
16. Spencer Arnold, quoted in "Notes on Special Board Meeting Monday, July 24, 1967, 10.30 A.M.," addition, box 2, folder Financial Records, Committee of Correspondence Papers.
17. See Kenneth Osgood, *Total Cold War: Eisenhower's Secret Propaganda Battle at Home and Abroad* (Lawrence: University Press of Kansas, 2006), for an excellent account of Eisenhower's long-running affair with psychological warfare.
18. Quoted in Athan Theoharis, "A New Agency: The Origins and Expansion of CIA Covert Operations," in Athan Theoharis, ed., *The Central Intelligence Agency: Security under Scrutiny* (Westport, Conn.: Greenwood Press, 2006), pp. 163–164. For more on the Doolittle Committee, see John Prados, *Safe for Democracy: The Secret Wars of the* CIA (Chicago: Ivan R. Dee, 2006), pp. 148–149.

19. Richard Immerman, "A Brief History of the CIA," in Theoharis, ed., *Central Intelligence Agency*, p. 25.
20. Minutes of meeting, 22 August 1952, 2.18, Committee of Correspondence Papers.
21. Rose Parsons, Dorothy Bauman, and Charlotte Mahon to "Friend," 24 November 1952, 7.213, Phillips Papers.
22. Quoted in Laville, *Cold War Women*, p. 177.
23. Annual Report, 1 March 1953–1 April 1954, 2.19, Committee of Correspondence Papers.
24. "About the Committee of Correspondence," Fall 1961, 1.3, Committee of Correspondence Papers.
25. Gertrude Protain to Alison Raymond, 5 June 1960, 1.7, Louise Backus Papers, Schlesinger Library, Radcliffe Institute, Harvard University.
26. See "Hattertown Training Session—October 16–17, 1959," 1.4, Backus Papers.
27. Zarina Fazelbhoy, oral history, 54.893, Committee of Correspondence Papers.
28. Jean and Harvey Picker, oral history, 54.901, Committee of Correspondence Papers.
29. See the splendid explanation of this shift in emphasis in Christina Klein, *Cold War Orientalism: Asia in the Middlebrow Imagination, 1945–1961* (Berkeley: University of California Press, 2003), chap. 1. For more on People-to-People and the Peace Corps, see, respectively, Osgood, *Total Cold War*, pp. 232–244, and Elizabeth Cobbs Hoffman, *All You Need Is Love: The Peace Corps and the Spirit of the 1960s* (Cambridge, Mass.: Harvard University Press, 1998).
30. Spencer Arnold, quoted in "Notes on Special Board Meeting Monday, July 24, 1967, 10.30 A.M.," addition, box 2, folder Financial Records, Committee of Correspondence Papers.
31. Bauman, oral history.
32. Minutes, 27 October 1953, 2.18, Committee of Correspondence Papers.
33. Minutes, 26 May 1953, 2.18, Committee of Correspondence Papers.
34. Minutes, 23 February 1954, 2.19, Committee of Correspondence Papers.
35. Annual Report, 1 April 1954–31 March 1955, 2.20, Committee of Correspondence Papers.
36. Annual Report, 1 April 1955–31 March 1956, 2.21, Committee of Correspondence Papers.
37. See "Foundations Which Have Supported the Committee of Correspondence," 1 March 1967, addition, box 2, folder Financial Records, Committee of Correspondence Papers.
38. Hester's departure in 1955 sounded a rare note of internal discord in the Committee. In her resignation letter to Rose Parsons, she complained of "a permanent confusion as to the responsibilities, organizational structure, policies, and procedures." Anne Hester to Rose Parsons, 3 January 1955, 2.20, Committee of Correspondence Papers.

39. "Committee of Correspondence," n.d., 1.3, Committee of Correspondence Papers.
40. Bauman, oral history.
41. "Notes on Special Board Meeting Monday, July 24, 1967, 10.30 A.M.," addition, box 2, folder Financial Records, Committee of Correspondence Papers.
42. Jean and Harvey Picker, oral history.
43. Alison Raymond, oral history, 54.895, Committee of Correspondence Papers.
44. "Recommendations of the Press and Public Relations Committee Concerning Any Change in the Present Policy," n.d., 2.19, Committee of Correspondence Papers.
45. Theodore C. Streibert to Rose Parsons, 16 April 1954, box 7, folder Committee of Correspondence, 1954, Phillips Papers; minutes, 27 April 1954, 2.19, Committee of Correspondence Papers.
46. Notes on meetings with Rose Parsons, 28 March 1960, and Jean Picker, 22 August 1960, 13.275, Anna Lord Strauss Papers, Schlesinger Library, Radcliffe Institute, Harvard University.
47. Raymond, oral history.
48. Rosalind Harris, oral history, 54.894, Committee of Correspondence Papers.
49. Jean Picker to Committee Members, 20 March 1967, 1.8, Committee of Correspondence Papers.
50. "SMcK at Special Meeting, 7/24/67," and Susan McKeever, "From meeting with Spence, Washington," 19 July 1967, both addition, box 2, folder Financial Records, Committee of Correspondence Papers.
51. "Notes on Special Board Meeting Monday, July 24, 1967, 10.30 A.M.," addition, box 2, folder Financial Records, Committee of Correspondence Papers.
52. Eleanor G. Coit et al., "Statement to go with Committee of Correspondence Files in the Sophia Smith Collection, Smith College Library," December 1970, 1.14, Committee of Correspondence Papers.
53. Harris, oral history.
54. Elizabeth Wadsworth, oral history, 54.902, Committee of Correspondence Papers.
55. Raymond, oral history.
56. Anne Crolius, oral history, 54.892, Committee of Correspondence Papers.
57. "Notes on Special Board Meeting Monday, July 24, 1967, 10.30 A.M.," addition, box 2, folder Financial Records, Committee of Correspondence Papers.
58. See minutes, 4 August 1953, 2.18, Committee of Correspondence Papers.
59. John H. Jamison to Rose Parsons, 4 January 1955, box 7, folder Committee of Correspondence, 1955, Phillips Papers.
60. Minutes, 27 December 1955, 2.20, Committee of Correspondence Papers.
61. Anderson, oral history; Jean and Harvey Picker, oral history.

62. Bauman, oral history; Anderson, oral history; Raymond, oral history; Crolius, oral history.
63. John H. Jamison to Rose Parsons, 7 March 1955, box 7, folder Committee of Correspondence, 1955, Phillips Papers.
64. Bauman, oral history.
65. Minutes, 24 October 1952, 2.18, Committee of Correspondence Papers.
66. Annual Report, 1 March 1953–1 April 1954, 2.19, Committee of Correspondence Papers.
67. Minutes, 31 January 1955, 2.20, Committee of Correspondence Papers.
68. Constance Anderson, 29 March 1960, 13.275, Strauss Papers; Susan McKeever, 18 April 1960, 13.275, Strauss Papers.
69. Dorothy Bauman, "Right or Wrong?" 29 October 1974, 54.888, Committee of Correspondence Papers.
70. See the historiographical discussions in Laville, *Cold War Women*, pp. 1–4, and Jane Sherron De Hart, "Containment at Home: Gender, Sexuality, and National Identity in Cold War America," in Peter J. Kuznick and James Gilbert, eds., *Rethinking Cold War Culture* (Washington, D.C.: Smithsonian Institution Press, 2001), pp. 124–128.

8. Saving the World

1. Seth Jacobs, *America's Miracle Man in Vietnam: Ngo Dinh Diem, Religion, Race, and U.S. Intervention in Southeast Asia, 1950–1957* (Durham, N.C.: Duke University Press, 2004), pp. 77–78.
2. Richard Gid Powers, *Not without Honor: The History of American Anticommunism* (New York: Free Press, 1995), p. 51.
3. James T. Fisher, *Dr. America: The Lives of Thomas A. Dooley, 1927–1961* (Amherst: University of Massachusetts Press, 1997), pp. 3–4.
4. Ibid., p. 2. Campus rumor had it that Dooley received his diploma only after pledging he would never practice medicine in the United States.
5. For more on Passage to Freedom, see Jacobs, *America's Miracle Man*, pp. 129–138.
6. See, for example, Thomas to Agnes Dooley, 12 May 1955, box 1, folder 7, Thomas A. Dooley Papers, Western Historical Manuscript Collection, University of Missouri, St. Louis. Dooley boasted, "So, mother dear, it is a long time since I flunked my senior year."
7. See, for example, Thomas to Agnes Dooley, 28 November 1954, 1.7, Dooley Papers, in which Dooley describes the horrible injuries of a Catholic priest tortured by his Vietminh captors. "I can't even write these things without getting all filled up with emotion," the doctor told his mother.

8. Jacobs, *America's Miracle Man*, p. 149.
9. Quoted in ibid., p. 152.
10. Evan Thomas, *The Very Best Men—Four Who Dared: The Early Years of the CIA* (New York: Simon and Schuster, 1995), p. 57. Among Lansdale's several accomplishments in the Philippines was producing a "Magsaysay Is My Guy" button and helping write "The Magsaysay Mambo." Jonathan Nashel, "Edward Lansdale and the American Attempt to Remake Southeast Asia, 1945–1965" (Ph.D. diss., Rutgers University, 1994), p. 70. Since completing his Ph.D., Nashel has published *Edward Lansdale's Cold War* (Amherst: University of Massachusetts Press, 2004).
11. For an account of Filipino politics that plays down Lansdale's contribution, see Nick Cullather, *Illusions of Influence: The Political Economy of United States–Philippines Relations, 1942–1960* (Palo Alto, Calif.: Stanford University Press, 1994), pp. 96–122.
12. Quoted in Nashel, "Edward Lansdale," p. 81; Edward Lansdale to Allen Dulles, 15 November 1961, 37.909, Edward G. Lansdale Papers, Hoover Institution, Stanford University.
13. For more on SMM operations, see Lansdale's own report, "Lansdale Team's Report on Covert Saigon Mission in '54 and '55," in Neil Sheehan et al., *The Pentagon Papers as Published by The New York Times* (New York: Quadrangle Books, 1971), pp. 54–67.
14. See ibid., p. 65; also Jacobs, *America's Miracle Man*, p. 133.
15. Cecil B. Currey, *Edward Lansdale: The Unquiet American* (Boston: Houghton Mifflin, 1988), p. 159; Lansdale quoted on p. 157.
16. Ibid., pp. 170, 188. Lansdale also had several clashes with French colonial administrators during his tour of Vietnam.
17. Edward Lansdale, report on Operation Brotherhood, 35.804, Lansdale Papers.
18. Fisher, *Dr. America*, p. 6.
19. Lansdale, quoted in ibid., p. 117. Referring to a more famous "jungle doctor," the U.S. ambassador to Laos dubbed Dooley "the Madison Avenue Schweitzer." J. Graham Parsons, quoted in ibid., p. 139.
20. Ibid., p. 60.
21. Dooley wrote his mother from Haiphong (in a letter that inadvertently proved his unsuitability for real espionage) "to the world, we are doing . . . medical triage to the refugees who are here in such large numbers awaiting their [transfer] to the Navy Transports down at Baie d'Along. . . . The second part of our job, and the real thing, is Medical Intelligence." Thomas to Agnes Dooley, 14 September 1954, 1.7, Dooley Papers.
22. Fisher, *Dr. America*, p. 49.
23. Norton Stevens, a naval intelligence officer, quoted in Jacobs, *America's Miracle Man*, p. 150.

24. See, for example, Thomas to Agnes Dooley, 11 February 1955, 1.7, Dooley Papers, in which the young doctor portentously explained to his mother that "just as important as the diplomatic table talks" in winning the Cold War struggle for hearts and minds were "the rice paddy talks [and] the sick call talks."
25. Thomas Dooley to "Rosa," 1 July 1955, 1.9, Dooley Papers.
26. "I tried to point out that our job in Asia is not a matter of money or hordes of people," Lederer wrote Lansdale in October 1957, following conversations with some U.S diplomats. "It only requires a small number of highly trained or skilled guys." William Lederer to Edward Lansdale, 28 October 1957, 38.992, Lansdale Papers.
27. Fisher, *Dr. America*, p. 74.
28. Quoted in ibid., p. 73.
29. Debate continues about the veracity of Dooley's atrocity stories: although their early appearance in letters to his mother suggests that they were not entirely fabricated after the event, a lengthy report on *Deliver Us from Evil* commissioned by the United States Information Agency in 1955 concluded that they were "nonfactual and exaggerated." Quoted in Jim Winters, "Tom Dooley: The Forgotten Hero," *Notre Dame Magazine*, n.d., 10.147, Dooley Papers.
30. For more on the extensive links between the CIA and *Reader's Digest*, see John Heidenry, *Theirs Was the Kingdom: Lila and DeWitt Wallace and the Story of Reader's Digest* (New York and London: W. W. Norton, 1993), pp. 470–474. In April 1963, Lansdale met with seven editors and senior writers at the Pleasantville, New York, headquarters of *Reader's Digest* and briefed them, "off the record," about U.S. counterinsurgency measures in Vietnam. He then proposed the publication of a number of short stories about individual Americans "who are in today's struggle abroad [and] who are doing the right thing unselfishly," explaining "that *Reader's Digest* was in a unique position to make situations in critical areas of the world understandable in warmly human terms." The editors and writers "were intensely interested in the subject matter and responded warmly to my suggestions," Lansdale reported to Deputy Secretary of Defense Roswell L. Gilpatric. "I trust that this leads to some further constructive working together in a quiet way." Edward Lansdale to Roswell Gilpatric, 17 April 1963, 48.1359, Lansdale Papers.
31. Quoted in Fisher, *Dr. America*, p. 90; Jacobs, *America's Miracle Man*, p. 153.
32. Fisher, *Dr. America*, p. 35.
33. Jacobs, *America's Miracle Man*, p. 154.
34. Fisher, *Dr. America*, p. 83.
35. Frank Mahon, "Legacy of a Legend," *Notre Dame Magazine* (Spring 1998), 23. See Randy Shilts, *Conduct Unbecoming: Gays and Lesbians in the U.S. Military* (New York: St Martin's Press, 1993), pp. 22–27, 517–521, 735–736.
36. Instead, in 1952 the CIA established a proprietary organization, Aid Refugee

Chinese Intellectuals, Inc. (ARCI); by 1955, when it curtailed its activities, ARCI had dispensed a total of $1,348,063 in aid. Anon., "Background of Committee to Aid Chinese Refugees," n.d., box 1, folder Background material, Aid Refugee Chinese Intellectuals, Inc., Papers, Hoover Institution, Stanford University; anon., "Purpose and Program of Aid Refugee Chinese Intellectuals, Inc.," n.d., box 1, folder Purpose and program of ARCI, ARCI Papers.

37. See, for example, Joseph Buttinger, "Memorandum on Indochina (Vietnam)," n.d. [probably early January 1955], box 83, folder IRC, 1954–1957, Asia Foundation Papers, Hoover Institution, Stanford University.

38. Quoted in Eric Thomas Chester, *Covert Network: Progressives, the International Rescue Committee, and the* CIA (New York: M. E. Sharpe, 1995), p. 164. Another important member of the "Vietnam Lobby"—and the Lansdale circle—was Wesley R. Fishel, a political science professor who was responsible for setting up a South Vietnamese police training program at Michigan State University, which would later be exposed by *Ramparts* as a CIA front. See below, chap. 10.

39. Ibid., p. 168.

40. Robert Scheer and Warren Hinckle, "The Vietnam Lobby," in *Ramparts, A Vietnam Primer*, n.d., n.p., box 17, Dooley Papers.

41. Joseph G. Morgan, in *The Vietnam Lobby: The American Friends of Vietnam, 1955–1975* (Chapel Hill: University of North Carolina Press, 1997), tends to downplay the AFV's influence. For a contrary view, see Jacobs, *America's Miracle Man*, chap. 6. An excellent brief treatment of the Vietnam Lobby is James T. Fisher, "'A World Made Safe for Diversity': The Vietnam Lobby and the Politics of Pluralism, 1945–1963," in Christian G. Appy, ed., *Cold War Constructions: The Political Culture of United States Imperialism, 1945–1966* (Amherst: University of Massachusetts Press, 2000), pp. 217–237.

42. One CIA-front donor was the Baird Fund. Chester, *Covert Network*, p. 165.

43. Oram's mere presence in the IRC and AFV is suggestive: his firm undertook public fund-raising for a wide range of CIA front organizations on the non-communist left, such as the American Committee for Cultural Freedom. Ibid., pp. 152, 163.

44. Fisher, *Dr. America*, p. 95; see, for example, Edward Lansdale to John O'Daniel, 3 January 1958, 21.547, Lansdale Papers, wherein Lansdale suggests that AFV attempt to discredit a reporter, Hilaire du Berrier, who had commented critically on U.S. support for the Diem regime.

45. Quoted in Morgan, *Vietnam Lobby*, p. 154; Jacobs, *America's Miracle Man*, p. 232.

46. Jacobs, *America's Miracle Man*, p. 329.

47. IRC Saigon Office Quarterly Report, January–March 1956, box 83, folder IRC, 1954–1957, Asia Foundation Papers; Edward Lansdale to Joseph Mankiewicz, 17 March 1956, 35.785, Lansdale Papers.

48. Quoted in Jacobs, *America's Miracle Man*, p. 110.
49. Quoted in Nashel, "Edward Lansdale," p. 290.
50. Edward Lansdale to Ngo Dinh Diem, 28 October 1957, 39.1052, Lansdale Papers.
51. Quoted in Jacobs, *America's Miracle Man*, p. 110.
52. Fisher, *Dr. America*, p. 96.
53. Ibid., p. 113.
54. Ibid., p. 182. See also Diana Shaw, "The Temptation of Tom Dooley," *Los Angeles Times Magazine*, 15 December 1991, 43–46, 50, 80.
55. Quoted in Fisher, *Dr. America*, p. 117.
56. Thomas Dooley, "Plans for the Medical Mission to the Kingdom of Laos," n.d., 2.35, Dooley Papers.
57. Quoted in Jacobs, *America's Miracle Man*, p. 167. Lederer and Burdick's *Ugly American* featured a tough Jesuit missionary, Father John. X. Finian, with more than a passing resemblance to Thomas A. Dooley.
58. Quoted in Fisher, *Dr. America*, p. 163.
59. See Chester, *Covert Network*, pp. 169–174.
60. Edward Lansdale to John W. O'Daniel, 5 August 1963, 21.547, Lansdale Papers.
61. The Asia Foundation had already inherited some programs originated by the IRC's Saigon office, including the popular cultural associations. See Robert Blum to Margaret Z. Cole, 20 September 1956, box 83, folder IRC, 1954–1957, Asia Foundation Papers. The history of the Asia Foundation, whose records have recently been opened at the Hoover Institution, awaits further exploration.
62. Paul Hellmuth to Thomas Dooley, 21 December 1960, 4.67, Dooley Papers. "I believe that you have talent, the imagination, and the dynamic, practical sales ability needed to imbue other leaders in this country with this great aim and ideal," Hellmuth wrote Dooley.
63. See, for example, Thomas Dooley to Paul Hellmuth, 18 November 1960, 4.67, Dooley Papers, in which the medic imperiously asks his attorney to buy his brother Malcolm a dinner service.
64. Quoted in Fisher, *Dr. America*, p. 217.
65. Jacobs, *America's Miracle Man*, p. 138.
66. Quoted in ibid., p. 140.
67. Quoted in Richard Gribble, *American Apostle of the Family Rosary: The Life of Patrick J. Peyton*, CSC (New York: Crossroad Publishing Co., 2005), p. 25. For more about Peyton's early life, see ibid., chap. 1.
68. Quoted in Patrick Peyton's autobiography, *All For Her*, excerpted on web site of Holy Cross Family Ministries, "Early Priesthood," www.familyrosary.org (accessed 20 July 2005).
69. "Early Life," www.familyrosary.org (accessed 20 July 2005).
70. "Founding of Ministries," www.familyrosary.org (accessed 20 July 2005).

71. See Jeffrey Burns, *American Catholics and the Family Crisis, 1930–1962* (New York: Garland Publishing, 1988).
72. Quoted in Gribble, *American Apostle*, p. 39.
73. Quoted in ibid., p. 129.
74. Ibid., p. 328.
75. Ibid., pp. 107–108.
76. Quoted in ibid., p. 115.
77. See Robert Waters and Gordon Daniels, "The World's Longest General Strike: The AFL-CIO, the CIA, and British Guiana," *Diplomatic History* 29 (2005): 279–307.
78. See Philip Agee, *Inside the Company: CIA Diary* (Harmondsworth: Penguin Books, 1975), pp. 243–245; George Morris, *CIA and American Labor: The Subversion of the AFL-CIO's Foreign Policy* (New York: International Publishers, 1967), pp. 92–97.
79. "Institute of International Labor Research, Inc.," n.d., Norman Thomas Papers, series 2, reel 65, New York Public Library; Steven V. Roberts, "Thomas Upholds CIA-Aided Work," *New York Times*, 22 February 1967, 17. "What we did was good work, and no one ever tried to tell us what to do," the eighty-two-year old Thomas told the *New York Times*. "I am ashamed we swallowed this CIA business, though."
80. See William H. Chafe, *Never Stop Running: Allard Lowenstein and the Struggle to Save American Liberalism* (New York: Basic Books, 1993), pp. 256–261.
81. Penny Lernoux, *Cry of the People: The Struggle for Human Rights in Latin America: The Catholic Church in Conflict with U.S. Policy* (New York: Penguin Books, 1982), p. 283.
82. See Gerard Colby with Charlotte Dennett, *Thy Will Be Done: The Conquest of the Amazon: Nelson Rockefeller and Evangelism in the Age of Oil* (New York: Harper Collins, 1995).
83. See Lernoux, *Cry of the People*, pp. 289–292.
84. Quoted in Richard Gribble, "Anti-Communism, Patrick Peyton, CSC, and the CIA," *Journal of Church and State* 45 (2003): 540–541, 542–543.
85. Penny Lernoux, *People of God: The Struggle for World Catholicism* (New York: Viking, 1989), p. 296.
86. Ibid., p. 297.
87. Grace said that he would tell "everyone I meet when I can buttonhole them for a minute" that "the Family Rosary seems to me to be the only answer to the situation in which we all find ourselves today." Quoted in Gribble, *American Apostle*, p. 70.
88. Quoted in Gribble, "Anti-Communism, Peyton, and the CIA," 545.
89. Quoted in Gribble, *American Apostle*, p. 165.

90. Quoted in Gribble, "Anti-Communism, Peyton, and the CIA," 543.
91. Peter Grace to Allen Dulles, 24 November 1958, 428 (FR) 14, Archives of the Holy Cross Generalate (hereafter AHCG), Rome, Italy. (Copies of papers in this collection were obtained from a private source.) Grace sent an almost identical letter to a banker, John Madden, on the same day, suggesting that he had still not given up hope of securing private backing for the Rosary Crusade.
92. Quoted in Gribble, *American Apostle*, p. 170.
93. Peter Grace, quoted in Gribble, "Anti-Communism, Peyton, and the CIA," 544.
94. Frip Flannigan to "RMW," 5 December 1958, box 298, folder J. P. Grace, Richard Nixon Vice Presidential Papers, National Archives District Branch, Laguna Niguel, California; Peter Grace to Allen Dulles, 24 November 1958, 428 (FR) 14, AHCG.
95. Peter Grace to Allen Dulles, 24 November 1958, 428 (FR) 14, AHCG.
96. Quoted in Gribble, "Anti-Communism, Peyton, and the CIA," 545.
97. Quoted in Gribble, *American Apostle*, p. 177.
98. Quoted in Gribble, "Anti-Communism, Peyton, and the CIA," 548n44.
99. Norman Carignan, quoted in ibid., 549.
100. Ibid.
101. Quoted in Gribble, *American Apostle*, p. 184.
102. Quoted in ibid., pp. 182, 185.
103. See ibid., pp. 182–191.
104. See William Blum, *Killing Hope: U.S. Military and CIA Interventions since World War II* (Monroe, Maine: Common Courage Press, 2004), chap. 27.
105. Quoted in Gribble, *American Apostle*, p. 191. In the weeks immediately before the coup, middle-class housewives concerned about the threat posed to the traditional Brazilian family by communism staged a series of anti-Goulart rallies, the "March of Family with God for Liberty." See Phyllis R. Barker, *Brazil and the Quiet Intervention, 1964* (Austin: University of Texas Press, 1979), pp. 63, 81.
106. Quoted in Gribble, "Anti-Communism, Peyton, and the CIA," 551.
107. Quoted in Gribble, *American Apostle*, p. 190. The fact that the CIA agreed to fund the Crusade in Brazil for a two-year period suggests that its estimates indicated that the Family Rosary was exerting an advantageous political influence there. See ibid., p. 186.
108. Powers, *Not without Honor*, pp. 304–305.
109. See Lernoux, *Cry of the People*, p. 31. According to Theodore Hesburgh, Câmara, the auxiliary archbishop of Rio, was one of the Brazilian prelates who "was dissatisfied with what he thought was the Rosary Crusade's part in arranging the recent coup in Brazil." Theodore M. Hesburgh to Germain Lalande, 7 October 1964, 428 (FR) 14, AHCG.

110. Germain Lalande to Richard Sullivan, 28 September 1964, Richard Sullivan to Germain Lalande, 3 November 1964, both in 428 (FR) 14, AHCG.
111. Grace had sought to assure Hesburgh that disclosure of the secret funding was impossible. "However, I reminded him that a number of people were talking about it, and that very few human happenings were free from disclosure these days," the Notre Dame president wrote Lalande. Theodore Hesburgh to Germain Lalande, 7 October 1964, 428 (FR) 14, AHCG.
112. See Patrick Peyton, minutes of meeting, 24 October 1964; anon. [probably Germain Lalande], "Meeting with Fr. Peyton and Fr. Mullahy," 24 October 1964; both 428 (FR) 14, AHCG.
113. Germain Lalande, "Meeting with Fr. Sullivan . . . 20, 21, and 22 February 1965"; Germain Lalande to Pope Paul VI, 6 September 1965; Germain Lalande to Richard Sullivan, 1 September 1965; all in 428 (FR) 14, AHCG.
114. Richard Sullivan to Germain Lalande, 16 September 1965; Germain Lalande to Richard Sullivan, 27 September 1965; both 428 (FR) 14, AHCG.
115. Joseph M. Quinn to Richard Sullivan, 19 October 1965, 428 (FR) 14, AHCG. After reviewing the Albany office's books, a Holy Cross religious arrived at a total figure of $996,450.
116. Germain Lalande, minutes of meeting with S.E. Mgr. Dell'Acqua, 14 October 1965; Germain Lalande to Richard Sullivan, 27 September 1965; both 428 (FR) 14, AHCG.
117. Richard Sullivan to Germain Lalande, 3 November 1965, 428 (FR) 14, AHCG.
118. Germain Lalande to Richard Sullivan, 20 December 1965, 428 (FR) 14, AHCG.
119. See, for example, Germain Lalande to Richard Sullivan, 22 January 1966, 428 (FR) 14, AHCG.
120. Germain Lalande, minutes of meeting in Montreal, 25 April 1966; Germain Lalande, minutes of meeting with Richard Sullivan, 20 June 1966; Germain Lalande to Richard Sullivan, 17 October 1966; all 428 (FR) 14, AHCG.
121. For details on the turn of U.S. missionaries against the CIA, see Lernoux, *Cry of the People*, p. 287. While considering the unintended consequences of this operation, it is also tempting to speculate—although, of course, difficult to prove—that some of the popular religious enthusiasm unleashed by the Family Rosary Crusade in South America later crossed over into the Church of the Poor advocated by liberationist theologists.

9. Into Africa

1. Quoted in Hazel Rowley, *Richard Wright: The Life and Times* (New York: Henry Holt, 2001), p. 521.
2. Quoted in Michel Fabre, *The Unfinished Quest of Richard Wright*, 2nd ed. (Urbana: University of Illinois Press, 1993), p. 519.

3. See Rowley, *Richard Wright*, pp. 525–526, and James Campbell, *Exiled in Paris: Richard Wright, James Baldwin, Samuel Beckett, and Others on the Left Bank* (New York: Scribner, 1995), pp. 241–247.
4. See Gerald Horne, *Communist Front? The Civil Rights Congress, 1946–1956* (Rutherford, N.J.: Fairleigh Dickinson University Press, 1988), chap. 6.
5. An extensive academic literature now exists concerning the links between African independence, the civil rights movement, and the Cold War. There is also a growing body of writing about overt U.S. cultural diplomacy in Africa, especially the State Department–sponsored tours of "jazz ambassadors" such as Duke Ellington and Dizzy Gillespie. This chapter represents the first scholarly attempt to document this effort's covert dimension. See, for example, Thomas Borstelmann, *The Cold War and the Color Line: American Race Relations in the Global Arena* (Cambridge, Mass.: Harvard University Press, 2001); Mary L. Dudziak, *Cold War Civil Rights: Race and the Image of American Democracy* (Princeton, N.J.: Princeton University Press, 2000); James H. Meriwether, *Proudly We Can Be Africans: Black Americans and Africa, 1935–1961* (Chapel Hill: University of North Carolina Press, 2002); Brenda Gayle Plummer, *Rising Wind: Black Americans and U.S. Foreign Affairs, 1935–1960* (Chapel Hill: University of North Carolina Press, 1996); Brenda Gayle Plummer, ed., *Window on Freedom: Race, Civil Rights, and Foreign Affairs, 1945–1968* (Chapel Hill: University of North Carolina Press, 1996); Penny M. Von Eschen, *Race against Empire: Black Americans and Anticolonialism, 1937–1957* (Ithaca, N.Y.: Cornell University Press, 1997); Penny M. Von Eschen, *Satchmo Blows Up the World: Jazz Ambassadors Play the Cold War* (Cambridge, Mass.: Harvard University Press, 2004).
6. For more on the pan-African movement, see Ronald Walters, *Pan Africanism in the African Diaspora: An Analysis of Modern Afrocentric Political Movements* (Detroit: Wayne State University Press, 1993).
7. For more on the trials of the CAA, see Von Eschen's excellent account, *Race against Empire*.
8. John Davis to Martin Kilson, 25 April 1962, 6.2, AMSAC Papers, Moorland-Spingarn Research Center, Howard University.
9. Anon., Council on Race and Caste in World Affairs, n.d., 20.1, AMSAC Papers, Moorland-Spingarn Center.
10. For more on the emergence of this new set of attitudes toward Africa, see Von Eschen, *Race against Empire*, chap. 7.
11. Von Eschen, *Satchmo*, p. 157.
12. See the judicious discussion of Wright's complex relationship with the African liberation struggle in Kevin K. Gaines, *American Africans in Ghana: Black Expatriates and the Civil Rights Era* (Chapel Hill: University of North Carolina Press, 2006), chap. 2. On the French African circle around *Présence Africaine*, see V. Y.

Mudimbe, *The Surreptitious Speech:* Présence Africaine *and the Politics of Otherness, 1947–1987* (Chicago: University of Chicago Press, 1992).

13. Rowley, *Richard Wright*, p. 363.
14. Borstelmann, *Cold War and Color Line*, p. 96; Plummer, *Rising Wind*, p. 254.
15. Telegrams of 8 May 1956 and 17 May 1956, quoted in Rowley, *Richard Wright*, p. 474. Wright was also in touch with Michael Josselson of the Congress for Cultural Freedom (and CIA). See Campbell, *Exiled in Paris*, p. 192.
16. "The Origin and Nature of the American Society of African Culture," enclosed with form letter by James T. Harris, Jr., 21 May 1958, box A197, folder Leagues and Organizations: AMSAC, Part III, General Office File, 1956–1965, NAACP Papers, Library of Congress, Washington, D.C. My thanks to Joe Street for providing me with a copy of this document.
17. Richard Wright to John Davis, 1 August 1956, 17.36, AMSAC Papers, Moorland-Spingarn Center.
18. See John Davis to Horace Mann Bond, 15 August 1956, 36.111A, Horace Mann Bond Papers, W. E. B. Du Bois Library, University of Massachusetts, Amherst. Bond was also president of the Institute of African-American Relations (later, the African-American Institute), another U.S. instrument of cultural diplomacy in Africa with links to the CIA. See Wayne J. Urban, *Black Scholar: Horace Mann Bond, 1904–1972* (Athens: University of Georgia Press, 1992), pp. 158–159. The reports proved slow in coming: Davis had not received a single one by 23 October. Orin Lehman made it clear to Davis that the former would not back proposals for a permanent society of African culture until he had received all the reports. See John Davis to Horace Mann Bond, 23 October 1956, 36.111B, Bond Papers.
19. John Davis to Richard Wright, 5 September 1956, 96.1276, Richard Wright Papers, Beinecke Library, Yale University.
20. James Baldwin, "Letter from Paris: Princes and Powers," *Encounter* 3 (1957): 52–53.
21. Horace Mann Bond, "Report on the First Congress of Negro Writers and Artists, Held in Paris, France, The Sorbonne, September 19–22, 1956," n.d. [1956], 36.111B, Bond Papers. Bond's report also makes mention of the fact that, just after arriving in Paris a few days before the conference was due to begin, the American delegation met with U.S. embassy officials, raising the possibility that some of their suspicions concerning fellow conferees were officially prompted.
22. Anon., report on Congress, n.d. [1956], 36.111C, Bond Papers.
23. Bond, "Report on the First Congress of Negro Writers and Artists."
24. Quoted in Margaret Walker, *Richard Wright, Daemonic Genius: A Portrait of the Man, a Critical Look at His Work* (New York: Warner Books, 1988), p. 280.
25. "Origin and Nature of the American Society of African Culture."

26. Baldwin, "Letter from Paris," 53.
27. Bond, "Report on the First Congress of Negro Writers and Artists."
28. "Origin and Nature of the American Society of African Culture."
29. Baldwin, "Letter from Paris," 58.
30. Richard Wright, observations about 1956 Congress, n.d. [1956], 104.1557, Wright Papers.
31. Quoted in Rowley, *Richard Wright*, p. 478.
32. Baldwin, "Letter from Paris," 58. Given the famously strained relationship between the two men (both African American writers in Parisian exile), the description Baldwin offered of Wright's predicament at the Paris Congress was notably sensitive and sympathetic. Wright's controversial interest in the modernizing influence on Africa of western colonialism, which he tried to explain in the final lecture of the Congress, "Tradition and Industrialization," is discussed in Gaines, *American Africans in Ghana*, pp. 65–66. For a summary of all the debates staged at the Congress, see Bennetta Jules-Rosette, *Black Paris: The African Writers' Landscape* (Urbana: University of Illinois Press, 1998), pp. 56–64.
33. Quoted in Rowley, *Richard Wright*, p. 480.
34. Diop's speech reported in Baldwin, "Letter from Paris," p. 60. See also "Origin and Nature of the American Society of African Culture."
35. Alioune Diop to John Davis, 25 January 1957, 36.111C, Bond Papers.
36. John Davis to Richard Wright, 31 January 1957, 17.36, AMSAC Papers, Moorland-Spingarn Center.
37. John Davis to Alioune Diop, 18 February 1957, 104.1557, Wright Papers.
38. Alioune Diop to John Davis, 19 April 1957, 36.111D, Bond Papers.
39. John Davis to Horace Mann Bond et al., 5 May 1957 and 20 May 1957, both 36.111D, Bond Papers.
40. McCloskey had agreed to join the board of directors of the American Information Committee on Race and Caste in March 1957, after receiving an invitation from Davis, Lehman, and Webster explaining that the organization's purpose was "to present an accurate picture of the development of race relations in the United States . . . [and] correct the distorted version of these relations which has such wide currency abroad." John Davis, Orin Lehman, and Bethuel Webster to Matthew McCloskey, n.d., 20.9, AMSAC Papers, Moorland-Spingarn Center.
41. Minutes of Coordinating Committee for the American Information Committee on Race and Caste, 24 September 1957, 20.10, AMSAC Papers, Moorland-Spingarn Center.
42. Minutes of Special Meeting of Directors of American Information Committee on Race and Caste, 24 October 1957, 20.10, AMSAC Papers, Moorland-Spingarn Center.

43. John Davis to Alioune Diop, 18 November 1957, 13.24, AMSAC Papers, Moorland-Spingarn Center.
44. John Davis to Richard Wright, 18 November 1957, 96.1276, Wright Papers.
45. Richard Wright to John Davis, 25 November 1957, 17.36, AMSAC Papers, Moorland-Spingarn Center. Wright also told Davis that Diop had heard the group of black intellectuals in Atlanta around the journal *Phylon* "describe me . . . as a Communist, an accusation that rendered him speechless."
46. Richard Wright to James Harris, 14 April 1958, 17.36, AMSAC Papers, Moorland-Spingarn Center.
47. James Harris to Richard Wright, 21 March 1958, 93.1173, Wright Papers.
48. "You know our French African brothers far better than we do," Davis pleaded with Wright. "Please come." John Davis to Richard Wright, n.d., 96.1276, Wright Papers.
49. Richard Wright to John Davis, 1 March 1958, 17.36, AMSAC Papers, Moorland-Spingarn Center.
50. Richard Wright to John Davis, 11 May 1959, 17.36, AMSAC Papers, Moorland-Spingarn Center.
51. Ibid.
52. John Davis to Richard Wright, 23 May 1959, 93.1173, Wright Papers.
53. Quoted in Fabre, *Unfinished Quest*, p. 490.
54. Quoted in Rowley, *Richard Wright*, p. 520.
55. "AMSAC: Its Purpose, Program, and Activities," n.d., 1.2, AMSAC Papers, Schomburg Center for Research in Black Culture, New York Public Library.
56. "Summary Report, Second Annual Conference," June 1959, 1.4, AMSAC Papers, Schomburg Center; Yvonne O. Walker, telephone interview with author, 9 May 2006.
57. "AMSAC: Its Purpose, Program, and Activities."
58. These volumes included the proceedings of the 1960 and 1963 conferences, entitled *Pan-Africanism Reconsidered* and *Southern Africa in Transition*, respectively. The 1963 event, held at Howard University, featured, among other southern African independence leaders, Oliver Tambo of the African National Congress. For the conference program, see AMSAC Newsletter (Extra Conference Issue), 15 March 1963, 1.12, AMSAC Papers, Schomburg Center.
59. Program, "Fifth Annual Holiday Party," 1961, 1.4, AMSAC Papers, Schomburg Center.
60. Walker interview; John Davis to Martin Kilson, 25 April 1962, 6.2, AMSAC Papers, Moorland-Spingarn Center.
61. "U.S. Culture Society Opens Office in Africa," *Chicago Defender*, 2 September 1961, 9; "AMSAC Opens Cultural Center in Nigeria," *Chicago Defender*, 30 December 1961, 7.

62. AMSAC Newsletter, January–February 1961, 49.9, St. Clair Drake Papers, Schomburg Center for Research in Black Culture, New York Public Library.
63. Alioune Diop to John Davis, 4 December 1961, 6.2, AMSAC Papers, Moorland-Spingarn Center.
64. Minutes of Postponed Annual Meeting of Directors, AMSAC, 2 July 1962, 31.86C, Bond Papers; John Davis to AMSAC Board, 14 November 1961, 13.26, AMSAC Papers, Moorland-Spingarn Center; AMSAC Executive Council minutes, 29–30 June 1962, 49.9, Drake Papers.
65. John Davis to Alioune Diop, 14 August 1962, 49.9, Drake Papers.
66. Alioune Diop to John Davis, 4 December 1961, 6.2, AMSAC Papers, Moorland-Spingarn Center.
67. Adelaide Cromwell Hill to John Davis, 19 December 1961, 6.2, AMSAC Papers, Moorland-Spingarn Center.
68. Martin Kilson to John Davis, 10 April 1962, 6.2, AMSAC Papers, Moorland-Spingarn Center.
69. Alioune Diop to John Davis, 4 December 1961, 6.2, AMSAC Papers, Moorland-Spingarn Center; John Davis to Martin Kilson, 25 April 1962, 6.2, AMSAC Papers, Moorland-Spingarn Center. The attitude of young Africans at Harvard toward AMSAC, as described by Kilson, is echoed in the account by Nigerian poet and playwright John Pepper Clark of his sojourn at Princeton on a Parvin Fellowship in 1962. According to Clark, the "social climbing and status-seeking" black Americans who belonged to AMSAC made "a profession of their identity, and indeed a booming business of it." J. P. Clark, *America, Their America* (London: Andre Deutsch, 1964), pp. 73, 71.
70. "Report on the Special Meeting Called by AMSAC," 27 May 1961, 49.10, Drake Papers.
71. Summary minutes, Business Meeting, 29 June 1959, 49.22, Drake Papers.
72. Minutes of Postponed Annual Meeting of Directors, CORAC, 10 March 1959, 37.113A, Bond Papers.
73. Matthew McCloskey to John Davis, 29 April 1959, 30.80B, Bond Papers; minutes of First Meeting of Directors, AMSAC, 22 June 1960, 31.82C, Bond Papers.
74. In 1962, AMSAC transferred its account to the Chase Manhattan bank in order to facilitate money transfers to Lagos. Yvonne Walker to Horace Mann Bond, 27 September 1962, 8.41, AMSAC Papers, Moorland-Spingarn Center.
75. James Baker to Frederick Van Vechten, 30 November 1962, 8.35, AMSAC Papers, Moorland-Spingarn Center.
76. AMSAC Budget, 1 June 1964–31 May 1965, 8.34, AMSAC Papers, Moorland-Spingarn Center. It is possible, indeed likely, that AMSAC's published budgets did not record all of the covert funds reaching the organization.
77. In 1964, for example, Webster asked "what was being done to spread the word of

AMSAC's work among other agencies in the field: he said he had recently seen a Ford Foundation paper which did not even mention AMSAC." Minutes of Postponed Annual Meeting of Directors, AMSAC, 15 October 1964, 37.113B, Bond Papers.

78. Financial Statement, 1 June 1962–31 May 1963, 6.8, AMSAC Papers, Moorland-Spingarn Center. These changes in AMSAC's funding should be viewed in the context of a general increase in CIA covert operations in Africa in the early 1960s, as the rate of European decolonization speeded up. According to one estimate, between 1959 and 1963 Agency activity on the continent grew by 54 percent. Kevin A. O'Brien, "Interfering with Civil Society: CIA and KGB Covert Political Action during the Cold War," *Journal of Intelligence and Counterintelligence* 8 (1995): 434.
79. Adelaide Cromwell Hill to Members of Board of AMSAC, 24 February 1967, 33.19, AMSAC Papers, Moorland-Spingarn Center.
80. Walker interview.
81. John Davis to Charles L. Frankel, 9 June 1967, 32.90E, Bond Papers. See, for example, James Harris to John Davis, Report on Accra Conference, 18 December 1958, 1.23, AMSAC Papers, Moorland-Spingarn Center.
82. Walker interview.
83. Adelaide Cromwell Hill to Members of Board of AMSAC, 24 February 1967.
84. While in Nairobi, Malcolm had a chance encounter with two members of a touring party sent by the Student Nonviolent Coordinating Committee, another U.S. civil rights organization interested in Africa and increasingly drawn to black nationalism. See Clayborne Carson, *In Struggle: SNCC and the Black Awakening of the 1960s*, 2nd ed. (Cambridge, Mass.: Harvard University Press, 1995), pp. 136–138.
85. For more details on the launch of the ANLCA, see Francis Njubi Nesbitt, *Race for Sanctions: African Americans against Apartheid, 1946–1994* (Bloomington: Indiana University Press, 2004), pp. 44–49.
86. There are other similarities between the CIA's labor operations in Africa and South America, including the creation in 1964 of the African-American Labor Center as a "counterpart . . . to the American Institute for Free Labor Development." Barry Cohen, "The CIA and African Trade Unions," in Ellen Ray et al., eds., *Dirty Work 2: The CIA in Africa* (Secaucus, N.J.: Lyle Stuart, 1979), p. 73. The African-American Labor Center was run for the first decade of its existence by Lovestoneite Irving Brown.
87. James Farmer, *Freedom—When?* (New York: Random House, 1966), p. 134.
88. Quoted in Dan Schechter, Michael Ansara, and David Kolodney, "The CIA as an Equal Opportunity Employer," in Ray et al., *Dirty Work 2*, p. 64.
89. Farmer, *Freedom—When?* p. 133.

90. See Calvin Raullerson to James Farmer, 29 December 1964, 8.31, AMSAC Papers, Moorland-Spingarn Center.
91. Carl Rowan to John Davis, 14 December 1964, 8.31, AMSAC Papers, Moorland-Spingarn Center.
92. "Generally, the idea of the Farmer trip is to give a true picture of the progress of civil rights in the United States and the true aspirations of American Negroes as distinct from what Malcolm X and Cassius Clay have said," Davis wrote. John Davis to James Baker, 1 December 1964, 8.30, AMSAC Papers, Moorland-Spingarn Center.
93. John Davis to James Baker, 7 December 1964, 8.30, AMSAC Papers, Moorland-Spingarn Center.
94. Farmer, *Freedom—When?* p. 135. Farmer's account of his tour in *Freedom—When?* was based on an article in AMSAC's magazine, *African Forum* ("An American Negro Leader's View of African Unity"), which was in turn based on an interview Farmer gave to Hank Raullerson shortly after his return to the United States. See transcript of interview, 10 February 1965, box 3, folder Articles, First Issue, AMSAC Papers, Moorland-Spingarn Center.
95. American Embassy, Lusaka, to Department of State, "Visit of Farmer," 14 January 1965, 3U247, FBI file, James Leonard, Jr., and Lula Peterson Farmer Papers, Center for American History, University of Texas, Austin.
96. James Baker to James Farmer, 13 May 1965, 8.30, AMSAC Papers, Moorland-Spingarn Center. AMSAC's grant to Farmer totaled $1,192, made up of a $24 per diem and $400 for incidental items. Calvin Raullerson to James Farmer, enclosing check, 23 December 1964, 8.30, AMSAC Papers, Moorland-Spingarn Center.
97. James Baker to Calvin Raullerson, 27 January 1965, 8.30, AMSAC Papers, Moorland-Spingarn Center.
98. Ibid.
99. Calvin Raullerson to John Davis, 21 October 1965, 8.31, AMSAC Papers, Moorland-Spingarn Center. For more on Bill Sutherland, a veteran civil rights activist and antinuclear campaigner, see Gaines, *American Africans in Ghana*, pp. 103–106.
100. See, for example, Farmer, *Freedom—When?* p. 163.
101. See, for example, American Embassy, "Visit of Farmer."
102. Farmer, *Freedom—When?* pp. 140, 158–159.
103. James Farmer, interview with Calvin Raullerson, 10 February 1965, box 3, folder Articles, First Issue, AMSAC Papers, Moorland-Spingarn Center. See James Farmer, *Lay Bare the Heart: An Autobiography of the Civil Rights Movement* (New York: New American Library, 1985), pp. 228–230, for a published account of this meeting.

104. Quoted in Farmer, *Lay Bare the Heart*, pp. 230–231; ibid, p. 234.

105. Schechter, Ansara, and Kolodney, "CIA as Equal Opportunity Employer," p. 66.

106. Calvin Raullerson to Martin Luther King, 26 April 1965; Calvin Raullerson to John Davis, 10 November 1964; both 8.29, AMSAC Papers, Moorland-Spingarn Center.

107. See Harold Cruse, *The Crisis of the Negro Intellectual* (London: W. H. Allen, 1969), p. 499.

108. See Von Eschen, *Satchmo*, pp. 150–160; and Gaines, *American Africans in Ghana*, pp. 251–254. For a scathing contemporary assessment of AMSAC's role in the Dakar festival, see Hoyt W. Fuller, *Journey to Africa* (Chicago: Third World Press, 1971), pp. 92–93.

109. Calvin Raullerson to Executive Council, 19 September 1966, 33.20, AMSAC Papers, Moorland-Spingarn Center.

110. Orin Lehman to John Davis, 28 June 1966, 33.20, AMSAC Papers, Moorland-Spingarn Center; Calvin Raullerson to Adelaide Cromwell Hill, 26 July 1966, 33.20, AMSAC Papers, Moorland-Spingarn Center.

111. Anon., "Memorandum for the Record," 17 June 1966, 33.20, AMSAC Papers, Moorland-Spingarn Center; Walker interview.

112. Executive Council minutes, AMSAC, 22–23 September 1966, 32.90E, Bond Papers.

113. Adelaide Cromwell Hill to Saunders Redding, 3 April 1967, 33.19, AMSAC Papers, Moorland-Spingarn Center.

114. Kala-Lobe to President of AMSAC, 14 April 1967, 33.19, AMSAC Papers, Moorland-Spingarn Center. "I can understand your position," Davis wrote in response, "but I would suggest that you ought not to judge AMSAC too quickly." John Davis to Kala-Lobe, 21 April 1967, 33.19, AMSAC Papers, Moorland-Spingarn Center.

115. John Davis to Charles Frankel, 9 June 1967, 32.90E, Bond Papers.

116. Executive Council minutes, AMSAC, 1 March 1969, 33.91B, Bond Papers.

117. Annual Report, 20 June 1969, 49.22, Drake Papers.

118. Minutes of Postponed Annual Meeting of Directors, AMSAC, 20 June 1969, 33.91E, Bond Papers.

119. Quoted in Schechter, Ansara, and Kolodney, "CIA as Equal Opportunity Employer," p. 55.

120. Quoted in Summary Report, First Annual Conference, June 1958, 49.13, Drake Papers.

121. See "Report on the Special Meeting Called by AMSAC," 27 May 1961, 49.10, Drake Papers. This report consists of two parts: a "Report on the Utilization of Negroes in the State Department and USIA as Overseas Representatives, Especially in Africa"; and "The Role of the American Negro Scholar and Africanist, and the Role of the American Negro and Foundation Leadership."

122. Von Eschen, *Race against Empire*, p. 148.
123. The 1959 conference "The Negro Writer and His Relationship to His Roots" was a case in point. See Gaines, *American Africans in Ghana*, pp. 137–140, and James Edward Smethurst, *The Black Arts Movement: Literary Nationalism in the 1960s and 1970s* (Chapel Hill: University of North Carolina Press, 2005), pp. 120–123.
124. Horace Mann Bond to John Davis, 20 May 1959, 30.80B, Bond Papers.
125. AMSAC Annual Report, 22 June 1963, 49.13, Drake Papers.
126. Von Eschen, *Satchmo*, p. 256.
127. Ralph Ellison, *Invisible Man* (Harmondsworth: Penguin, 1952), p. 119.

10. Things Fall Apart

1. Quoted in Carl Bernstein, "The CIA and the Media," *Rolling Stone*, 20 October 1977, 57, 60. The loyalty cut both ways: when Alsop became the victim of a homosexual "honey-trap" by the KGB during a visit to the Soviet Union in 1957, the foreign policy establishment closed ranks around him, Wisner in particular helping to protect him from the attentions of the FBI. See Robert D. Dean, *Imperial Brotherhood: Gender and the Making of Cold War Foreign Policy* (Amherst: University of Massachusetts Press, 2001), pp. 157–158. For more biographical information about Alsop, see Joseph W. Alsop, *I've Seen the Best of It: Memoirs* (New York: W. W. Norton, 1989); Leann Grabavoy Almquist, *Joseph Alsop and American Foreign Policy: The Journalist as Advocate* (Lanham, Md.: University Press of America, 1993); Edwin M. Yoder, Jr., *Joe Alsop's Cold War: A Study of Journalistic Influence and Intrigue* (Chapel Hill: University of North Carolina Press, 1995); Robert W. Merry, *Taking on the World: Joseph and Stewart Alsop—Guardians of the American Century* (New York: Viking, 1996).
2. Hugh Morrow of the *Saturday Evening Post*, quoted in Rhodri Jeffreys-Jones, *Cloak and Dollar: A History of American Secret Intelligence*, 2nd ed. (New Haven, Conn.: Yale University Press, 2003), p. 161.
3. Quoted in Evan Thomas, *The Very Best Men—Four Who Dared: The Early Years of the CIA* (New York: Simon and Schuster, 1995), p. 63.
4. Quoted in Loch Johnson, *America's Secret Power: The CIA in a Democratic Society* (New York: Oxford University Press, 1989), p. 305n5.
5. Ibid., p. 185.
6. For other important 1970s investigative pieces on the CIA and journalists in addition to Bernstein's, see Stuart H. Loory, "The CIA's Use of the Press: A 'Mighty Wurlitzer,'" *Columbia Journalism Review* 13 (September–October 1974): 9–18; and a series of *New York Times* reports by John M. Crewdson and Joseph B. Treaster, "The CIA's Three-Decade Effort to Mold the World's Views," 25 December 1977, 1, 12; "Worldwide Propaganda Network Built by the CIA," 26 De-

cember 1977, 1, 37; "CIA Established Many Links to Journalists in U.S. and Abroad," 27 December 1977, 1, 40–41.

7. Bernstein, "CIA and Media," 60–61. The *Times* also agreed on several occasions to kill stories deemed unfavorable to the CIA. See, for example, Victor Marchetti and John D. Marks, *The CIA and the Cult of Intelligence* (New York: Knopf, 1974), pp. 357–358, and Thomas, *Best Men*, p. 117.
8. Bernstein, "CIA and Media," 62; Nancy E. Bernhard, *U.S. Television News and Cold War Propaganda, 1947–1960* (Cambridge: Cambridge University Press, 1999), p. 186.
9. Quoted in Bernhard, *U.S. Television News*, p. 187. CIA officer William Bundy believed the Alibi dinners with the CBS executives were "very useful in giving the feeling of Allen's thinking without giving them secret material." Quoted in Thomas, *Best Men*, p. 185.
10. See Steve Weissman, "The CIA Makes the News," in Philip Agee and Louis Wolf, eds., *Dirty Work: The CIA in Western Europe* (Secaucus, N.J.: Lyle Stuart, 1978), pp. 204–210, and Russell Warren Howe, "Asset Unwitting: Covering the World for the CIA," *More* (May 1978): 20–27.
11. Philip Agee, *Inside the Company: CIA Diary* (Harmondsworth: Penguin Books, 1975), p. 78.
12. Richard P. Davis to Conrad Christiano, 16 May 1961, box 113, folder 6, American Newspaper Guild Papers, Part 2, International Series, 1940–1959, Archives of Labor and Urban Affairs, Wayne State University, Detroit (hereafter ANG Papers).
13. Anon., "Amounts Received by the American Newspaper Guild International Affairs Fund," n.d., 116.2, ANG Papers.
14. Bernstein, "CIA and Media," 66; Loory, "CIA's Use of Press," 13.
15. Almquist, *Joseph Alsop*, p. 49; Burton Hersh, *The Old Boys: The American Elite and the Origins of the CIA* (St Petersburg, Fla.: Tree Farm Books, 2002), p. 288; Thomas, *Best Men*, p. 105; C. D. Jackson, log, 22 April 1953, box 68, Log 1953 1, C. D. Jackson Papers, Dwight D. Eisenhower Library, Abilene, Kansas. CIA officer Desmond Fitzgerald would get his own back by deliberately feeding Alsop disinformation, remembers Fitzgerald's stepdaughter, Barbara. "At breakfast he'd amuse himself reading the papers to see if Alsop had taken the bait." Quoted in Thomas, *Best Men*, p. 200.
16. In April 1963, DCI John A. McCone tried to persuade Stewart Alsop not to run an article about him in the *Saturday Evening Post*. "Alsop refused," states a White House memorandum, "said he had seen several people and intended to see more; he had a great deal of information because of his own personal experience in OSS; he was convinced the article would be informative to the public, and therefore intended to go forward." Anon., memorandum, 12 April 1963, box

271, folder CIA general, National Security File, Arthur M. Schlesinger, Jr., Papers, John F. Kennedy Library, Boston.

17. Quoted in Bernstein, "CIA and Media," 60.
18. See Hugh Wilford, *The CIA, the British Left, and the Cold War: Calling the Tune?* (London: Frank Cass, 2003), pp. 133–134.
19. C. D. Jackson to Allen Dulles, 21 February 1956, box 48, folder Allen Dulles, Jackson Papers.
20. Sidney Hook to Irving Brown, 31 October 1951; and Irving Brown to Sidney Hook, 3 November 1951; both 13.10, International Affairs Department, Irving Brown Papers (RG18-004), George Meany Memorial Archives, Silver Spring, Maryland. It was James Burnham who first proposed, in November 1949, that the "*New Leader* should immediately receive immediate and adequate financial aid." See James Burnham, "The Financial Condition of the *New Leader*," 21 November 1949, 11.1, James Burnham Papers, Hoover Institution, Stanford University.
21. Frances Stonor Saunders, *Who Paid the Piper? The CIA and the Cultural Cold War* (London: Granta, 1999), p. 163.
22. Bill Furth to Henry Luce and C. D. Jackson, 24 July 1956, box 80, folder *New Leader*, Jackson Papers.
23. Franklin Lindsay to C. D. Jackson, 13 December 1956, box 80, folder *New Leader*, Jackson Papers. "I am delighted to hear of the progress that has been made in seeing that it has support," Allen Dulles informed Lindsay. Allen Dulles to Franklin Lindsay, 20 December 1956, 38.18, Allen W. Dulles Papers, Seeley G. Mudd Manuscript Library, Princeton University.
24. C. D. Jackson to Allen Dulles, 21 February 1956, box 48, folder Allen Dulles, Jackson Papers.
25. Philip Horton to Arthur Schlesinger, Jr., 22 March 1950, box 16, folder Philip Horton, Schlesinger Papers.
26. For more information about *The Reporter*, see the excellent essay by Elke van Cassell, "In Search of a Clear and Overarching American Policy: *The Reporter* Magazine (1949–1968), the U.S. Government, and the Cold War," in Helen Laville and Hugh Wilford, eds., *The U.S. Government, Citizen Groups, and the Cold War: The State-Private Network* (London: Routledge, 2006), pp. 116–140.
27. C. D. Jackson to Henry Luce, "Your Memo to Stillman on *The Reporter*," 24 January 1955, box 71, folder Henry and Clare Luce, 1956, Jackson Papers.
28. Philip Horton to Arthur Schlesinger, Jr., 10 January 1951, box 16, folder Philip Horton, Schlesinger Papers.
29. Quoted in Cassell, "In Search," p. 128.
30. For more on *The Reporter*'s and *New Leader*'s links with the Vietnam Lobby, see Robert Scheer and Warren Hinckle, "The Vietnam Lobby," in *Ramparts*, *A Viet-*

nam Primer, n.d., n.p., box 17, Thomas A. Dooley Papers, Western Historical Manuscript Collection, University of Missouri, St. Louis.

31. See Chap. 5 above and Bernstein, "CIA and Media," 63.
32. Anon., "*Ramparts:* Gadfly to the Establishment," *New York Times*, 20 February 1967, 1.
33. Warren Hinckle, *If You Have a Lemon, Make Lemonade* (New York: G. P. Putnam's Sons, 1974), p. 103.
34. Ibid., p. 160. For more information about the resurgence of muckraking journalism in the 1960s, see James L. Aucoin, *The Evolution of American Investigative Journalism* (Columbia: University of Missouri Press, 2005), chap. 2.
35. Hinckle, *If You Have a Lemon*, p. 50.
36. Ibid., pp. 160, 100, chap. 5.
37. Arthur Schlesinger, Jr., to John F. Kennedy, "CIA," 21 April 1961, box WH-3a, folder CIA General 1, White House File (WHF), Schlesinger Papers.
38. Quoted in Hersh, *Old Boys*, p. 404.
39. William Colby and Peter Forbath, *Honorable Men: My Life in the CIA* (New York: Simon and Schuster, 1978), p. 187.
40. Ibid., p. 184.
41. Rhodri Jeffreys-Jones, *The CIA and American Democracy*, 3rd ed. (New Haven, Conn.: Yale University Press, 2003), p. 153.
42. Godfrey Hodgson, "Cord Meyer: Superspook," in Agee and Wolf, *Dirty Work*, p. 57. See, in addition to Hodgson's brilliant portrait, Merle Miller, "One Man's Long Journey," *New York Times Magazine*, 7 January 1973, 9, 53–55, 63, 70; anon., "A Hidden Liberal," *New York Times*, 30 March 1967, 30; and Saunders, *Who Paid the Piper?* pp. 341–342.
43. Paul Sakwa, "Chief/Covert Action/Vietnam," 2 August 1976, 63.5, Victor G. Reuther Papers, Archives of Labor and Urban Affairs, Wayne State University, Detroit.
44. Anon. [Paul Sakwa], "CIA: Problems of a Clandestine Agency," n.d., box WH-3a, folder CIA General 5, Paul Sakwa, WHF, Schlesinger Papers.
45. Cord Meyer, journal, 21 March 1963, box 5, Journal, 1945–1967, Cord Meyer Papers, Library of Congress.
46. Sakwa, "Chief/Covert Action/Vietnam."
47. See contents of 63.9 ("CIA—Sakwa, Paul—Dismissal Case, 1979"), Victor Reuther Papers.
48. Lawrence de Neufville, quoted in Saunders, *Who Paid the Piper?* p. 357.
49. Quoted in E. W. Kenworthy, "Hobby Foundation of Houston Affirms CIA Tie," *New York Times*, 21 February 1967, 32.
50. Richard Helms with William Hood, *A Look over My Shoulder: A Life in the Central Intelligence Agency* (New York: Random House, 2003), p. 345; Ben A. Frank-

lin, "CIA Aid Backed by White House as Legal Policy," *New York Times*, 24 February 1967, 16.

51. Helms, *Look over My Shoulder*, p. 346.
52. Anon., "On Secrecy and Censorship," *Near East Report*, 21 March 1967, 21–23.
53. Scheer and Hinckle, "Vietnam Lobby," Dooley Papers.
54. See Hinckle, *If You Have a Lemon*, pp. 165–170.
55. Quoted in Angus Mackenzie, *Secrets: The CIA's War at Home* (Berkeley: University of California Press, 1997), p. 17. McCone had left his position the previous year, following a difference of opinion with the Johnson administration about Vietnam policy.
56. Richard Helms to Bromley Smith, "Actions of the Faculty of the University of Washington Concerning CIA," 31 May 1966, box 9, folder CIA Vol. 2 [1 of 2], National Security File (NSF), Agency File (AF), Lyndon B. Johnson Library, Austin, Texas.
57. Raborn, quoted in Mackenzie, *Secrets*, p. 19.
58. Tom Wicker, "The Story behind the Story behind the CIA Spooks," *Times Talk* 18, no. 12 (May 1966): 3.
59. See Saunders, *Who Paid the Piper?* pp. 367–368.
60. Quoted in Nelson Lichtenstein, *The Most Dangerous Man in Detroit: Walter Reuther and the Fate of American Labor* (New York: Basic Books, 1995), p. 408.
61. Ken Metzler, "Campaign against Covert Action Division No. 5," *Old Oregon*, May–June 1967, 7, 29.208, Allard K. Lowenstein Papers, Southern Historical Collection, Wilson Library, University of North Carolina at Chapel Hill.
62. Sherburne later told historian William Chafe that Allard Lowenstein was among those advising him against severing the relationship between the NSA and CIA. Other interviewees of Chafe disputed this claim. See, for example, William Dentzer, Columbia University Oral History Project, 1989, add. 3.1, folder 165, Lowenstein Papers.
63. Anon. [Allard Lowenstein], handwritten notes, n.d. [1967], 29.208, Lowenstein Papers.
64. W. Eugene Groves, "President's Report to the Twentieth National Student Congress," 1967, box 62, folder President's Report, U.S. National Student Association Papers, Hoover Institution, Stanford University.
65. Hinckle, *If You Have a Lemon*, pp. 172, 173.
66. See ibid., pp. 175–177; Saunders, *Who Paid the Piper?* pp. 353–354; Cord Meyer, *Facing Reality: From World Federalism to the CIA* (New York: Harper and Row, 1980), p. 88.
67. Hinckle, *If You Have a Lemon*, p. 174; Mackenzie, *Secrets*, p. 21.
68. Mackenzie, *Secrets*, p. 21.
69. Groves, "President's Report."

70. Hinckle, *If You Have a Lemon*, p. 180.
71. Sol Stern, "A Short Account of International Student Politics with Particular Reference to the NSA, CIA, Etc.," *Ramparts* 5, no. 9 (March 1967): 29–38.
72. Meyer, *Facing Reality*, p. 89. "It will take a long time before we all understand what has happened in the last few months and why," reads Meyer's diary entry for March 10, 1967. It then goes on to note that "the *New York Times* and the *Washington Post* are committed to the proposition that the CIA is a worse danger to American democracy than any conceivable external enemy and must be exposed as such." Meyer, journal, 10 March 1967, box 5, Journal, 1945–1967, Meyer Papers.
73. "In the Pay of the CIA: An American Dilemma," *CBS News Special Report with Mike Wallace*, 12 March 1967.
74. George E. Brown, Jr., et al. to Lyndon B. Johnson, 14 February 1967, box 44, folder Ramparts-NSA-CIA, NSF, Johnson Library; Hubert Humphrey quoted in "In the Pay of the CIA."
75. Quoted in W. Eugene Groves, "NSA and the CIA: On People and Power (Second Thoughts after the Storm)," box 62, folder President's Report, NSA Papers.
76. Quoted in Morrill Cody to Howland H. Sargeant, 28 February 1967, box 44, folder Ramparts-NSA-CIA, NSF, Johnson Library.
77. Quoted in Jeffreys-Jones, *CIA and American Democracy*, p. 162.
78. Richard Helms to Lyndon Johnson, 28 March 1967, box 9, folder CIA Vol. 3 [1 of 2], NSF, AF, Johnson Library. According to an internal CIA report, coverage of the affair in South Africa emphasized the secret funding of AMSAC and the African-American Institute, "two organizations which South African media note as opposing . . . apartheid." "Foreign Press Reactions to Revelations about CIA," n.d., CIA Records Search Tool (CREST), National Archives, Washington, D.C.
79. International Federation of Journalists, Statement, 25 February 1967; International Executive Board, ANG, Statement, 12 March 1967; both 108.32, ANG Papers.
80. Mark Hawthorne to Directors, ANG, 26 February 1967, 114.8, ANG Papers; 24 signatories, *Look* Magazine Unit of ANG, 20 February 1967, 116.3, ANG Papers.
81. Notes of telephone conversation between Jimmy Breslin and Charles Perlik, 19 February 1967, 116.3, ANG Papers.
82. Jimmy Breslin, "The Guild's CIA Money," 20 February 1967, 116.3, ANG Papers.
83. See Tony Brenna, "Guild Irresponsibly Smeared by CIA Story, Leader Claims," *Editor and Publisher*, 25 February 1967, 9–10.
84. Ed Torres to Victor Reuther, 27 September 1967, 33.8, Victor Reuther Papers.

85. When Cater passed the information on to the president, the response was typically Johnsonian. "Why, aren't you the lucky one," LBJ told his assistant. "You let that fellow come into your office and lay a big, fat turd right in your lap." Quoted in John Prados, *Safe for Democracy: The Secret Wars of the* CIA (Chicago: Ivan R. Dee, 2006), p. 371.
86. Nicholas Katzenbach to Lyndon Johnson, 13 February 1967, box 193, CF Oversize Attachments, Packet 3, White House Central File (WHCF), Confidential File (CF), Johnson Library.
87. Mike Mansfield to Lyndon Johnson, "Clandestine or Covert Financing of Government Activities," 22 February 1967; Lyndon Johnson to Mike Mansfield, 23 February 1967; both box 55, folder FG11-2 CIA [1 of 2], WHCF, Johnson Library.
88. United Press press release, "The Big CIA Scandal Growing," 20 February 1967, CREST.
89. In late March, Nicholas Katzenbach told Dean Rusk, presumably using intelligence gleaned from CIA informers in *Ramparts*' offices, that the magazine "may soon publish an exposé of CIA support channeled to [the] Asia Foundation." Nicholas Katzenbach to Dean Rusk, 21 March 1967, box 44, folder Ramparts-NSA-CIA, NSF, Johnson Library.
90. Mackenzie, *Secrets*, p. 24.
91. George C. Denney, Jr., to Nicholas Katzenbach, 15 February 1967, box 44, folder Ramparts-NSA-CIA, NSF, Johnson Library; Mackenzie, *Secrets*, p. 22. The National Security Archive in Washington, D.C., holds copies of memoranda written by an anonymous CIA officer in February 1967 recording meetings with senior IRS officials about *Ramparts*. For example, a memo dated February 2 describes a meeting held the previous day in which the author briefed IRS representatives on "information and rumors we have heard about RAMPARTS," "impressed upon them the Director's concern and expressed our certainty that this is an attack on CIA," and "suggested that the corporate tax returns of RAMPARTS, Inc., be examined and that any leads to possible financial supporters be followed up by an examination of their individual tax returns." Although another memo dated February 15, presumably written after the IRS had reported to the CIA, stated that the author was "satisfied that there is no information on either the corporation or individual returns which would justify an official request for access to the returns," the Agency and Service were still exchanging information about *Ramparts*' financial affairs on May 18. Given what we know from other sources, it seems reasonable to assume that the author of the memoranda was Richard Ober. Anon., "IRS Briefing on RAMPARTS," 2 February 1967, 9.C-48, Center for National Security Studies (CNSS) Collection, National Security Archive, George Washington University, Washington, D.C.; anon.,

"RAMPARTS Tax Returns," 15 February 1967, 9.C-48, CNSS Collection; anon., "Miscellaneous Matters Discussed at IRS on 18 May 1967," 19 May 1967, 9.C-48, CNSS Collection.

92. Edward Applewhite, quoted in Thomas, *Best Men*, p. 330; Louis Dube, quoted in Mackenzie, *Secrets*, p. 24.
93. See Saunders, *Who Paid the Piper?* p. 382.
94. M. M. Morton,"The Inside Story of *Ramparts* Magazine," *Human Events*, 8 April 1967, 216. After reading the *Human Events* article, White House aide Peter Jessup, presumably ignorant of the source of its inspiration, recommended "that some agency of the government [pursue] the threads involved here." Peter Jessup to Walt Rostow, "A Right Cross to Left Temple," 4 April 1967, box 44, folder Ramparts-NSA-CIA, NSF, Johnson Library.
95. This fact was also noted in a widely syndicated column by Carl Rowan, and probably lies behind later claims that the *Ramparts* exposure of the NSA was inspired by the Czechoslovak secret service, acting at the behest of the KGB. Mackenzie, *Secrets*, p. 23; Brian Crozier, *Free Agent: The Unseen War, 1941–1991* (London: Harper Collins, 1993), p. 5.
96. Hinckle, *If You Have a Lemon*, p. 104. Also see ibid., pp. 111–118, for more detail on *Ramparts*' search for angels, including an unsuccessful approach to Hugh Hefner.
97. Anon., "CIA Man Who Told," *New York Times*, 8 May 1967, 37.
98. Thomas W. Braden, "I'm Glad the CIA is 'Immoral,'" *Saturday Evening Post*, 20 May 1967, 10. Braden trailed the article with a widely reported interview in the *Los Angeles Times*. See Harold Keen, "Braden Reveals He Set Up CIA Aid to Students, Unions," *Los Angeles Times*, 7 May 1967, 1, 19.
99. Victor Reuther to Joseph Walsh, 4 May 1967, 17.30, Victor Reuther Papers. For an account of the impact of Braden's article on the circle around *Encounter*, see Saunders, *Who Paid the Piper?* p. 403.
100. Transcript of President George Meany's Press Conference, Executive Council Meeting, 8 May 1967, box 98, folder AFL-CIO, ANG Papers.
101. Cord Meyer to Allen Dulles, 1 May 1967; Allen Dulles to Joan Braden, 20 June 1967; both 8.27, Dulles Papers.
102. Walt Rostow to Lyndon Johnson, 19 April 1967, box 44, folder Ramparts-NSA-CIA, NSF, Johnson Library.
103. See Thomas, *Best Men*, p. 124.
104. Saunders, *Who Paid the Piper?* p. 398.
105. Victor Riesel, "Reuther-Meany Feud and the CIA," *World-Journal-American*, 2 May 1967, box 570, folder U.S.–Central Intelligence Agency, Jay Lovestone Papers, Hoover Institution, Stanford University.
106. John P. Roche to Lyndon Johnson, 17 February 1967, box 193, CF Oversize Attachments, Packet 3, WHCF, CF, Johnson Library.

107. Lichtenstein, *Most Dangerous Man*, p. 422.
108. Quoted in Saunders, *Who Paid the Piper?* p. 402.
109. Douglass Cater to Lyndon Johnson, 21 February 1967, box 10, folder CIA Funding of Private Organizations, CIA Vol. 3 [2 of 2], Office of the White House Aides, Johnson Library; Jeffreys-Jones, *CIA and American Democracy*, p. 163.
110. Nicholas Katzenbach to Lyndon Johnson, "Report of Your Committee on CIA Relations with Private Voluntary Organizations," 17 March 1967, box 193, CF Oversize Attachments, Packet 3, WHCF, CF, Johnson Library.
111. Jeffreys-Jones, *CIA and American Democracy*, p. 186.
112. Dean Rusk to Lyndon Johnson, 4 June 1968, box 192, CF Oversize Attachments, Packet 1, WHCF, CF, Johnson Library.
113. Michael Warner, "Sophisticated Spies: CIA's Links to Liberal Anti-Communists, 1949–1967," *International Journal of Intelligence and Counterintelligence* 9 (1996–97): 426.

Conclusion

1. Anon., "Presentation to the Rusk Committee: The Problem and the Alternatives," 6 May 1967, box 192, CF Oversize Attachments, Packet 1, White House Central File, Confidential File, Lyndon B. Johnson Library, Austin, Texas.
2. Ibid.
3. The kidnapping and gruesome murder in Pakistan in 2002 of American journalist Daniel Pearl, based on the mistaken belief that he was a CIA agent, is a recent case in point.
4. See, for example, Robert D. Putnam, *Bowling Alone: The Collapse and Revival of American Community* (New York: Simon and Schuster, 2000).
5. *Final Report of the Select Committee to Study Governmental Operations with Respect to Intelligence Activities, United States Senate* (Washington, D.C.: U.S. Government Printing Office, 1976), pp. 188–191.
6. See Ernest Volkman, "Spies on Campus," *Penthouse* (October 1979), www.cia-on-campus.org/ (accessed 28 October 2005).
7. See Loch Johnson, *America's Secret Power: The CIA in a Democratic Society* (New York: Oxford University Press, 1989), p. 159.
8. Daniel Golden, "In from the Cold: After Sept. 11, the CIA Becomes a Growing Force on Campus," *Wall Street Journal*, 4 October 2002, 1. The two most outspoken critics of clandestine links between the CIA and academe are University of Arizona political scientist David N. Gibbs, and distinguished University of Chicago historian Bruce Cumings.
9. See Hugh Wilford, "'The Permanent Revolution?' The New York Intellectuals, the CIA, and the Cultural Cold War," in Helen Laville and Hugh Wilford, eds.,

The U.S. Government, Citizen Groups, and the Cold War: The State-Private Network (London: Routledge, 2006), pp. 194–209.

10. See Richard Byrne, "A Collision of Prose and Politics," *Chronicle of Higher Education*, 13 October 2006, 12.
11. Serge F. Kovaleski, "Young Muslims in Britain Hear Competing Appeals," *New York Times*, 29 August 2006, 3.
12. Quoted in Burton Hersh, *The Old Boys: The American Elite and the Origins of the CIA* (St. Petersburg, Fla.: Tree Farm Books, 2002), p. 269.

Acknowledgments

I want to thank some friends and colleagues who, as well as helping review the manuscript, made other crucial contributions to the writing of this book. Robert Cook was a model of professional scholarship and collegiality; Dominic "RN" Sandbrook dared me to write for a larger audience and provided some excellent entertainment along the way; Brandon High offered his usual erudite commentary; Rhodri Jeffreys-Jones was a sympathetic guide through the maze of American intelligence history; and Nelson Lichtenstein allowed me to pick his vast brain mercilessly over the tennis net.

I am hugely grateful also to the following, who have read chunks of the manuscript, offered good advice, or simply been there during my peripatetic existence of the past few years: Pertti Ahonen; Richard Aldrich; Mike Braddick; Richard Carwardine; Flurin Condrau; Penny Croxson; Richard Cummings; Ken Curtis; Kathleen DiVito; George Fujii; Andrea, Martha, and Daniel Greengrass; Patrick Gribble; Karen Harvey; Tim Keirn; Ian Kershaw; Helen Laville; Dan Leab; Scott Lucas; Richard Maltby; John Munro; Karen Paget; Inderjeet Parmar; John Sbardellati; Barbara Schmucki; Lise Sedrez; Tony Shaw; Sean Smith; Joe Street; Howard Tolley; Brian Vick; Michael Warner; and Cath, David, Gilly, and Peter Wilford. My students, both at my previous institution, the University of Sheffield, and my new one, California State University, Long Beach, have in turn indulged and stimulated my interest in the hidden history of the Cold War.

Among the institutions that supported me while I researched and wrote, the British Academy provided several small grants that enabled me to visit archival collections in the United States; the University of Sheffield granted me a semester's research leave and additional assistance with travel costs; the Arts and Humanities Research Council matched my institutional leave so that I could spend a whole year researching in the United States; the Cold War Studies Center at the University of California, Santa Barbara, under the directorship of Tsuyoshi Hasegawa, extended me a wonderfully warm welcome as a visiting scholar and proved an outstandingly congenial research environment; and California State University, Long Beach, has been generous in giving me the time and space during my first year of appointment to lick the manuscript into shape. Administrative staff in the Sheffield, Santa Barbara, and Long Beach History Departments have provided invaluable practical support and unfailing good cheer. I am also grateful to the librarians of these three institutions for their assistance in tracking down a vast and strange assortment of publications, as well as to the uniformly courteous and efficient archivists who have aided me as I trawled manuscript collections throughout the United States.

My literary agents, Felicity Bryan and George Lucas, deserve special thanks for their faith in this project and support in bringing it to fruition. Assisted with great efficiency by Kathleen Drummy, Kathleen McDermott of Harvard University Press has been a model editor, and Donna Bouvier an exemplary copyeditor.

Finally, my heartfelt gratitude to two women: my mother, Jan Wilford, who has always been a vital source of solace for me, but never more so than in the past few years; and Patricia Cleary, who, in addition to being my most dedicated and expeditious reader, has brought untold happiness into my life.

Index